Camp
in Literature

Camp in Literature

GARY MCMAHON

McFarland & Company, Inc., Publishers
Jefferson, North Carolina, and London

The work of Chloe Poems is quoted by permission of Chloe Poems and the publishers Route and the Bad Press. The work of Rosie Lugosi is quoted by permission of Rosie Lugosi.

LIBRARY OF CONGRESS CATALOGUING-IN-PUBLICATION DATA

McMahon, Gary, 1959–
    Camp in literature / Gary McMahon.
        p.   cm.
    Includes bibliographical references and index.

    ISBN 0-7864-2466-4 (softcover : 50# alkaline paper)

    1. English literature — History and criticism.   2. Camp (Aesthetics) in literature.   3. Literature — History and criticism. I. Title.
    PR149.C34M37   2006
    820.9'11— dc22   2006001878

British Library cataloguing data are available

On the cover: Oscar Wilde illustration by Frederick B. Opper of *Puck* magazine (*Library of Congress*)

Manufactured in the United States of America

McFarland & Company, Inc., Publishers
    Box 611, Jefferson, North Carolina 28640
        www.mcfarlandpub.com

To All Good Friends, Yours and Mine

Acknowledgments

Many thanks, Peter Burton; Peter Bush; Robert Cochrane at Bad Press; Kevin Craig; Kendal Eaton; Norma McMahon; Manchester University Computing — Education Department and Owens Park; Joan Needham; Gerry Potter; Swinton Public Library; and of course the Polar Bar.

Contents

Preface

In the twilight of the 20th century, in my godforsaken city of Manchester, England, New Bohemia was happening on Saturday nights at the Green Room Theater. New Bohemia was a cabaret celebration of ingenious human diversity, like Berlin between the Wars, with artistes like dominatrix Siren Rosie Lugosi, booted and catsuited and crop-fisted, and androgynous anarchist The Divine David, looking and moving like Stravinsky's Firebird. The host was the writer in residence, a performance poet with some radical ideas about camp. Playing to type in transvestite gingham, bob wig and falsetto tenor, with a tone of domesticity familiar to anyone raised around women, yet this sorcerer was sweeping generalizations with a new broom. Chloe Poems made camp look quaint like Margaret Rutherford, an agony aunt for your sins and woes, then suddenly as blasphemous as the end of the world.

And while I sat at a table on Saturday nights at New Bohemia, teatotaling in the dark, my tricoteuse eyebrows knitted a conundrum. What does camp look like set down on the page? In all the discourse on camp performance, it seems nobody had classified camp as a literary genre. How does camp scan as a style of writing? The writer in residence, who hated writing and only wrote poetry to serve his stage persona, would soon find out for himself. Chloe Poems' first publications would lead to a strange, fateful association with Spain's foremost writer, Juan Goytisolo...

Juan Goytisolo fraternized, in exile, with the Paris set of Genet and Sartre and Camus and all. His prose ponders weighty concerns, yet increasingly overstated in symbolism and taboo sexuality, tongue in cheek. As Juan Goytisolo published *A Cock-Eyed Comedy* in the U.K. in 2002, his crowning camp achievement, Chloe Poems went to press with *Adult Entertainment* and a C-D of live, ironic readings. It occurred to Peter Bush, Goytisolo's notable English translator, that Poems personified much that was represented in

1

the book, the ideal voice of *A Cock-Eyed Comedy*. And so they toured together, these cavalier mountebanks, an unlikely contrast of cultures, taking camp literature into the 21st century in progressive and provocative style. They signal an agenda of insurrection that challenges my own ideas about camp and begs to differ with fellow men of scented letters.

Looking at novels, short stories, essays, drama, poetry, and memoir, this book compiles a canon of writers in the camp tradition. I invite the reader to pull up a divan and appreciate their amazing blasé artistry. Part One applies the history and definition of camp to literature. In principle and by example we discover traits and variations of camp style. Part Two applies our observations to six featured writers and plots the development of camp over a hundred years.

This comparative study is something of a fantasy cocktail party, hosting anachronistic introductions: Max Beerbohm and Juan Goytisolo compare notes while Brigid Brophy notes their asides; yes and Christopher Isherwood takes tea with Saki and Aubrey Beardsley passes the opium to a bemused Alan Bennett as Chloe Poems tries to convert Lord Berners (or is that Ronald Firbank?) to socialism behind Noël Coward's back; yes and Amanda McKittrick Ros jabs a hatpin in a critic while Marie Corelli wonders why she hasn't got her own chapter, which comes as no surprise to E.F. Benson, as Leopold von Sacher-Masoch admires Ed Wood's angora and Quentin Crisp arches a disdainful brow across the room where Oscar Wilde is holding court... The miracle is that this singular, secular, marginalized style can accommodate such temperamental diversity. Fortunately, all writers unite over a common enemy, the critics.

Oscar Wilde is as famous for his personality as for his epigrammatic writing. His dialogue on and off the page expounded the camp aesthetic, and his oeuvre and his personage modeled it. Even before his trial, critics deplored his stylized bluff. Noting the poor reception of *The Duchess of Padua*, Wilde demonstrated how aloof camp must be to endure cultural prejudice, "The play in itself was a great success, but the audience was a profound failure."[1]

A generation later, under Wilde's shadow and too frivolous to cast a shadow of his own, Ronald Firbank was, his biographer reveals, "irrevocably and personally hurt by non-notice from critics and public." Firbank paid for publication of nine out of ten of his books, and his reputation remains as "a minor novelist."[2] He deconstructed dialogue in the 20th century novel and his fluent prose is generously poetic, by the way.

Quentin Crisp was rejected as a writer for twenty-five years before television made him famous. His subsequent publications are considered accessories to his media persona. Dare I suggest, his work may be classic literature within a hundred years, when no one can recall his televisionary status and cinema cameos?

Edward D. Wood is the unlikely American in this camp sextet. No stranger to criticism, Ed Wood is better known as the worst director of all time: *Plan 9 from Outer Space* (1957) is reputedly the worst film ever made. He was also a fantastically prolific author, whose cult pulp books are trash classics. Not altogether wittingly, yet beyond the capability of any other author, his sensational penmanship raises the question of when camp becomes kitsch.

None of the writers is purely camp, eclectic influences see to that, yet they are all as camp as ninepence, as the saying goes. These chapters are selective in their inventory and not especially biographical, but each writer enlightens our consideration of what can be achieved with this form. Literary criticism, I discovered in the course of this book, may exercise veiled moral reproach as well as mistranslating one aesthetic, camp, by another more ascetic set of values. Imagine my lack of surprise.

My first observations on literary camp were published as the Foreword to *Adult Entertainment*. I said there that camp is so misunderstood that any artist donning its guise faces a gruelling battle for recognition. *Camp in Literature* sets the frame of reference for this coherent and fabulous genre.

PART ONE

An Introduction to Camp

*A history ... camp or Decadence? ... French borrowings
in camp ... art for art's sake ... camp narrative ... irony
... an exposé on seriousness ...*

You have probably met before but, in literature, you have never been formally introduced. Allow me...

Camp is common currency in mainstream culture now, though it was the language of marginalized misfits, theater luvvies, the effete elite of the 19th century, and the French baroquery that you find at Versailles. It has been politicized on that account. "Parody becomes the process whereby the marginalized and disenfranchised advance their own interests by entering alternative signifying codes into discourse."[1] Moe Meyer is the cultural prospector who stakes a separatist claim on camp: straight camp is fraudulent and Susan Sontag's celebrated essay only undermined the political currency of camp as a gay statement, so it seems.

Sontag's landmark "Notes on Camp" in 1964, and then the Aubrey Beardsley exhibition at the Victoria and Albert Museum in 1966, signaled a camp renaissance, with its epicenter in London. Post World War II, Powell and Pressburger and later camp auteurs like Ken Russell elevated this remarkable aesthetic in cinema. The mid–20th century started talking about "high camp." It staged personhood, society and process as performance, disdaining identification with character or motivation or narrative. Pop Art and Warhol's surface aesthetics legitimized lowbrow culture, spilling over into kitsch and spelling out its colorful impact, *blam*! to parody comic-strips and advertising, complicating camp definition. Generically, camp can apply to any format in popular culture: how can we use it as a definitive literary term? Polari, a Romany term for talk, is an esoteric camp idiom of burlesque innuendo, elaborate euphemism and pun, harking backwards, perhaps, to *comedia del'arte.* Polari has an underground gay subtext yet is popular entertainment, at home in theater, where exhibitionism goes in disguise and acts with impunity. Arched and sinuous intonations distance the speaker tonguc in cheek from surface meaning and allude to something risqué, taboo, frivolous. It seldom flirts with literature: Polari was promiscuous in BBC radio comedy broadcasts in the 1960s. By the '60s, the most performative decade of the 20th century, camp writing was most evident in the scriptwriting of tongue in cheek British television and cinema like *The Avengers* and *Modesty Blaise.* Camp makes the 21st century laugh with tongue in cheek innuendo and precious inflection and gender-bending parody. It is dismissed on that account. "Camp self-parody presents the self as being wilfully irresponsible and immature, the artificial nature of the self-presentation making it a sort of off-stage theatricality, the shameless insincerity of which may be provocative, but also forestalls criticism by its ambivalence."[2]

Many critics enforce a puritanical set of aesthetics, with unbending measurements of what is art and what is base, and base their reviews on a mistranslation. This book seeks to better understand a style of writing that has not been validated by classical or realist or academic aesthetics. To appreciate and criticize a crafted work, adopt its pose, assume its attitude, step into the author's rhythm before engaging your critical faculty. What is camp? What value does it have? What's the difference between *camp* and *kitsch?* Is there such a literature, a camp style of writing?

Colorful and contrary themes and motifs decorate this thesis: the nature of artifice ... style over content ... feminine styles of writing ... ironic distance ... theatricality ... narcissism as a detached perspective ... ecclesiastical camp ... domestic-fantastic juxtaposition ... the social pertinence of camp ... an impertinent re-evaluation of the cult of seriousness in literary criticism and in philosophical enquiry against the throwaway frivolity of camp...

Moe Mayer[3] finds the debut of "camp" in Ware's 1909 dictionary of Victorian slang, *Passing English to the Victorian Era:* "Actions and gestures of exaggerated emphasis. Probably from the French. Used chiefly by persons of exceptional want of character," a likely euphemism for homosexuality. Honoré de Balzac underscored the French association with formative camp in 1830, when he identified four signifiers as badges of identity: posture, gesture, costume and speech. Mark Booth[4] finds *se camper* ("to camp it up") in Théophile Gautier's *Capitaine Fracasse* of 1863, a rather theatrical take on the Romantic novel.

The Decadent school of writing is steeped in French. Camp too, though a particularly English inclination, is partial to soigné French dressing to convey savoir faire, that je ne sais quois too recherché for English. Oscar Wilde (1854–1900) wrote *Salomé* in French and left the English translation to Alfred Douglas. Lord Berners (1883–1950) composed a "wild Ossianic lament" in boyhood: "I wrote it in French, for I thought that a foreign language would be a more suitable vehicle for such lofty invective."[5] The esoteric accent keeps banality at arm's length. Droll French intonation appeals to a delicate palette a tad aloof from semantics, outré yet blasé. None of the pulverizing impact of German or the abrupt fervor of Italian and Spanish. Opening Act II of *The Importance of Being Earnest,* Cecily objects to German lessons, "It isn't at all a becoming language. I know perfectly well that I look quite plain after my German lesson." It seems a question of sound over meaning: camp was well ahead of Marshall MacLuhan in determining the medium as the message. Max Beerbohm (1872–1956) can't speak highly enough of French as "a supreme means to slighter ends," whose "feminine" inclination "to such lighter tasks as ordinary conversation" leaves "graver tasks" to masculine languages.[6] Camp English aspires to this elegant levitation of domesticity. How pretentious: in the quaint novel *Lucia's Progress,* by E.F. Benson (1867–1940), a friend petitions Elizabeth Mapp "'to drop that silly habit of putting easy French phrases into your conversation.'"[7] In Benson's *The Oakleyites,* Mrs. Andrews "regarded the use of French language by anybody but herself rather an invasion of her privileges."[8]

If we describe masculinity as extrovert, then masculinity in camp English exerts itself theatrically, in the *performance* of language writ large, not in the assertion of meaning. Mayer traces camp to theatricality with Francois Delsarté's voice training for actors and speakers in 19th century France. Steele Mackaye added physical movement to this classification of gestures and postures when he introduced it to America in 1870, where Mackaye also produced the plays of Oscar Wilde.

Oscar Wilde is often nominated as the founder of camp. Camp is also circulated as not only exclusively gay but necessarily male too and always transvestite. None of those propositions is true, but look how persuasive they are. Wilde heralds our first chapter in Part Two; all those writers featured are male; five of them are gay and the other is transvestite. Yet camp influenced Oscar Wilde before Wilde influenced camp; gay culture is the vanguard of camp but not exclusively so; women can be camp artistes too; and transgender motifs like transvestism are among many incongruent juxtapositions that camp plays with. Long before "camp" was minted in the language, John Bulwer's manual of gestures in 1694 describes a syndrome of effeminate and exaggerated physical language.[9] Bulwer appreciates "the art of manual rhetoric" like conservative critics and scholars appreciate a reserved kind of writing; he distrusts effeminate gesturing and recommends it "should disqualify a man" from military service, much as we may find critics who discount camp style from the literary canon.

Camp is a superficial aesthetic; it is not to be found in Russian literature. It is a tilling of the topsoil, but it blossoms in Shakespeare. A century before John Bulwer went to press, Shakespeare was courting dandified language with flourishing courtiers like Osric in *Hamlet*: "Sir, here is newly come to court Laertes; believe me, an absolute gentleman, full of most excellent differences, of very soft society and great showing. Indeed, to speak feelingly of him, he is the card or calendar of gentry, for you shall find in him the continent of what part a gentleman should see," (*Hamlet* Act V, scene ii, 105–11). This deft yet superlative stroke of the quill suggests that Quentin Crisp (1908–1999) did not invent *Crisperanto*, "speaking with a courtly flourish — artificial and insincere like all the best things in life."[10] Camp is indeed a language of "very soft society and great showing," which nicely enunciates its feminine-masculine dynamic with preciousness and showmanship. Shakespeare, toasted by Virginia Woolf as a paragon of "androgynous style" (1929), put Crisperanto on stage in the 16th century. Richard Le Gallienne, a chronicler of the aesthetes, reminded Edwardian Britain that the novel derives from drama and "remains a drama — with extended stage directions,"[11] especially true of camp novels, I find. Who can fail to see camp heritage — theatrical relish, wordplay like swordsmanship, flourishing similes with a limp wrist and a sharp tongue — in the plum-cheek enunciation, the mannered effeminacy and the tart and fruity evil of Olivier's Richard III? Not that Olivier is overacting, mark you: it is Richard who overacts in the cavorting rhetoric of the text. With a whimsical tinkling of dashing "t's"and a narcissist flirting with fashion, "I'll be at charges for a looking glass, /And entertain a score or two of tailors /To study fashions to adorn my body," Shakespeare puts his looking glass on a lectern to make up his Iambic rhetoric. A punning couplet affects to be aspirate in its blasé assonance: "Shine out, fair sun, till I have bought a glass, /That I may see my shadow as I pass." (*Richard III*, Act I, scene ii, 255–263)

In lush descriptions of costumes and idealized flora and landscapes, camp literature acknowledges the Romantic period, though rarefying its tragedy to a case of ennui. In poetry, before "camp" was coined, we can find camp touches in Tennyson's flamboyance. A self-effacing but alter-ego-aggrandizing Quentin Crisp regrets that his grand and highbrow reflections were beyond "my sub–Tennysonian style."[12] Byron and Coleridge and Shelley and Blake, however, were too grave or stentorian or abrupt or breathless or preoccupied with epic narrative or, in the case of Wordsworth, just too lost in urgent sincerity, to be camp. Woolf finds Wordsworth and Milton and Jonson and Tolstoi "had a dash too much of the male in them."[13]

When poets do assume camp traits, they clash with critics of classical sensibility. Scholar J.R. Watson criticizes John Keats' "Hymn to Pan" in *Endymion,* "the extraordinary use of adjectives, and especially compound adjectives, together with the sense of abundance which comes from the piling up of one image upon another... Here its overwhelming richness can be cloying: the imagery becomes an obstacle to the narrative, and it is sometimes difficult to see the wood for the trees," at least, until he matures to "a classical simplicity."[14]

Camp was an English literary fashion of the late 19th-early 20th century that partied with Decadence, a *fin-de-siècle* art style. They are usually conflated, tied by tendrils of art nouveau and art for art's sake. Decadence too is amoral and larger than life. *The Picture of Dorian Gray* proclaims, "'A new hedonism — that is what our century wants.'"[15] Camp or Decadence? Angela Carter's radio play about Ronald Firbank in 1984 aligns him with Decadence and never refers to camp. In 1933 Mario Praz calls *Under the Hill,* by Aubrey Beardsley (1872–1898), "the essence of the English Decadent school." *Under the Hill* is the most camp writing in the canon. Yes, and it would seem "the classic of the Decadence in England is *The Picture of Dorian Gray.*"[16] J.K. Huysmans (1848–1907) was the French ambassador of Decadence who influenced Wilde: *Against Nature* discloses, "As a matter of fact, artifice was considered by Des Esseintes to be the distinctive mark of human genius."[17] Camp too prefers Art over Naturalism, yes, but camp is seldom in opposition to anything; *Against Nature,* even in its title, defines a tonal difference between Decadence and camp. Camp glories in artifice, to be sure, yet cultivates flowers more than any other genre outside gardening books. Traits of Decadence common to camp include esoteric decoration; effeminacy; a predisposition to ennui; and extremism — though camp *poses* polarities while remaining stylistically detached. Camp is supremely ironic; Decadence loses irony in the saturation of its detail and its absorbing sensual and philosophical quests, more inclined to decay while camp blooms, and the intensity and occasional occultism of Decadence is not in the camp remit.

Marquis de Sade pioneers Decadence but Sacher-Masoch gets closer to the camp ideal, I will suggest later. Sade has his moments— the phallic and ecclesiastical innuendo that climaxes his short story "Retaliation"— but even theatrical analogies and gender role subversion are over-laden with anguish and saturated with lust, lacking reflective distance even in his famous disquisitions: the transgressions too desperately seek sacrilege to find the aloof temperament of camp. Sade's dialectic passages of philosophical elucidation of cruel and carnal scenes are dense and turgid — not the camp ambiance — and call on the work ethic of the reader to plough through the text. Camp, we'll see, flouts the work ethic. Roland Barthes observes of Sade, "Throughout his work, the author, the characters, and the readers exchange a dissertation for a scene: philosophy is the price (i.e. the meaning) of vice...."[18] Camp would never subscribe to such penitence. Camp never strains to make a point; Sade puts the point on the rack. Ronald Firbank and Juan Goytisolo's chapters will model camp sadomasochism.

Academics analyze schools of aesthetics in terms of movements: after Naturalism, Decadence peaked in the 1880s, say, borrowing from Gothic Romanticism, then acceded to the Symbolist movement. No one, ever, talks of a Camp movement. Practitioners never drafted the manifesto. That would have been unbearably political and too *too* serious. You can sample most literary genres in edited anthologies— but there is not a single anthology on camp writing. O, there are disquisitions on camp as performance art and a subject for gender studies— but the number of collected critical essays on camp as a *literary* style, should you wish to consult your library, is zero. Camp has aristocratic relations yet no political influence. Its drawing-room heroes pose life as theater and find meaning, if not political or moral meaning, and perhaps psychological insulation, in stylized detachment. If camp appears historically ineffectual, it represents the abdication of an elite and effete minority and dismissal by serious scholars. Camp is problematic to reference as a genre: its historical range is epic and amorphous. The rise and decline of Naturalism or Decadence or Symbolism or even New Journalism is more obliging to classification. The fashionable locus of camp is the "aesthete generation," which lasted two generations, from Wilde to Beerbohm. This is when camp aesthetics coalesced into a literary initiative that nurtured many of the names in this book: Sacher-Masoch, Corelli, Beardsley, Saki, Benson, followed by Berners, Firbank, Ros, Coward, Isherwood ... the greatest concentration of camp writers so far. E.F. Benson reminds us that nobody who was there conceived of the aesthete movement as a school.[19] Benson likens all literary movements to puppeteering, manipulating cultural history to portray a commentator's vision in patently artificial categories. Decades do this. These approximations allow us to distinguish trends and periods, though distortedly, inexactly. The aesthete movement pools the writings and paintings of the *fin de siècle,* with pre-- Raphaelite nostalgia, but this generic term is too loose for a literary definition. Camp roots are at least Shakespearean. Its faltering, marginal development is still, demonstrably, active, and I contend its style is coherent enough for us to talk intelligibly about a cogent force in literature.

Camp fashion declined with the invention of World War: rationing, which endured until the '60s, was not as conducive to camp as the dandyism of the turn of the century. Benson's biographer considers our alienation from his first novel, *Dodo*, "unrecognizable to modern eyes. The characters seem arch and artificial, their manner ridiculous and their speech contrived," but Brian Masters maintains that *Dodo* is an historic artifact of the aesthete period, now as dead as the Dodo: in 1893, mannered style was all the rage.[20] The enduring fact is that Benson's arch and artificial style was not fashioned for *Dodo* only: even in maturity this remained a distinctive signifier of his voice. I hear it in his 1930 memoir *As We Were*, as he charts the rise and swoon of the era that shaped his aesthetic, and ends it with World War I. In 1930, a biographical profile of Ronald Firbank (1886–1926) records the devastation of Firbank's equilibrium in World War I, when Art was drafted into propaganda. To his credit, Firbank produced novels that had nothing meaningful to say about the political situation. They did not sell. Firbank recoiled from the oppression of mass banality, the lowest common denominator that he called "the mob," and his friend and biographer conceded, "The war was their triumph."[21] Armistice was a reprieve while the mob regrouped. Now Lord Berners, an aristocratic camp dilettante with some talent but no convictions, retreated: Berners' biographer puts the rumblings of World War II in a context that personifies the decline of camp,

> not just the eclipse of an attractive way of living, but a world in which the things he revered and admired simply did not exist. It was not only that everything would be difficult and drab—though there was that, too, and he felt that he would not be suited to coping with it—it was that his sort, his style, would be pointless, too marginal to be noticed and then gone altogether, like the Russian aristocrats living in Paris after the revolution.[22]

And so, between 1920 and 1939 in the popular *Mapp and Lucia* saga of E.F. Benson, Lucia presides over flippant village life unaffected by World War. Lucia reigned "with a secure autocracy pleasant to contemplate at a time when thrones were toppling, and imperial crowns whirling like dead leaves down the autumn winds."[23] Even the simile for revolution is picturesque. In "London Revisited" in 1935 and "Speed" in 1936, broadcast on radio and published as essays, Max Beerbohm draws a camp portrait of old London and mourns the extinction of the boulevardier, overtaken by a faster pace, the industrial urgency that renders obsolete the poise and detachment of camp.

Noël Coward wonders how Saki—pen name of Hector Hugh Munro (1870–1916)—would have fared had he survived World War I. Modernism "wouldn't really have been his cup of tea." Coward summarizes Saki for a new generation, fey in his lamentation: "His articulate duchesses sipping China tea on their impeccable lawns, his witty, effete, young heroes Reginald, Clovis Sangrail, Comus Bassington, with their gaily irreverent persiflage and their preoccupation with oysters, caviar and personal adornment, finally disappeared in the gunsmoke of 1914."[24] Noël Coward too (1899–1973) would languish in obsolescent devotion to the camp aesthetic. He was after all a big fan of the *Mapp and Lucia* saga that expired with Benson in 1940. And in 1940 *The Sunday Express* was considering spokesmen for the new age: "In any event, Mr. Coward is not the man for the job. His flippant England — Cocktails, Countesses, Caviare — has gone. A man of the people more in tune with the new mood of Britain would be a better proposition...." Coward responds tongue in cheek to this and another snipe by *The Daily Mirror,* at some distance from his public image,

> These sinister references to caviar — once with an E and once without — struck at my conscience like a dagger when I remembered the two large tins I had bought in Shanghai, also there were countesses I had left behind, presumably in a series of Mayfair luxury-flats.[25]

His dramatic reference to a dagger is a classic theatrical prop of a metaphor, made ironic by his pause to note a spelling discrepancy, playing to type, flippant indeed. The question of modern credibility is not a pressing concern. An incongruent feature of this thesis, in challenging the critical disdain for camp, is that camp would dissociate itself from any such protestation. (I take my lead from that brazen philosopher Wittgenstein, who concluded a treatise with peerless hypocrisy by kicking away the ladder of his methodology.)

What accounts for the critical blind spot around the caprices and devices of literary camp? Appraisal from a realist or minimalist aesthetic, from a perspective of understatement and academic rigor, is ideologically bound to dismiss camp as counterfeit. However, camp suggests that all aesthetics are counterfeit in the artifice of their representations. Aldous Huxley associates conspicuous artifice with primitive development — which supports the dismissive body of criticism, though it does not anticipate the self-reflective structures of postmodernism. Huxley finds, "The first attempts of any people to be conspicuously literary are always productive of the most elaborate artificiality."[26] He defines mature aesthetics as "art without artifice." Oscar Wilde said exactly the contrary fifty years before. Necessarily, the delineation of representation deals in aggrandizement: when we focus, we magnify; when we elaborate, we exaggerate. Wilde enlightens our discourse: "Art itself is really a form of exaggeration; and selection, which is the very spirit of art, is nothing more than an intensified mode of over-emphasis."[27]

And so the most camp character in *The Importance of Being Earnest,* Algernon, declares in Act II, "If I am occasionally a little over-dressed, I make up for it by being always immensely over-educated." Huxley's ideal was simplicity. Camp is remarkably superficial, but Huxley's modest simplicity does not countenance exhibitionism. Huxley's simplicity comes down to a conventional ideal that the artifice shouldn't show.

Aesthetics oversees several sensibilities: there is more than one measure of what is appealing or correct. Susan Sontag classifies three aesthetic movements. Each pitches a different ideal: the "straightforward relation between intention and performance" seeks "truth, beauty and seriousness" in high art like Homer and Rembrandt. There is also the distorted seriousness of "anguish, cruelty, derangement," such as the disharmonies of Kafka and, Sontag adds, Sade. Lastly, there is the frivolous elevation of "artifice as an ideal," camp.[28] The application of one aesthetic to the form of another provokes the culture clash we saw in Watson's assessment of Keats' early work such as "Imitation of Spenser," which "luxuriates in description but completely lacks the high and serious morality which gives backbone to the description in *The Faerie Queene*."[29] (Saki recommends *The Faerie Queene* for insomnia in his much shorter story "Louise.") Art for art's sake is not enough for traditional academicians. Ira Grushow, in academic consideration of Max Beerbohm, invokes "a core of general truth ... that underlies the novel from *Tom Jones* to *Ulysses* ... which alone validates our troubling ourselves with the behavior and fortunes of invented beings."[30]

Quentin Crisp, a most provocative pacifist, disagrees: "the difference between 'a truth' and 'a lie' is as inconsequential as the difference between 'non-fiction' and 'fiction': as long as it's 'a good read' and pleases an audience who cares how it may be classified by pedants?"[31] This is fundamentally subversive, the relativity of truth and the artifice of sincerity. Crisp took his lead from Wilde, who wrote, "One of the chief causes that can be assigned for the curiously commonplace character of most of the literature of our age is undoubtedly the decay of Lying as an art, a science, and a social pleasure."[32] Wilde is alluding to irony. Lack of this gleaming commodity excludes some flamboyant writers— Frederick Rolfe, for instance — from these considerations: camp demands irony. Cynthia Morrill[33] obliges with a definition: "By speaking the opposite in order to expose an asserted standard, irony relies upon establishing a critical distance ... between an ostensible standard and a point of commentary." In this polarity, she says, irony is "inflexible." Paradox, however, is not. Paradox exposes truth in the opposite of a truthful position: irony speaks the opposite of its intent and paradox reflexively finds truth there. Camp exponents are arch manipulators of irony in badinage and persiflage, with the aloof touch that Morrill calls "distance." Camp remains aloof from the script, often posing ironic inversion of intention in an exhibitionist aesthetic of extremes, drawing attention to its posturing. Oscar Wilde made ironic paradox fashionable in *fin de siècle* high society. Firbank and Coward also specialize in persiflage, that is, flippant banter — Shakespeare too: persifleurs, all.

Irony renders some euphemisms camp by a conspicuous correspondence between understatement and brazen allusion, paradoxically. Consider two oblique rhetorical structures that may express euphemisms. *Cockney rhyming slang* is too discreetly tangential to be camp: it diverts the reference to the subject with evasive and surreal juxtaposition — and so "tea leaf" is a picturesque, innocuous term for "thief." *Innuendo* upstages the function of the euphemism with double entendres and metaphoric references that *dramatize* the impact of the subject which the euphemism only appears to downplay, assuring an ironic reading. Innuendo is not merely insinuation; it is a *display* of insinuation that more pointedly references the subject than if it was named directly. The usual sexual connotations don't account for the camp of innuendo as substantially as this key ironic dynamic: it stages the expression and its rhetorical genre overtly, like theater, yet remains aloof from the implications. This is camp irony, and it preempts the critics by dismissing its subject on delivery.

Three aesthetic principles put camp out of favor with orthodoxy: camp prefers transparent *artifice* (exhibitionism) over discreet guile; prefers *flippancy* over seriousness (or *style* over content); and prefers *excess* (exaggeration) over minimalism.

A principle of aesthetics considers when is enough too much. "More is less" is the ascetic maxim of minimalism and of moderate, figurative and functional aesthetics, especially of a postgraduate pedigree that is the grounding of many literary critics and publishing houses. The orthodox editorial role prunes clichés and purges artistic transgressions such as repetition, redundancy, and any appearance of effort or art for art's sake. "Trying too hard" by reaching for another phrase to evoke atmosphere or define character dilutes the effect. Camp, however, plays on repetition with showboating excess, flaunting redundancies. Is repetition an admission that the writing is not honed enough to "get it" the first time? Not unless the koan or the haiku is an admission of the paucity of a poet's imagination. In camp, more is more, and more and more is moreso. By any orthodox judgement, camp is overwritten. Camp always comes back for an encore: why use one word or sentence where five will do— and none of them are likely to qualify the expression, unless ironically ("quite appalled" or "somewhat filibustered"). In punctuation, camp amplifies the pause between the thought and the deed. Camp puts the cliché on the stage. It exposes the masquerade of portrayal ... the grandiose pose, precise and public diction, ironic overstatement, which paradoxically scales down the subject yet oversees character, narrative, ideology, and the form itself.

The conventional maxim "Show, Don't Tell" downplays narrative to conceal the author's hand and let characters speak and react for themselves. If it doesn't advance plot or argument or inform character, strike it out. "Show, Don't Tell" became mandatory once television showed us everything, and narrative went the way of the art of conversation. Camp, however, upstages plot with stylistic authors loath to abdicate narrative personality: it's one of the antiquated niceties of camp. *The Times Literary Supplement* couldn't even wait for John Logie Baird to complain of Ronald Firbank, "He seems more concerned to get out smart remarks than to tell the story, or even to let the reader know what is really going on," (1 November 1917) but Leslie Fiedler sees strength in the weakness in *Nation* (12 April 1951): "We need the example of his splendid inconsequence ... to deliver us from the dull consequence of plot." Plot is concerned with *what happens next*. In *Odette: A Fairy Tale for Weary People,* Ronald Firbank reports the premise of the story as gossip overheard by the narrative. *Inclinations,* not a play but a *tour de force* of dialogue with narrative as flimsy as stage directions, can be read as one long verbatim exchange of gossip. In "Lady Appledore's Mésallaince," Firbank relegates the conclusion of *what happens next* (did they or didn't they get together?) to a summary piece of tattle, an afterthought, an incidental diversion from the *style* of the story.

Saki typically compresses the plot of "The Elk" in Mrs. Yonelet's quotation marks. Plot is nothing but a passing conversation piece. Charles Maude helped Saki write *The Watched Pot,* and Maude prefaces the play by recalling that Saki "was so full of witty remarks that it was a cruel business discarding some of his *bons mots.*" Finally, Maude notes, "Shortly before the war Saki at last gave in on the question of plot."[34] Still, to my reading, Saki delightfully subverts the exigencies of plot and the dramatic dynamics in *The Watched Pot,* which never boils but favors flippant characterization and salvaged *bons mots.*

In a collection of film reviews, Quentin Crisp, obliged to relate the plot even of an unfavorable film to his readers ("Although everybody knows that I am only masquerading as a film critic"), must pause to sigh, "Shall I go on?"[35]

Many a camp author has sighed the same. J.K. Huysmans[36] says of his literary experiments, "the necessity of coming to a conclusion did not appeal to me," and all his analyses of literature in *Against Nature,* his scathing criticisms and his eulogies, focus on style.

Brigid Brophy objects, "The 20th century narrative-drug is so strong that it slugs its readers into near-unconsciousness," where "the content must be almost all plot, and plot must be convoluted into the form of a maze."[37] Brophy credits psychology with exposing even naturalistic narrative as make-believe, breaking the collusion between author and reader and leaving us self-conscious about the process. One Victorian device to counter our canny cogniscence of narrative was a wearisome authentication of it in "a narrator-I within the narrator-I," Brophy notes. This nests the writing deeper in convoluted testimony.

Realism is out of the question. Wilde's style of criticism makes the point, "There is such a thing as robbing a story of its reality by trying to make it too true, and *The Black Snow* is so inartistic as not to contain a single anachronism to boast of, while the transformation of Dr. Jekyll reads dangerously like an experiment out of *The Lancet*."[38] Like Wilde before him, and like Huysmans' graduation from Naturalism to Decadence before Wilde, Juan Goytisolo (1931–) rejected realism in the mid–1970s: "The old-fashioned novel (with 'round' characters developed psychologically, with its verisimilitude and its 'realism,' etc) no longer interests me," and he declared, "The only 'novelistic' works which I am interested in now are those which show a new and audacious elaboration; those in which the creative imagination of the writer manifests itself not through an outside referent in reality, but above all, through the use of language."[39] From this period, with Goytisolo's pedigree established, his books became camp. Had camp come first in his development, critics would find it easier to diminish as the splashes of an ingenious novice, like Watson's critique of early Keats. Though highly acclaimed, Goytisolo does like to satirize the conventional critical reaction that would turn Brecht over in his grave and make camp shed its boa: "precisely! readers of novels, like television serial addicts want to be gripped by a sustained and interesting plot, tense, human scenes, oodles of emotion!" proclaims *The Marx Family Saga*.[40] Goytisolo is sufficiently scholarly to construct a justifying rationale for his audacious development and build it into his narratives, a postmodernist bridge between classical aesthetics and irreverence, which qualifies the camp and pacifies academics. Wilde too secured a place in the classic canon with another tip to the scholastic major domo. Yes, but their intellectual discourse on camp should read aloof from commitment or closure, free of the unbecoming frown of Rodin's Thinker.

Camp snubs the moral imperative of Milan Kundera, an earnest and influential intellectual novelist who asserts, "A novel that does not discover a hitherto unknown segment of existence is immoral. Knowledge is the novel's only morality."[41] Chloe Poems (1962–) will reassess the value of knowledge in poems like "Stupid Intellectual," but Kundera's orthodox valuation always finds comrades in criticism and on campus, though not in camp. Seriousness is an act like any other rhetoric and no more valid than whimsy, Oscar Wilde knew. Perhaps less so, lacking in style: Lord Darlington says in Act I of *Lady Windermere's Fan*, "Who are the people the world takes seriously? All the dull people one can think of, from the Bishops down to the bores." Lord Darlington models the author's attitude for the audience: seriousness is too irresponsible an attitude to take seriously: "I think that life is too important a thing ever to talk seriously about it."

An Ideal Husband sets the limitations on seriousness when Lord Goring cautions, "I only talk seriously on the first Tuesday in every month, from four to seven."[42] Any extension on this doctor's surgery of seriousness "makes me talk in my sleep," implying equivalence and contesting the common school of thought that esteems seriousness as truth itself. As Wilde premiered *Lady Windermere's Fan*, young E.F. Benson was writing a wonderfully frivolous novel called *The Babe*, whose protagonist wants to lose his baby-faced innocence. His Cambridge friend advises, "'But you should take yourself more seriously. I believe that is very aging.'"[43] Perhaps that is the untold moral of *The Picture of Dorian Gray*, too.

Camp poses the exposure as the aesthetic. Style is the enlightenment of deportment in artifice and process, which is why Gwendolen remarks, in Act III of *The Importance of Being Earnest*, "In matters of grave importance, style, not sincerity, is the vital thing." Algernon speaks for Wilde when he opens Act I on the piano, "I don't play accurately — but I play with wonderful expression." Wilde is remarkably honest in affirming style over content: in making the expression overt, paradoxically, camp shows a certain integrity that I challenge you to find in, say, politics.

Noël Coward makes it clear in a revue with an announcement to the audience that "new ideas are not necessary, and that it is only the *treatment* that is important."[44] There follows an extramarital scene of "the Eternal Triangle," enacted three times in the style of J.M. Barrie, Frederick Lonsdale, and (*"played at lightning speed"*) a French Farce. The dramatic revelation of a wife's infidelity is theatrically subverted each time by caricature of the featured author's style. In *We Were Dancing*, a two-scene comedy of manners, Noël Coward presents style over content by preserving decorum even in unseemly situations, as another husband discovers his wife's infidelity. Karl, the lover, was played by Coward in the premier. We never leave the drawing-room, but as Karl prepares to elope with the husband's wife, the husband can only say,

HUBERT: Then I shan't be seeing you again.
KARL: Not unless you come and see us off on the boat.
HUBERT: I shan't be able to on Wednesday, I have to go up-country.[45]

The cock-eyed notion of a cuckolded husband in attendance on the docks to wave farewell to the elopers is topped by the reply that only a prior engagement prevents Hubert from obliging. Impeccable manners prevail over sensational content, detached from the eternal triangle. Quentin Crisp in his Edwardian decorum would approve. "It is the *style* with which anything is said or done that matters most," he said.[46] Functionalism is dismissed with aristocratic disdain. Immanuel Kant too preferred a "useless" definition of art in the 18th century, if we want to bestow heavyweight credibility on this whimsy — though the cosmetic notion was truer *before* Kant said it, I feel.

The sight of musical notes in flight on the stave inspired Lord Berners to compose, not its sound, and his influences are "compositions which seemed to consist for the most of arpeggios, glissandos and cadenzas."[47] Lord Berners' disclosure of style over content assumes the guise of Lord FitzCricket in *Far from the Madding War:* "When traveling on the Continent he had a small piano in his motor car, and on the strength of this he was likened in the popular press to Chopin and Mozart."[48] In edifying conversation, his biographer reports, Berners "was relieved to hear that he could regard Nietzsche as a wit and poet and ignore the philosophy."[49]

Camp courts epigrammatic conversation, urbane, succinct and throwaway. Meter and aloof delivery register more than content. In Benson's *Trouble for Lucia,* Lucia demonstrates her love for aesthetic effect in the epigram, popularized by Wilde, quite aside from meaning. She tells Georgie she never hedges but comes down one side or the other...

> "A hedge may save you from falling into a ditch," said Georgie brilliantly.
> "*Georgino,* how epigrammatic! What does it mean exactly? What ditch?"[50]

Style over content is even more prevalent in camp narrative. Max Beerbohm[51] interrupts a dandy simile with a commentary on the narrative, "The moon, like a gardenia in the night's button-hole — but no! why should a writer never be able to mention the moon without likening her to something else — ..." although his protesting disclaimer is too involved to be aloof. Personalizing third person narrative was a charming 19th century fashion and occasionally comments on the genre, but camp narrative must be aloof from its own image. Beerbohm is a borderline case: inverted classical and even Biblical phrasing in *Zuleika Dobson,* his only novel, is anachronistic to his contemporary tale, with tragedian posturing. Classical, titled pronouncements set up a dandified prose from page one:

> An ebon pillar of tradition seemed he, in his garb of old-fashioned cleric. Aloft, between the wide brim of his silk hat and the white extent of his shirt-front...

I find Beerbohm more fixed on his tale than major camp players, not so self-reflective. He is occasionally closer to camp in his ornamental detail and feminine attention to wardrobe in larger than life yet effete characters. He does set up the character theatrically, "He alone was worthy of the background." His hero the Duke, described in feminine detail, values style over content in accepting the Order of the Garter and shows no recognition of political responsibility. Neither does Beerbohm. "The dark blue riband, and the star scintillating to eight points, the heavy mantle of blue velvet, with its lining of taffeta and shoulder-knots of white satin, the crimson surcoat, the great embullioned tassels..." When the Duke revives his beloved with a water jug — "(Dew-drops on a white rose? But some other, sharper analogy hovered to him)" — Beerbohm's analogy draws more attention to the writing than to the scene, and the Duke himself indulges the writer's frivolous evaluation of the metaphor. "He dipped and flung, then caught the horrible analogy and rebounded." The variable "analogy" reminds us that all sentences are compounds of variables selected by deliberation to spin the author's yarn. Ironically, here, a fictional character contemplates an alternative analogy, even in the drama of his fainted beloved. But then, to the camp temperament, personality is art, and all art is artifice, and so personality is a fiction. Beerbohm's effect distances us from the domestic drama.

Wry reflective narrative subverts the drama again later, teasing a moment of crisis: "I am loath to interrupt my narrative at this rather exciting moment — a moment when the quick, tense style, exemplified in the last paragraph but one, is so very desirable." The commentary reframes that "quick, tense style" with ironic distance. Beerbohm advocates the classical school for delivering tragic messages, "graphic verses unimpeachable in scansion," so dramatic news that the Duke has drowned himself is undercut by snooty narrative criticism:

> Blank verse, yes, so far as it went; but delivered without the slightest regard for rhythm, and composed in stark defiance of those laws which should regulate the breaking of bad news.

Charles Dickens caricatured this manner of speech with Mister Jingle in *The Pickwick Papers,* but Beerbohm parodies the entire artifice of representing speech and exhibiting behavior in narrative. "'The river,' gasped Clarence. 'Threw himself in. On purpose. I was on the towing-path. Saw him do it.'" Dramatic potential is upstaged by commentary and sent up by melodrama as women model their reactions like tragediennes: "Mrs. Batch had a keen sense of the deportment owed to tragedy. Katie, by bickering with Clarence, had thrown away the advantage she had gained by fainting."

Is style over content insubstantial? It's a common dismissal of Lord Berners' writing, the relegation of Firbank as "a minor novelist," and disdain for camp altogether. Jack Babuscio looks deeper to perceive, "Style is a form of consciousness,"[52] echoed by Quentin Crisp in *How to Have a Lifestyle*. When Babuscio polarizes the camp dynamic, "In terms of style, [camp] signifies performance rather than existence," on reflection I'd put it differently. Performance and existence, to be sure, but camp is too aloof to be polarized. This is the transcendental distance between performance and existence in camp revelations of the masquerade of personality and the artifice of process. Overplaying its hand ironically, camp charges this detachment, in the tension between aggrandized performance and everyday existence, the dynamic in the static, which sparks consciousness.

Critics and Clerics

Academic tradition ... puritan criticism ... ecclesiastical
camp ... punning ... shirking the work ethic ...
aloof disposition ... rewriting criticism ...

Quentin Crisp was often invited to speak at universities. "There I explained that education is a mistake. Cluttering one's skull with facts about any subject other than oneself I hold to be a waste of time."[1] Saving his careless dismissal for the end of the sentence is equivalent to a sweep of the hand that brushes the matter aside, so typically Crisperanto. (Self-awareness and narcissism are incestuous bedfellows, and the sentiment is anticipated by Saki in "Reginald On Worries.") Chloe Poems, punning on "campus Christmas" in "Further Education," following the poet's damning admission of never attending higher education, frivolously equates being "campus a row of tents" to a most superlative degree. Even while planning a didactic recital at Harvard, Poems challenges the marketing of certificated knowledge on "credit" as a consumer commodity in brainwashed, remedial notions of *lifelong learning* and *education-education-education.* Poems takes the Socratic view without citing Socrates. Camp authors flout the notion of studiousness as an edifying virtue and knowledge as the scripture of wisdom, their skepticism related to their irreligious sentiments. And the dons and deans of Oxbridge frown.

Max Beerbohm was a caricaturist as well as a writer. Beerbohm sends up academia in a 1925 illustration, captioned, "Logic and Mathematics Reconciled Through the Bitterness of Beholding the Passionate Advances Now Made By Mr. Bertrand Russell to Physics." I'd like to draw your attention to this scenic diversion from literary camp: it signals the flouting of academic decorum so characteristic of camp aesthetics. Bertrand Russell is the subject: his famous intellectual eclecticism looks like gratuitous promiscuity with that camp device, innuendo. A caricature of Russell importunes an effete Athenian male in classical toga and sandals who represents Physics. Three robed figures look on in statuesque disdain. Logic and Mathematics embrace: wiry seniors with the pinched intensity and round, squinting spectacles of academicians. In dialogue balloons, Logic says, "How unlike dear Mr. Mill!" and Mathematics responds, "Odiously incontinual and fluxional!" Politics, standing aloof, arms folded, remarks, "He even had the impertinence to flirt with *me* once. And no man ever understood me less well."[2] The classical Athenians look imperiously studious but they pose like effeminate male whores, conspiring to make the great Bertrand Russell look like a solicitous lecher.

Academia is affronted by the camp attitude to art and learning. Camp liberates the restrictions of dominant aesthetics that is traditionally austere, masculine, serious, didactic, clinical and clerical in naturalistic detail ... aesthetics to disguise rather than expose artifice. Beerbohm applauds his "frivolous" youth spent in music halls and he is inclined to believe, "a young man who desires to know all that in all ages and all lands has been thought by the best minds, is laying up for himself a very miserable old age."[3] His teasing rhetoric sets up a laudable ambition whose sophisticated clauses lead, ceremoniously, to a decrepit conclusion. Beerbohm succeeded George Bernard Shaw as drama critic for *The Saturday Review* and introduced himself to his readers, "I am not fond of the theater."[4] Just as Crisp declared his periodical role as film critic to be a masquerade, Beerbohm enjoys the irony, aloof from anything so practical as consequences or what I imagine as the consternation of his editor. "I, who have never left a theater with any definite impression of pleasure or displeasure, am curious to know how on earth I am going to fill so much as half a column of this paper, week by week, with my impressions," followed by a snipe: "My self-respect and my ignorance of bygone formulae of drama will prevent me from the otherwise easy task of being an academic critic." That snide aside is not the last we will hear on academia. Beerbohm is not above a stage analogy, a minor music-hall artist sent on as an extra-turn. He does bring camp pedigree to the appointment: "Though I have no theoretic knowledge of the drama, I am a rich mine of theatrical gossip." And so, favoring "a voice of thunder and an imperial manner of walking about the stage" over understated realism, and reflecting on criticism as often as exercising it, he continued in the post for twelve years.

Noël Coward's plays seem most unconvincing when he is being sincere — sentimental and patriotic. Only theatrical sensibility dissociates his style from unseemly lapses into sincerity to save many plays from foundering. *Conversation Piece* puts it in domestic terms, "Emotion is so very untidy."[5] Coward adjusts the sentiment to reflect on process in *Relative Values,* "Dearest Cynthia. You really must not let righteous indignation play such hell with your syntax."[6] Camp doesn't suppress but rather gives itself to the gesture so generously that the performance cultivates a witnessing consciousness, grandly overseeing the moment. It's a matter of taste, Coward explains in *Design for Living,* and we find the same attitude displayed by Quentin Crisp, Lord Berners, Ronald Firbank, in both lifestyle and writing. Accused of frivolity, and what is worse, bad taste, Otto, an artist in *Design for Living,* responds, "Certain emotions transcend even taste, Ernest. Take anger, for example: look what anger's doing to you. You're blowing yourself out like a frog!"[7] The importance of being earnest would seem overestimated.

Consider motifs, consistent themes that give identity and subliminal coherence to a work. The author is expected to disguise these sublimated fetishes under the narrative. The critical eye appreciates their discovery, and a wily part of the critic's congratulations may be preening conceit at his detection as he takes credit for the edifying revelation. Camp, however, displays its fetishes like an exhibitionist. If there is a redundancy, it could be the critic.

Quentin Crisp disarmed many a critic by being the first to dismiss his own writing, even as he wrote it. Siegfried Sassoon complains about Firbank's conversation, "His most rational response to my attempts at drawing him out about literature was 'I adore italics, don't you?'"[8] Camp is so frivolous that serious critics can do nothing with it. Lord Berners commends his favorite author, "Ronald Firbank is frivolous par excellence. Frivolity combined with beauty, humor and fantasy. One should not expect to find in his work any weighty sociological or philosophical judgements." Berners' biographer says of Berners too, "Certainly his flight from Victorian heaviness and emotion, his refusal to preach, his fear of boring, let alone becoming pompous, stripped him of the trappings of seriousness...."[9] Seriousness: that indispensable tone of heavyweight classical aesthetics described by Sontag as antithetical to camp. Camp looks at reflections, not depth. Chloe Poems' unruly work, and the flippant and militant nome de plume Aunty Establishment, react to the pre-fabricated media structures of meaning, such as royalty and capitalism and the cult of celebrity, the presentation of fabrication not as artifice but as political, cultural realism. The angst of meaning-lessness is not lack of meaning but the telling deceit of unsustainable false meaning that leaves us displaced, in a state of ideological yearning. Lord Berners dramatizes the dichotomy in *Far from the Madding War:* "Lord FitzCricket was a dilettante and had always been interested in the pleasurable aspects of art, and he thought that a work of art should never be tedious. Francis, on the other hand, held that art should be austere, and he felt that he himself had a mission." FitzCricket is Berners' self-portrait.[10] His own biographer takes the critical role, "The plot is slender, indeed inadequate, more a series of incidents that give rise to conversation, and in this perhaps reminiscent of Firbank."[11] And, in *The Listener* (8 June 1961), W.H. Auden said this about Ronald Firbank: he created "a private vision of Eden" that was "no place for literary critics." This rare and dandy aesthetic, with aloof poise and aristocratic heritage and retrospective flourishes of fanciful Romanticism, seems rather conservative literature, and yet it frustrates and offends conservative critics at every arabesque turn.

A camp Cambridge Fellow is no exception, and so E.F. Benson's *The Weaker Vessel* is dismissed as "surface polish, all Benson Brilliantine" by *The Gentlewoman* in 1913, while the *Western Gazette* complains, "Mr. Benson attacks no problem, but merely paints portraits remorselessly." The analytic school feeds on problems. Benson's biographer records that with a biography of Charlotte Bronte in 1932, Benson overcame "years of being tartly dismissed as lightweight," and Brian Masters sees this triumphantly: at last, "he was now the subject of earnest scholarly discussion," albeit for non-fiction. "His critics had never bothered to look behind the ease and superficiality of his novels," Masters complains.[12] My complaint is this: ease and superficiality are aesthetic effects that many novelists cannot fashion to save their lives: its accomplishment should be meritorious enough. Critics overlook the superficial in search of something serious and secreted that will yield to analysis.

Well, *The Babe* indulges the Cambridge lifestyle, culled from Benson's distinguished background, but the only episode where characters actually study is frivolously comic. Reggie and Ealing undertake to study together with ineffectual resolve, easily distracted by superficial diversions. Ealing waits for Reggie to sharpen his pencil, don't you know: "'I can't go on till it's ready. I'm in the middle of underlining something.'" They sign off after fifteen minutes, and their resolution to resume after lunch for a further six hours is framed ironically. "'And six hours steady work a day,' said Reggie cheerfully, 'is as much as is good for any man. I begin not to attend after I have worked, really worked, you know, for six hours.'" The Babe's tutor credits his papers with "'a certain power of giving plausible and voluminous answers to questions of which it was obvious you know nothing whatever...'" Another tutor advises Reggie to read two classics, *Phaedrus* and the *Symposium:* "'The former you should read on the upper river under a plane tree if possible, the latter after dining wisely and well in your rooms...'"[13] *The Babe* sold remarkably well and the book adopted the tutor's sound advice with some charming pictures of Cambridge bridges. *The Inheritor*[14] bemoans the suffocation of fancy in Oxbridge, "that aseptic academical air of Cambridge, in which surely no germ of the fantastic could live." And in Benson's sagas of Lucia, his bourgeois heroine flouts the value of higher education by her very pretensions to it: so vague and confused and rife with anachronisms are her references to art and philosophy that Lucia cultivates a profound impression of flippancy.

Mario Praz was a distinguished scholar who disparaged form over function even in his appreciation of Decadence, *The Romantic Agony*, in 1933. "The style of *The Picture of Dorian Gray* alternates between the fanciful and the witty ... making one pun after another, and in his descriptive passages assuming the false naivete and picturesque bombast of an adult who wishes to appear ingenuous and surprising to the children whom he is trying to amuse. Wilde's point of view is always scenic; he sees things as in stage-perspective; he is all the time arranging his characters, his landscapes, his events, and making them pose." Praz perceives the details of camp without recognizing an evolved aesthetic: punning, frivolity, indulgence of the picturesque, bombastic narrative, theatricality and artificiality are all equally evident in Firbank, for instance. And so Praz discounts Wilde's (and camp's) tremendous irony, beyond the vision of Decadence.

Praz cannot understand why Wilde would introduce "into the midst of a scene which he wishes to make horrifying, an opium-tainted cigarette, a pair of lemon-yellow gloves, a gold-latten match-box, a Louis Quinze silver salver, or a Saracenic lamp studded with turquoises, which brings the whole edifice to the ground by revealing the fact that the author's real interest is in the decorative." These are camp emblems that take the decorative foreground in camp aesthetics. What falls is the orthodox construction of Praz, not Wilde, the ivory Babel of high seriousness. Praz can only conclude, "These inopportune decorative images are proof of a lack of seriousness in Wilde's conscience and of the superficiality of his hedonism, and show him to be greedy and capricious as an irresponsible child."[15] Charged and chaste ethical terms like "greedy ... irresponsible ... conscience..." are signs of moral reproach in criticism that has a theological aesthetic. They are impurities, by other aesthetics.

Orthodox critics and clerics share the same objections to camp. Camp has, in fact, been excommunicated.

The earliest universities were monasteries, where specialized Biblical learning and calligraphy required ascetic sacrifice from dedicated brethren. What I call orthodox academic aesthetics is bedeviled by Puritan Christian tradition. Scholars are theologians in sheep's clothing. The literary canon is canonical, and the ordination of camp may have to wait for the Apocalypse.

Camp is pagan. Camp is carnival. Camp pilgrims upstage canonical tradition but keep the pretty vestments, like Dorian Gray who, despite his hedonism, "had a special passion, also, for ecclesiastical vestments, as indeed he had for everything connected with the service of the Church."[16] I find ecclesiastical imagery in such kinky canons as Ronald Firbank, Juan Goytisolo and Chloe Poems—and especially among excommunicable exiles from the Catholic Church and misfit converts like Wilde and Beardsley and Firbank: flouting solemnity whimsically with hearsay heresy. Alan Bennett's (1934-) Anglican sensibility is less sensational, though E.F. Benson was spectacularly placed: his father was Archbishop of Canterbury. Saki explains, "The fashion just now is a Roman Catholic frame of mind with an Agnostic conscience: you get the medieval picturesqueness of the one with the modern conveniences of the other."[17] Lord Berners critiques that classic of literature, the Bible:

> The ugly, common bindings, the villainous print and the double columns were not calculated to arouse aesthetic interest, while the rigid numbering of the verses seemed to impart an unpleasantly didactic tone to the contents. Having been told that the book had been written by God himself, I often wondered why One who had shown himself, in most respects, lavish to the point of extravagance should have been so economical in the presentation of his literary efforts to the public.[18]

J.W. Lambert finds this aesthetic aside in Saki: "People may say what they like about Christianity; the religious system that produced green Chartreuse can never really die."[19] *The Unbearable Bassington* offers a Saki epigram that echoes the art of camp, "The art of public life consists to a great extent of knowing exactly where to stop and going a bit further."[20] Christian humility is too modest to complement the camp aesthetic. How *do* you solve a problem like Maria? Quentin Crisp breaks diplomatic relations with God, "from whose territory I had withdrawn my ambassadors at the age of fifteen. It had become obvious that he was never going to do a thing I said."[21] His grand agnosticism brings color and wit to a nondescript concept. The flagrant egocentricity that would have God do his bidding, on reflection, echoes many a congregation that exhorts God to satisfy our wishes on His day off.

Noël Coward[22] recalls his showstopping audition as a choirboy: "I remember giving way to a certain abandon on the line 'There was no other goo-oo-oo-ood enough to pay the price of sin,' and later, lashing myself into a frenzy over the far too often repeated—'Arnd terust in His redeeming blood.'" The incongruous contrast of his barnstorming audition with the holy post is camp. The frenzied commitment to the rendition would not qualify but for the ironic distance that Coward projects through retrospect, fully aware now of his larger than life formative ego, portrayed as a character. The precise insertion of "a *certain* abandon" qualifies Coward's abandonment preciously, while singing "a shade too dramatically" ironically exaggerates the impression by undercutting it: the genteel qualifier of "a shade" is so incongruous and impotent against its dramatic subject. Exaggerated pronunciation spells out the artifice on the page, "Arnd terust...." juxtaposing the sweeping gesture with the aloof touch. The ecclesiastical association becomes a camp motif when subverted by pagan impropriety or theatrical trappings. Ascetic values are flouted by a frivolous relish for ecclesiastical costume and ritual performance.

Christopher Isherwood (1904–1986) makes irreverent holy icons of his Berlin lodgings: his washstand is "a Gothic shrine"; even a cupboard has "carved cathedral windows"; and, "My best chair would do for a bishop's throne." Sally Bowles features in several irreligious analogies in *Goodbye to Berlin*. Addressing a millionaire, "Sally's features began to assume, with increasing frequency, the rapt expression of the theatrical nun."[23] Max Beerbohm's dandy Duke in *Zuleika Dobson* is celibate, but even in celibacy, narcissism is his religion, framing his devout vocation as ironically (though of course never so promiscuously) as Goytisolo's hedonistic narcissism. "The dandy must be celibate, cloistral: is, indeed, but a monk with a mirror for beads and breviary."[24]

Alan Bennett's superbly understated offering of ecclesiastical camp is a memorial service story in 2001. *The Laying on of Hands* is a *double entendre:* the deceased subject, in life, procured salvation by sexual ministrations under the guise of masseur. Bennett confides hushed prose and discreet asides from Church pews. He observes fame and prestige among the unlikely congregation come to bid farewell to a gay male prostitute, with the author's domestic perspective on life, the universe and everything: "The small-screen gardeners knew the big-screen heart-throbs but none of them recognized 'someone high up in the Bank of England' ('and I don't mean the window-cleaner,' whispered a man who did)." That would be Bennett, our invisible parishioner-chaperone through the service. He notes ever so wryly, "Diffidence was very much to the fore," and spies a leading architect ("one of whose airports had recently sprung a leak"),

> his self-effacing behavior and downcast eyes proclaiming him a person of some consequence humbled by the circumstances in which he currently found himself, and which might have been allegorically represented on a ceiling, say (although not one of his), as Fame deferring to Mortality.[25]

Bennett defrocks the memorial reverence: that word "proclaiming" exposes the self-effacing architect, making bombast of his humility, and then a fantastic metaphor, extending like Michelangelo across the church ceiling, sends up the pretense most high. The asides gossip about the architect's projects in the deflated decorum due in a pew, and they ground the pompous humility in Bennett's accustomed banal tones, like the one about the window-cleaner who identifies a man high up in the bank of England. Bennett's mock solemnity, paraded like a Royal Command performance, recalls Benson's *Mapp and Lucia,* where Lucia models bereavement impressively for a year. Like her sham modesty, it is self-aggrandizing; like the Queen being seen to be sad or humble with bejeweled sincerity, Lucia wears her widowhood as her artistic black period, "when grief forbade her to play golf."[26]

The Laying on of Hands upstages Alan Bennett's monotone commentary with fantastical touches.

> Much noticed, though, was a pop singer who had been known to wear a frock but was today dressed in a suit of stunning sobriety, relieved only by a diamond clasp that had once belonged to Catherine the Great....

Casting a transvestite pop star, distinguished by "stunning sobriety" and embellished by a sensational accessory from the decadent reign of Catherine the Great, upstages solemnity beautifully. The priest himself regards the service as a performance and the congregation his audience, but he distrusts the deity and His melodramatic temper. Indeed, "on one of his reports at theological college his tutor had written, 'Tends to confuse God with Joan Crawford.'"[27]

Brilliantly self-contained, Bennett gets color and character from his monotone narrative delightfully, incidentally irreverent without once betraying the reverent tone, as if every ecclesiastical faux pas were attributable to Tourette's syndrome.

In *A Question of Attribution* in 1988, where "saints brandish the emblems of their suffering, the cross, the gridiron and the wheel," Alan Bennett observes the old masters: "these martyrs seldom lose a drop of their *sang froid,* so cool about their bizarre torments, the real emblems of their martyrdom a silk dressing-gown and a long cigarette-holder."[28] In a lecture at the National Gallery in 1993, he confides his relief that one can give an intellectual and not just aesthetic response to paintings because "saying who's who and what's what in a painting, could be taken as a higher form of that very English preoccupation, gossip." Bennett gossips about art throughout the lecture delightfully. He reads fey effeminacy in all those depictions of St. Sebastian: "Invariably his response to the arrows is quite inadequate, no more than wincing as yet another bolt finds its mark, as if to say, 'Oh, really. Must you?'" Having domesticated intellectualism, he domesticates Divinity. In representations of the Crucifixion, he worries "why one of the Holy family couldn't occasionally walk over and pay one of the other crosses a visit." After all, "it's what we did if we went to see someone in hospital and there was someone on the ward with no visitors."[29]

E.F. Benson admires a representation of the resurrected Christ in a church window in *The Babe*: "To the right kneels Mary Magdelene gaudily dressed, just having turned and seeing that he was not, as she supposed, the gardener," whose irony observes the hushed decorum that Bennett delights in a century on. Benson goes further: "By a quaint but curiously felicitous idea of the artist, the figure of Christ is holding a spade in his hand, as if to give color to Mary's mistake," while Christ waits for recognition like many an aspirant to celebrity.[30] In 1934, Ronald Firbank also perceived the camp aesthetic of the Crucifixion — camp martyrdom makes theater of suffering — but skirted this side of blasphemy by merely observing its artistic representation by a pupil of Felicien Rops:

> — a pale woman stretched upon a Cross in a silver tea gown, with a pink Rose in her powdered hair; the pearls about her throat bound her faster to the Cross, and splendid lace draped her bleeding hands and feet.[31]

Feminized, flamboyant and exhibitionistic, marrying domestic and exotic detail, tea gown and splendid lace adorning the iconic magnitude of the spectacle, camp symbols laid in offering at the feet of the icon: a fan; a letter; a kinky handkerchief "tortured into a knot till it looked like a white flower." How fey.

Camp finds other places of worship for its outcast practitioners. In "Faith Is A Toilet," in the *Adult Entertainment* collection, Chloe Poems makes a church of a temple of convenience. We will also find this indiscriminate embrace of mind, body and soul in Juan Goytisolo's trips to the toilet, rather Rabelaisian. The book launch for *Adult Entertainment* was conceptual art: it happened in The Temple of Convenience in 2002, a Victorian underground public toilet converted to a bar, in the godforsaken city of Manchester. It was a far cry from the author's readings at the Cheltenham Literature Festival, and a farther outcry from Goytisolo's tour with Poems in the Cervantes Center for Spanish Studies and the Royal Festival Hall. The Temple of Convenience was inconveniently narrow, standing room only, punters packed together as in a urinal after last orders. It was an aesthetic, not strategic, location for a book launch, driven by thematic inevitability as surely as historic determinism: some ironies are too irresistible to camp. Poems courts controversy like a coy exhibitionist, outrageously, yet with poetic decorum.

In the years before his flat became his dressing room, the public toilet was where Quentin Crisp made up his face and turned into a bird of paradise, and where gay prostitution paid dividends. The public toilet (sanctified again by Poems in "The Effeminate") is sanctuary to outlawed homosexuals, where they can kneel and find succor in peace. Rhyme in "Faith Is A Toilet" telegraphs a blasphemous epigram like music-hall call and response.

> So if you're terribly evangelical
> I don't wish to spoil it
> But quite simply
> For some of us
> Faith is a toilet.[32]

The naked and knowing simplicity reads like graffiti on a toilet wall, the scripture of the underworld. The lines stand aloof, with line breaks as arched as an eyebrow, from their likely and not altogether undesirable impact on evangelical sensibility. Chloe Poems' "No Stranger To Sequins" takes an epiphany in a public toilet. The prostitute protagonist is moved to evaluate his life by toilet graffiti as holy as Benedictine calligraphy —

> Some people find it in books
> I found it on a toilet door:
> There must be room for love[33]

— despite the promiscuous proximity of gay oral sex in the happy stanza.

The public toilet is the sanctuary of the repressed unconscious and the persecuted bodily functions— and the last refuge of the pun. "Mark my words," a headmaster remarks in Alan Bennett's *Forty Years On,* "when a society has to resort to the lavatory for its humor, the writing is on the wall."[34] Bennett's memoirs marry our holy and bodily postures in pew and cubicle with an analogy. Cubicles are hallowed places of confessional intimacy and contemplation, no matter how irreverent the result and however fantastically scholastical.

Brigid Brophy (1929–1995) puts her Irish lilting prose onto a public toilet wall in her novel *In Transit.* "And facing him, just above the lavatory itself, there was a positive scholar's palimpsest.

"The original hand had written

> BUT YOU'D LOOK SWEET
> UPON THE SEAT.

"To this a scholiast had supplied

> OF A BISEXUAL MADE FOR TWO."[35]

Camp transgresses thrifty campus values like "restraint," celebrates all manner of parsimonious pejoratives as honest generosities: "Self-indulgent ... self-referential ... prurient ... obvious ... naïve ... contrived ... fluffy ... overwritten..." camp models them all as comely style accessories.

Camp art disdains church morality. "I believe in good food. I believe in sex. I believe in the freedom to explore its many recipes. I believe in overeating," Chloe Poems' personal manifesto introduces *Adult Entertainment* ... including this belief: "I believe the world is sick with greed."[36] Poems gets away with paradox like Wilde, thanks to camp's ironic and dégagé disposition. Ronald Firbank satirized morality as a chattering mantra that impedes discourse; the very word was always on the President's lips in *Concerning the Eccentricities of Cardinal Pirelli,* and it left an impression:

> The serenity of my moral. The prestige of my moral. The perfection of my moral. She has no dignity of moral. I fear a person of no positive moral. Nothing to injure the freshness of her moral. A difficulty of moral. The etiquette of my moral. The majesty of my moral, etc, etc —

The moral:

> Beware of a facile moral![37]

Angela Carter notes, in her play on Firbank, "The American publisher, Brentano's, turned down *Cardinal Pirelli* on 'religious and moral grounds.'"[38]

A significant heredity in camp genealogy is queer subculture, and so, historically, the amoral perspective may reflect the homosexual as outsider. I rather think, though, that this gay context does not explain the aloof disposition that stands off the enactment of roles and ideology half as well as the tradition of theater. Morality is one mask, immorality is another.

The work ethic, with all its Lutheran and capitalist and communist endorsements, is another flouted code in camp. Camp tills the topsoil and leaves the rest to Turgenev and Tolstoy. Oscar Wilde, in "The Remarkable Rocket," voices one of those paradoxes that takes a position without making a stand: "Hard work is simply the refuge of people who have nothing whatever to do."[39] Camp satirizes the rat-race from outside: to depict Sisyphean labor from within would be laborious, and so camp forgoes the proletarian perspective. Saki looks to the Sermon on the Mount to sanctify the point that aesthetics should be useless: "Reginald recalled the lilies of the field, which simply sat looked and looked beautiful, and defied competition." Reginald becomes a martyr to camp before the paragraph is out: "'You don't know what a world of trouble I take in trying to rival the lilies in their artistic simplicity.'"[40] Clovis, another serial camp protagonist in Saki, is scathing of booming industry and utilitarianism. "Clovis On the Alleged Romance Of Business" opens,

"It is the fashion nowadays," said Clovis, "to talk about the romance of Business. There isn't such a thing. The romance has all been the other way, with the idle apprentice, the truant, the runaway, the individual who wouldn't be bothered with figures and book-keeping and left business to look after itself."

His epic vision of the industrial massacre of souls would rival Saki's experience in the trenches of world war, the legions of apprentices who "married early and worked late" and sacrificed style and individualism to somebody's idea of progress:

"He is buried by the thousand in Kensal Green and other large cemeteries; any romance that was ever in him was buried prematurely in shop and warehouse and office. Whenever I feel in the least tempted to be business-like or methodical or even decently industrious I go to Kensal Green and look at the graves of those who died in business."[41]

And so the foremost female in Saki's novel *When William Came* knows that "to be governed by ambition was only a shade or two better than being governed by convention."[42] Even when "the woman behind the man" in *The Watched Pot* urges a bachelor to become more eligible by being socially useful, all her suggested occupations are absurdly impractical ... painting (regardless of his inability to paint), founding a new religion, inventing a scoring system for county cricket, breeding a new fox terrier.... When René loses his maternal benefactress, his camp uncle says to his camp nephew, with camp decorum (avoiding vulgar practicality), "'I don't like to suggest anything so unbecoming as an occupation, but can't you manage to get entangled with a salary of some sort?'"[43] Saki flips the point on its whimsical head in "The Infernal Parliament," where Barton Bidderdale manages to die of a new disease: "'We always knew he would do something remarkable one of these days,' observed his aunts."[44]

There would be more candidates for the camp canon if only they would work at putting their perspective on paper instead of into the droll convenience of conversation — which is where Wilde claims his best work went — and the camp ideal of lifestyle as art. Exceptionally, E.F. Benson was prolific but fortunately most of his output was gloriously superficial. Aubrey Beardsley flouted the work ethic so much that his only novel is unfinished. Beardsley remains famous for his art, including illustrations of Wilde's work, in a more democratic medium open to different ways of seeing. For example, if Beardsley had *drawn* this passage — from his obscure novel, *Under the Hill* — it would be better known:

The coiffeur Cosmé was caring for her scented chevelure, and with tiny silver tongs, warm from the caresses of the flame, made delicious intelligent curls that fell as lightly as a breath about her forehead and over her eyebrows, and clustered like tendrils round her neck.[45]

And the hero is "troubled with an exquisite fear lest a day's travel should have too cruelly undone the labored niceness of his dress," as fey as Ophelia.

Brigid Brophy[46] makes the case for Beardsley's art, flouting "the Pre-Raphaelites' reliance on displaying the dignity of labor through the artists' laboriousness." Beardsley was all about *flair* and the notion of "artist as aristocrat." Orthodox aesthetics enforces the utilitarian work ethic that you can trace to fallen man's toil in atonement — which is why pleasure for pleasure's sake, or art for art's sake, is sinful or superficial. Art must have meaning, rational or moral design, to justify itself in puritan aesthetics — though its message should be veiled. After two expurgated instalments, posthumously published, a critic lambasted Beardsley and *Under the Hill*: "This labored literary indecency ... this fantastic drivel, without cohesion, without sense, devoid of art as meaning — a sheer labored stupidity, revealing nothing — a posset, a poultice of affectations."[47]

An unfinished novel is the perfect ending when the last thing Beardsley was concerned about, in his ornate style, was the plot. What a striking example of art nouveau in literature, from coiffeured curls "clustered like tendrils round her neck," to floristry, "and the rose-trees were wound and twisted with superb invention over trellis and standard," made baroque by asymmetrical and superabundant patterning in a fountain, "the water played profusely, cutting strange arabesques and subtle figures."[48] Beardsley heralds most of camp's preoccupations and effects: the ennui and narcissism of the hero; fetishistic attention to fashion; inclination to French culture; sensual decadence ("delicious" and "exquisite"); ornate decadence ("banqueted upon tapestries"); aloof touches ("caresses" and "lightly as a breath"). I might add delicate alliteration and flamboyant metaphor, or what amounts to the same thing, a preening fan or an exotic bird. In Beardsley's poem "The Three Musicians" (1895), "The charming cantatrice reclines," feminine and blasé, "And fans herself, half shuts her eyes /And smoothes the frock about her knees."[49] (A "cantatrice" is a female singer and the cantata is her musical narrative — but the sound and the look of "cantatrice" on the page is so much greater than its definition that you don't need to know that.)

The reclining pose, a camp motif to flout the work ethic: such an effete and fey position seems contrary to overstatement, but as Saki says, "Gracefully asprawl on the ottoman, in an attitude of almost exaggerated repose, was the boy of the woods."[50] One of Saki's cats "lay in considerable ease in a corner of the divan" in "The Philanthropist and the Happy Cat."[51] Exaggerated; considerable. The pose lends a droll tone to Coward's play *Point Valaine* (1944), when Linda reclines on a chaise lounge and laments the monotony of life's tranquility.[52] Max Beerbohm observes the camp pose of Zuleika Dobson who, "in a white peignoir tied with a blue sash, lay in a great chintz chair, gazing out of the bay window," and posing the attendant attitude: "There was ennui, and there was wistfulness, in her gaze."[53] In *Goodbye to Berlin*, by Christopher Isherwood, "Sally yawned languidly. 'People make me feel so tired.'" Even in impoverished surroundings, Sally's décor reflects the decadence of her divan demeanor, in a faded battle picture, "with the wounded reclining on their elbows in graceful attitudes,"[54] a tad masochistic.

In the 1950s, Sax Rohmer's serial novels about the queenly villainess *Sumuru* depict the divan demeanor, sounding tongue in cheek now: Sumuru is frequently found reclining across the pages on her divan, contemplating world domination from the end of a cigarette-holder. The effortless pose of the dominatrix is cultivated by Rosie Lugosi, in modern performance poetry, and worshipped classically by Leopold von Sacher-Masoch (1836–1895) in *Venus in Furs*. Marie Corelli (1855–1924) confers the divan demeanor on many a queenly heroine in her romance novels: "In a half-reclining attitude of indolently graceful ease, the Princess Ziska watched from beneath the slumberous shadow of her long-fringed eyelids...."[55] In *Ardath,* Corelli depicts a male character almost inanely detached even in the face of an haranguing *femme fatale:* "Like an enraged Queen she stood — one white jeweled arm stretched forth menacingly — her bosom heaving, and her face aflame with wrath, but Theos, leaning against Sah-lûma's couch, heard her with as much impassiveness as though her threatening voice were but the sound of an idle wind."[56] Corelli aggrandizes Theos's tranquility by pushing the melodrama over the top with the *femme fatale's* rage. Such an extreme contrast of attitudes suggests theatrical scaffolding around the space and scale of a dramatic performance too overt for the novel, exposed as absurdly unfeasible on the concentrated space of the page.

Corelli overplays Christ's equanimity in a consensual crucifixion in *Barabbas,* presenting the ordeal as if One were lay on a divan: "As peacefully as a weary traveler might stretch himself upon a couch of softest luxury, so did the Conqueror of Time stretch out His glorious limbs upon the knotty wooden beam of torture...."[57] This penchant for exaggeration sabotages her reverence for the Awesome time and again in *Barabbas*. Not even camp would ordinarily claim this level of transcendence, so beyond the fey. Corelli opens *The Secret Power* in 1921 with a camp cloud that models the aloof disposition:

> A cloud floated slowly above the mountain peaks. Vast, fleecy and white as the crested foam of a sea-wave, it sailed through the sky with a divine air of majesty, seeming almost to express a consciousness of its own grandeur.[58]

Quentin Crisp, ostensibly as humble as Sacher-Masoch's Severin, reclined even when standing at a bus stop, in his matter of fact mission to bring flamboyance to the banal. Told to pose as if waiting for a bus, in his duties as a fine arts model, he reflects, "What kind of injunction was that when, at a bus stop, I looked as though I were on the dais of some life room?"[59] The expression is perfectly poised between the advice and the ironic interpretation, staged by a rhetorical question. Taking the bus stop metaphor, literalizing it, and inverting the fine arts studio itself into metaphor, he transcends both with easy irony, balancing their equivalence in the idea and in the weighting of the phrasing. Aloof disposition, so emblematic of camp, is simply the measure of detachment required by irony to dissociate from singular focus and meaning. It differs from academic or scientific objectivity because, though easily as skeptical, it does not attach itself to the quest for facts that concentrates scientific objectivity ever so seriously: it remains aloof even from that. The reclining pose is equidistant from two polarities and detached from their vying gravitation by equalizing their weight. Paradoxically, this gives equal merit to each perspective while discounting them both.

Noël Coward seeks to distance himself from this effortless aesthetic — only to sound even more aloof in *Bitter Sweet*. With the accuracy of an insider, the last Act satirizes those elements of Decadence and Symbolism that are, actually, camp. "*Four over-exquisitely dressed young men*" enter Act III, aesthetes all, and all "so entrancingly late":

VERNON: My silk socks were two poems this evening and they refused to scan.
HENRY: It's going to be inexpressibly dreary, I can feel it in my bones.[60]

Melodramatic adverbs like "entrancingly late" and "entirely Vernon's fault" and "inexpressibly dreary" are so overtly disingenuous in overstating their emotions that they actually emphasize how aloof they are from being late, being culpable and being bored. A poem made of silk socks satirizes the domestic though aristocratic material of many a camp artifact — but the sharpest satire is the pose of the aesthete — art as a way of being — which Coward objected to in Wilde and his disciples. Coward gives these "blasé boys" self-reflecting lyrics that sing about their heroes — "We like Beardsley and Green Chartreuse" — and, above all, flaunt their aloof disposition and attendant ennui, "Exquisitely free" from the dreary morality of "the common herd." If Coward finds their pose objectionable — suggested by the arched satire — could it be that their indiscretion makes a decadent exhibition of his own private elitism? In any case, their song "We All Wore a Green Carnation" voices these emblematic characters, so dégagé that they are asexual, too "bored to bill and coo."

Coward's irony was crucially aloof. These are the stage directions for Charles after the death of his wife in *Blithe Spirit:*

> *He is in deep mourning. He finishes his coffee, puts the cup down on the mantel-piece, lights a cigarette and settles himself comfortably in an arm-chair. He adjusts a reading lamp and with a sigh of well-being, opens a novel and begins to read it.*[61]

An actor could only interpret such grief ironically with blasé demeanor. In Saki and Maude's play *The Watched Pot*, René announces his mother's dramatic disappearance more for effect than assistance: when others demand what he is doing about it, René lists the practical measures underway and adds, with no sense of relegation, "and we've told the dairy to send half a pint less milk every day till further notice." Saki and Maude stage theatrical reactions all around René's equipoise: "Disappeared! What an extraordinary thing to do. Had she any reason for disappearing?" to which René retorts, "Oh, several, but my mother would never do anything for a reason."[62] Saki played hatred with the same elegant decline of the petitions of drama and masculine verve. The first sentence of "The Bull" sets the dramatic parameters: "Tom Yorkfield had always regarded his half-brother, Laurence, with a lazy instinct of dislike, toned down, as years went on, to a tolerant feeling of indifference."[63]

Lord Berners[64] recalls the equidistant temperament of Ronald Firbank. "He seemed to dread being pinned down to any positive assertion even of the most simple nature. 'Where does So-and-so live?' one might ask. 'Why should one live anywhere?' he would reply..." an attitude shared by his authorial voice. The reclining pose — and the reclining pause that occasionally punctuates camp writing — suggests a blasé surfeit of decadence as well as effeminate reserve from uncouth masculine force: ennui: grandstanding spectatorship with its own droll commentary. Firbank is fey in *The Flower Beneath the Foot* in 1923: "With a slight sigh, the lectress took up the posture of a Dying Intellectual," where the capitals put the divan on a dais.[65] When Lord Berners[66] took a spell of psychoanalysis ("Four times a week I visited an amiable Viennese Jewess, a pupil of Freud, and lay on a sofa in a small room in the Woodstock Road and was invited to say anything that came into my head...."), free association was perfect treatment for the camp disposition to hold court carte blanche on a sofa.

In Crisp's novel *Love Made Easy*, Lady Drea is supine on the analyst's couch. The masculine force of psychoanalysis is eroded by femininity, which Freud too admitted is stubbornly "resistant." The diagnosis for Lady Drea:

> "In our little talks you have described the ways in which you try to alleviate your boredom. Some of them would have added color to the lives of the

Borgias but your *ennui* only increases, so I suggest a change of occupation —
kindness— but only as another doctor might suggest a diet of oranges— only in
search of a cure."[67]

In Crisp's philosophy of equivalence, aloof from opposing polarities,
a change in morality is no more evangelical than a change of posture on a
divan.

Firbank would have appreciated the whimsy of that. Firbank sports the
whimsy of P.G. Wodehouse with a flamboyance and theatricality that Wodehouse wouldn't wear. In defense of Firbank's silliness and skeptical of literary conservatism, Arthur Waley jeers in 1929, "The critics, in their natural
fear of being hoaxed, have invented what they consider to be an infallible
method of self-protection; they will admit no one who does not carry the
passport of solemnity, countersigned by two octogenarians."[68] Camp writing jeopardizes a good review, if the critic has an orthodox schooling. "The
problem seems to reside in the fact that Firbank joins radical technique to
apparently frivolous content" (John Ash, *Voice Literary Supplement*,
November 1986). Firbank didn't set out to mock the critics, but how could
they know that? Even compliments from critics and peers like Evelyn Waugh
(1929) and Anthony Powell (1956) were often self-conscious and backhanded. Once Harold Nicolson had finished deriding E.F. Benson's *The Outbreak of War* in 1933 (abjectly apologizing to the author beforehand)[69], he
said favorable things about Firbank, and then Nicolson said this: "Ronald
Firbank, even today, is regarded in America as one of our important literary figures. I question whether such a reputation will prove durable."[70]

Camp's affinity to paradox further intimidates critics from staking
their reputation on an affirmation. Quentin Crisp peruses reviews of his
first memoir: "One said it was full of self-pity; someone else remarked upon
its freedom from precisely this emotion. One critic was delighted by the
aphorisms with which the pages were riddled; the *Times Literary Supplement* deplored the arch and jaunty style in which the story was told." *Love
Made Easy* "received bad notices even in New Zealand," he reflects.[71] Saki
satirizes literary critics in "For the Duration of the War": they studiously
verify and date a ludicrous literary hoax of ancient text even when the verse
is preposterously banal, inferring sanctimonious gravitas in frivolity.

Camp should be so lucky. Noël Coward complains to his diary in 1957
of critical bias against "lightness." He's working on his only novel: "It is gay
and irreverent and with little sentiment and *no* significance." On its publication he notes, "Patronizing, dismissive reviews of *Pomp and Circumstance* continue to arrive from England," as anticipated, "but I am well used
to that."[72] Chloe Poems warns, in music-hall tradition in *I'm Kamp,* "Don't
Put Your Laurels on the Page, Mr. Birmingham." Coward does like to snipe

back at critics who frisk innocent phrases "like old ladies peering under the bed for burglars, and are not content until they have unearthed some definite, and usually quite inaccurate, reason for my saying this or that."[73] Coward has a point. Analytical critics just can't forgive camp for leaving them no intellectual Easter eggs to find and feel smart about.

Like the Magic Circle, the literati avows an ideology of legerdemain. Experimental highbrow literature like *Finnegans Wake* exposes process cleverly, reinventing narrative convention and deconstructing genres and linguistics itself. Its saving grace, for the cloistered cognoscenti, is that it is infinitely obscure: not demonstrative but inscrutable with introverted guile. Kurt Vonnegut, the master of downbeat irony (though not florid in the camp tradition), frowns: "It has been my experience with literary critics and academics in this country that clarity looks a lot like laziness and ignorance and childishness and cheapness to them. Any idea which can be grasped immediately is for them, by definition, something they knew all the time."[74]

Saki frames the point askance against the cultural fashion of *angst:* "'One of these days,' he said, 'I shall write a really great drama. No one will understand the drift of it, but every one will go back to their homes with a vague feeling of dissatisfaction with their lives and surroundings. Then they will put up new wallpapers and forget.'"[75]

Lowbrow literature may expose facades too, but always front of house. Joyce pioneered stream of consciousness, while Firbank wrote without an unconscious at all. In Noël Coward's novel, *Pomp and Circumstance,* the female protagonist reflects on her fictional status in relation to the traditions of the novel: "I am frequently saddened when I realize the width of the gulf that separates me from the heroines of those modern psychological novels written by our leading women novelists."[76]

Literary criticism has designs on the modern novel. Metafiction is a postmodern term for fiction that expresses consciousness of its form. Critic Mark Currie defines metafiction as "writing which places itself on the border between fiction and criticism," and therefore he decides, "The reciprocity of this relationship indicates that metafiction is only half, the fictional half, of a process of challenging the boundary between fiction and criticism."[77] Currie bestows on critics an essential role in the development of fiction that I find ironic considering the lack of style and endemic seriousness in most criticism. While claiming overlap between critics and novelists, Currie never affirms anything other than the traditional analytic, reductionist expression of criticism in his anthology of metafiction.

Postmodern self-awareness develops from the catalogue of literature, writers' knowledge of predecessors, but this has more to do with what fiction writers have written than what critics have observed. I suggest the exposure of artifice reflects theater and narcissism, not criticism. Currie's claim for the centrality of criticism is an assertion of *academic* narcissism.

Mark Currie has serious allies, and Max Beerbohm is no longer around to satirize them. David Lodge, a novelist and academic critic, reduces the historic influence of academic criticism to the selection of a literary canon which then governs the reading (which influences the writing) of new novelists.[78] However, there is no literary genre for camp and many writers remain outside academic respectability. It is quite possible to complete under- and postgraduate literary studies without encountering camp style. Yes, and while literary criticism traditionally pursues theoretical content to the utter detriment of style, metafiction —fiction with a postmodern consciousness— indulges style over content and none moreso than camp. Perhaps it is publishers and editors who are more influenced by literary criticism and the canon. Even in the reduced sphere of academic influence circumscribed by Lodge, this shadow has been negative, making publication difficult for aesthetes of irreverent whimsy and style. Firbank's output was entirely self-funded, after all.

Patricia Waugh too wants to revise the dependence of literary criticism and the subsistence of the critic on the novel by contriving their interdependence. Waugh supports her definition of metafiction as "a *theory* of fiction through the *practice* of writing fiction" by suggesting, "The term 'metafiction' itself seems to have originated in an essay [by William H. Gass],"[79] as if this baptism proves a pre-eminently theoretical nature of metafiction and that the modern novel owes its creative development to literary criticism. It reads like fake I.D. at the Pearly Gates. All the assertion demonstrates, really, is that critics have observed and named a modern trend in fiction, and by renaming it, in a born-again moment of evangelism, they seek to appropriate its form and genesis. Richard Le Gallienne speaks for the aesthete generation, "Literary criticism is man's sulky complaint that he was not invited to the creation."[80] Waugh's discourse, like her peers, observes the usual formalities: the systematic suppression of style, shrouded in content and seriousness whose authority equates to truth, here, as it is in theology. It is endemic to criticism and yet so antithetical to metafiction, especially camp metafiction.

Carl van Vechten prefers to stylize creative evaluation. Succinct yet evocative, affectionate, more impressionistic than analytical, he conjures incongruous comparisons in the camp tradition. He calls Firbank the master of the light touch, "the Pierrot of the minute. Felicien Rops on a merry-go-round. Aubrey Beardsley in a Rolls Royce ... Sacher-Masoch in Mayfair. *A Rebours* a là mode. Aretino in Picadilly. Jean Cocteau at the Savoy."[81] Lush like a Rolls' upholstery, these juxtapositions catch Firbank's aesthetic with more resonance than analysis, describing rather than explaining. "Sacher-Masoch in Mayfair" creams the sadomasochistic whip off *Venus in Furs* and presents it as a kinky soufflé without Sacher-Masoch's beseeching intensity. If there is a touch of Magritte in the review, well, that comparison has been drawn with Firbank too, all whimsical surface and fantastic invention and tongue in cheek. We need these endeavors to reform Old Testament criticism, heaven knows. Angela Carter cites van Vechten's remarks in her biographical evocation, "A Self-Made Man," and portrays Firbank laughing gleefully at the description. And the dons and deans of Oxbridge frown.

Oscar Wilde himself promotes the critic's profile in his 1890 paper "The Critic as Artist." Wilde is advocating a figurative, evocative critical agenda that favors style over the uninspiring function of explanation. He is rewriting the critic — as someone better able to describe his work and gossip more eloquently about it. Six years later Le Gallienne listed "Criticism is the Art of Praise" as maxim one in his tenets of criticism.[82] What else would we expect a narcissistic aesthetic to say? Another narcissist, Marie Corelli, complains— in chapter one of a romance novel —"In all criticism it is an understood thing that the subject to be criticized must be *under* the critic, never above —" and Corelli wants to be on top.[83] Critics stamped several penalizing endorsements on Corelli's poetic license but she was possessed by three Muses: Shakespeare; vengeance; perfect female beauty; and her authorial mirror image. (I don't believe she was conscious of how much the ideal female form embellished her work.) She wrote to her publisher after a bad review, "I shall never write another novel till I have whipped the malicious little puppy-scribblers of flippant criticism into something like a wholesome terror of me."[84] Corelli accomplished the threat, chiefly by inspiring the work of Amanda McKittrick Ros. Amanda McKittrick Ros (1860–1939) believed that critics had a hand in sending Corelli, her heroine, to an early grave. Ros has something to say about all this:

> Mark the fact, the great fact, that "classic" critics never allow their pens to depict their conclusions re strong or weak forms of thought or traits of talent with the ink of ignorance, revenge or blackguardism "macassored" over with the oil of odium as their less-endowed insignificant "crowdrop" contemporaries do. Oh no![85]

Ros writes to publisher J.S. Mercer in 1927, "Their bayonets of bastard sheen with their scurrilous punctures of jealous jadery affect neither the Book nor its Author financially but, on the contrary, will not be overlooked by me in the near future."[86] Ros and Corelli pay back the critics in full in our chapter "Camp By Misadventure," but first, with respect to camp women writers, we instigate a search for Shakespeare's sister.

Shakespeare's Sister

A feminine writing style ... floristry, couture and color ...
masculine women and feminine men ...
bitchcraft ... camp women?

E.F. Benson flourishes a flamboyant adverb, grown in his own greenhouse, when a diva is socially delayed by acclaim for her performance: showered in "a blaze of bouquets" and encores, "it was late when Olga came florally out."[1] Camp writing is an effeminate style, rich in floral arrangements. It is not incapable of excess, as Ronald Firbank has it, yet the cultivation is precious, not reckless:

> With vine-sprays clinging languorously to the candle-stands, rising from a bed of nespoles, tulips, and a species of wild orchid known as Devil's-balls, the Chicklet, to judge from his floral caprices, possessed a little brain of some ambition, not incapable of excess.[2]

Even solemn occasions for Saki have a lush satin lining, even in bereavement: "At the same time, there was a rainbow of consolation irradiating our grief."[3]

Robin Lakoff [4] notes gendered differences in language use: women "make far more precise discriminations in naming colors than do men; words like *beige, ecru, aquamarine, lavender,* and so on are unremarkable in a woman's active vocabulary, but absent from that of most men" ... excepting, I say, male camp writers. The *Glasgow Herald* congratulates Firbank's "delicate descriptive power, a fine perception of the value of color...."[5] Just as Huysmans' hero in *Against Nature* "had always been excessively fond of flowers," so he rhapsodized about color and philosophized about the spectrum's relation to the psyche. "The blue of the woodwork was stabilized, so to speak, warmed up by the surrounding orange tints, which for their

41

part glowed with undiminished brilliance, maintained and in a way intensified by the close proximity of the blue."[6] This novel of sheer Decadence is also occasionally camp, when it can find the irony.

Beardsley's writing is sumptuously scented and decorated and garmented, flagrantly fetishistic:

> She wore a gown of white watered silk with gold lace trimmings, and a velvet necklet of false vermilion. Her hair hung in bandeaux over her ears, passing into a huge chignon at the back of her head, and the hat, wide-brimmed and hung with a valance of pink muslin, was floral with red roses.[7]

Camp takes such feminine attention over décor and costume. When Edward D. Wood, Jr. (1924–1978) reports,

> I read an article in a Glendale paper the other day of a character dressed in a green dress, red sweater and blonde wig who held up a liquor store. THE TOUGHS — THE INVADERS. The police picked him up in a telephone booth still dressed as such — and a mighty poor combination of clothes I might add,[8]

the crime of uncoordinated dress is equated to the robbery in that arched addendum. Chloe Poems stitched a colorful gingham metaphor to reflect socialism that is egalitarian yet individualist, choosing the most banal tablecloth design and making an array of technicolor in equilateral patterning. The gingham diva observes gay boys on the game in "No Stranger to Sequins," "who wear street corners like clothes," an iconic relation between identity and environment as intimate as one's wardrobe.[9] Impeccable timing cuts the lines like sharp-suited tailoring in "London Is Paranoid." The fashion capital is looking over its shoulder to look you up and down, and,

> That's not because it's caring
> it just wants to check out
> what you're wearing.[10]

Max Beerbohm finds the London of his youth, the 1880s and '90s, in a quainter state of camp. "There was a demure poetry about her," until she surrendered her femininity to become an "it" under "later-nineteenth-century utilitarianism and efficiency." Old districts "were places of leisure — of *leesure,* one might almost have said in the old-fashioned way." He salutes the exhibitionism of promenades: "High-swung barouches, with immense armorial bearings on their panels, driven by fat, white-wigged coachmen, and having powdered footmen up behind them; signorial phaetons; daring tandems; discreet little boughams, brown or yellow." This grand procession of detail borders on pageantry and heraldry but not solemnity: "flippant high dog-carts; low but flippant Ralli-carts; very frivolous private hansoms shaming the more serious public ones." He doffs his plumed prose to the showboating dandyism of these travelers in contrast to the seriously banal occupants of modern, enclosed vehicles. The bygone "man-about-town" whose dandyism Beerbohm championed was unhurried by industry, "a leisurely personage, attired with great elaboration," who was "not necessarily interesting in himself; but fraught with external character and point."[11]

It is not fashionable to generalize but, just as women are more preoccupied than men with the mirror image, even if only a socialized condition as feminism has it, so we find narcissism writ large in camp writing too. "The Pervasion of Rouge," a eulogy posturing as an essay on artifice, appeared in the first issue of *Yellow Book* in 1894. Here Beerbohm exercises his dandy style to characterize the aesthete's attention to surface as feminine. This rapturous identification with fetishized feminine cosmetics is rather transvestite:

> Loveliness shall sit at the toilet, watching her oval face in the oval mirror. Her smooth fingers shall flit among the paints and powder, to tip and mingle them, catch up a pencil, clasp a phial, and what not and what *not,* until the mask of vermeil tint has been laid aptly, the enamel quite hardened. And, heavens, how she will charm us and enscorcel our eyes![12]

E.F. Benson holds the plot while Georgie, a favorite character whom we'll get to know, soliloquizes what to wear with his new dinner suit in *Trouble for Lucia:* "One of my pleated shirts, and a black butterfly tie, and my garnet solitaire. And my pink vest. Nobody will see it, but I shall know it's there. And red socks. Or daren't I?" As far as Georgie is concerned, it's a dramatic moment.[13]

As Quentin Crisp calls the law expediency in a long white dress, I must draw your attention, rather like a fashion commentator, to word selection in camp literature. More a matter of couture than semantics—"of *leesure,* one might almost have said"—where writers cut a phrase according to the patterning and tone of syllables. Words are modeled as comely accessories to style. Crisp explains his own dashing haberdashery, "Crisperanto is a manner of speaking in which a sentence gets all dressed up to create a pleasing impression." Enlightening his particular bittersweet tone, "Euphemisms are unpleasant truths wearing diplomatic cologne."[14]

Camp extends its feminine delight to exotic scents and floral fragrances,

> tropical spices such as the pungent odors of the Chinese sandalwood and Jamaican hediosmia with French scents such as jasmine, hawthorn, and vervain; olefying climate and season to put forth trees of different smells and flowers of the most divergent colors and fragrances; creating out of the union or collision of all these tones one common perfume, unnamed, unexpected, unusual....

writes J. K. Huysmans.[15] And so Brigid Brophy takes a butterfly net to Ronald Firbank's work, "The butterfly was an obvious self for Firbank: it shares his passion for flowers,"[16] and so The Divine David, camp avant garde performance artist, dedicates his bohemian Foreword to Chloe Poems' *Universal Rentboy* "To Nasturtium everywhere."

Camp alights on subjects with precious prose, skipping like a Morris dancer. Beardsley courts terms like "quite the daintiest ... quite the prettiest ... delicate perceptions ... as lightly as a breath ... slender voices of the fairies ... Tannhäuser became a little triste."[17] A paradox of my investigation is that male writers are pre-eminent in camp and they write in a feminized style. Female narrative is inclined to lateral detail with a lighter touch than a typically direct male hand, I suggest — which is extended by ornate camp style. Yet this conspicuous facility to *exaggerate* feminine traits is a bold, masculine promotion. And so camp excess is always offset by irony, the exclamation qualified by a pause, an aside or a clause: delicate, discrete, arched. Consider Saki's short story, "Excepting Mrs. Pentherby." Mrs. Pentherby and her faux pas are the source of local gossip and bitchy irritation ... until one lady finally tells Mrs. Pentherby exactly what she thinks of her. "The object of this unpent storm of accumulated animosity waited patiently for a lull, and then remarked quietly to the angry little woman —

"And now, my dear Mrs. Gwepton, let me tell you something that I've been wanting to say for the last two or three minutes, only you wouldn't give me a chance; you've got a hairpin dropping out on the left side. You thin-haired women always find it difficult to keep your hairpins in."[18]

"You thin-haired women" generalizes the personal remark with a grand perspective. Mrs. Pentherby's response builds up a full head of rhetoric, "And now, my dear Mrs. Gwepton, let me tell you something..." only to deflate it with "two or three minutes" instead of years (it must have felt like years): this too diminishes the showdown that the narrative has escalated, to put the domestic scene (and Mrs. Gwepton) in its place. Finally, the critical observation that she bided her time to deliver couldn't be more trivial — yet damning to the camp aesthetic, for it exposes a distinct absence of style. The mannered phrasing sets up the confrontation with propriety, a tad aloof itself from events. It belittles the outburst with a waspish description of "the angry little woman" and contrasts her "unpent storm" with her opponent's poise, until Mrs. Pentherby's repost. *Aloof* becomes arched. The scene is a feminine domestic encounter of the type that took place in the absence of men, yet penned by a man whose droll, domesticated style gives no portent of an author who was to die in World War I.

The style fits a sub-type of *gossip* that Deborah Jones[19] calls "bitching."

Its sniping is less principled than the idealized feminist expression of resistance to oppression that Jones prefers. Ms Jones sees such language as sisterhood bonding, but Mrs. Pentherby demonstrates how divisive the bitchy quip, the *acid drop* that Kenneth Williams prescribes, can be. E.F. Benson seems to affirm the benevolence of bitching too, at least as far as *Mapp and Lucia:* "To those not acquainted with the usage of the ladies of Tilling, such bitter plain-speaking might seem to denote a serious friction between old friends." He domesticates any such drama: "Such breezes, even if they grew far stronger than this, were no more than bracing airs that disposed to energy, or exercises to keep the mind fit. No malice."[20] And Benson is acquainted enough with the bracing bitchcraft of the ladies of Tilling to fill books with their conversation. After Lucia poses for a self-aggrandizing portrait as Mayor, seated at her piano and surrounded by emblematic objects— the scarlet robe and chains of office, her new bicycle, Bridge cards, paint box — Elizabeth Mapp remarks on its exhibition: "'A pity the whole thing looks like a jumble sale, with Worship as auctioneer.'"[21] *Lucia's Progress* dares some dashing imagery when the rivalry between Mapp and Lucia extends to shareholding, not immediately adventuresome until Benson's fantastical conceit raises the domestic stakes: "waged as on some vast battlefield consisting of railway lines running between the shafts of gold mines, Lucia, so to speak, on the footboard of an engine on the southern railway shrieked by, drawing a freight of Burma Corporation, while Elizabeth put lumps of ore from Siriami on the metals to wreck her trains."[22] What a dynamic and masculine metaphor for bitchcraft, drawing the lengths that these women go to outdo the other, while the distance between the perilous, hysterical image and their poised, domestic machinations makes the whole passage scatty.

Benson evoked a harsher definition of bitchcraft when he wrote "The Jamboree" for *The Tatler* in 1924: "Caroline had an apt and acid wit and a soft, dreamy meditative way of saying the nastiest things, which made them doubly telling...." He admonishes and admires the "modern" woman.[23] At its most rarefied, bitchcraft is urbane, aloof from slander and anger: to lose one's cool is to lose face. Camp never makes a fist (except to make a lewd innuendo), but its manicured nails are sharp. Personal spats between Sybil and Agatha are a delectable highlight of Saki and Maude's play *The Watched Pot:* Sybil scorns Agatha's marital ambitions, "Because a man has refused you twice there's no particular reason for supposing that he'll accept you at the third bidding. It's merely a superstition." Agatha fancies a husband could escort her everywhere but Sybil replies, "A woman who takes her husband about with her everywhere is like a cat that goes on playing with a mouse long after she's killed it." A wicked implication of lack of style is slander to the camp sensibility, "Why is it that plain women are always so venomous?" but Agatha counters, "Oh, if you're going to be introspective, my dear."[24]

No surprise, in this androgynous art, that male protagonists too may turn their hand to bitchcraft in Saki and Wilde and Coward. In *Blithe Spirit*, Charles' wife tells him, "As far as waspish female psychology goes, there's a strong vein of it in you."[25] The stagecraft of bitchcraft makes a performance of disdain. In Coward's *Bitter Sweet*, Hansi perverts Sari's superior entrance with camp imagery, "Here comes the snow queen."[26] The camp bitchy quip is concise and above all disdainful — and above all. Quentin Crisp calls it "stylized cattiness," cosmetic jibes by effeminate peers: "Nothing at all was meant by it. It was a formal game of innuendos about other people being older than they said, about their teeth being false and their hair being a wig. Such conversation was thought to be smart and so very feminine."[27] Years later, Crisp went to dinner with director John Waters and sketched a catty exchange "which might have been positively venomous had not Mr. Waters been aware that I might repeat everything he said."[28] This, in a book laced with catty snipes at England from New York.

Bitchcraft often spikes a disarming compliment with a barbed twist. In *Jane* in 1900, Marie Corelli's third person narrative takes a dislike to Mrs. Maddenham, "gorgeously attired and ornamented after the style of a jeweler's window with diamonds."[29] Bitchcraft highlights Corelli's superior tone in characterization and narrative voice. In 1896, *Delicia* displays a ravishing slight on a wretched husband,

> he was absolutely devoid of all ambition, save a desire to have his surname pronounced correctly.[30]

Epically emphatic, "absolutely devoid" oversees her observation from an imperious vantage. Corelli sketches two society women like pantomime dames who specialize in sardonic disdain and cutting quips to steal another scene: "La Marina" is introduced before a long mirror, "so as to completely block the view for anybody else, a brilliant-looking, painted personage in a pale-green costume, glittering with silver," who delights in urbane insults to Delicia's wretched husband. He attempts a rather futile masculine explosion:

> "You wild cat!" he said savagely. "If you have *dared*—"
> "Puss, puss! Pretty puss!" laughed Marina. "Cats have claws, my Lord Bill, and they scratch occasionally!"

The other pantomime dame, Lady Brancewith, with fan, "was undoubtedly very lovely, despite her artificial flesh tints and distinctly dyed hair." Delicia's husband assents to escort her home with a show of indifference, whereupon she tops his pose with sardonic poise of her own, simply dripping with irony: "'How sweet and condescending of you!' and Lady Brancewith threw on her mantle gleaming with iridescent jewels and showered with perfumed lace. 'So good of you to bore yourself with my company!'" He registers that "she was in a dangerous mood."[31]

Corelli sneers best in quotation marks that serve, like "so-called," to indict the integrity of the quoted subject, conjuring ironic skepticism. Misanthropic disdain spikes Delicia's amusement at "the droll little units that call themselves 'society.'"[32] With a grand and gothic stroke of her superior pen, arched quotations structure heavy irony like flying buttresses arching over the sentence. People who get scratched include "'society' ... 'select people' ... 'a candid friend....'" *Delicia* sets the tone in the Preface: "The following slight and unelaborated sketch of a very commonplace and everyday tragedy will, I am aware, meet with the unqualified disapproval of the "superior" sex."[33] Those sneering quotations relegate the superior sex beneath even equality.

The passive aggression in bitchy jibes is usually attributed to femaleness because, until lately, women didn't have the status to force a confrontation. Crisp himself declares his latent hostility as a persecuted minority too disempowered to afford a confrontation[34]—but his barbed wit is more potent than blunted masculinity on the page. Chloe Poems makes the point, pointedly, in a seminal portrayal of effeminacy that warns "never underestimate the effeminate." A eulogy to Crisp, to effeminates everywhere and to the author's reflection, "The Effeminate" models the passive and aloof disposition that belies the quick-witted flourish, "always two steps ahead /While seeming to lag behind." Albeit dance steps,

> The effeminate can structure the most intricate ballet
> Out of his silliest dillies and dallyings
> A marrying of wit and movement.

Alliteration and rhyme and sudden changes of pace ("dallyings" advancing into "marrying" where rhyme anticipates the echo ahead of the line break, and then the curt consonant where "wit" takes an arched stance against "and movement") make words pirouette with a cavalier flourish. It has the parrying and piercing of the rapier, wordplay as swordplay, or at least a tongue-lashing. "Silliest dillies and dallyings" flaunts the frivolous, effeminate style, structured like gossip, where rhyme itself dillies and dallies.[35]

Fin de siècle female writers Ada Leverson, George Egerton, Victoria Cross, and Kate Chopin, emblematic of the 19th century New Woman, conflate gender traits a la camp, yet not camp. Decadent: sensual, esoteric, poised and fanciful, yet their indulgence falls short of flamboyance and the grand distance from motivation and process that camp achieves through stagecraft. Brigid Brophy's 1963 novel *The Finishing Touch* cultivates the occasional camp bud early on before it is nipped by experimentation, before she gets her style caught in her clauses. Female masculinity flexes the text: Miss Braid sounding "like a precocious voice-broken schoolboy," against a general tone of ennui with a fey "gesture of ultimate exhaustion." Antonia's masculine couture indulges "the dandy in her soul," à la "hussars (or was it lancers?)," fetishizing the "hint of mess jackets" with "an epaulette here, a high collar there? or merely a straight, a darkening line of braid? (though not, one could feel sure, in honour of *Miss* Braid)...." Brophy's breeze carries "the sound of fans," as "The southern night fell, like a fruit"; there is a cultured smattering of French; and we identify a cameo butterfly, self-appointed symbol of Firbank. "Scurrying pens on the paper made a noise like cicadas," and in the next sentence, outside, "cicadas made a noise like scurrying pens."[36] In this last touch, demonstrative writing makes *noises off,* frivolously reflexive. Brophy's 1969 novel *In Transit* is a tad camp, too. The author-as-narrator-as-character reflects on her dependent and incorporeal relation to the reader, parodying Sacher-Masoch along the way: "Why should I not appear to you as a free-moving figure in costume?

> My pelt, could it move away from you, might by its narcissistic unconcern with what it provoked in you, by the mystery of its self-movingness, excite you into admiring pursuit. Free-standing, my plumage might curl into crests and cartouches and thus cut a dash on the retina of your imagination.[37]

In Transit is a tad camp on those occasions when it puts some distance between its intellectualism and consciousness: reflection on process need have nothing to do with analysis, Brophy could have noted from her favorite subject, Firbank. "So much for the strategy of this narration," engrossed in experimentation without his frivolous yet no less novel invention. (She does like to pun, as does Shakespeare, as does camp — but then, so does Sigmund Freud.)

Contemporary British poet Rosie Lugosi is a rare exponent of female camp in verse, traditionally in costumed performance. Her androgynous authorial voice may recall brusque Mancunian tones of John Cooper Clark or the sinuous innuendo of Fenella Fielding. "There's a plaice for us" puns and parodies Shakespearean sonnet 87: "Farewell! thou art too dear for my possessing," to extol the less highbrow English tradition of fish and chips. "Thy self gav'st, thy own worth not knowing," her Shakespeare quotation, sends up the notion of romantic sacrifice with a kinky twist insinuated by the author's dominatrix persona, which is high profile in her work. "Yet focussed on the place where thy'd be going, /The yellow batter in which thou'd be dropped," mocks the torturous fate of her eponymous prey with sadomasochistic relish that makes a banal subject decadent, "Self-sacrificed for me, hot oil demanding." Hot oil that simmers like subliminal sadism highlights, by ironic contrast, the author's aloof whimsy. She rests on music-hall tradition, which in turn may rest on Shakespearean jesting, "The piece of cod which passeth all understanding."[38] Sadomasochism teases the delicate genre of the sonnet with a dominant streak of female masculinity. Rosie Lugosi models aloof and epigrammatic and exhibitionistic style that requires performance. "I'm reclaiming the power of being a show-off— that sign of ego and expression of energy so much frowned upon in female children."[39] The bold counterpoint to femininity creates the androgynous voice in its aloof yet exaggerated dynamic. How did Shakespeare put it, in our Introduction, "very soft society and great showing." Showboating is essential to camp, schooled in theatrical tradition, yet rare among women writers, I find.

In *I Capture the Castle* in 1949, in the space of a page, Dodie Smith typically defines an apologetic narrator who admits the limitations of her narrative, confesses to inadequacy unequal to the demands of the novel, and deferentially declines a comparison to Jane Austen (whose own voice was muted by decorum). Robin Lakoff concludes, "Women's speech is devised to prevent the expression of strong statements."[40] The pantomime villainess of *The One Hundred and One Dalmations* flaunts her sadism like a fashion statement, posing like a snow queen to make the children boo and hiss: Cruella de Vil, aloof from compassion and parading her furs like Shirley Bassey while her diminutive husband is little more than a furrier, appears iconically camp, a parody of Wanda in *Venus in Furs,* but Dodie Smith's narrative remains unassuming even in irony, never so bombastic as the "unassuming" Sacher-Masoch. Rosie Lugosi's authorial voice assumes the archetype with music-hall bravado— her perverse listing of "favorite things" rhymes "Turning cute puppy dogs into warm mittens" gleefully with what she does to kittens,[41] while only Wagneresque "death and destruction" can dramatize the author's pre-menstrual tension in "queen of the night"— tongue in cheek, kinky.

Camp literature flirts with precious qualifiers that pose feminine reserve in counterpoint to overstatement, staging dramatic impressions only to qualify their impact, with mannered and supremely reflective punctuation. Take this sentence by Max Beerbohm from his 1896 essay "Poor Romeo": "I did not, at the time, suffer my fancy to linger over the tessellated document."[42] Punctuation qualifies the retrospection, "at the time," more preciously in its precise and portentous timing than if the sentence began, "At the time, I did not..." the kind of pastoral dalliance that would pause to pick daisies in Ronald Firbank's landscapes. "Suffer my fancy" is a precious contrivance and "tessellated document" is a delicate poetic flourish.

Virginia Woolf idealized an "androgynous" writing style, before revising her evaluation from a position of sexual difference. "Shakespeare's Sister" is Woolf's metaphor for the suppressed potential of female writers. Marie Corelli stakes her claim: she lived in Avon and appointed herself custodian of Shakespeare's heritage. She was a best-selling novelist and her romance fiction aspires to classical imagery. Amanda McKittrick Ros confides similar delusions of grandeur to publisher J.S. Mercer, in November 1927, that her first novel was now, finally, "sistering Shakespeare, Milton and Blake."[43] Corelli complained, "I do not write in a ladylike or effeminate way, and for that they hate me ... and now that I know how criticism is done, I care not a jot for it!"[44] As effete male camp writers appropriate feminine style, women must summon their masculine energies to conjure camp androgyny. These wishful Shakespearean sisters show rare masculine verve in prose that showboats their style, though the irony so essential to camp is all the reader's. Not quite what Woolf had in mind.

Shakespeare's Sister turned out to be a transvestite who blends feminine-masculine tones in the camp aesthetic. When Woolf says of woman's literary training in early 19th century, "Her sensibility had been educated for centuries by the influences of the common sitting room,"[45] I recall the drawing-room demeanor of camp. Wilde's heroes rarely venture from the drawing-room: "Egotism itself, which is so necessary to a proper sense of human dignity, is entirely the result of indoor life."[46] In Saki's novella *The Unbearable Bassington,* "Francesca herself, if pressed in an unguarded moment to describe her soul, would probably have described her drawing-room."[47] Saki subverts any metaphysical meaning that the trained critic might extrapolate in the alcoves of even a domestic analogy. He insists instead on the surface interpretation: he doesn't leave the drawing-room, but he makes it iconic. "Louise" sets the tone of English bourgeois femininity win the opening sentence, "'The tea will be quite cold, you'd better ring for some more,' said the Dowager Lady Beanford."[48] It's a typical Saki sentence. In 'The Elk,'"On the afternoon of Christmas Day, Mrs. Yonelet dashed into the drawing-room, where her hostess was sitting amid a circle of guests and tea-cups and muffin dishes."[49] Take Saki's "Tea," if you like, preoccupied with the finer points of afternoon tea — written by the man who braved the front line of World War I:

> Cushat-Prinkly had read of such things in scores of novels, and hundreds of actual experiences had told him that they were true to life. Thousands of women, at this solemn afternoon hour, were sitting behind dainty porcelain

and silver fittings, with their voices tinkling pleasantly in a cascade of solicitous little questions.[50]

And Ronald Firbank, says G.C. Hadlow, has "the eyes and ears of a gossip columnist, a feminine delight in the chic and modern."[51] Not Woolf's vision, yet uninhibited by gender prescription and without the anguish of woman's voice under patriarchy, camp models "the man-womanly mind."

Quentin Crisp negotiates the parlor parlance of two women whose bland exchanges keep up appearances while sniffing out truffles of gossip: "In a group of women, whether of two or two hundred, there is almost always a different atmosphere from that which prevails if so much as one man is present — even such an apparently sexless man as Davies," Crisp reveals in his androgynous style ... but how does he know? Is it the insider privilege of an effeminate celibate, unlike Mr. Davies in his gothic fantasy *Chog?* In Crisp's two published novels, characters are mostly surface — reflecting the author's suspicion of intimacy, perhaps — but women take the strongest roles. In *Love Made Easy* Lady Drea is, as they say, the part to play, and altogether too much for her psychoanalyst, who disintegrates. In *Chog,* Raina the prostitute is defined as heroine among men weaker than herself.[52] Chloe Poems bequeaths heroic status on prostitutes in poems like "Whore," and champions effeminacy in women and men alike. Indefatigable housewifery in "Something Red in a Tart's Glass" rebels against banality. Assuming the character of Audrey Pringle, wilfully bawdy and tawdry behind her bourgeois seemliness, Poems lends his considerable energy to celebrate the "flip-side of motherhood,"

> I'm siren
> Byron
> poetry and violence
> indulgent
> effulgent
> an angel of profanity.[53]

Drag stands accused of misogyny in its grotesque caricature of women but literary camp seems frequently feminist. Conceived by men, yet wilful women dominate the literature, with transvestite focalization and an occasional stereotype, all frills and gossip, fussing over the melodrama — while male heroes tend to be effete. Crisp[54] says of Noël Coward, "His greatest gift was for writing lines that actresses long to say. This ensured that his dialogue was always spoken with the utmost gusto." Evident in all his books, Crisp himself, the most effeminate stylist of them all, was inspired by icons of charismatic femininity. He glimpses Joan Crawford arriving at the National Film Theater:

She looked at me for only a moment before her hosts took her attention, but when she had gone through the stage door I felt impelled to turn around and see if my silhouette had been burned on the wall behind me as were the images of certain victims of Hiroshima.

The gorgon was a beautiful woman in original mythology. Behold in Joan Crawford awesome associations with goddesses channeled through the intensity of theatrical personality and the power of feminine energy, for Crisp is not merely star-struck by celebrity but enthralled by this paragon of stylized femininity.

In *Blithe Spirit,* Madame Arcati is a spiritual medium with masculine verve and maternal assurance. Even the maid secretly manipulates the plot, and the male lead is led by women throughout. His wife tells him, "Just because you've always been dominated by them it doesn't necessarily follow that you know anything about them."[55] Noël Coward wrote "The English Lido" in 1928 for a musical revue, where Daisy leads the Chorus like Boadicea through "Britannia Rules the Waves," predicting a feminist future for Britain: "Up girls, and at 'em," is the rallying cry, for men must surrender to the feminine. Daisy fashions camp nationalism with this whimsical confluence of masculine-feminine, patriotic yet not patriarchal: "We'll put a frill on the Union Jack."[56]

Sally Bowles is stylized femininity, "With her poised self-conscious head and daintily arranged hands." Yet Bowles was a real woman, freely irreverent about marriage, abortion and fidelity, a "larger-than-fiction public character," Christoper Isherwood called her. She tells her author in *Goodbye to Berlin,* "'You know, Chris, you do understand women most marvelously: better than any man I've ever met....'"[57] Here, and in *Mr. Norris Changes Trains,* effete males make way for strong women; Mr. Norris is as effeminate as a Beardsley hero, who gladly defers to the dominance of Olga and Anni. Isherwood is camp in his characters, not his technique. Frl. Schroeder reads now like a German impression of Irene Handl, but as men stand rooted in shock it is Frl. Schroeder who protects Norris from physical assault.

Like Saki, E.F. Benson populates many a short story with chattering bourgeois women, though Benson's women are keener social climbers. Men attend with servile Edwardian decorum. Women came to the fore when men went to war in 1914 and 1938, but — just as Corelli and Ros didn't wait for men to go to war before waging war with the critics — in Benson's cityscapes women were always on top. In "Bootles" in 1904, "Lady Maizie Ferrars took a cigarette from the gold box by her and lit a match on the sole of her very high-heeled shoe," while her husband is likened to a collie or a poodle. Mrs. Grantham, their guest, "got up, and stood in a rather masculine attitude, feet apart, in front of the fire."[58] The ladies of Benson's village of Tilling, eccentric and assertive, have a habit of outliving their husbands. They tower over their men, even ex-military: the Major reflects on bridge games in Miss Mapp's house, "'Bless me, when I think of the scoldings I've had in this room for some little slip....'" He is outflanked by the gentler sex, "Irene forging on ahead with that long masculine stride that easily kept pace with Major Benjy's...." though we must let the sentence run its course, in respect of Benson's artistry, as he follows a straggler behind Irene, "the short-legged Diva with that twinkle of feet that was like the scudding of a thrush over the lawn."[59] (Benson fashions humor from his poetic turns of phrase, but don't let that depreciate his delectable expressions.) Elizabeth Mapp marries the Major in *Lucia's Progress*. It's a feminist wedding: "At the marriage service she had certainly omitted the word 'obey' when she defined what sort of wife she would make him."[60] She moulds the Major to her preferences—tea instead of whisky and church instead of golf—calling him to heel at parties. The domestic status of these parochial *femmes fatales* is playfully elevated to royalty with scatty, catty eccentricity. Irene, local artist, changes her painting of women wrestlers to men, and Isabel Poppit almost knocks the novel's leading man down on her motorcycle: "she looked like a sort of modernized Valkyrie in rather bad repair."

Unrestrained male masculinity is uncouth to urbane camp aesthetics, which also refines nature, and so effete males are an advance in evolution. Amanda McKittrick Ros cautions us not to disparage them, for once, when we encounter an effete chap in *Helen Huddleston*—unless one happens to be a heart surgeon:

> She thought Maurice Munroe's heart far too effeminate for any man to posses and that such a heart was only owned by women; but to dive into the human heart and extract therefrom an opinion of its nature is a very difficult and problematic triangle to solve or tackle, for to judge either man's or women's heart dodges the most dogmatic, the most energetic, clogs the veins and the veriest, thickens the glands of the presumptive, strains the sinews of the sneakiest, blanks the bravest and ends in dim defeat.[61]

I think we can all agree on that.

Benson wrote "Mr. Carew's Game of Croquet" for *The Tatler* in 1924, pausing to sample the perfume of flowering limes—"There was the hint of the country about them, but also the hint of Bond Street; you would have said that they had been touched up at some scent manufactory and thus rendered the more palatable to civilized nostrils." The protagonist too "looked very civilized," we read: "his rurality was more suggestive of Richmond Park than of the untamed moorland."[62] Not, then, D.H. Lawrence. Benson was satirizing this society from the inside, and how his voice blends with his subjects. Georgie is introduced to the public in 1920 in *Queen Lucia,* "Such masculinity as he was possessed of was boyish rather than adult, and the most important ingredients in his nature were feminine."[63] In *Mapp and Lucia,* Georgie is inert without the inspiration of dynamic women: Benson describes "the eclipsed condition of his energies," abandoned by his affianced housemaid and listless in the absence of a local operatic diva who is off to tour America and lost without Lucia. "Even the prospect of impersonating Francis Drake at the forthcoming fête aroused only the most tepid enthusiasm in him." The contrast with his heroic subject comically establishes his effete stature, as Georgie complains that rehearsals for his knighthood as Sir Francis Drake are hurting his shoulder. "A book of Elizabethan costumes, full of sumptuous colored plates, had roused him for a while from his lethargy, and he had chosen a white satin tunic with puffed sleeves slashed with crimson, and a cloak of rose-colored silk...." With his "very nautical-looking cap," the role inspires his dress sense about town, not his sense of adventure: "There was a hint of seafaring about Georgie's costume as befitted one who had lately spent so much time on the pier at Folkestone." It is Mapp and Lucia who take to sea heroically, swept through the village during a flood. In a transsexual and actorly simile, Georgie is left to utter woe "like Cassandra."[64]

This echoes Benson's early novel *The Babe,* whose androgynous protagonist takes time out from rugby to give a stage performance as Clytemnestra so convincing that a young man "fell in love with her on the spot, and was disposed to take it as a personal insult that the Babe was of the sex that Nature made him."[65] Benson's mannered expression, "disposed to take it as an insult," accepts the antagonism as predisposition instead of confronting or objecting to it: this is the camp attitude to conflict that Quentin Crisp will demonstrate peerlessly. Even when he curses, the Babe's language is "Aristophanic."

Amiable Georgie approximates a protagonist in *Mapp and Lucia* but he capitulates to Lucia every time: "He did not want to go away, but when Lucia exhibited that caliber of determination that he should, it was better to yield at once than to collapse later in a state of wretched exhaustion." Not the sexualized submission of Sacher-Masoch (even though, in Tilling, "Mr. Wyse bowed so low that his large loose tie nearly dipped itself in an ice pudding"), Benson prefers celibacy. Still, Georgie is as spellbound as Severin: "He had never been the least in love with her, but somehow she had been as absorbing as any wayward and entrancing mistress."[66] They marry in *Lucia's Progress,* and by their next novel Georgie is reflecting contentedly — or ambivalently, depending how you read him — "Marriage, in fact, with Lucia might be regarded as a vow of celibacy."[67] Closest of platonic friends, the happy couple specify "No caresses of any sort," preserving Lucia's celibacy and Georgie's innocuous ambiguity. It's true, when Georgie retires to bed, "A random idea of kissing Lucia once, on the brow, entered his mind, but after what had been said about caresses, he felt she might consider it a minor species of rape," made funnier because Lucia is more masculine than Georgie.[68] In their first novel together they share a sigh, more intimate than a kiss in camp aesthetics. The series is often summarized as tales of Mapp and Lucia's rivalry, but they are more about the touching relationship between Lucia and Georgie. Benson frames two beautiful portraits of the pair in *Lucia's Progress:* "Lucia and Georgie were seated side by side on the bench of the organ in Tilling church. The May sunshine streamed on to them through the stained glass of a south window, vividly coloring them with patches of the brightest hues, so that they looked like objects daringly camouflaged in war-time against enemy aircraft...." Lucia was lit by the stained glass tints of Elijah bound for heaven in a chariot. "Georgie came under the influence of the Witch of Endor."[69] Georgie grows a beard especially for this novel. It could be to recollect his gender, just as, during his needlework, "He remembered that he was a man." At the end, Lucia is trying on hats for a ceremony, and Benson proves how moving whimsy can be in a land where appearances are everything: he frames the pair in Lucia's bedroom mirror exquisitely for the final image of the book:

> "Georgino! Your beard: my hat," cried Lucia. "What a harmony! Not a question about it!"
> "Yes, I think it does suit us," said Georgie, blushing a little.

And *Lucia In London* ends with the pair sharing an inside joke.

Mapp and Lucia gives gay hints of transvestism that get bolder as the series develops and readers acclimatize. There is a subtle aside after Georgie's enchantment with flamboyant Elizabethans, "Even Georgie, who had a great eye for female attire...."[70] The aesthetic that refines men's masculinity also voices the most striking details in asides, couched in clauses that upstage the rest of the sentence as if incidentally. We have strained an ear to Alan Bennett's memorable hushed asides, but Benson writes more assertively in "The Exposure of Pamela," "Lady Lorimer, who resembled a dissipated bird of Paradise...."[71] and, in "The Male Impersonator," pointedly, "'We really must make a compromise,' thought Miss Mapp, meaning that everybody must come round to her way of thinking, 'or our dear little cosy bridge evenings won't be possible.'"[72] Benson exhibits masculine assertion in the narrative that doesn't wait for Miss Mapp to speak before disclosing the meaning of her sentiment, but the vehemence is deflected by punctuation, like a piercing glance over a fluttering fan.

"An Entire Mistake" makes husbands redundant with a whimsical yet potent "elopement" between two wives. In "The Male Impersonator" women make greater advances on masculine territory, couched in harmless whimsy. And here is how women laugh together: "The three ladies rocked with laughter. Sometimes one recovered, and sometimes two, but they were re-infected by the third, and so they went on, solo and chorus, and duet and chorus, till exhaustion set in."[73] Benson discloses his inspiration for Mapp and Lucia, "As an external observer I had seen the ladies of Rye doing their shopping in the High Street every morning, carrying large market baskets, and bumping into each other in narrow doorways, and talking in a very animated manner."[74] Benson's women bloom from chattering social climbers to larger than life icons. He writes striking portraits of "great ladies" from the Victorian era in his illustrious memoir *As We Were*. Stately houses and guests were "material props and scaffoldings to that stage," framing those women like divas: "she was a marchioness from top to toe and was playing the part to perfection." Lady Londonderry was "enamored of power" and "its insignia," true to the decorative aesthetic, and like Joseph Mankiewicz directing Bette Davis in a grand entrance, Lady Londonderry stands at the head of the stairs, pausing before one of her prestigious parties "with the 'family fender,' as she called that nice diamond crown gleaming on her most comely head, and hugging the fact that this was her house...." Effeminate phrasing nicely crowns "her most comely head" with the lady's own domestic conceit for a tiara, "the 'family fender,'" as flippant as Firbank. Benson had already borrowed the tiara and its expression as an attribute of his serial character Dodo, in 1921 in *Dodo Wonders*. *As We Were* likens the woman's formidable verve to "a highwaywoman in a tiara," for, "She liked violence and strong color, and sweeping along with her head in the air, vibrant with vitality." A baroque and frivolous montage shows the domestic-fantastic, masculine-feminine range of her lifestyle, "on a plane of high-pitched sensation of the most catholic kind: sailing a small boat in a gale wind, the twelve o'clock Communion at St. Paul's Cathedral, the state-coach in which she attended the opening of Parliament, a loud noise on the organ, all these were of the quality which gave her sustenance." Another portrait exhibits his preference for style over content as well as Lady Rippon's, for the sound and appearance of her fickle and various names are more significant than their legitimacy:

> She had a series of beautiful names: first she had been Lady Gladys Herbert, then she was Countess of Lonsdale, now in the nineties she was Countess de Grey, and presently became Marchioness of Ripon — who ever had such lovely names or so well became them?[75]

Even in a smallish house she rises above banality "with a touch of that apotheosized Bohemianism of which nobody else ever quite had the secret." Naturally she smokes cigarettes from a long amber holder.

Ronald Firbank's protagonists are predominantly female. "Clad in full black, with a dark felt *chapeau de résistance* and a long Lancastrian shawl, she felt herself no mean match for any man,"[76] Firbank attends to feminine costume flamboyantly, and presents woman as a formidable force. Women dominate the formative autobiography of Lord Berners. Women in Beardsley's novel *Under the Hill* are even more sexually explicit and autonomous than in his art. Women can be brutish in Ed Wood's pulp fiction, particularly in *Devil Girls* and *Hell Chicks*, though his most aggressive heroines are male transvestites. Alan Bennett's play *Getting On* pays tribute, between cups of tea in Act I, to the ingeniously adaptable womanly strength of "those firm capable hands." Wilde's women rule the roost: Aunt Agatha seems more masculine than the men in *The Picture of Dorian Gray;* and so does Lady Windermere and indeed the Duchess of Paisley in "Lord Arthur Savile's Crime"; Mrs. Erlynne, in *Lady Windermere's Fan,* is an anti-heroine who flouts the prescription of motherhood and Christian penitence; Mrs. Cheveley is wickedly assertive in *An Ideal Husband* and steals her scenes admirably; and Salomé is a favorite *femme fatale* of the *fin de siècle.* Even Mario Praz, who decries Wilde as an imitator, grudgingly concedes, "It was Wilde who finally fixed the legend of Salomé's horrible passion."[77] Matriarchs intimidate Saki's drawing-rooms with female masculinity: Mrs. Thropplestance in "The Elk" "suggested a blend between a Mistress of the Rhobes and a Master of the Fox-hounds, with the vocabulary of both."[78] Cicely in *When William Came* is remarkably self-contained for a woman in 1913, and several Saki grown sons, here and in other stories, defer to their keepers and benefactors, their mothers. Saki opens "The Easter Egg," "It was distinctly hard times for Lady Barbara, who came of good fighting stock, and was one of the bravest women of her generation, that her son should be so undisguisedly a coward."[79] In *The Watched Pot,* Claire rejects the maternal stereotype with vehement disdain for infants and their species: "I hate babies. They're so human — they remind one of monkeys." Not even Medea gets a line like that. And Madame Hortensia is not only "a sort of Governor-General and Mother Superior and political Boss rolled into one. A Catherine the Second of Russia without any of Catherine's redeeming vices," she is also based on a real acquaintance. Her domestic influence is epic, and when she takes offense even the senior male character steers clear: "She has settled comfortably into a glacial epoch which will transform Briony into a sub-arctic zone in which I, for one, am not tempted to remain."[80] Another female in *The Watched Pot* will finally release her matriarchal hold over the estate — by establishing a matriarchy of her own.

Not quite the feminist role-model for Dodie Smith, yet the strongest character in *The One Hundred and One Dalmations* camps it up and makes her husband change *his* name to de Vil to retain her iconic identity. Feminism brought critical awareness to the gendering of pronouns that assumes the male viewpoint, but in Victorian literature there is a quaint segregation of nouns that invents a feminine turn of phrase to many a specialist noun. Camp writing inclines to a feminine view and preserves this dated habit: camp writing genders nouns in flamboyant inflections that give women arched and exotic expertise in contrast to their banal male equivalents. Aubrey Beardsley sings the praises of a "cantatrice" in "The Three Musicians." Lord Berners encounters a "Tricoteuse" in *Percy Wallingford*, a noun that sounds out revolutionary resonance in the domestic activity of hand-knitting in tricot. When unisex nouns are feminized, a dated practice now — "creator," "poser," signify either sex — the grammatical contrivance seems painted on thick like a transvestite who catwalks every gender signifier, not merely self-conscious but explicitly culturally conscious, and so Beerbohm discusses the "creatrix"[81] and Coward finds a "poseuse" in *Hay Fever*.[82] Crisp acknowledges his influential "editress,"[83] and *Irene Iddesleigh* stands accused as a "traitoress" by Amanda McKittrick Ros.[84] Benson discusses the "citizenesses" of Tilling.[85] Marie Corelli sneers at "snobesses" in *Jane*[86]; she is charmed by a "*charmeresse*" in *Ziska*[87] and a "danseuse" in her short story "Mademoiselle Zephyr"[88]; Corelli underscores the holier than thou capacity of a "*religieuse*"[89]; she stakes a feminist claim on the specialism of an "ancestress" in *God's Good Man*[90] and an "improvisatrice" in *A Romance of Two Worlds*.[91] Ronald Firbank puts a "lectress" on a pedestal in *The Flower Beneath the Foot*. Enter Firbank's "ambassadress.... Clad in the flowing circumstance of an oyster satin ball dress, and all a-glitter like a Christmas tree (with jewels)."[92] Besides a "poetess," in *The New Rythum*, the narrative announces, "Benefactress, arbitress, patroness, wielding international influence, Mrs. Otto van Cotton."[93] Feminine specialisms, role reversals and androgynous synergy in characters and narrative voice put a kink in the language, a camp exhibition of gender as a role to play in the pageantry that is, when it gets the chance, life.

Saki's Cat

Fantasy, banality & camp ... domestic-fantastic
juxtaposition ... the personification
of camp ... narcissism ...

In camp, the axiom "be yourself" is an invocation to performance. Oscar Wilde discloses "the great drama of my life" to Andre Gide: "I've put my genius into my life; I've put only my talent into my works."[1] Wilde, such an influential personality, describes man himself as symbolic and the self as "the ultimate realization of the artistic life. For the artistic life is simply self-development."[2]

Camp is easier to understand — and stereotype — when personified: abstract principles manifested as personality traits. Lucia's effete and latent transvestite sidekick in *Mapp and Lucia*, amiable Georgie, draws from experience. In 1916 Benson wrote a whimsical and poignant and occasionally catty series of portraits, *The Freaks of Mayfair*. "Aunt George" is the most extraordinarily frank, funny and touching chapter that comes out about the lifestyle of an effeminate homosexual. He personifies the coalescence of masculine-feminine energies in camp aesthetics and in Benson's narrative. He utters "tarsome" just like Georgie in *Mapp and Lucia;* and just as in the *Mapp and Lucia* saga, Georgie loves to do needlepoint in *The Freaks of Mayfair*, where you can watch Georgie doing *petit point* in an effete ink drawing, one of several illustrations by George Plank.

> He was in fact an infant of the male sex according to physical equipment, but it became perfectly obvious even when he was quite a little boy that he was quite a little girl.

The sentence carries the breezy temperament of the subject, with just the right glib turn of phrase to remain aloof from that last upstaging trans-

gender word: Benson lets the rhythm trip blithely by the rhetorical match-
ing pair that switches "boy" to "girl," unpunctuated, without qualification
or objection, it's all the same to the author as it is to Georgie. Benson hosts
Georgie's biography with a remarkable marrying of plain-speaking with
frivolous rhetoric, poised between a plotless short story and an essay, read
it as you please, it swings both ways. We follow Georgie through boys'
school, where he fought quarrels not by punching but by slapping and
pulling hair. He ran like a girl but, like *The Babe*, he was good and strong
at sports. Benson reports that school encouraged Catholic confession and
shows how feminine energy in camp adapts the forces of society, or adapts
the rhythms and expressions of language, ironically, to accommodate a genteel sensibility. Seduction by confession: "Georgie conceived a sort of passion for this athletic young priest, poured out to him week by week a farrago
of pale and bloodless peccadilloes, and thought how wonderful he was."
"Farrago" exotically embellishes Georgie's fanciful confessions until "peccadilloes" domesticates his fancy in this Edwardian glimpse into homosexuality. We watch Georgie pass "from girlhood into womanhood" and thence
into auntihood: "Here he lived a kind and blameless life, but the life of a
sprightly widow of forty, who is rich and childless, and does not intend to
marry again."

Benson's ironic construction deviates from the innocuous direction of
a blameless life to elaborate on his status as a widow. "His auntishness was
of the proverbial maiden-aunt variety, and was touched with a certain acid
and cattish quality that now began to tinge his hitherto good-natured gos-
sipy ways." Each stage of Georgie's development is put honestly as natural
progression. As for the perennial party guests, "slightly effeminate young
men and old ladies," well, "Those were the sections of humanity with whom
he feels most at home, because he has most in common with them." Clearly
put in a simple, airy tone with Benson's ubiquitous leisurely authority, it
implies acceptance as the only rational response, without a fuss. However,
this son of the Archbishop of Canterbury knew that the Bible was a tad
scalding of homosexuals. He concludes his portrait of this most camp personality by musing on his life after death:

> It would be a very cruel thing to think of sending poor Georgie to Hell; but it
> must be confessed that, if he went to Heaven, he would make a very odd sort
> of angel.[3]

This is not a tortuous "coming out" story, more matter of fact than a
plea for understanding — though the piece does have some of Ed Wood's
later educative remit on the lifestyle of effeminacy and transvestism.

Ed Wood, whose life was camp enough for filming and whose character is now inseparable from his oeuvre, joined the Ice Capades as an under-cover agent in the Cold War. Our patriotic American author showboats over the ice on a paranoid mission to investigate communist spies, glori-ously, obliviously, camp. Gerry Potter/Chloe Poems as author/performer converges the camp ideal of lifestyle and persona as art with literature, via drama. Camp writers make an ironic performance of wordsmithery, which is why punning is such a camp penchant. Ira Grushow, studying the essays of Beerbohm, notes his "propensity to perform while criticizing."[4] Beer-bohm was a dandy, "the last of the aesthetes" after Wilde, and his prose was somewhat dandified — though not so camp as his persona. In later genera-tions, performance of composition and authorship on the page becomes more demonstrative. Gerry Potter, and before him Crisp, fashioned an artis-tic confluence of lifestyle, persona and literature. Potter presents his sub-personality on stage, blending Chloe Poems' past with autobiography and fashioning speech into poetry, which is delivered and then published. Pot-ter even interviews Poems in *How to Be a Better Gay*.

Fictional portraits of camp writers contribute to the genre as substan-tially as their authors. Benson was a tad self-conscious about the glorious superficiality of his best work, and he compensated with some darker, intro-spective tales and historical non-fiction (often considered his best work). Before he did, Benson wrote about a writer in *The Oakleyites* whose "genial sunshine shed itself impartially on all kinds of subjects. He gardened, he golfed, he played the piano with great fluency, yet again with no passion." Wilfred kept emotion at arm's length in and out of his books. His charac-ters "did not strive or cry; they looked out of the window, or talked to each other, or played charades." Note the telling lack of plot too, a minimum of conflict: his trains "ran punctually and smoothly, and got to their destina-tions as advertised, after a journey made short for his travelers by much delightful and witty conversation." His severest critic, his mother, objected to his preoccupation "with things that lay outside himself; he was a bystander with an admirable eye, quick to perceive, extraordinarily deft to describe."[5] Now there is much to admire in the overseeing eclecticism and the light touch of a dilettante. There is a delectable fluency in the work of the best superficial writers that is crystal clear in the best of Benson and Berners and Firbank and Crisp. Wilfred could be a self-portrait or a por-trayal or foreshadowing of many a camp writer.

Here is Benson's indifferent sketch of Lucia's first husband, Peppino the poet: his poems are published locally by "Ye Signe of Ye Daffodille," we learn in *Queen Lucia*, and *Lucia in London* observes Peppino's profound moment of creativity in the garden: "He had given up the crossword, and was thinking over the material for a sonnet on Tranquility...."[6] Passion, angst and hard labor are *inartistic* traits to camp sensibility. Like Lucia, Benson's portrait of Susan Leg in *Secret Lives* in 1932 precisely describes the real life style of Marie Corelli — a satirical salute. Corelli herself was first to model characters after her self-image, and they are all writers of rare genius. One such aggrandized disguise is Delicia, worshipped by the narrative, reflexively narcissistic:

> Admirers of her genius were too dazzled by that genius to see anything but the glow of the spiritual fire burning about her like the Delphic flames around Apollo's priestess.[7]

The lighting is kitsch but the imagery boasts her classical pretensions and the rhetoric is enraptured by the sound and the notion of "genius." The writer herself becomes a camp character, invisible yet exhibitionistically omnipresent. Delicia rises above banality, "As a writer she stood quite apart from the rank and file of modern fictionists. Something of the spirit of the Immortals was in her blood — the spirit that moved Shakespeare, Shelley and Byron...." Despite her "brilliant brain-work," Corelli notes, Delicia was "one whom certain distinguished noodles of the Press were accustomed to sneer at from their unintellectual and impecunious standpoint as 'a lady novelist' not mentioning the name of 'author,' and who, despite sneers and coarse jesting, was one of the most celebrated women of her time."[8] When she dies a martyr's death, public clamor for her last novel "entirely overwhelmed the ordinary press cackle...." which equates to "You'll be sorry when I'm gone."

You'll find rarefied projections of Corelli as Alwyn/Sah-lûma in *Ardath* and, in *The Sorrows of Satan*, Mavis Clare: "Cleanness of thought, brilliancy of style, beauty of diction, all these were hers, united to consummate ease of expression and artistic skill...."[9] Madame Irene Vassilius suggests the most camp of these portraits in *The Soul of Lilith* in 1892: "She was an authoress of high repute, noted for her brilliant satirical pen, her contempt of press criticism, and her influence over, and utter indifference to, all men." She engages in cutting debate, correcting the male antagonist loftily while keeping her cool: "'That is a mistaken idea — one of the narrow notions common to men,' she answered, waving her fan idly to and fro."[10]

Camp elevates personality into personage, whose signal traits are as emblematic as a Wilde epigram, as representative of camp as an open book on the subject. Lord Gerald Berners wrote autobiographies and novels and stories and plays when he wasn't painting and winning plaudits from Stravinsky and commissions by Diaghilev for his musical compositions. Friend Ronald Acton recalls his camp persona: "His manner was detached and urbane.... He could make startling remarks in a matter-of-fact voice,"[11] which coincidentally describes the narrative voice of camp on the page.

"I suppose there is a caricaturial self in nearly everyone (perceptible, or not, to its owner)," Nancy Cunard says in relation to her friend Ronald Firbank. Theatrical irony in camp is a *knowing* performance of the self: it confirms our connection with the caricaturial everyman and his status as a character in the scripts and drama of his lifetime. "In such exits and entrances, Firbank could appear enchantingly caricaturial, as if everything about him were heightened in tone."[12] Firbank's characters are writ large too, signified by their fantastical and punning names. We have already met Dodie Smith's arch antagonist whose name puns on "cruel devil" with a wink at her iconic mirror image.

Before we meet Saki's cat, it is time to consider a most familiar peculiarity about camp. Two opposite elements synthesize vitally in camp composition: the domestic banality of everyday life ... and the fanciful daydream. Combine them and you have it, the domestic-fantastic juxtaposition. It is key to understanding camp in all its forms and it takes us to another level.

Style is the transcendence of the nondescript, and style over content raises imagination over realism. As seriousness often equates to realism, camp has an affinity with the mythology and romanticism and pageantry of fantasy. Insofar as Quentin Crisp acknowledged literature, he fell under the spell of fairy tales.[13] Lord Berners recalls the formative lure of fantasy literature, where many a flight of fancy escapes the gravitational pull of banality. Even aside from "the Oriental voluptuousness of the illustrations," Beardsley too would have understood Berners' remembrance, "more interested in the pageantry of fairyland than in the personality of its inhabitants. In the story of Cinderella, I was far more thrilled by the pumpkin coach, by the glass slippers, than by the young woman who rode in the former and wore the latter." Décor looms larger than the books in his impressions of a library, "its elaborate gas chandeliers with their luminous globes like gigantic incandescent fruit on Gothic branches...."[14] Leopold von Sacher-Masoch was so adept at writing and romanticizing his sexual fantasies that the culture made a generic term of his most personal fantasy. Sacher-Masoch enjoyed the fantastic tales of history, too, and tales of real-life dominatrix tsarina Catherine the Great excited his world — but his formative personal history is where his infatuation with fantasy begins. In infancy, a Ukranian nurse "told me the wondrously beautiful Russian fairy tales," Sacher-Masoch recalls in *Souvenirs,* cited by Larry Wolff.[15]

A sense of wonder is vital to camp as to fantasy, and realism sometimes closes the window on wonderment, which is why fairy tales take place "Far away." Firbank winks at the traditional signifiers immediately in *Odette: A Fairy Tale for Weary People* in 1905:

Far away, at the end of a long avenue of fragrant limes, wound the Loire, all amongst the flowery meadows and emerald vineyards, like a wonderful looking-glass reflecting all the sky; and across the river, like an ogre's castle in a fairy tale, frowned the chateau of Luynes, with its round grey turrets and its long, thin windows, so narrow, that scarcely could a princess in distress put forth her little white hand to wave to the true knight that should rescue her from her terrible fate.[16]

Not the Gothic Romanticism of E.T.A. Hoffmann but camp romanticism, in a sentence winding like the Loire: after Tennyson, tongue in cheek was the only place left to go for Firbank and the fairy tale. A note of Christian compassion peals for the poor beyond the chateau walls, without actually venturing beyond. (Only Oscar Wilde ventured beyond, unwillingly, in Reading Gaol.) Firbank is concerned with the aesthetic effect on Odette of her act of mercy. As "she ran swiftly down the avenue of lime trees, her untied hair drifting aerially behind her as she ran," you can almost see the slow motion. Encountering a pitiful old woman, young Odette now knows that life is a struggle for millions less fortunate than she.[17] It discounts politics by talking about life being cruel, not society. "And as she passed down the avenue of over-arching limes a thousand thrushes sang deliriously amidst the branches," a pastoral delirium of hosannas that makes Christianity kitsch. "Millions" of wretches and "thousands" of thrushes indulge the epic scale of camp.

Most of Oscar Wilde's fairy tales speak to children, which curtails his flamboyance, but "The Fisherman and His Soul" indulges his baroque flair, not to say Beardsley. Even a phantom can be camp:

His face was strangely pale, but his lips were like a proud red flower. He seemed weary, and was leaning back toying in a listless manner with the pommel of his dagger. On the grass beside him lay a plumed hat, and a pair of riding gloves gauntleted with gilt lace, and sewn with seed-pearls wrought into a curious device.[18]

The effeminate simile that ripens his lips like a sensuous flower, and the dégagé pose of decadent ennui, as well as the opulent dress sense that admires the phantom as a period dandy, are familiar camp attributes and all prolific in the format of the fairy tale.

Above all, camp is seduced by the fairy tale's facility to take kitchen domesticity and turn it into *Cinderella*. Half-way through *Zuleika Dobson*, third person narrative comes out as first person all along, told by a retiring male servant. (It would have been more camp with a maid, but still), this is a metaphysical servant to a mythological mistress, a classical and analogous perspective to the romance—the Bigger Picture from the servant's quarters. Huysmans' alter ego in *Against Nature* designs an apartment that transcends banality: "This dining-room resembled a ship's cabin, with its ceiling of arched beams, its bulkheads and floorboards of pitch-pine, and the little window-opening let into the wainscoting like a porthole."[19] Berners and Firbank have camp company in their inclination to fantasy — Saki's favorite theme is anthropomorphic animals; Beardsley saturated domestic detail with grandeur and fabulous creatures; Goytisolo time-travels and genre-hops like a dapper Doctor Who, who happens to be a cultural hero for Chloe Poems, and Poems is not aversed to metaphysical metaphors and outlandish juxtapositions to enhance existence; Ed Wood's favorite genre was science fiction; Wilde's elevation of Lying is a fantastical antidote to the "common-place" literature of his age. A superlative adjective can do it. A fantastical adverb mythologizes Mrs. Packinton in *The Watched Pot:* "She's fabulously old and fabulously rich, and she's been fabulously ill for longer than any living human being can remember."[20] Domestic-fantastic metaphors artic-ulate a delectable dialectic between the commonplace and the eccentric to counterbalance banality. Saki's first sentence in "For the Duration Of the War" — written, amazingly, on the front line of World War I — defines the unassuming, parochial ambitions of the story: "The Rev. Wilfrid Gaspilton, in one of those clerical migrations inconsequent-seeming to the lay-mind, had removed from the moderately fashionable parish of St. Luke's, Kensin-gate, to the immoderately rural parish of St. Chuddock's, somewhere in Yondershire." ("Yondershire," such a frivolously transparent netherworld term, somewhere, anywhere, over the next hill.) Similes soon aggrandize the situation with a cavalier appropriation of a royal Court: "The Rev. Wil-frid found himself as bored and ill at ease in his new surroundings as Charles II would have been at a modern Wesleyan Conference."[21]

Camp, you see, abhors the uniformity of mediocrity. The real heart-break of Wilde's incarceration in Reading Gaol is just that: "I used to say that I thought I could bear a real tragedy if it came to me with purple pall and a mask of noble sorrow, but that the dreadful thing about modernity was that it put tragedy into the raiment of comedy, so that the great reali-ties seemed commonplace or grotesque or lacking in style." Even "The Soul of Man Under Socialism" (1891) calls for the universal right to individual development, not mass conformism to standardized equality: Wilde's pam-phlet is as much a strike against the nondescript Everyman as against the ruling classes. It puts a different gloss on Gwendolen's snobbery in *The Importance of Being Earnest,* when she disdains the mundane: "No, there is very little music in the name Jack, if any at all, indeed. It does not thrill. It produces absolutely no vibrations.... I have known several Jacks, and they all, without exception, were more than usually plain."[22] She is content to judge a book by its cover to insure against a nondescript encounter.

Refashioning his persona, which rises above petty prejudice and witless lack of style all around him, one of the first acts of Quentin Crisp was to change his name—from Denis "(as my name was before I dyed it)."[23] His autobiographies face the tyranny of mediocrity, the brutish majority that democracy gives the mandate to oppress individuals, eccentrics, scapegoats. Thanks to the cult of celebrity and the brave survival of his self, his story is a rare triumph over uniformity. "I have passed from being an outcast to being almost universally acceptable with such speed that I have had no time to experience ordinary life."[24]

One of many paradoxes in this most unassuming writer is that anything democratically called "a great leveler"—including political correctness and, probably, socialism — would appall Crisp's sensibility. "We have eaten the bitter apple of equality to the very core, dragging the gods down to our own mean level," he reflects in a book on film, where cinemagoing and glamorous artifice escape the mundane.[25] His occasional anti-socialist sentiment merely expresses his disdain for mobs and the oppression of mediocrity, not in terms of content but style. It is an aristocratic sensibility, and so Beerbohm says of his Duke in *Zuleika Dobson*, "Never had he given ear to that cackle which is called Public Opinion."[26] Another of E.F. Benson's artful camp characters, Lord Cookham this time in *Dodo Wonders,* makes the point with a Freudian slip. First, Benson presents his camp credentials in a single sentence:

> Lord Cookham bowed precisely as a butler bows when a guest presents him on Monday morning with a smaller token of gratitude than he had anticipated.

Here's the slip, with Lord Cookham in full flow with impressive propriety: "Your father, in fact, Lady Chesterford, is typical of the aristocracy of industry. Sprung from the very dregs— I should say from the very heart of democracy, he has risen to a position attained by few of those who have been the architects of their own fortunes." Dodo (Lady Chesterford) does not let him forget that word "dregs." Lord Cookham has a lofty manner of addressing the space a foot above the head of his interlocutor. Here is how removed from the fray this wonderful character can be, when a phone call from a mutual friend interrupts Lord Cookham's conversation, and even as Dodo mentions that Lord Cookham is right here with her:

> During this remarkable conversation Lord Cookham's long practise in dignity and self-possession had enabled him to appear quite unconscious that anything was going on. By the expression on his face he might have been sitting on the slopes of Hymettus, contemplating the distant view of the Acropolis, and hearing only the hum of the classical bees, so detached did he seem from anything that Dodo happened to be saying on the telephone.[27]

Ifan Kyrle Fletcher[28] recalls of Ronald Firbank, "He hated 'the mob,' as he called the vulgarians of all classes," their blunted sensibility a measure of banality. Fletcher visited his Cambridge lodgings and describes "the strange beauty which he created out of the drabness of college rooms." His writing embellished literature, just so. "His room was arranged with old red silks, masses of flowers, and a number of dainty tables, covered with books and statuettes ... Gothic religious figures, but sometimes they were Pompeian and Tanagra work, paganly attractive." Fantastic.

Banality: Sherlock Holmes called it "the dull routine of existence," but he abhorred florid case histories and so the staid prose of Arthur Conan Doyle is not camp, and the camp solution, although somewhat of a scandal in Bohemia, is not to be intently detective, nor even 7 percent of cocaine. Holmes may yet be a theatrical exhibitionist of narcissistic proportions in *The Sign of Four* and more — there is a case to be made — but camp does not reject banality: camp conflates the fantastic and domestic to subvert it. Even when nothing much is going on and nothing profound is discussed, banality is bent by innuendo, tea is served with an arabesque extension of the wrist, a pedestrian conversation saunters with soigné delectation of its syllables in diction seldom found outside theater. Style over content, larger than life: the fantastic-domestic conceit is another take on our definition of flamboyant exaggeration (fantasy) offset by irony (domesticity). The avant garde persona of The Divine David, in monologue on stage and television, is just such a flamboyant confluence: "There's more to life than buttering bits of bread," one such droll, homespun refrain as homely as a housewife's aphorism.

This bohemian banality, the domestication of the fantastic, the aggrandizement of make-believe only to be exposed as artifice, makes camp similes capriciously asymmetrical. Reading *The Artificial Princess,* where regal Herodias had a passion for motoring with her crown on, Brigid Brophy[29] finds the "essential Firbankian technique of a domesticity deflationary yet bizarre." Yet the domestic-fantastic "technique" is a world-view long predating Firbank. It expedites the opinion, voiced from a lectern in Alan Bennett's *The Laying on of Hands,* that death is not the end at all but more like "popping next door."[30] Incongruous juxtaposition becomes camp, not Surrealist or absurdist, when grounded in domesticity and presented theatrically. For a superficial aesthetic, there's more to camp than meets the eye.

Brophy does find an association with the "ambivalence" of *baroque* style (she credits Titian with "inventing" baroque in the 1550s), another translation of the incongruous juxtapositions we see in camp. *Baroque* and *rococo* "were used as often by way of insult as of description," and camp aesthetics languish under similar disdain.[31] "Ambiguity and puns are its raw material," she says of baroque, true, too, of camp.

Benson presents a domestic-fantastic gathering in *Dodo Wonders* as a couple dine at an elite restaurant:

> Here was a Cabinet Minister, Hugo Alford, lunching with a prima-donna, there an Australian tennis-champion with an eclipsed duchess, a French pugilist and a cosmopolitan actress of quite undoubtful reputation dressed in pearls and panther-skins. Then there was old Lady Alice Fane bedizened in bright auburn hair and strings of antique cameos....[32]

The unlikely pairings are completely whimsical and as flamboyant as a West End musical casting session. Benson's expressions are quite bedizened with literary glory. A "prima-donna" is always good camp mileage, while "an eclipsed duchess" may have seen grander days but never so fantastically represented, and a gallant assertion of the reputation of the cosmopolitan actress is undermined by "undoubtful," which contrives more doubt than it dispels, further indicted by her panther-skin costume.

Climbing down a social class or two, Quentin Crisp juxtaposes the banal and fantastic in his title, *The Naked Civil Servant,* conjuring an exhibition of nudity where one would least expect to find it, among the upstanding bowlers and umbrellas and anal regularity of the English civil service. His public speaking voices the domestic-fantastic conceit: "I was merely domesticating the high-flown precepts of the great thinkers of the past. " His own manner of speaking, *Crisperanto,* "wears a bit more eyeshadow, rouge and lipstick than is absolutely necessary (some people even say, 'That's laying it on a bit thick')...." and he contrasts it with *Esperanto,* "which reduces several European languages to their common denominator with the aim of producing a basic vocabulary of simple words and concepts...."[33] The people most likely to stand at their gates sniding, "That's laying it on a bit thick," of course, are literary critics.

Crisp even offers some rare literary criticism, a domestic-fantastic analogy of D.H. Lawrence's momentous oeuvre conflated with his domestic circumstances. It's an effeminate make-over of the celebrated author's masculine style, dusting over F.R. Leavis and reams of intellectual analysis:

> Mrs. Lawrence described her husband as almost impotent. Once you have seen that famous photograph of the two of them standing side by side — she so huge, so self-confident, he so thin, so haunted — you understand his entire literary output. He never got his wife to do a damned thing he wanted.[34]

Each camp writer finds his own domestic-fantastic signature. Noël Coward binds droll bourgeois Englishness to barking eccentricity, itself stereotyped as a national characteristic. In *Blithe Spirit,* Madame Arcati's spiritual earthiness revels in domestic-fantastic juxtapositions. The medium arrives for a séance on a bicycle. Her first demonstration of fantastic pre-science is rather pedestrian: "I'm afraid I'm rather late, but I had a sudden presentiment that I was going to have a puncture so I went back to fetch my pump." Madam Arcati is also a writer: she gave up her memoir of a Princess when her subject suddenly died. "I talked to her about it the other day and she implored me to go on with it, but I really hadn't the heart." Her matter of fact tone in discussing it, the other day, beyond the grave, almost overlooks the ghostly status of her subject.

The séance is a theatrical medium that lends even greater melodrama to lights down than the stage, though staged in the domesticity of a living room populated predominantly by women. Madame Arcati will have you know she is a professional who cannot tolerate the word "amateur," and her celebrated "Sudbury case" séance "was what you might describe in the-atrical parlance as my first smash hit!" The supercilious lead, Charles, pro-vides distance from Madame Arcati's performance. Charles is a writer who, for the purposes of research and the expediency of his next book, hopes that she is a real professional charlatan. Charles embodies the insincere and leisurely aesthetic that Coward so disdained in Wilde's generation. Elvira, the ghost of his first wife, delivers urbane detachment from the aloof after-life, though she continues an interest in domestic affairs like flower arrang-ing. She is a droll antidote to the spooked hysterics of Charles' current wife who extends jealousy to include ghosts, while Elvira makes barbed remarks from her invisible vantage. Coward contrasts Elvira's spiritual state with her careless pose and down to earth attitude as she "*sits in arm-chair with her legs over the left-arm.*" Those ghostly manifestations of Madame Arcati's hocus pocus are the most irreverent and skeptical witnesses of her esoteric rituals, with rather pedestrian cynicism in contrast to her theatrical div-inations. The domestic-fantastic confluence continues as Charles' current wife informs Madame Arcati of the ghost's whereabouts and mundane transport: "My husband has driven her into Folkstone — apparently she was anxious to see an old friend of hers who is staying at the Grand."[35]

"The Tube" (1928) is a sketch for another Coward musical revue, set in a railway station, where a song by a Bank Clerk and Chorus takes the national banality of waiting in queues and ironically recommends queuing as the latest eccentric craze. It's a novel perspective on banality through the eyes of the elite who are customarily insulated from mundane experiences. With all the roads up, "We must just be brave and do what the common people do," says the Honorable Millicent Bloodworthy. A routine transac-tion with a news vendor (he's never heard of *Vogue* magazine) appears, to our elite, quite fantastic.[36]

Now take Saki's cat, if you will, in a short story called "Tobermory."

Tobermory is an anthropomorphic personification of camp, domestic and quite fantastic: our urbane cat was, regrettably, taught how to speak — and quite able to "make startling remarks in a matter-of-fact voice" to rival Firbank. Enjoy the contrast between Saki's cat's incongruous *sang froid* and the rattled astonishment of the house guests. Imagine their embarrassment at "addressing on equal terms a domestic cat of acknowledged dental ability." A nervous offering of milk provokes a droll response, "'I don't mind if I do,'" from the cat's pajamas, "couched in a tone of even indifference." The lady of the house spills the milk and finds herself apologizing to the cat, who remains blasé, "'After all, it's not my Axminster,' was Tobermory's rejoinder."[37]

This bizarre comedy of manners is a study in camp delivery, modeled by the most qualified creature to make the most of a divan. Saki celebrates "The Achievement of the Cat" in a whimsical essay and dramatizes it in several short stories. A cat flaunts its Persian pedigree in "The Reticence of Lady Anne,""basking in the firelight with superb indifference." It royally disdains an invitation to lick up spilt milk: "Don Tarquino was prepared to play many roles in life, but a vacuum carpet-cleaner was not one of them."[38] Saki says of this breed, "If you want a lesson in elaborate artificiality, just watch the studied unconcern of a Persian Cat entering a crowded salon, and then go and practice it for a fortnight."[39] On the other paw, when a guest offends Tobermory's drawing-room sensibility, we are reminded that camp does a bitchy line in compromising gossip. Bitchcraft has claws. Aloof poise becomes arched:

> "How about your carrying-on with the tortoise-shell puss up at the stables, eh?"
> The moment he had said it everyone realized the blunder.
> "One does not usually discuss these matters in public," said Tobermory frigidly. "From a slight observation of your ways since you've been in this house I should imagine you'd find it inconvenient if I were to shift the conversation on to your own little affairs."[40]

That genteel but insidious phrase, "From a slight observation," suffices to sum up so slight and obvious a person. The signal euphemism "inconvenient" for downright disturbing and a condescending allusion to "your own little affairs" implies ironically that they are, morally, no small matter. Saki's cat models what Kenneth Williams called "the acid drop ... the tart retort which puts down the pompous, the pretentious, the dishonest and ... the innocent blunderer."[41]

Christoper Isherwood's portrait of Sally Bowles makes *Goodbye to Berlin*, his 1935 novel, camp. She makes her entrance in "a little cap like a pageboy's stuck jauntily on one side of her head," a cross-gender accessory whose oblique angle signals frivolous irony, too. The masculine German language becomes androgynous and kinky on her lips, on the phone, which Isherwood brings into decadent and artificial close-up on the page: "'Hilloo,' she cooed, pursing her brilliant cherry lips as though she were going to kiss the mouthpiece....." All the while, "Fritz and I sat watching her, like a performance at the theater."[42] She speaks from that culture of ironic superlatives and melodramatic absolutes: "'He makes love marvelously. He's an absolute genius at business and he's terribly rich — .'" Sighing into the cushions, "'I'm simply dying of thirst,'" the dramatic superlatives are camp in frivolous contrast to their domestic application.

The camp stand-off from its own upstaging effects is adopted by many camp authors, as well as their pets, outside their work. Berners is remembered now for painting his live fantail pigeons in multi-colors and playing piano in his car, in a biography inspired by his persona and literary connections but not by his books. Yet the camp signature may flourish on the page. Even Tobermory, it is speculated when he's late home, is probably at the local newspaper office, "dictating the first instalment of his reminiscences."[43] Quentin Crisp, who cut his personality to the camp template, augmented his persona with epigrammatic memoirs more distinguished than himself. When he relates camp to effeminacy to observe "the meaning of the mannequin walk and the stance in which the hip was only prevented from total dislocation by the hand placed upon it," his writing assumes the posture: his hip-swinging rhythm and the extreme "total dislocation" is flaunted then ironically subverted by precise and precious articulation of "the hand placed upon it," posing the preening manner of camp with prim awareness of his readership.

The same autobiography[44] sketches a camp acquaintance in a monocle and decorated discourse with quotations from French and Latin from his "Penguin scholarship." Rounding off the caricature, he was "snobbish beyond the wildest dreams of the Mitfords, sentimental and oozing with sly, circuitous jokes about sex." When he is institutionalized and Crisp comes to call, camp characterization and prose style come together beautifully:

> We were careful not to look out of the window because among the laurel bushes that luxuriated in the grounds men were in the habit of exposing themselves to the visitors — a sight which tended to interrupt my train of thought. We drank tea. He purchased three cups explaining, "The place is an absolute madhouse."

Here is the layering of camp elements in the passage: incongruity between luxuriant laurels and lewd exhibitionism; in this case absence of commas (we might expect one after "grounds," at least) removes any especial

emphasis in the matter of fact tone; precious, rather English phrasing akin
to Alan Bennett is seen to do its best to observe decorum despite the dramatic setting, and only serves to highlight the faux pas and the institution — the dash is the graphic depiction of distraction while the delicate
construction "which tended to" tries to restore English propriety by understatement: the extreme dynamic sets up the humor; a simple, laconic sentence pauses to sip tea and seems to observe a staid and distracted silence
beside itself, further domestic contrast with the compulsive naturism
through the window; and a final dogmatic utterance by his committed
acquaintance, even as he inexplicably delivers one cup too many, emphasizes the location obliviously, projected by "absolute" to the point of theatricality, putting the institution on a proscenium stage. The author's
passive persona in all this takes the aloof perspective so exquisitely essential to the aesthetic. Wonderful.

Crisp is adroit in the art of detached engagement, a stylized form of
consciousness, and his authorial voice exceeds Wilde in this form, I think.
Crisp recalls his arduous past in memoir but he never proceeds for more
than a few sentences before interposing the relief of a maxim or juxtaposing yesterday against his current circumstances. He is open about his past
yet aloof from it, beyond its determinism. Crisp's preferred genre, autobiography, is egocentric, and his fashioning of his effeminate persona as art
is narcissistic, yet the perspective on egocentricity in his literature is a paradoxical detachment from self. Is he merely posing as a narcissist? But then,
persona *is* a pose. The customary definition of narcissism is self-absorption
that does not conceive philosophic distance from the reflection. Camp writers are ever ready to reflect on the reflection.

The mirror image in *Against Nature,* in an apartment whose Decadent
décor is a shrine to the aesthetics of the one rounded character in the book,
the author's alter ego, is fathomless: "where mirror echoed mirror, and
every wall reflected an endless succession of pink boudoirs...."[45] Beardsley's
hero in *Under the Hill* looks to the looking glass for confirmation. "'Would
to heaven,' he sighed, 'I might receive the assurance of a looking-glass before
I make my debut!'" Later, he does, in a series of frivolous poses.[46] A furtive
glance behind his back, photographed in the glass, cannot be wholly
absorbed in ego as long as self-image requires focal distance to be appreciated and reflective distance to be set down on the page.

Beerbohm contrives mirror poses so that *Zuleika Dobson* can "see herself from beneath her eyelashes," posing expressions and acting the emotions. Her paramour the Duke is "too much concerned with his own
perfection ever to think of admiring anyone else."[47] It is the caricaturist
author and the readership who project askance distance. Saki projects it in

overblown narrative in "The Byzantine Omelette": "Now and again she glanced mirror-ward at the reflection of her wonderfully coiffed hair, as an insurance underwriter might gaze thankfully at an overdue vessel that had ridden safely into harbor in the wake of a devastating hurricane."[48] On the casual commencement "Now and again," Saki's sentence blithely docks with a fantastical simile almost as a whimsical afterthought after a leisurely comma — tongue in cheek: Saki is fully aware of what an upstaging comical comparison this is in the best camp tradition of the domestic-fantastic conceit. The sentence preens before the mirror just like the ostensible subject.

Marie Corelli's *Ziska* uses portraiture to frame narcissism when a painter comes to call. After a theatrical demonstration that she is "not without protection"— Ziska claps her hands and a wall slides open to reveal "twenty or thirty gorgeously-costumed Arab attendants," fully armed — then claps again to conceal them behind walls once more — she laughs at the painter's bewilderment, and before he or we can recover, "'Paint me now!' she said, flinging herself in a picturesque attitude on one of the sofas close by; 'I am ready.'"[48]

Narcissism is a likely theme in a literature that applies "Show, Don't Tell" not to the tale but more flamboyantly to show the writer writing. The style of some writers, from Wilde to Wood, from Crisp to Poems, becomes so iconic that it makes a protagonist of the author. Mark Amory[50] says of Lord Berners, "In practice he turned out to be not only his best subject but his only one." Berners devoted himself to two autobiographies, glossed by a tone more concerned with literary style than the incidental facts of a lifetime. *First Childhood,* widely considered his best work, births his self-awareness, acquired in much the same way as "the technique of riding a bicycle or of performing some trick of juggling, when, at a given moment and without any apparent reason, it is suddenly found that the thing can be done." He adds, "The condition in which this epoch-making event in my mental career took place could not possibly have been more trivial."[51] Incongruity between his profound rhetorical structure, toppling in the subsidence of an absurd analogy between the psychic foundation of identity and riding a bicycle ... then a full-blown declamatory "could not possibly" deflated by "more trivial," upstages the ego with a presiding tone of tongue in cheek: how finite and brittle ego really is, despite its grand allusions to Genesis.

Noël Coward recalls the chief attraction of Broadway, "flashing in myriad lights, with unfailing regularity, the two words, 'Noël Coward.'"[52] Those words are presented as a symbol, like the theatrical personality they represent, and this consciousness is implicit in his memoirs as in the memoirs of Crisp or Berners. Crisp regards his own one-man show, "Even with my name in lights and my countenance plastered around New York on posters (now peeling — how fleeting is fame) I remain the same: Your Humble Servant."[53] Larger than life, his visage on posters and name in lights (with wry despair in parenthesis), the tone remains servile, supremely, in uppercase. The show called him out of retirement, "a stand-in for Gloria Swanson" in this, "my glorious swan song," sending up his effeminacy but all the same hitching it to a star.

Writing one's memoirs would seem the most narcissistic process in art, and the most reflective. Curiously, Coward's autobiographies show narrative detachment that his long, story-driven paragraphs of prose fiction, lacking style, do not. In an anthology introduction, Coward recalls his new fame and suggests the media manufacture of his camp image, though I note some reclining collusion. He was photographed everywhere...." In my dressing-room. At my piano. With my dear old mother, without my dear old mother — and, on one occasion, sitting up in an over-elaborate bed looking like a heavily doped Chinese Illusionist."[54] How exotic. Like Crisp, he observes the camp tradition of appearing passive in the face of events and not at all responsible for the indelicacies of an unlikely plot.

Coward's memoirs transcend egoism, even in the reflection of narcissism. "I was photographed in every conceivable position." The glamor of celebrity is upstaged by innuendo at Coward's cheerful expense. His blithe indulgence of fame is made ironic in retrospect, like Tannhäuser's whimsical backward glance in the mirror in Beardsley's novel. Ahead of his time, for once, Coward exposes the ludicrous public equation of the celebrity figure with the Renaissance man, consulted like an oracle. He is happy to play the role as role, "smiling and burbling bright witticisms, giving my views on this and that, discussing such problems as whether or not the modern girl would make a good mother, or what would be my ideal in a wife, etc."[55] Coward's diaries cast Brechtian seriousness as heavy and humorless (and distastefully left-wing). Petitioned to describe the ideal wife, his irony is as discreet as a raised eyebrow if the reader is privy to Coward's homosexuality. Celebrity, like many a social interaction and like ego itself, is a theatrical masquerade.

Firbank's story, "A Study in Temperament," begins and ends with contemplation that either poses the self as art (the tenet of Oscar Wilde) or questions whether one loses one's self in the superficial and artificial attendance to ego...

> Lady Agnes Charters leaned back in a Louis XIV chair and critically glanced at herself reflected in a tall mirror. Certainly the delicate green brocade of the *grande siécle* made a foil for her crown of golden hair which her women friends charitable attributed to Art.[56]

Consider Wilde's *Salomé* of 1893: as the Page of Herodias grieves over the Young Syrian, "The sound of his voice was like the sound of the flute, of a flute player. Also he much loved to gaze at himself in the river. I used to reproach him for that," so Herod tells Salomé, "Only in mirrors should one look, for mirrors do but show us masks."[57] Juan Goytisolo unmasks the protagonist, whose "ostentatious extravagances won over the European fauna flourishing at the time," in *The Garden of Secrets*. "Daily he reconstructed himself a character and lived it with the conviction of an actor on stage."[58] The mirror image is never far from the transvestite masquerade of *Killer In Drag* and the sequel *Death of a Transvestite*. Ed Wood's prose colludes with the feminized ideal yet separates the performer from the image: "Holding the brush expertly in her hand she touched the corners of her lips then smiled at the lovely reflection who smiled back at her."[59]

Marie Corelli wrote *The Young Diana* in 1918, with sublimated homoeroticism, it seems to me: "Standing before the mirror she deliberately let the shining 'robe of ordeal' slip from her body to the floor. Nude as a pearl, she remained for a moment, gazing, as she knew, at the loveliest model of feminine perfection ever seen since the sculptor of the Venus de Medici wrought his marble divinity."[60] *Delicia* sounds like the likely name of a transvestite, but it is the name of Corelli's novel and its heroine of 1896. When Delicia learns that her husband is a cad, she addresses a heart-broken soliloquy to her mirror for moral support. "And, moved by a quaint compassion for herself, she leant forward and kissed the reflection of her own quivering lips in the mirror."[61]

Sentimentality was all the rage in the Victorian era, but Corelli's sensual narcissism, a kiss away from lesbianism, rather stands out.

Chloe Poems is nervous and inspired by the prospect of intimate contact with the self on a very personal blind date in "Me," and feigns confidence in the face of his own shyness:

> And although I'm pleased to see me
> And find myself really rather attractive
> I'm reminded by my eyes
> Just how many times I've failed love
> And how it's failed me....[62]

Narcissism is considered a shallow and regressive state of mind, but *expression* cultivates objectified revelation and distance from ego of at least the focal length of a mirror or a scanned page. "Me" winks at narcissism in a jaunty aside ("And find myself really rather attractive"), paradoxically deflecting the fixation on self-image. A touching declaration of shyness and an honest fear of intimacy in the middle of such an exhibitionist poem, written for public performance, is one more irony for us to negotiate.

Alan Bennett presents the most self-effacing narcissism, if I may. At an elite Oxford University voting ceremony, Bennett flashes a perfect likeness of his stylized banality to confirm his identity: his Camden Town bus pass—which is scrutinized "as grimly as an Albanian border guard."[63]

Bertolt Brecht muses on theater and recommends, "Using the third person and the past tense allows the actor to adopt the right attitude of detachment.... Everything to do with emotions has to be externalized, that is to say, it must be developed into a gesture.... The emotion in question must be brought out, must lose all its restrictions so that it can be treated on a big scale. Special elegance, power and grace of gesture bring about the "A" effect."[64] "Me" finds another form for the Alienation effect, first person singular conflated with third person objectivity that Brecht preferred. Line by line like a southern belle fanning a zephyr, Chloe Poems carefully loses all restrictions in those coy yet cumulative emotional disclosures, until the scale of the stanza is as big as Brecht...

The "Ahh" Effect

*The alienation effect ... theatricality ... cross-dressing
between genres ... camp diction & oral tradition ...
stage directions ... political camp?*

Camp and Brecht seem unlikely bedfellows. Yet when Brecht[1] observes of traditional Chinese theater, where actors use masks, "The Chinese actor achieves the A-effect by being seen to observe his own movements," I recall camp's ironic preoccupation with narcissism. Saki notes of a bore, "I used to listen to him with a rapt attention that I thought rather suited me,"[2] subverting the "rapt" import to cast an askance mirror image, for the singular concentration of rapt attention is actually *un*becoming to camp aesthetics and only made seemly by the dissociating observation of it.

Brecht complains, "The bourgeois novel in the last century developed much that was 'dramatic,' by which is meant the strong centralization of the story." Rather than "implicate the spectator in a stage situation" in dramatic theater, Brecht advocates *epic* theater, which "turns the spectator into an observer, but arouses his capacity for action." In dramatic theater, "the spectator is in the thick of it, shares the experience." In epic theater, "the spectator stands outside, studies." Brecht achieves distance as a director and playwright by exposing the artifice of theater. In 1931 he says, "The actor must not only sing but show a man singing. His aim is not so much to bring out the emotional content of his song ... but to show gestures that are so to speak the habits and usage of the body."[3] It's not what Brecht had in mind, but I recall the transvestite tradition in camp cabaret that lip synchs the songs of showboating divas. The "Ahh" Effect is camp's pronounced, opiated reading of the "A" Effect: the aesthetic alienation of Bertolt Brecht becomes aspirate and sibilant in the performative diction of camp, too blasé for ideology, too dégagé to summon much capacity for action.

Saki and Maude's play *The Watched Pot* satirizes the playwright's exigency of the telegram or the letter — so dependable for Oscar Wilde. The Butler reports the dramatic reception of a telegram just as the plot is floundering: "She held it for a long while looking at it, sir, theatrical like, and then said there was no answer." René parodies the dramatic exit line, "*[tragically]* Yes, let us go and dance on the edge of our volcano," just as his camp uncle "*holds up his hands in mock despair*" as he exits Act II. There is even an objection to bourgeois plays when a member of the servant class tells Agatha, as she exits, "What I envy about you, miss, is your play-going way of taking things." Play-going way? "Yes, miss. You just sit and wait till things has been brought to a climax and then you put on your hat and gloves and walk outside. It's different for those who've got to go on living with the climax."[4] (And, more horribly, with the banality of anti-climaxes.) Saki's droll and precious narrative "outs" the telegram device again in "The Unrest Cure," as a character intrudes with a telegram, "and in that household telegrams were recognized as happening by the hand of God. This particular telegram partook of the nature of a thunderbolt." More telegrams shape the plot and barely disguise the hand of the showboating author, who observes, in third person, "Telegram? It seemed to be a day of telegrams."[5] Like an arched brow, his ironic question mark distances the author from the design even as he draws attention to himself, even as he tells as he shows.

On stage, actors in dialogue vicariously address the audience: volume, inflections and gestures are designed to reach beyond the environs of the set; theatricality exhibits this awareness of being seen. Camp thrives in English tradition; theater too runs deep in English culture. Camp enacts an ancient wisdom passed down from Athens to Zen that all the world's a stage and its sincere practitioners, players. Art metaphors aggrandize camp narrative above any vestige of naturalism. Wilde and Saki sketched metaphors of portraiture in characterization. In Marie Corelli's precious Victorian prose in *The Mighty Atom*, "The leafy branches of the trees were delicately outlined in air as with an artist's careful pencil."[6]

Playwrights can be just as conspicuous. Noël Coward gives supremely mannered stage directions in the second Act of *Conversation Piece*. An otherwise not very camp musical comedy stylizes behavior, character, and form itself in a tableau vivant:

(*When the Curtain rises the* GUESTS *are grouped, with* JULIA *and* PAUL *in the center, forming a beautiful "still" picture. This attitude is held through a phrase of music, when, at a given point, the "picture" comes to life, and the party is in progress.*
(*Note: Throughout this Scene there are musical "stops" to allow the dialogue to be heard. All guests, etc, not actually concerned in the dialogue, remain immovable, in whatever positions they may be.*)[7]

Oscar Wilde found ways to liken scenes and characters to portraiture to similar effect, elevating artifice. Essentially theatrical, *I Am a Camera* is John van Druten's adaptation of Isherwood's Berlin story, where we may order coffee "Black, black, black, like Otello."[8] Beardsley's florid and fabulous writing is as vivid and visual as his drawing: *Under the Hill* creates then dispels the enchantment of a wooded lake that fantastically changes shape until the narrative reflects, ever so casually, "Perhaps the lake was only painted after all. He had seen things like it at the theater."[9] The enchantment of artifice and the alchemy of irony bewitch the wonderment of the camp artist. Camp transgresses in breaking the spell of realism and our conviction in the story. Philosophic insights into the performance of existence in *As You Like It* are high camp, translated by Eric Berne in the 1960s as a psychology of scripted social transactions. All the world's a stage, but camp juxtaposition of the domestic-fantastic makes *fringe* theater with a cast of outcasts. Quentin Crisp observed the masses who are "miscast for the roles they are offered in the Broadway drama of Life, and that they would be better off declining a part in an overrated mediocrity. There are great roles off-Broadway."[10]

Even derrieres are stage struck by camp: Chloe Poems muses, "Why Do Roughs Have Such Tight Buns?" whose fey theatrical analogies play up the disparity between the author and the Roughs:

> If they could be measured theatrically
> Roughs' bottoms are Shakespeare,
> Mine a bedroom farce.[11]

Noël Coward put camp into mainstream production, but his protagonists, buffered by aristocracy, remain aloof and eccentric. His later mediocre play *Waiting In the Wings* is set in a charity home for retired leading ladies of the theater, and the theatricality of their biographies and temperaments offsets their uneventful, waning lives, waiting in "The Wings" for their final curtain.

> SARITA (*descending the stairs*): Out damned spot! Out I say! One two: why then, 'tis time to do 't.
> MISS ARCHIE (*firmly*): You must *not* quote Macbeth in this house, Miss Myrtle. You know how it upsets everybody.[12]

The play feels mediocre because, despite occasional ironies that play to the gallery — "Dierdre can make even a game of draughts sound like a Lyceum melodrama" — the imbalance of domesticity-fantasy flounders in nondescript scenes and impotent pathos that can only summon the shadow of theater in the twilight of Coward's career. Least camp of all Coward's motifs is his wistful observation of life's and love's passing moment that becomes tomorrow's nostalgia and the ember of an old flame. This theme accounts for epic time lapses between Acts, where he seeks philosophical distance form the sentimental moment. It haunts his work — and much of any poet's output — engaging but often saturated with sentiment, like the *Bitter Sweet* lyrics ("I'll See You Again" and "Alas the Time Is Past"). Camp, saved from drowning by aloof disposition, would not hold the lapsed moment long enough for poignant reverie, any more than it holds onto plot to wonder what happens next. This detached perspective is the view from the wings, set up by staging the process as theatrical artifice.

Waiting in the Wings is at least typically Coward and camp in its overtly theatrical presentation. He draws on his theatrical world with actors who play characters who are also actors who make melodrama out of banality and appear to be performing even "off stage." (One of his funniest plays, *Hay Fever* portrays a most theatrical family who revel in hystrionics but remain detached from any import in the aloof aftermath, as shell-shocked houseguests leave like escapees the morning after.) The trappings of theater is camp vocabulary, and in Coward's autobiographies, half his life is spent in rehearsal: from his days as a child actor through to maturity, theater pervades like home.

Lord Berners recalls a homecoming in his autobiography, using imagery most familiar to his sensibility to capture a subtle yet material change in ambiance, "just as scenery on the stage is transformed by a change in the lighting."[13] Alan Bennett opens *An Englishman Abroad* with an actress who makes a frivolous theatrical analogy of the Iron Curtain and the fashionable tenure of a dictatorship:

> CORAL: Stalin died in 1953. I was in *Affairs of State* at the time, a light comedy that had a decent run at the Cambridge. Stalin had a decent run too, though I'd never been a fan of the old boy, even during the war when he was all the rage.[14]

Should Alan Bennett feature more in this study? Droll Coral Browne and dry and dandy Burgess in *An Englishman Abroad* are self-reflective camp characters. Bennett, I suggest, is often a master of banality without the counterpoint of exhibitionism, without the showboating image of the writer writing, without the outrageous innuendo of Goytisolo's intellectual camp. Bennett's nondescript presentation of himself — in monologues in *Telling Tales,* say, where he recalls an attraction to priesthood because he looked introverted enough for the role and entertained the notion of becoming a don on the same principle — is congruent with his shy, fine writing style, sounding his "rather wet and lackadaisical accent" without the outrageous eccentricity in Crisp's clipped tones, without those extrovert incongruities of camper writers.[15] Even his recent encounter with cancer downplays the drama, aloof from kitsch sensationalism: "I think I was a dull case, though I make no apology for that. With cancer, a challenge isn't what you want to be."[16] Shyness "will keep cropping up in this book," Bennett comes out to this degree in his latest book.[17] His ruminant tone sounds like Beckett at a bus stop, and afterthoughts occur in lieu of a bus. Brilliantly understated, but not especially camp until the bus comes. *Forty Years On,* his first play, does allow the flagrantly theatrical device of an amateur play-within-a-play, parodying droll lines, innuendo and larger than life characters. And so, when Gerald enters in military uniform and bids her good morning, Lady Dundown responds, "Gerald, do I detect a somewhat military note in your appearance? What is the reason for these warlike habiliments?"[18] Understated, "somewhat military" becomes camp in ironic contrast to Gerald's flamboyant scarlet uniform, pith helmet and plumes, and "warlike habiliments" sounds as grandly theatrical as his attire.

Sometimes a fantastic tangent explodes his banality to stage the camp perspective. Memories of "picture-going" aggrandize his parochialism as he employs Bette Davis to serve in a Bradford shoe shop:

> With her clipped tones, raised eyebrow and mocking smile Bette was a standard bearer for shop assistants everywhere and in the 1940s you could find her presiding over the counters of the smarter shops— Marshall and Snelgrove, Matthias Robinson or, in my aunties' case, Mansfield's shoe shop and White Ladies' Mantles.[19]

Recalling encounters with celebrities hitherto encountered only in "the pictures," Bennett meets the Burtons at a party with sparse furnishing, where Elizabeth Taylor perches on his knee. His own incredulous recollection would seem more persuaded if the roles were reversed: "I find myself wondering whether I am recalling it correctly: did she sit on my knee or did I sit on hers?" Another encounter featured a *different* Mrs. Burton on the eve of announcing their divorce. Mrs. Burton required an innocuous evening partner with whom no hanky panky would likely be construed by the columnists. Bennett fit the bill. He sees the symmetry of the situations:

> One wife hitting on me as having a suitably flavorless companion for the evening, the other sitting on me as a knee that would raise no eyebrows, both made me a prop in the drama of their lives far more interesting and celebrated than my own.[20]

"Hitting" and "sitting" replicate the symmetry, but the notion of a knee that would raise no eyebrow is charmingly cock-eyed; the author as theatrical prop for the Burtons' dramas is a delightful conceit — recalling those ironic but passive reflections and reminiscent tones of Quentin Crisp. Bennett's camp candidacy is up for debate: the joy of compiling a camp canon at this late stage is that all candidates are under review.

A clear case of theatricality, Osbert Sitwell notes the embellished urbanity of Ronald Firbank: "There is surely to be traced in all his books a marked love and understanding of the stage and its personalities. Just as virtuosity and style were for him the chief merits of literature...."[21] "With considerable coquetry," the heroine of *The Artificial Princess* stretches an arm,

> as if — any student of the theater would recognize the movement — to ward off some disgraceful proposition made by an indelicate person, invisible to the eyes, yet mentally no doubt an abomination of sin. She was evidently fussing over a stage gesture for her forthcoming play.[22]

It reads like an encore for Sybil Vane in *The Picture of Dorian Gray*: "Mrs. Vane glanced at her, and with one of those false theatrical gestures that so often become a mode of second nature to a stage player, clasped her in her arms."[23]

Not all extravagance is camp. Charles Dickens sketched zestful caricatures in prose too committed to epic narrative and social reform to be so aloof, plunging into sentiment that equates to a fall from grace in camp. On the other hand, anticipating transactional analysis which in turn translated Shakespeare's world view, Lord Goring "*plays with life*" in Wilde's play *An Ideal Husband*, as Mrs. Cheveley opines, "This is the game of life as we all have to play it."[24] Saki's first sentence in "The Occasional Garden," a character commentates on her own dialogue to generalize a common social trait, exposing the irony of a familiar expression: "'Don't talk to me about town gardens,' said Elinor Rapsley; 'which means, of course, that I want you to listen to me for an hour or so while I talk about nothing else.'"[25] Camp achieves the distance from character, motivation and narrative that Brecht idealized without his ideology. Vitally, Susan Sontag saw, "Camp sees everything in quotation marks,"[26] which puts transcendental distance between consciousness and experience, between reflection and action. This ironic framing is how camp stages excess or extravagance, and the stagecraft that promotes this view from the wings is the perverted art of incongruous juxtaposition.

Camp expertise in gay culture suggests an outcast view from the wings that is more adaptable to morphic incongruities. Each literary genre has a linguistic and thematic dress code — academic writing, for instance, disavows a fictional fetish for adjectives, and first person narrative qualifies the dogmatic rhetoric found in political argument by scientific measures that balance logical contrasts and never venture into exaggeration. Camp inclination to cross-dress transgresses these genre codes. Juxtaposing genres and posing polarities like classical-contemporary, being-acting, feminine-masculine, young-old ... camp dissociates our cultivated habit of selective identification — our fixation on protagonist or mood or plot — to show the masquerade of behavior, media, and personality, and the relativism of the status quo. Masquerade is as key to camp as to carnival. The *plot* of Saki's tale "Excepting Mrs. Pentherby" exposes masquerade. We have already weathered Mrs. Pentherby's penchant for objectionable remarks, fixing on a loose hairpin, which ruffles female society. Well, it turns out that Mrs. Pentherby was hired for that very purpose by the lord of the manor. He required a bonded party of women but, acting on forebodings of a shrewish female stereotype, knew the sniping and gossip had to be localized. Mrs. Pentherby is the hired scapegoat of their concerted hostility, which would otherwise disintegrate the group. The revelation, turning on the dichotomy of being-acting, reprised in the Saki story "Quail Seed," gives a proscenium perspective to the whole story and to socially ascribed roles. Not feminist, this unflattering stereotype, but a role, like any other.

You can hear camp's penchant for theater in its prose. The traditional tone of voice, male or female, sequestered in any respectable book in any genre, is hushed like a library, bound by introspective communion between writer and reader, like an encounter in an art gallery or Catholic confessional booth. The secluded writing process is meditative like prayer. Juan Goytisolo, whose intellectual prose never quite stops germinating, it must be said, concludes, "Quarantine for the author, quarantine for the reader, quarantine for the book, vital to the active, transforming power of the written word!"[27] His earlier work was couched deep in thought until his murmuring narratives grew more vocal, even unto the susurrant sentences of *Count Julian* in 1970. Goytisolo's prose came out camp (more or less) in middle age, influenced by "a prosody of orality stretching from the Middle Ages, when texts were read aloud." He even chaired a UNESCO committee to preserve oral literary traditions.[28] Camp has an oral heritage, fanned by gossip, that rarefies the skill of the raconteur to the art of the throwaway yet indelible epigram. Camp is not always so pithy; it may be baroque with lavish detail that makes art nouveau of sentence structure — Goytisolo sees to that. Goytisolo's association with Chloe Poems stresses the indispensable orality of their compositions. Camp diction is theatrical. Exaggerated pronunciation may cut a formal precision, like grandiloquent utterances of a modern actor when stylizing Shakespeare. Camp embouchure, tongue in cheek, may tout the meaning of words by onomatopoeia or enlarge and contort a word to signal a pun or clip it to sharpen the irony or a pointed epigram; it may sound fruity in its tart rolling of vowels and tangy chewing of consonants, all exaggerated on the page by alliteration and assonance and placing and punctuation. Oral tradition validates the single-draft process of writers like Poems and Wood, transgressing the work ethic that requires three years of gestation and toil to legitimize the work. "Whore" by Chloe Poems[29] speaks of the Queen Mother "Ceremoniously parading her wares" with Balmoral intonations,

> Arrogantly staggering
> And immorally soliciting the Mall
> Ostentatiously looking after the family business,

where the royal procession of "r's" and "g's" of "Arrogantly staggering" treads the boards, while "immorally soliciting the Mall" chews the "l's" and "m's" like minted truffles. We may scan camp diction on the page through excessive sequences of alliteration, assonance and rhyming, composed according to the aesthetic of Poems' theatrical training and ever so fruity embouchure.

The aphoristic memoirs and commentaries of Quentin Crisp germinated in recorded monologue, broadcast on radio, precipitating a new life of public speaking engagements. We hear Crisp's matter-of-fact monotone equilibrium in his narratives. Max Beerbohm's style inclines to radio broadcasts, and the author doesn't wait for critics to advise the reader to read him aloud: he urges it in the "Author's Note" to *Mainly on the Air,* as does Chloe Poems in the introduction to *I'm Kamp.* It was appreciated in 1915 that Ronald Firbank's novels benefit from being read aloud, especially for dialogue.[30] J.W. Lambert observes of Saki, "Like those of that far weightier decorator of trifles, Henry James, Saki's prose narratives seemed to lean towards the theater...."[31] Camp makes a drama out of an ellipsis, grandstanding to the gods, and even asides— those especially — play to the gallery.

Camp dialogue is overheard in gossip, repartee, superlatives, melodrama and those stage asides, amplified by the echo of narcissism, concisely pointed or florid, though never lost in emotion: either the character or the narrative stands aloof. Bourgeois drawing-room dialogue is too *too* superlative and wryly effusive in *The Vortex,* more than any other Noël Coward play, parodying the voguish vocabulary of 1923, made even more conspicuously theatrical as the vogue became outmoded so that now *The Vortex* appears to parody Coward himself. Florence: "Take off that perfectly divine cloak and have a cigarette — I've got to rush and dress now, because I'm *terribly* late...."[32] Domestic drama is underscored by exclamation and cast aloof by irony, so that every sentiment artfully glosses the surface no matter how "too too" or *wildly* thrilling. Parody or the anachronism of the convention puts the contrivance, not the characters or the news, in the footlights. In *Quadrille,* Coward's play from 1952, Hubert accuses his wife of some rather masculine metaphors: "You have rent the fabric of romance into a thousand pieces; you have trampled brutally on a dream, stamping it into the ground, mangling it beyond recognition. You have ridden roughshod through my private heart, swaggering and looting and burning until there is nothing left but emptiness and desolation...."[33] The artifice of the rhetoric isn't so aggrieved that it ever forgets to aggrandize the drama, which distances reader and audience from any possibility of social realism.

Ronald Firbank is exceptional in the free hand he gives to dialogue in novels, though lines are always persiflage, never exposition; laconic yet flamboyant repartee:

> "You were asleep."
> "Was I horrid?"
> "You looked too perfectly orchidaceous."
> "Orchidaceous?"
> "Like the little women of Outa-Maro."[34]

("Too perfectly" is so very superlative.) His droll tone gives succinct whimsy even to his narrative: "A beehive in Brompton, a tray of gleaming fish, the way the wind blew — everything that morning seemed extraordinarily Greek."[35]

In Berlin between the Wars, Christopher Isherwood parodies human expression with cabaret performance in a manner and a milieu not a million miles from Brecht: "With absurd, solicitous gravity, the dancers performed their intricate evolutions, showing in their every movement a consciousness of the part they were playing." The singer, "charging his voice with innuendo, rolling his eyes in an epileptic pantomime of extreme joy," obliges Brecht in form though not in political purpose. Even Nazism is rather a backdrop: *Goodbye to Berlin* suggests theatrical analogies to highlight the artifice of gender attributes and the cult of personality.[36] Brecht conceived of "gestus" as both gist and gesture, posing an ideological attitude as well as an action that distances the spectator from emotional engagement. Pamela Robertson[37] makes the distinction in camp: "The self-conscious masquerade discovers a discrepancy between gesture and 'essence' and not simply between anatomy and costume." She makes a feminist application: "Gender parody would utilize masculinity self-consciously in order to reveal the absence behind the mask and the performative activity of gender and sexual identities." Karen Laughlin returns the principle to Brechtian theater with "the value of "alienating" actor and character through cross-gender casting,"[38] a point not lost on Chloe Poems.

Camp exposes the cultural subtext of language that Jacques Lacan spoke about, which shapes our personal development as we express our selves.

Cora Kaplan[39] puts Lacan's view, "In each speech act the self and the culture speak simultaneously or, to put it another way, each time we speak we are also spoken." This is a psychological take on "gest" and "gesture." Camp performs language, overtly crafting the written word to show the "gestus." Stage directions by many camp playwrights warrant narration by a performer, I feel, they are so extrovert beyond their functional remit. We've read Noël Coward's directions for "deep mourning" in *Blithe Spirit*. Now he describes the setting for Act I scene i of *Point Valaine*, including battered shutters "*imparting to everything an atmosphere of strange gloom, almost as though one were at the bottom of the sea. During the rainy season this faintly obvious simile is used several times a day by the majority of guests.*" The faint-hearted declaration of the simile as if smuggled through critical customs sets the playwright wryly aloof from the directions to cast an atmosphere (to the reader) not only of "strange gloom" but of tongue in cheek awareness of the media. When characters subsequently quote the sentiment,

MORTIMER [*with a glint in his eye*]: It feels exactly as though one were at the bottom of the sea, doesn't it?
MRS. BIRLING: That's what I always say.[40]

— they reflect their author's hand in the self-conscious process of fashioning a play.

Director Joseph Losey was an advocate of epic theater who worked with Brecht but, noting his "austerity," warmed the emotional hues closer to camp, dressing the proletariat in fuchsias and pinks.[41] Losey cites an *Observer* article (23 October 1960) by Kenneth Tynan, which plots the influence on Brechtian theater of Berlin cabaret between World Wars. He doesn't make the camp connection — but look at the blasé decadence and juxtaposed gender traits and sheer exhibitionism of Berlin cabaret. Motivation, somber tone and an analytical subtext distinguish Brechtian theater from camp consciousness. Camp has no such clinical attitude as Brecht recommends in 1926: "I aim at an entirely classical, cold, highly intellectual style of performance."[42]

Brigid Brophy's *In Transit* sometimes favors camp but often inclines to intellectual analysis of process. She refers to "the machinery of my narration," where camp would tend to floral or haute couture metaphors of process. The novel is a missing link between camp and Brechtian aesthetics. "I've muttered to you, my dear Reader, several asides on the subject of the technique of fiction, including some about alienation effects...."[43] Brechtian theater foregrounds the social context of character and interaction to catalyse political analysis and action. Camp has been politicized by gay and feminist culture but its detachment is traditionally apolitical, I contend, and so does Sontag. Camp felt quite at home in the court of Louis XIV and Regency England, aloof from labor and physical force, we know, and too dandy for Brecht's revolution. The crucial issue is good manners to Quentin Crisp's rather Edwardian philosophy. Good manners tame masculinity, cultivate reflection and refine communication to Crisp's own dry irony: "There is much more at stake here than whether one should pour tea from left to right, or right to left." Still, his remit is domestic diplomacy, not international — though his tea service sounds decadent: "The fact that someone may drop the Bomb in the middle of our mad tea party should in no way deter us from serving the best tea and the best conversation in our best manner — for ever."[44] It is not Brecht's cup of tea but it does venture beyond Saki's drawing-room. The English penchant for tea is book-ended fantastically between Apocalypse and — in a flouting addendum — eternity. Benson's *The Babe* begins with a fatuous chat over tea, where a Cambridge tutor cautions, "'High tea, if frequently taken, will make anyone a nonconformist, in the same way as incense induces Roman Catholicism.'"[45]

Saki introduces the champagne socialist protagonist of "The Byzantine Omelette," "When she inveighed eloquently against the evils of capitalism at drawing-room meetings and Fabian conferences she was conscious of a comfortable feeling that the system, with all its inequalities and iniquities, would probably last her time."[46] Lord Berners caricatured this position in 1941 in *Percy Wallingford*. The "violently subversive" authoress of *The Rising of the Masses* nonetheless had a weakness for high society:

> She meant to make the most of capitalism while it lasted and her solicitude for the idle rich almost equalled her concern for the down-trodden workers; a Tricoteuse knitting scarves for the Aristocrats to keep them cosy on their way to execution.[47]

That's a fantastic line. The force and conviction in "violently" is, within a sentence, upstaged by hand-knitting and the incongruity of a devout Marxist who does indeed believe in the historic inevitability of the rise of the proletariat but therefore intends to make the most of inequality while it lasts — like Lord Berners himself, knitting whimsical tales for a retreating elite as world war and socialism advanced. A "Tricoteuse" is a hand-knitter of woolen tricot, associated with spectators of executions in the French Revolution — but again, you don't need to know that to appreciate the poetic impact of this domestic take on the Tricoteuse Trotskyist. (Noël Coward courted this word in *We Were Dancing* in 1935.)

Quentin Crisp reminds us that askance humor also conjures distance: "A true humorist is so totally disengaged that he can relax in any situation and evaluate every crisis — even those that are brought about by his own folly—from at least two (possibly opposed) points of view."[48] Crisp, like Wilde, is fond of epigrammatic and exhibitionist generalizations, frivolously unqualified so as not to spoil the gleaming aesthetic of a global assertion by the clutter of a clause. His passive authorial voice makes even cavalier generalizations noncommittal, as if, should you take exception to it, he will gladly sweep the sweeping statement under the carpet. He remains aloof even from his antipathies, distanced by his ironic phrasing, such as the wry, colloquial refrain "I don't hold with it," incongruous against his prim and proper prose and so implicitly tongue in cheek in *The Naked Civil Servant*, as in, "I don't hold with art."[49] Oscar Wilde applies the attitude to aesthetics: "To art's subject matter we should be more or less indifferent. We should, at any rate, have no preferences, no prejudices, no partisan feeling of any kind."[50] That's a nice qualification: "more or less." While the protagonist of *The Babe* paints his bicycle in white enamel "and presented a very elegant appearance on it every morning in Battersea Park," E.F. Benson writes, his father is contesting an election for the Conservatives. "But party questions did not interest his son, and the Babe, reflecting that whether the Liberals or the Conservatives governed the country, Battersea Park would still be open to him and his bicycle, pursued his calm course on a moderately evenly-balanced wheel."[51] By the decorum of this leisurely pace, political rhetoric is altogether uncouth. Saki's politician in *The Unbearable Bassington* takes this equanimity into the House of Commons, on a zephyr of ennui, it seems, so that "the most attentive observer of Parliamentary proceedings could scarcely have told even on which side of the House he sat."[52] A senior political character in *The Watched Pot* dismisses the electoral process, "Government by democracy means government of the mentally unfit by the mentally mediocre tempered by the saving grace of snobbery."[53] In "The Jesting of Arlington Stringham," Saki reduces Parliament to a forum for droll quips. There is, too, a legend that Lord Berners took his seat in the House of Lords only once, and vowed never to return after a bishop stole his umbrella. So much for political intervention.

"Context and content" crucially inform conflict and its communication, Bradley Epps tells us, for "it is only through the persistence of specificities and differences that conflict can beat all."[54] Such language determines whose side you're on. Camp stays above the fray by elevating style over content. Camp language is more aerated, generalized and precious than the divisive specifics of argument. The distance that Joseph Losey finds in past tense and third person in Brechtian theater, and by extravagant gesture that reveals characters as players and ego as a role, has other agents. Distance from emotional involvement or intellectual commitment is promoted by esoteric detail and, too, by incongruities such as anachronisms and dated genre conventions. Ed Wood inadvertently puts himself outside the crime and horror genres he writes in by exposing their conventions with such obvious artifice, making outsiders of his readers, too.

Coward is camp both by design and by obsolescence. His overstated theatricality is crafted but the milieu of his characters, like the world of Lord Berners, is now so removed from our society that we interpret every gesture as bourgeois caricature and artifice. The defunct mannerisms, highly stylized to begin with, now seem fantastical. Coward's 1928 comedy revue included "The English Lido," a patriotic yet tongue in cheek defense of England's holiday resorts against exotic competition. It expands into a caricature of bourgeois culture in theatrical call and response: "Topping! ... Righto! ... Good egg!"[55]

Camp engages with life generously yet towers above realism, seriousness and allegiance. In 1931 Lord Berners built "the last traditional folly-tower in England." He describes the virtue of his folly, "The great point of the Tower is that it will be entirely useless."[56] Beyond decoration over functionalism, the folly-tower is a rich camp metaphor. You can see four or five counties from the viewing platform: camp style finds aloof elevation in the scale of its exaggerations to offer just such an overview. I find the view edifying, even though it doesn't urge the spectator to action as Brecht advocated. Berners' notice on the entrance is the only message posed by his tower, somewhat short of being Brechtian: "Members of the Public committing suicide from this tower do so at their own risk."

Quentin Crisp declared three reasons for becoming a writer: you need money; you have something to say; and lastly, "you can't think what to do with the long winter evenings."[57] Crisp claims the first; a Brechtian could claim a political message, perhaps written in a winter of discontent; but *camp* books *read* as though motivated by shades of ennui during those long evenings. Yet camp does imply a fanciful ascension to higher consciousness that exposes and disowns what the proletariat's champion would call "false consciousness." Camp is frequently appropriated to expound gay politics in academic disquisitions that are far from camp in style. I pose the question, can the aesthetic of style over content ever be political or partisan? Rebuked for calling Margaret Thatcher "a star," Crisp reflects, "I was obviously supposed to take politics seriously; I never have."[58]

Bradley Epps finds, "The struggles in Goytisolo are also influenced with a profound sense of fatalism and defeat" and call on ethereal transcendence rather than political revolution to transform them.[59] From a camp perspective, that Goytisolo should struggle at all is remarkable. The fatalism of Quentin Crisp, if not his effacing persona, precludes intervention: his writings are the commentaries of a bystander, a "resident alien" more alienated than Brecht had imagined. Banalities and crises get equal weighting in his novels *Love Made Easy* and *Chog;* protagonists do not enjoy catalytic import in their destinies and all deaths are matter-of-fact. His irony is deadpan, his resistance is passive and his passivity is obliging. His authorial voice treats misfortune and fortune and strangers and friends much the same. Although antipathies ripple his serene tone of indifference, they are always understated. When, in his forties, Crisp notices his social network begin to disband according to social mobility, he equates demographics with cosmic inevitability, "I had just started to feel the pull of the expanding universe."[60]

Epps reminds us that "Brecht's alienated detachment is not, of course, dis-interest." Epps objects that in Juan Goytisolo's writing, "The expanding chains of equivalents, linking injustice to injustice" in expanding metaphors, will forestall the Brechtian response to injustice as "'appalling' and 'unnecessary,' as in need of and open to change," and instead "the universalizing spectator" will see suffering and injustice as "'inescapable' realities of the human condition." This is indeed Crisp's fatalism, though Goytisolo, I think, does believe the exposure of historical events to consciousness can catalyse change. Chloe Poems makes a distinction between humanity and society (one is a structural system and the other a species of organism, after all), identifying even to the point of collective consciousness with humanity but alienated from even the everyday conventions of society. Even while coining the refrain "Society is evil," injustice is not written in the stars, there is an exhortation to change the social system. Poems does receive audience testimonies to personal change through this catalytic poetry. Society, of course, continues much the same as before.

Alan Bennett's trustworthy memoirs make his cosy socialism sound so quaint, post–Attlee, there is even room for royalty, more about nostalgia than reform. But then socialism *is* nostalgic, nowadays. His 1971 play *Getting On* chisels his ambivalence to revolution in an iconic analogy:

> There is something wrong, I suppose, if we have to be dragged into the future. We ought to go forward with firm jaw and clear brow, all in profile like a Soviet Poster.[61]

The sentiment is too tongue in cheek to carry off a firm jaw, too nonconformist to be serious about it, and too skeptical of the work ethic to lend its art to communist propaganda. Yet Bennett can sound positively outspoken — in comparison to Crisp anyway — in these trying times. Diary entry, 8 March 2003: "A phrase often in the mouth of Bush and Blair is 'Our patience is exhausted.' It's a phrase that is seldom used by anyone who had much patience in the first place; Hitler was quite fond of it."[62] Bennett's tone maintains reserve from the reported statement and too from indignation at it, defusing the skepticism in a generalization about any such someone's patience. Citing the arch nemesis of the 20th century is a fantastic counterpart to the matter of fact tone — fantastic in the sense of most extreme. I don't presume to doubt its validity in terms of the act of invasion, Bush and Blair's militant clout or their rhetoric: Bennett is also an historian, remember.

Close to the source of Bennett's comparison, Christopher Isherwood wrote his "Berlin novels" in 1930s' Germany. As Sally Bowles makes camp of *Goodbye to Berlin,* Mr. Norris performs this service in *Mr. Norris Changes Trains.* He is trafficking for Communists in Nazi Germany, even though "'Class distinctions have never meant anything to me.'" Still, Nazism "'offends my sense of the beautiful.'" Mr. Norris preserves Wilde's elevation of aesthetics over morality — and his appreciation of paradox. He enjoys a more stylized presentation of Nazism in his sexuality: he is a masochist who makes a fetish of the uniform and icons of the women who whip him in scenes of fascist theater. In a daring moment of spy hijinks, his friend rallies him to be brave and think of Lenin. Norris replies, "'I find more inspiration in the Marquis de Sade.'"[63] Norris considers it peerless sabotage when, speaking of Hitler's hotel the Kaiserhof, he reveals, "'Do you know, I have lately made a point of being manicured there.'"

In Wilde camp is philosophical rather than political, unaffiliated. "The Soul of Man Under Socialism" is a political tract but not camp (though Wilde does seem to object to capitalism as unaesthetic); the political subtext of *An Ideal Husband* is incidental to its camp appeal; and committed pieces like "The Ballad of Reading Gaol" are political to be sure but not camp, whereas the protagonists of his plays are often Lords and Ladies. Yet when we discuss Goytisolo and Poems, writers with an agenda as left-wing as Brecht, and as Bennett is finally pushed too far and raises a septuagenarian objection, I must review how active modern camp intends to be. The distinction between Brechtian theater and camp coexists with surprising similarities, which calls for a second glance from those who look camp up and down and dismiss it on appearances — and too from people like me and Lord Berners who describe camp as apolitical. The camp sensibility of Lord Berners, who was, his biographer records, "rather put out when it was made clear to him that he was expected if not exactly to earn his living, then to find some occupation," while in a position "to avoid what he found unpleasant,"[64] is going to feel more detached from earthy and political realities than the social backdrop of Chloe Poems, a rationed working class Liverpool heritage either side of the Winter of Discontent. There are substantial differences between Lord Berners, whose response to war was to have a nervous breakdown (as valid a response as any, it seems to me), and American war hero Ed Wood, or then again Goytisolo, whose response to war in Croatia was to land in the war zone and report what he saw; between Saki, who was killed on the front line in World War I, and Firbank, who was made exempt from active service due to "sunstroke," and Quentin Crisp, who was exempted due to "sexual perversion." Crisp recalls the momentous outbreak of World War II, whereupon he went out and bought two pounds of henna.[65]

There is a world of difference between the Englishness of Noël Coward, stereotypically eccentric and just an oblique stage aside away from jingoism, and the multi-cultural diversity of Juan Goytisolo. Meanwhile, Ed Wood's pulp characters linger in the underworld a stone's throw from skid-row, but Wood never settles for such a mundane expression as "You can't take it with you," o no: "From the time she was old enough to grasp the meaning of the monetary, she realized that there were no cash drawers in the casket."[66] He shows no left-wing allegiances, however, reluctant to relinquish the American Dream even when impoverished. The American Dream is Wood's insurance against banality. Coward's plays happen in bourgeois households or in luxury hotels; Saki's households are bourgeois too and Berners' are altogether aristocratic. Firbank features royalty — the arch enemies of a raft of poetry by Chloe Poems, who begins that sensational portrait of the Queen Mother with the signal accusation, "A hundred years of whoredom this madam."[67]

In *Bitter Sweet* in 1929, Coward gives footmen and cleaners and waiters a voice — a collective chorus befitting the indistinct lower classes — to complain of their ill-paid labors, the merest tincture of Brecht, whom Coward disliked. Their choruses are interludes in the drama that is, as always, driven by the bourgeoisie. Waiters soon make way for Carl and Sari's dream of owning a chic café. Coward presents his conclusions on British class divisions in *Relative Values* in 1949. The butler is a marvelous camp character who remains aloof even when he is obsequious, as if waiting for better employment to come along, yet he is, after all, content with his place. The butler shows a different sensibility to Saki's servant who observes the entrances and exits of the bourgeoisie in *The Watched Pot*. The butler in *Relative Values* proposes a toast to the maid: to the "disintegration of the most unlikely dream that ever troubled the foolish heart of man — Social Equality!"[68] The play snubs socialist reform, a topical movement in postwar Britain — and it seems particularly cynical to make the servant class mouth bourgeois propaganda. Poems prefers a toast to "true equality" — the individual socialism that Wilde proclaimed — in "What Is This Called Gay?": "This is for the rent-boys/Disadvantaged, and the poor/This is for the people our magazines ignore" (and lack of coverage *is* deprivation to the camp temperament).[69] I can't imagine Chloe Poems or Juan Goytisolo raising their glasses with Noël Coward with the redistribution of wealth on their minds. Amanda McKittrick Ros, of course, thought socialism meant high society and so applied it to socialites: when Sir John Dunfern is cuckolded in *Irene Iddesleigh,* he fears he can never again "stare socialism in the face."[70]

How can one aesthetic describe the artistry of all these authors? How amazing that camp entertains such diversity yet remains an identifiable aesthetic, and could be so representative yet remain marginalized.

Now we can classify this fanciful genre and debate the candidates, now that we recognize camp on the page, familiar with its indiscretions, on speaking terms with some major players. We have catalogued the marvelous ways that literature may be creatively camp — with florid characters all flexing gender and hosting subjects such as royalty, dress sense and narcissism and modeling drawing room accoutrements like fans and divans and cigarette-holders with droll and frivolous tone and precious language that keeps identification at arm's length; with plentiful alliteration and assonance uninhibited by an ascetic conscience; with baroquery and exotica that defies mediocrity; with domestic-fantastic conceits; and, across the board, with audacious theatricality.... This is how camp scans as a style of writing. The best of camp conjures all these attributes and enunciates their exaggeration.

However, there is another dimension of camp that is revealed only in its worst examples...

Camp by Misadventure

Low camp ... writerly behavior ... exalted superlatives ...
transgender narrative voice ... deranged camp ...
when camp becomes kitsch ...

We are about to discover just how bad camp writing can be. Yet all four exemplars of artless camp — Leopold von Sacher-Masoch, Marie Corelli, Amanda McKittrick Ros, and Edward D. Wood, Jr.— are unreservedly recommended reading: entertaining, enlightening, and breathtaking.

Camp revelation of the writing process is more ironic than postmodernism. Let's call this ironic reflection "high camp," in cahoots with highbrow culture. In the case of artlessness for art's sake, *unwitting* revelations take an inglorious swan-dive into *low camp*. Cynthia Morrill obliged us with a definition of irony that speaks the opposite of an intention to establish critical distance and signpost the ulterior meaning. Camp ironic distance may occur between a character and the author, which is then picked up by the reader, or between the author and the process of writing. In extreme cases that tend to bloom after a time lapse, irony is projected over the head of the author by a hip readership. Inadvertent camp voices its literal intent with such extremism or incongruous imagery or overt devices that the reader's incredulity generates the distance that allows wry interpretation. Our attention to plot and character is deflected to the artifice of the artifact. In "Notes on Camp," Susan Sontag compares the camp *object,* which is unaware of its camp translation, with the camp subject that is camp by design. Most authors in our discussion fashion camp subjects, but we have already sampled works whose camp effect happens behind the author's back. This chapter demonstrates how authors with no camp inclination, who show no awareness of its aesthetic, get railroaded into a camp interpretation. I don't describe as *low camp* all writing that exposes itself indiscreetly: some of the variable traits that signpost camp by design expose themselves in low camp too— theatricality and narcissism and transgender inversions in narrative voice or characterization, and such like.

Romance novelists Marie Corelli and Amanda McKittrick Ros are feisty Victorian contemporaries; they sublimated their sadomasochism, whereas Leopold von Sacher-Masoch was a debauched romantic; and half a century later, Edward D. Wood, Jr. served pulp fiction to the rock 'n' roll generation and the swinging '60s. Their camp status is debatable and subjective because the reader must provide the ironic interpretation: each writer is sincerely committed to a serious narrative. They are camp by misadventure.

Sacher-Masoch and Corelli flagged their classical ambitions with metaphors that aspire to the purist aesthetic that Susan Sontag identified with Homer and Rembrandt. Sacher-Masoch, like Corelli, elevates femaleness with classical metaphors: statuesque heroines sculpted in marble or figuratively depicted like painted portraits. A Belgian painting is the foreshadowing allegory of the sadomasochistic relationship in *Venus in Furs* in 1870. Poses are staged artificially and the animation of the characters reads like stage directions. "The sublime being had wrapped her marble body in a huge fur," he succinctly signals the fetishized triumvirate of his heroine as divinity, classical subject, and model in furs. Sacher-Masoch, like Corelli, aspires to the ultimate classical symbol when he deifies his heroines— there are even two "divine sneezes" in *Venus in Furs*. This classic novella that aspires to classicism introduces the leading lady,

> Opposite me, by the massive Renaissance fireplace, sat Venus: not, mind you, some demimondaine who, like Mademoiselle Cleopatra, had taken the pseudonym of Venus in her war against the enemy sex. No: my visitor was the Goddess of love — in the flesh.[1]

Lofty ambition over-reaches and, tripping over classical feasibility, stumbles into camp aesthetics. Sacher-Masoch claims the mythic and metaphoric as literal, his infatuated vision reaching for one more superlative, and so, in *Don Juan of Kolomea* in 1864, a happy couple have a child and "Our parents literally melted with joy...."[2] Exaggeration is the prime culprit in camp by misadventure — excess in assertion or lush description or mood swings on a theatrical scale, unable to sustain the intensity of Decadence in their preposterous gambits of incredulity that trigger unimagined irony. Sacher-Masoch is rapturous in prose worship of the perfect female. "But why speak in superlatives— as if something that is beautiful could be surpassed?" he asks,[3] but this turns out to be one more superlative that draws attention to the narrative addiction.

Literary commentary on *Venus in Furs* prefers to fixate on the psycho-
dynamics of its compelling sexual relationship; hardly anyone talks about
its literary style. Its style is camp. It is made camp not by the author/Sev-
erin's desperate passion for masochism — which is pitched at Decadence —
but by the ironic and complicit distance that arches over his abandon in the
manner of his Mistress, imperious and aloof, reclining on an ottoman.
Ennui is her aristocratic emblem: it affirms her feline disdain of the work
ethic and all who yoke themselves to its petty tyranny and masculine energy.
Gender roles are stressed and overturned as Wanda grows beyond his control and Severin surrenders his manhood as an offering. Theatrical analogies take a bow with demarcated roles and iconic symbology and lines
rehearsed by generations of archetypes. When the anguished masochist
becomes indignant at losing his Mistress, she makes dramaturgy of his
protests: "'What play are you quoting?' she mocked." Sadomasochism is
melodrama, extreme contrasts of emotional tones between Mistress and
slave. James Joyce parodied the transaction in *Ulysses* but Sacher-Masoch
is in earnest:

> "Wanda!" I hurried toward her, trying to throw my arm around her, to kiss
> her. She took a step back and scrutinized me from top to bottom.
> "Slave!"
> "Mistress!" I knelt down and kissed the hem of her robe.
> "That's the ticket."
> "Oh, how beautiful you are!"
> "Do you like me?" She went to the mirror and viewed herself with proud
> delight.
> "I'm going insane!"
> "Her lower lip twitched scornfully, and she gave me a mocking glance
> through half-closed eyelids.
> "Give me the whip."[4]

Translator Joachim Neugroschel finds a pun in "top to bottom," which
are sadomasochistic terms for Mistress and slave — other translations lose
the pun in "from head to foot." The whip-wielding coda is obligatory in
the sadomasochistic scenario, made theatrical by the cursory punctuation
to this script-in-hand exchange. Wanda portrays the narcissistic notion of
persona as the ultimate art idealized by Wilde and staged by theater. "Half-
closed eyelids" pose such aloof distance from his stammering passion that
the extreme contrast is potentially hilarious to the ironic modern reader.
My reading of Sacher-Masoch never goes more than a page without recalling the weird and wonderful works of Edward D. Wood, Jr. Those crazed
exclamations— as Wood once said, "as frustrated as a transvestite in a nud-
ist camp"[5]— sound inanely incongruous to Wanda's self-assured supremacy.

The slave's tributes explode on the page, prompting her response from the star-struck haze of her mirror image, "'Do you like me?'" that barely corresponds to his entreaties. Nevertheless, their staged transaction observes the formal traditions of this underground sexuality, covered by his famous fur fetish.

Sacher-Masoch's furry masochism strokes the text, often as innuendo or incidental asides made conspicuous by strange contrivance, "she sarcastically retorted, her white fingers playing in the dark fur," including a transvestite disclosure that our hero rather enjoys wearing her furs.[6] His light, feminine touch further exposes those mannered asides, winking to post-Krafft-Ebing generations. The weather is fetishized in the landscape of *The Man Who Re-Enlisted* in 1868: "The wintery ermine cloaked it in supreme majesty. It was completely covered in snow; only the bare trunks of the low-growing willows, the long-armed country wells further off, and away in the distance, a few rust-colored stray huts made black dots on the snowy white fur."[7] Thanks again to Neugroschel's English translation of *Venus in Furs,* an incidental pun makes us see the fetish behind every tree, so to speak: "Full moon! There it was, peeping over the top of the lower firs that edged the park...."[8] *Moonlight* indulges a little more deliberately, observing Olga, "enveloped in the dark, Siberian sable and the soft furs of the sleigh," so when she "continued with a muffled voice," we're not surprised.[9] Driven to distraction by his own teasing innuendos, the author casts off insinuation and drapes his fetish all over the reader: "When he turned around in surprise, Olga was standing before him. She took off her big, heavy fur and threw it over him," a dress rehearsal for a scene in *Venus in Furs.* Olga in *Moonlight* and the wife of *Don Juan of Kolomea* are prototypes of Wanda: *Venus in Furs* is the work that really "comes out" kinky. Wanda binds her victim: "'And remove this heavy fur from me,' Wanda continued. 'It's in my way.'" The imperious gravity of her command is superseded, in my sensibility at least, by another gaze at her furs: even shedding the fetish is one more purring pretext to noticing it. In this same scene, within a page of shedding her fur, "With savage grace she now hiked up the fur-trimmed sleeve and lashed my back." The lashing is upstaged as the dramatic flashpoint by the eternal fetish object that dogs the text even after it is shed.[10]

Leopold von Sacher-Masoch reveals he was publicly mistaken "for almost everything ... for a Jew, a Hungarian, a Bohemian, and even for a woman." And in his writing? In his *Jewish Tales* collection, the master masochist eyes those Hassidic women "dressed in silk morning-gowns and long caftans made of silk or velvet and trimmed and lined with expensive furs. One could see all colors and kinds of furs: yellow and pink silk, green, red and blue velvet, squirrel, ermine, marten, and sable," he purrs. Larry

Wolff, whose task it is to introduce Sacher-Masoch to a Penguin Classic readership, satisfies himself that at least he "restrained his literary instincts and impulses" from "envisioning a rabbinical harem for masochistic Hassids."[11]

Marie Corelli also exalts her heroines as goddesses of perfect female beauty and spirit. Contrived lighting fashions halos or else crowns the heroines in symbolic coronation. The heroine of *The Sorrows of Satan*, who happens to be a great writer, is canonized when "the sunlight caught her fair hair and turned it to the similitude of a golden halo circling her brows"[12]; and in *Ardath*, "a dim golden suffused radiance seemed to hover like an aureole above that dazzling white brow...."[13] and in *Temporal Power*, "with the afternoon sun-glow bathing her in its full mellow radiance, sat a visibly enthroned goddess of the landscape — a girl, or rather a perfect woman, more beautiful than any he had ever seen, or even imagined"[14]; and in *Delicia*, who happens to be a great writer, extraordinarily contrived lighting poses as natural light and

> flicked across a pearl-inlaid mandolin that hung against the wall, as though it were playing an unheard melody in delicate *tremolo* on the strings; then, settling a crown of light on Delicia's hair, it flung an arrowy beam at the head of Hadrian's "Antinous," whose curved marble lips, parted in an inscrutable half-mocking smile, seemed about to utter a satire on the ways of women.[15]

Whatever satire Antinous had in mind, Corelli was unaware of any satirical interpretation of her writing. The lighting often stages the heroine's martyrdom, and so Delicia is a long-suffering wife whose righteous indignation finally awes her husband, as the narrative prepares her for ascension: "She looked as if during the past few minutes she had risen above and beyond him to a purer atmosphere than that of earth."[16] This is the ultimate state in aloof disposition.

Even in housewifery, Delicia demonstrates fantastic domesticity, "as she made the tea and with a few quick touches here and there altered the decorous formality of the breakfast table into the similitude of an Arcadian feast of beauty by the mere artistic placing of a vase of flowers or a dish of fruit, and this done, handed him the morning's newspaper with smiling and courteous punctilio."[17] Her fastidious chores are exotically rounded off with a Mary Poppins flourish by that exquisite dash of "punctilio," which seems to take a bow on Delicia's behalf.

Corelli too assumes lofty levitation in third-person narrative. *The Young Diana* sneers like a parody of haughtiness with a right royal "We":

> Life, as we all know, is a curious business. It is like a stage mask with two faces— the one comic, the other tragic. The way we look at it depends on the

way it looks at us. Some of us have seen it on both sides, and we are neither edified nor impressed.[18]

Queen Victoria was a fan of Corelli. The quote above is equivalent to Queen Victoria's most traveled remark, "We are not amused."

Ziska begins a chapter with a sneering put-down across the bows of the reader: "For the benefit of those among the untraveled English who have not yet broken a Soda-water bottle against the Sphinx...." Having evoked the enchanting middle-east with mystic lighting across the desert over the inscrutable Sphinx, Corelli blows the mood in a rant about "the wandering biped who swings through the streets of Cairo," that is, the western tourist who behaves "as if the whole place were but a reflex of Earl's Court Exhibition."[19] What a wonderful juxtaposition of that mystic mood and exotic lighting dashed against the frivolous domestic reference to a banal and uncouth London exhibition. It isn't the finely balanced juxtaposition of camp by design in, say, Saki; Corelli has simply lost her temper, irresistibly, and since her resentments motivated her writing as much as did her spiritualism or her classicism, these melodramatic polarities stretch the text of every novel.

Anachronisms are domestic-fantastic accidents. Marie Corelli wrote *Barabbas* in devout sincerity: ancient Jerusalem is a stage where profound truths and miracles were afoot that would change the world, in Christian terms. The awesome scale is rather domesticated when Corelli writes cosily, "Meanwhile the city of Jerusalem was pleasantly astir. Lights twinkled from the windows of every house"—in a period before windows existed. Historical research is so tedious that no self-respecting camp personage would stoop to it. Embellishing the Bible, she gives Judas Iscariot a sister, and follows western convention in surnames even if it doesn't historically apply. She even copies Judas's initials and alliteration to stress the family resemblance. The revelation brings the whole mythic scale of the piece down to corner-shop familiarity. She embellishes feminine beauty superlatively before naming the sister, in Corelli's rarefied style:

> Nothing more beautiful in the shape of woman could be imagined than she— her fairness was of that rare and subtle type which in all ages has overwhelmed reason, blinded judgement, and played havoc with the passions of men. Well did she know her own surpassing charm — and thoroughly did she estimate the value of her fatal power to lure and rouse and torture all whom she made the victims of her almost restless attractions. She was Judith Iscariot —[20]

Judith Iscariot sounds so close to Judas's name that it puts one in mind of Judas in drag. *Barabbas* is a case of ecclesiastical camp by misadventure. When religious art is animated by narrative it is more answerable to reason.

Corelli nails artistic analogies with a hammer. Even from the mouths of the executioners at the Crucifixion, "'One would think Him made of marble,' muttered one, pausing, hammer in hand."[21]

The pause doesn't help: the pause in camp (even inadvertently) is a proscenium elevation of whatever follows—a stage pause. The brutal punctuation makes the tableau even more mannered as the executioner reveals his poetic sensibility at the contrary moment of hammering the nail.

Brian Masters, Corelli's biographer, documents criticism of her "weighty nouns, guarded not infrequently by a triple escort of epithets."[22] It's a nice phrase that warns how formidable her prose could be. Corelli's command of superlatives outflanks the peerless Sacher-Masoch. In *Vendetta!* from a male perspective, "But fairest where all were fair, peerless in the exuberance of her triumphant vanity, and in the absolute faultlessness of her delicate charm, was my wife—the bride of the day, the heroine of the night. Never had she looked so surpassingly beautiful...."[23]

Corelli wrote with Shakespeare conspicuously in mind. Fey references to Ophelia adorn her tone and characterization and plotting—in *Wormwood, The Soul of Lilith, Vendetta!* and *The Avon Star*. In *Ziska*, perhaps Corelli's campest novel, Dr. Dean reminds Dr. Denzil of *Hamlet*: "'There are more things in heaven and earth than are dreamt of in your philosophy, Horatio,'" and then he adds, in something of a climb-down from Shakespeare, "'The Princess Ziska is one of those "things."'"[24] Benson knew Corelli and based his serial character Lucia on her: in Lucia's home "you had to be in a fanatically Elizabethan frame of mind to be at ease there"; outside, a flower-bed in "Shakespeare's garden" is called "Ophelia's border, for it consisted solely of those flowers which that distraught maiden distributed to her friends when she should have been in a lunatic asylum."[25]

Corelli's real name was Minnie Mackay, and her exaggerated rhetoric seems an elaborate bid to disprove that in every novel. Corelli created the persona of a classic writer and lived it with the commitment of Wilde's notion of lifestyle as art. Lofty metaphors pitch her claim to the classical aesthetic. In *Vendetta!* set in contemporary Naples, she sends a plume of smoke up from the crater of Vesuvius to signal some classical foreboding. She favors the Medusa metaphor to signal feminist vengeance, assimilating Greek myth into ancient Egypt in *Ziska*. In softer tones, she aggrandizes "the model of perfect womanhood" superlatively: "her fair head poised proudly on regal shoulders, while the curve of the full bosom would have baffled the sculptural genius of a Phidias."[26]

Camp auteurs like E.F. Benson use the icons of classicism ironically, artfully, to explode a frivolous, fantastical comparison: he explodes Miss Mapp's pose, "Elizabeth rose and pointed at her like one of Raphael's

Sibyls,"[27] and Lucia's parochial role in village life: "Just as the painter Rubens amused himself with being Ambassador to the Court of St. James's (a sufficient career in itself for most busy men), so Mrs. Lucas amused herself, in the intervals of pursuit of Art for Art's sake, with being not only an ambassador but a monarch."[28] You find this untouchable royal poise in all Corelli's heroines, impassive as marble before narrative adoration and attendant male admirers ("With all my soul I reverenced her genius—with all my heart I honored her pure womanliness!"),[29] stoic against injustice, and disdainful of the banal masses. When the Queen in *Temporal Power* puts a man in his place, her "half-disdainful" smile makes embittered remarks like this seem nonchalant:

> "You are a man, Sir Roger de Launay," she said after a pause, "And man-like, you propound any theory which at the moment happens to fit your own particular theory."[30]

The half-disdainful smile, a familiar expression of Corelli's heroines, is the equivalent accessory to a long cigarette-holder to an aloof disposition. It's another measure of extreme distance from the content. Princess Ziska preens her ego with it:

> She was amused at the small spites and envies of the malicious and unsuccessful, and maintained her philosophical and classic composure under all the trumpery slights, ignorant censures and poor scandals put upon her by the less gifted of her own sex.[31]

That sentence is laced with a deal of spite, yet the heroine rises above retaliation because the narrative snipes on her behalf. Corelli preserves the ideal of implacable feminine poise by projecting it onto her heroine and venting her vengeance in third person, as conspicuously as a manifesto. When the great Delicia reads aloud a scathing review of her new book, the hot-tempered hero rages on her behalf while Delicia remains impervious to insults. Sniping at critics and social groupings-— the upper class, chauvinist men (most men, in her time), women who don't use their brains but also women who won't stay home — Corelli wasn't a model Suffragette, but she was, I believe, a model misanthrope, rising above the common denominator like a rarefied fraction on its way to infinity.

Corelli's magnificent ego dominates her characters and articulates her melodramatic polarities. Characters model her spiritual and physical idealism or they illustrate her prejudices in conspicuous ventriloquism, extending to anthropomorphism if no person is at hand. It's a poetic thing to do, but poetic devices, like theatrical devices, can seem fantastically artificial in prose. Corelli's sensationally presumptuous narrative voice articulates Mother Nature in *The Mighty Atom,* a dog as disdainful as Saki's cat in

Delicia—"Had he been able to answer his new master then, he might have said—'Honesty is an ordinary quality in dogs, but it is exceptional in men'"[32]—and a representation of the crucified Christ in *Vendetta!* "that seemed to say...." *Barabbas* adds a monologue for Christ beyond the remit of the Bible for several enraptured pages, couched speculatively, "Had He spoken at that thrilling moment, He might have said...." And then, with superb irony that is all the reader's, "But no words such as these were uttered...." the author conscientiously, grudgingly returns to the Biblical interpretation lest she should sound like an Apostle with a scoop.[33] She may have thought it remiss of the Messiah not to have taken the opportunity and spoken the lines.

Her Elizabethan aesthetic plays to the gallery over the reader's shoulder. Delicia addresses a soliloquy to a marble bust: "'Yes, Antinous, I can read in your sculptured face the supreme Egotism of manhood, an Egotism which fate will avenge in its own good time!'" Delicia says, "'I should have made a very bad actress,'" and I agree. The hero is a bona fide actor, even off-stage,

> staring at his own classic face and brilliant, dark eyes in the little mirror which dominated his "make-up" table. "And I no more than mime!—stage-puppet and plaything of the public! Wait, though! *I am* something more! I am a MAN!"[34]

Dramatic revelation is a dated feature of romance fiction. In *Ziska*, after a sensational description of exotic dancing, the dancer turns out to be "no other than the Princess Ziska!" (Ziska will make another dramatic entrance to clinch Chapter XV!) The revelation is all too much for the hero at the close of the chapter: "The great French painter, Armand Gervase, had suddenly fainted."[35] Theatrical faints punctuate romance fiction, but to a modern readership they may parody the drama.

Vengeance, essential to Elizabethan drama, is intrinsic to Corelli's voice too. Short story "The Song of Miriam" tells of a diva who enacts her revenge on a killer from her past. Naturally, "she looked like a goddess, and sang like an angel." She assimilates his fate in a performance that climaxes in a revenge murder, for the killer is now an operatic actor—with a bad case of stage fright this night. The greatest theatricality is reserved for the courtroom denouement, where the guilty diva is granted extenuating circumstances. The judge "wound up the case by a panegyric on her 'superb talent,' and let her go scot-free."[36] The diva didn't take a bow in the dock—because it was never intended as comedy.

In times of male oppression, ambitious women overcompensate to compete in patriarchal domains, which shows in the writing of Corelli and

Ros. In *The Sorrows of Satan,* a brazen male chauvinist of the type that held sway in 1895 reads the superior novel of Mavis Clare, who enjoys the initials of her author. "And that she should force me, by the magic of her pen to mentally acknowledge, albeit with wrath and shame, my own inferiority!"

Granted this first person narrative is past tense, allowing repentant reflection, but that such a pronounced chauvinist should see through his own prejudice so cogently and without excuses reads like transparent ventriloquism. "Women, I considered, should be kept in their places as men's drudges or toys—as wives, mothers, nurses, cooks, menders of socks and shirts, and housekeepers generally—."[37] A writer himself, he vows to assassinate her in a review—exposing the churlish motive of many a sour critic of Corelli, I take it. "This Mavis Clare, 'unsexed,' as I at once called her in my own mind simply because she had the power I lacked—wrote what she had to say with a gracious charm, freedom, and innate consciousness of strength—a strength which forced me back upon myself and filled me with the bitterest humiliation." The aggrandizement of M.C.'s talents, from the very mouth of her detractor, sounds like a forced confession, blurted out under torture at the author's hands. Such chinks in the curtain of the drama expose the writer studiously fashioning writerly devices that unwittingly call on camp aesthetics. The first edition of *The Sorrows of Satan* served notice that no copies were sent to the press, who must purchase their copy just like the rest of the public, thank you.

"Unsexed" is a telling catalyst. A year later in 1896, Corelli's opinionated Preface to *Delicia* snarls, "This word 'unsexed' is always cast at brilliant women by every little half-penny ragamuffin of the press that can get a newspaper corner in which to hide himself for the convenience of throwing stones."[38] She stokes up a formidable head of steam to drive the memorable rhythm of her castigation, so when the "unsexed" slur echoes in the narrative of *Delicia* as a dramatic trigger for a marital showdown the word becomes a theatrical prop. Delicia eavesdrops behind a curtain in theatrical tradition as her disrespectful husband finally goes too far with that loaded taboo: "'I think a clever woman—a writer of books, you know, like my wife—is a mistake. She is always unsexed.'" It's a dramatic moment of confrontation, but the set-up is comic when the reader is apprized, by the Preface, of Corelli's loathing for that chauvinist term. It recasts the scene as cathartic ventriloquism. The revelation of Delicia's gorgon gaze makes her husband "shrink within himself like a beaten hound," though the heroine must preserve her aloof disposition and leave the vengeance to Corelli's barbed narrative, and so "with an unshaken grace of bearing and queenliness of movement, she turned away, her soft satin train sweeping them by...."[39] The dynamic between these attitudes, counterposed in one sentence, strains when Corelli bristles with contempt yet pulls back to reach for Romanticism and recall the heroine's placid poise. It's a compelling derangement in the rhetorical structure of her novels.

The Avon Star: A Literary Manual for the Stratford-on-Avon Season of 1903 begins at the pace of a gondola gliding down the Avon, with lush lighting, fluent Romanticism, Shakespearean name-dropping and a dramatic exclamation:

> Long lines of rippling light and waves of sweeping shadow — pale green reflections of trailing willow-tresses, such as Ophelia might have bound about her fair hair ere she sank to death — delicate gleams of blue where the peeping clusters of forget-me-nots grow, amid soft feathery glints of mauve and golden-white from the purple loose-strife and meadowsweet, as they bend their blossoms to the drifting weight of the slowly moving water!

The exclamation after such delicacy looks like a rhetorical cue for applause. Within two pages, her contempt for modernity breaks the dreamy spell. She pauses a eulogy on Shakespeare to damn the clergyman who demolished his house and felled his tree, and she notes curtly of Stratford,

> The "new" street called Evesham Place, is like a cheap bit of Clapham.[40]

The extreme mood swings and writing styles may dislocate a reader's credulity. The domineering impression is not Shakespeare or Avon but the author's temperament: what mood will waken in the next chapter? *The Avon Star* wants to span the philosophical scale of Shakespeare's paradigm but the ambition is distracted by petty bourgeois propriety and parochial sniping. An article on "Where to Buy Pretty Things in Stratford" warns,

> Visitors should not run away with the idea that the only things to buy in Stratford are cheap busts of Shakespeare, models of the Birthplace, photographs, and picture postcards. It is not a kind of "Lowther Arcade" got up specially for American trippers.

The Avon Star was a guide to Stratford and Shakespeare's haunts. In her queenly editorial capacity, Corelli mixes Shakespearean essays (written mostly by herself but also featuring Emerson) with some extraordinary Commandments to American tourists: "Don't expect to buy picture postcards, photographs, or sweeties at Shakespeare's Birthplace. It is a shrine — not a shop." Yes, and, "Don't go into the confectioners' shops fourteen at a time, and order two glasses of milk and one bun for the whole party, so that those who don't want to pay for a drop of the milk or a crumb of the bun, may ask for a glass of water gratis. This way of serving refreshments to the wealthy American makes Shakespeare's townspeople tired." Most intimidating of all,

> If you believe Bacon was Shakespeare, or Shakespeare Bacon, get right out of Stratford-on-Avon as fast as you can and take the train to London.[41]

This translates as a Wild West warning. Indeed, Mark Twain enjoyed her work — Twain was a connoisseur of what he called "hogwash" literature — but Corelli's biographer reports that when they met, Twain couldn't get out of Avon fast enough.[42]

The Corelli reader must adapt to dramatic extremes in feminine-masculine energies. The original owner of my first edition of *Temporal Power* writes in smitten penciled handwriting dated September 1902, "For me it seems even impossible that this book could have been written by a woman. What argument, what fine feelings— she has strength of purpose in it all." I can see why an Edwardian man or woman would be impressed. At a time when women were seen and not heard, Corelli's masculine narrative verve is compelling: vehement, bombastic, patronizing, this transgender trait is superbly authoritative and always fluent with exhilarating pace, inspiring Amanda McKittrick Ros by the time of *Temporal Power*. "A soft laugh rippled on the air," but sooner or later we must reckon with the force of the author's most un-camp puritan indignation.

> Alas, poor Snob-world! How often has it fancied that with show and glitter and brazen ostentation of mere purse-power, it can quell the rage for Justice, which, like a spark of God's own eternal Being, burns forever in the soul of People! Ah, that rage for Justice!— that divine fury and fever which with strong sweating and delirium shakes the body politic and cleanses it from accumulated sickly humors and pestilence![43]

In their hapless extremism, camp *objects* often translate as grotesque the picturesque language and imagery of camp by design. Spiked with exclamations and distorted by the grotesquerie of "fury and fever ... strong sweating and delirium ... sickly humors and pestilence!" Corelli's language and visions disorientate perspective. In Sontag's tripartite system this would qualify not as classicism nor as camp but as the "distorted seriousness" of Kafka and Sade.

Corelli and Ros appropriate the masculine initiative of Sacher-Masoch's Wanda not in characterization but in narrative voice — wilful, disdainful, formidable, swinging moodily from lush Romanticism to the macabre, from genteel femininity to ranting assertion and misanthropic venom. If you seek a cinematic equivalent to their deranged scope, I give you *Whatever Happened to Baby Jane?* Marie Corelli and Amanda McKittrick Ros are the Joan Crawford and Bette Davis of camp letters. It's a kitsch thing to say, but their works are now kitsch artifacts, for during the course of this book I will equate *camp objects*, as Sontag would have it, with *kitsch*.

Circa 1920s but posthumously published, *Helen Huddleston* focalizes the ponderous exposition and unhinged psychodrama of Amanda McKittrick Ros. She stretches credulity and coherence yet compels our attention with great authority:

> That she whom he stole from the straight and narrow path upon which she unquestionably trod was now about to walk on the crooked and broad road of destruction, driven thither by his daring desire to stab the life out of his chum, Maurice Munro, with the steel of distrust in order to gratify his licentiousness by the purity of his stolen, enforced prey distressed him even to the edge of distraction.[44]

It's the perfect conclusion to the sentence, for the sentence itself is stressed to the edge of distraction.

Camp by misadventure approximates Aldous Huxley's notion of naive aesthetics, self-consciously contrived artifice. I call it naive not because the artifice is overt, as Huxley has it, but because the effect is not the intent. Huxley compared Amanda McKittrick Ros to the Elizabethan novelists who first fashioned the novel form, and neither her biographers nor Ros herself notice the patronizing slight. Ros credited Huxley as a rare critic who understood (appreciated) her. He took her seriously. It is, though, a backhanded compliment, "the result of the discovery of art by an unsophisticated mind of its first conscious attempt to produce the artistic...."[45] Huxley is saying Ros is primitive. Ros did, though, define her voice inimitably, whose compelling rhythm carries the fluency despite deranged constructions and bizarre expressions and the most excessive alliteration in all literature.

Her work never concedes that poetic devices, exposed to excess in prose, look ludicrously contrived. Look at her titles: *Irene Iddesleigh; Delina Delaney; Poems of Puncture; Fumes of Formation; Saint Scandalbags; Helen Huddleston; Donald Dudley.* Her biographer, after the pleasure of meeting Ros, credits her with formidable humorlessness: her show-stopping alliteration is consciously crafted, but not to derail the narrative and provoke humor where she wanted drama. Once past the titles, you might typically read this:

> The theft of such a character-coral he, in his moments of passion abstracted from the sacred store-rooms of his victims never taxed for a moment his designing brain with one thought of wrong or pity until he stood supporting himself against this leafy queen that so often had hid him from the eyes of the many patrolling profligates who patronizingly paced past him on their way to the seductive sanctum of searching sham, scandal and sin.[46]

You have just read Lord Raspberry, no less, leaning against a tree and assessing his career of robbing rich women, though the plot doesn't advance the interpretation much. Ros intrigues the reader with outlandish figures of speech, not altogether explained by the period and her colorful Belfast blarney ... "such a character-coral, he" is a curious expression with quaint poetic inversion; use of "abstracted" sounds distracted; "this leafy queen" is a coy curiosity that alludes to the tree as sinuously as innuendo; "his designing brain" sounds more bizarre now than it did to Victorians who equated "brain" with the more abstract "mind," and Corelli and Ros used "brain" abstractly — but now the objective physicality of "brain" fairly pulses, trepanning the subject to get inside his head. The finale of the sentence that should clinch the meaning, "the seductive sanction of searching sham, scandal and sin," leaves readers looking for closure. A single sentence establishes her unique voice and demonstrates that the pen is mightier than the gun, and more plosive. Each alliterative sequence loads her blunderbuss with more buckshot. For some, it stops the fluency dead in its tracks. I find each addictive alliteration shovels more coal into her steam engine for another exhilarating ride, hurling health and safety to the winds. In her greatest alliterative fits each word mirrors its pairing in self-referential double-exposures; each attendant adjective is like an understudy waiting in the wings, hoping for the spotlight should the lead noun take ill or go insane with the tension of these deranged constructions.

Lofty aspiration projects her poetic sensibility all over the prose. A corpse is called "the rigid sleeper," and in a blush, "The hot hand of bewilderment again pasted its crimson patch suddenly on both her cheeks...."[47] and a dramatic exit takes its ponderous leave, "Heavily laden with the garb of disappointment did the wandering woman of wayward wrong retrace her footsteps from the door for ever, and leisurely walked down the artistic avenue of carpeted care, never more to face the furrowed frowns of friends who, in years gone by, bestowed on her the praises of poetic powers."[48] The poetic presumption extends to dialogue as the author's voice dubs her characters in hot pursuit of her Muse. Situations and characters are posed like mannequins on which to hang the most flamboyant embellishments. When Helen Huddleston despairs of lax clergymen, a puritan objection after Ros's own heart, her uncle takes a deep sigh before his awesome alliterative lines,

> "Ah dear Helen, I feel heart sick of this frivolous frittery fraternity of fragiles flitting round and about Earth's huge plane wearing their mourning livery of religion as a cloak of design tainted with the milk of mockery," wiping his moistened brow with a crimson handkerchief, while Helen acquiesced, Henry Jr. remaining silent.[49]

There is in Ros a deranged psychological dimension that thankfully unhinges Victorian romantic tradition like a creative psychosis, preserving her from banal mediocrity for all time. Perhaps this is why she fancied, in a letter to friend Norman Carrothers in December 1933, having noted her name in that week's *Newsletter,* "I expect I will be talked about at the end of a 1,000 years."[50] She was aware of her idiosyncracies but not of their effect, and so rises supremely above banality in a letter to publisher J.S. Mercer in December 1927, "Personally, as a writer, well I know, my writings are wholly different from the common-place everyday novel. I also know that I write absolutely different from any known writer or organizer of prose."[51] This letter also claims the common touch, but the nature of her ego that imprints its patent on her work claims extremism in opposing directions.

Though not as theatrical as Corelli, Ros upstages her fainting fits in *Delina Delaney'*s denouement. The exemplary heroine is unjustly condemned of murder, whereupon all melodrama breaks loose in court. In the pantomime pandemonium,

> Ladies became hysterical, some fainting, others weeping copiously, and nothing was heard save sobbing and wailing. One young girl named Fanny Fowler, who had been a companion of Delina's at school, died from shock as the words fell from the clerk's lips.[52]

When it comes to exaltating femaleness, *Helen Huddleston* lets Lord Raspberry rhapsodize a preference for his wife over any harlot:

> "I say — give her me with a robe of rags, a mind of modesty, a heart of horror for all things unclean and hands untainted by the gruesome grasp of vice, rather than a princess— a duchess— a countess— a mimicking Madonna decked with diamonds of the purest, rubies the rarest, pearls of matchless luster (produced by mechanical and mischievous means) and the defiled non-trappings some of our ugly-faced have-you-believe cream of aristocracy don to impersonate heaven's purest virgin of what is disgusting in the all-vacilating team of kindred humanity. I say, Madam, give me my wife rather than all these sistered as aforesaid mentioned!"[53]

This is a heavier hand than Corelli, but I find the rhetoric breathtaking. As meaning is deranged by bizarre constructions, parenthetic distractions and fantastic elaborations on exotic beauty to aggrandize his preference yet further, the rhythm gathers pace, rolling over any critical reflection the reader might have, accelerated by hyphenated slurs and cumulative alliteration, inexorably, like the pull of the moon. Long sentences teeter on the brink of the author's temperament, martialing her energy magnificently. Even a short sentence rings exceeding strange: "Gently ringing the bell, the door was attended by a strange face."[54]

Biographer Jack Louden attributes some incoherence to bad grammar: "She has an extraordinary manner of beginning a sentence with a phrase that belongs to the previous sentence and is unrelated to the subject it governs." Louden favors *Irene Iddesleigh,* where Sir John lies on his death-bed as the nurse enters: "On entering the chamber of sickness with a new bottle of medicine sent from London, Sir John raised himself slightly on his left elbow...."[55]

Another aspect of derangement, alarming exclamations seize the reader's lapels, not entirely under the author's control. A poem from *Fumes of Formation* in 1933 upstages solemnity, indecorously bonny in Westminster Abbey, and so suddenly macabre that Ros may startle the unwary reader. Her vigorous masculine voice makes a stunning comparison with Alan Bennett's hushed tones in the pews of *The Laying on of Hands.* "On Visiting Westminster Abbey" begins, "Holy Moses! Have a look! /Flesh decayed in every nook!" Portraying death as the great leveler of rich and poor and fame as no insurance against decay, "bits of brain" decorate her ghoulish inventory of the illustrious dead. In the end, poets, politicians, rogues, "Kings— Queens, all of them do rot, /What about them? Now — they're not!"[56] The emphatic exclamation mark nails the coffin, and the startling interplay between question and exclamation snaps on that closure with unceremonious ruthlessness, taking "rot" as the basis for a frivolous rhyming dismissal of any such sentiment as grief or tragedy ... as if they all got what they deserved. Ros seems unaware of her deranged impact on the reader: when in 1910 she writes to a fan, treasuring his letter "amongst the many thousands of which I hold," having assured him that, "In fact I hold letters concerning my works from all crowned heads except the Czar of Russia and the Emperor of Austria," Ros gives her fan a peak of her next project and signs off on a startling note — if you imagine for a moment unfolding the letter on your doormat: "The hero is a bastard and writes poetry while in hell but I mustn't tell you too much."[57] The coy discretion that belatedly qualifies the alarming pronouncement is not tongue in cheek but is likely to be read that way; the sudden discrepancy is the kind of construct that typifies Sontag's second aesthetic.

Distorted seriousness is stretched on the rack between interrogation and exclamation marks in Ros's first novel in 1897, *Irene Iddesleigh.* Sir John summons his wife to confront their estrangement. His wounded ego is about to become ridiculous as Ros blows pathos into bathos— in one of the most sustained passages of camp by misadventure in the accidental canon. The extraordinary speech gathers pace uninterrupted by Irene or by narrative observation: bombastic righteous indignation and exposition resembling a trial summary for the defense as Sir John discloses his marital angst. A distinctive authorial voice, so prized by aspiring writers, gets in the way of characterization as we see the author's lips move to voice a character bereft

and distressed but still preening his poetic form. Who but Ros would articulate how, "'during these six months, which naturally should have been the
pet period of nuptial harmony, it has proved the hideous period of howling dislike!'" Sir John's commentary proudly presents self-pity:

> "I, as you see, am tinged with slightly snowy tufts, the result of stifled sorrow
> and care concerning you alone; and on the memorable day of our alliance, as
> you are well aware, the black and glossy locks of glistening glory crowned my
> brow."

"Snowy" was Ros's favored synonym for "white," but she didn't recognize its comical incongruity with the character, the pitch of his mood and
the situation. With lighting styled after the Corelli halo, he recalls better
times when "'black and glossy locks of glistening glory crowned my brow,'"
an effete dandy martyr to his narcissism — like Oscar Wilde in "De Profundis." And now the rhetorical questioning and crazed exclamations begin
to derange his seriousness.

> "But alas, now I feel so changed! And why?
> "Because I have dastardly and doggedly been made a tool of treason in the
> hands of the traitoress and unworthy!"

Stress is congruent with the character's situation, as anguished as
Sacher-Masoch's Severin, but the text too is fraught with obsessive and preposterous alliteration and ruptured cogency. Don't misunderstand me: I
wouldn't change a word of this.

> "Was I falsely informed of your ways and worth? Was I duped to ascend the
> ladder of liberty, the hill of harmony, the tree of triumph, and the rock of
> regard, and when wildly manifesting my act of ascension, was I to be informed
> of treading still in the valley of defeat?"

Ros is now sailing full mast with escalating alliteration and those
totemic phrases that loom in my mind like the spines of a shelf-full of Victorian poetry — The Ladder of Liberty, The Hill of Harmony, The Tree of
Triumph, and The Rock of Regard — alongside Patience Strong.

As the demanding questions continue — "'Can it be that your attention
has ever been, or is still, attracted by another, who, by some artifice or other,
had the audacity to steal your desire for me and hide it beneath his pillaged
pillow of poverty, there to conceal it until demanded with my ransom?'" —
we become aware that Irene has not said a word in response or been noticed
by the narrative for three pages. There are good reasons for this. Irene is
put on the spot, since her heart belongs to a third party. The author wants
to build dramatic tension: what is Irene thinking? what will she say? will
all be revealed? Instead, this is likely to trigger hilarity — because another

reason for Irene's silence during this poetic, dramatic, rhetorical speech is that she can't possibly get a word in edgewise.

> "Speak! Irene! Wife! Woman! Do not sit in silence and allow the blood that now boils in my veins to ooze through cavities of unrestrained passion and trickle down to drench me with its crimson hue!
>
> "Speak, I implore you, for my sake, and act no more the deceitful Duchess of Nanté, who, when taken to task by the great Napoleon for refusing to dance with him at a State ball replied, 'You honored me too highly'—acting the hypocrite to his very face."[58]

It could be that Irene has lost the thread of his question. For all Sir John's angst and passion, those fine-tuned parenthetic clauses qualify his rhetoric in Ros's construction that covers every eventuality and links more carriages to the train of thought. This gives Sir John a contradictory semblance of composure that splits his psyche. The ironic reader may picture Irene's unwritten expression, speechless during this literary tirade, as I did, irresistibly.

When Sir John runs out of rhetoric, Irene composes her reply. As theatrical and mannered as her counterpart, she begins with ponderous formality, "'Sir and husband,' she said, with great nervousness at first...." the kind of nerves experienced before a public address. This conversation, composed of two monologues before the reader, *is delivered* as a public address. Irene upstages his rhetoric with a dramatic revelation about her life —foxily, it seems to me, like an actor vying for limelight. A staged revelation of her aristocratic background with its scrupulous formal phrasing in the midst of marital strife maintains Victorian decorum — but its lofty posturing treads the boards with the strange, compelling gravitas of bad theater. Irene even takes issue with Sir John's snowy tufts, the stressed emblem of his martyrdom:

> "You speak of your snowy tufts appearing where once there dwelt locks of glossy jet. Well, I am convinced they never originated through me, and must surely have been threatening to appear before taking the step which links me with their origin."[59]

The construction is so delectably studied that the dialogue may also be read as an exchange of long-distance correspondence, like *84, Charing Cross Road*.

Reviews of *Irene Iddesleigh* were inevitably mocking — their bland language and obvious jeering all banal while Ros emblazoned her eccentricities on the reader's memory. Barry Pain wrote a one-page review in 1898, "Book of the Century." In response, Ros consumed a nine-page Preface to her second novel *Delina Delaney* that same year. It's an extraordinary counter-attack on "the scathing trade" of criticism and a vindictive personal slander of Pain as "a ranting schoolboy." When Pain sarcastically takes his hat off to her work, she pushes his irony further than it was ever meant to go.

> I should think this sentence of elegance more at home, practically, were a sweep seen to doff his cap to a critic cad whilst momentarily asking me if I had a job in store for him. I consider he'd wholly degrade the modesty of a female by attempting to doff his filthy headgear even to that god of scathers, Barry Pain.[60]

The key meaning here is not to be found in the warped syntax but in the expressions: the sooty sweep is rather a schizophrenic image, nominated as more suitable employment for a critic but the sweep doffs his cap to a critic such as Barry Pain. The overriding impression of a woman's scorn spikes a Dickensian caricature of the sweep-critic: the contempt that spits "critic cad" and "doff his filthy headgear" couldn't be clearer. She tries to dispatch her sentences with curt dismissal but she is too stung to keep aloof: "*I* care not for the opinion of half-starved upstarts, who don the garb of a shabby-genteel, and feign would feed the minds of the people with the worthless scraps of stolen fancies." The imagery is plagued with something medieval, "...Barry's monotonous disease ... a cancerous, irritant wart ... deadly sting...."[61] When Pain mocks, "*I shrank before it in tears and terror,*" Ros rises to the irony with alarming imagery that may unnerve the reader, "Just think of Barry *Pain* shedding tears, or being in terror, either, even at the sight of a butchered mother!" After Pain describes *Irene Iddesleigh* coming at him out of the night, Ros indulges a deranged fantasy:

> But perhaps it is Irene in person he refers to, who slipped into his bedroom one night, to be sure. Nothing remarkable, either, nothing awe-inspiring, nothing revolting, in this nineteenth century of ours, to know of an innocent young girl being decoyed even by a critic![62]

The attack extends from punning on his name to insinuating illegitimacy, bigamy, molestation, and speculation that Pain is friendless and perhaps he has fleas. None of this has anything to do with literary criticism — but to Ros much of literary criticism has nothing to do with literature. I make the case that camp by misadventure is oblivious of its irony but Ros is never more deranged than when she labors irony. Her riveting voice and barbed wit are not far from her usual seriousness: are we sure the heavy irony is not in fact in earnest? She doesn't resolve the ambivalence when she asserts that Barry Pain "must either have been in love, desperate love, with Irene or the author."[63] She takes Pain's antipathy and inverts the irony — or does she? Our knowledge of the author's deranged narcissism may wonder how tongue in cheek that conclusion really is.

Reviewing the illustrated edition of *Irene Iddesleigh,* D.B. Wyndham Lewis noted the lambasting of Pain and resolved to critique the pictures only, whimsically implying the slight on the novel. Ros responded with *Saint Scandalbags,* her pejorative term for Lewis. She wrote to publisher J.S. Mercer in January 1928 that it would preface her next novel, "which I presume will silence this erratic fool as I did Barry Pain."[64] Alas it wasn't published in her lifetime, for it gallantly outstrips Lewis's mediocrity. A few insults warm up the reader: she calls Lewis "this egotistical earth-worm, this aspiring asset in the world of conceit"; she calls him "a thick-witted, evil-minded snapshot of spleen"; she proclaims "not the faintest respect for a man, posing as a critic or cadger to introduce such filthy super-blackguardly remarks towards even harlots or the drossiest drabs who inhabit the blighty Brothels of the damned."[65] Beside the familiar diseased imagery, "blackguard" always finds favor with Ros, and now she conjures a fantastic superlative, "super-blackguardly," which sounds to modern ears like the language of superhero comic strips intent on exploding the perspective beyond earth. In another magnifying variation on the art of superlatives, Ros doesn't slow at the approach of a period but accelerates with a dramatic sense of resonance that ends a sentence on "the damned," which echoes its vehemence beyond the full stop.

She flaunts the very art the critics were mocking, staking her claim to immemorial fame on the basis of her first novel emphatically:

> Nor is it beyond a dram of doubt that *Irene* must inevitably possess the art, the *undoubted art* of arousing the passions of, not alone St. Scandalbags, but, of the whole character-clipping-combination including its creamiest genius-beetlers to an uncontrollable degree — as the dogs on the street — while *she* still lives to *fool* them and *force* them through capes of comparison and on the rocks of revenge.[66]

You see how her mood has turned since her first novel, for "the rock of regard" has become "the rocks of revenge." The meter trips along those hyphenated conceits with terrific momentum; one must repeat them to fully appreciate their bizarre invention: the likes of "creamiest genius-beetlers" intrigue interpretation, like a William Burroughs hallucination. Her writing does outlast her criticism —for all the reasons the critics pointed out before they faded away. The narcissism of her claim to classic status is, like every aspect of her imperious art, imperviously extreme, and consistent with her accidental motif of derangement. Ros writes like an author with forearms like cricket bats. The arched opening sentence of *Delina Delaney* puts the reader on the spot, as we experience how it feels to be Irene Iddesleigh, tracking a tenuous question through its journeying clauses:

Have you ever visited that portion of Erin's plot that offers its sympathetic soil
for the minute survey and scrutinous examination of those in political power,
whose decision has wisely been the means before now of converting the stern
and prejudiced, and reaching the hand of slight aid to share its strength in
augmenting its agricultural richness?

Before we can recover, the author subjects her readers to a disdainful
put-down to establish her authority from page one:

If you have not already reached the western borders of your native and beloved
isle of green and striking grandeur, you are hardly worthy of permission to
dawdle in your existence or dwindle your lives of dull monotony into hoped-
for futurity.[67]

Her judgement is delightfully *Sacher-Masoch* in its supremacy, infan-
tilizing the untraveled reader with schoolmistress tones; "...dwindle your
lives of dull monotony into hoped-for futurity" might mean, at a guess,
relieve your boring lifestyles by dreaming of better days, but the fantastic
sound and pose alone merits the expression. The presumptuous condescen-
sion in that opening is astonishing, at once alienating and compelling, I find.
     Half-way through *Delina Delaney,* a pamphlet blows across the path
of our protagonists like a leaf from that virulent Preface. Lord Gifford seizes
on the theatrical prop, a work of mischievous criticism: "'Ah, by heavens!
and this is that scathing ridicule on the production of 'The Stockbroker's
Son,' by May Marchmont, my clever cousin, who has won the praises of all
nations—yea, the congratulations of crown heads—by her talented pen.'"
May Marchmont doesn't figure at all as a character in the novel, but this
illustrious if invisible cameo graces the page with a reflection of the author's
ego, like Corelli's characterizations of great writers. Lord Gifford catharts
a histrionic tirade against "'the babbling brays of a bastard donkey-headed
mite, that helps to swell the rotten retinue of a maggoty throng who
endeavor to fester the heart with their verminy outbursts of wordy black-
guardioms, and infuse a scabby halo around the minds of a cleanly major
race!'"[68] The author's spite could not be contained by a nine-page Preface,
and just as Corelli's Preface to *Delicia* catharts about the accursed term
"unsexed" so that we recognize the "plant" in the narrative, so in *Delina
Delaney* the pamphlet is signposted as a contrived prop by the Preface. The
exclamation that dramatically punctuates the virulent imagery, and another
conjugated coinage on "blackguard," catches the reader short because it
leaves the sentence a tad incoherent. No matter: immediately after his two-
page tirade, Lord Gifford was "laughing loudly as he went along" to convey
that the criticism is not worth his anger—but it sounds insanely distracted
by sudden contrast to his prolonged outburst.

"The throbbing twitch of constant criticism"[69] so agitated her work that *Donald Dudley,* the story of an impoverished, unscrupulous critic whose soul is claimed by a visit from the Devil, was logically inevitable. Donald Dudley was an embittered caricature of critic Thomas Beer, whose unkind and petty comments, she wrote to J.S. Mercer, are "well deserving of the tyrannical and diabolical fate of Anne Boleyn."[70] The first sentence is short of an axe: it taunts literary criticism for one hundred and forty-five words. The first person narrative deflects any criticism of the language onto the critic himself. Misanthropic imagery festers in *Donald Dudley,* the ventriloquism is obvious—"...I said, with as much innocence as becomes a critic..."—and perception is skewed surreally. The Devil, in the guise of Mr. Devildinger, scorns Dudley's profession for many pages, but the most frightful revelation is that only Lucifer could express Ros's depths of livid scorn. A tirade gathers pace by running a sequence of adjectives that register like inverted superlatives:

> What the misery do the public care in this age of enlightenment for the brainless, thoughtless, worthless, senseless numskull, rattle-tat opinions of a pack of illiterate tooters who call themselves "critics," a paltry crew of wretched beggars—not a particle.[71]

They say the devil is in the detail, but in *Donald Dudley* the grotesquerie is even moreso in the contrived language of the Devil's detail: "His teeth were a touch tusky and kept in unsightly check by a couple of lips which at first struck me to be well stuffed sausages that he meant every moment to reduce. These he kept nicely damped by periodical tongue exercise."[72] A "couple" of lips suggests a variable number, not putting us in mind of two lips only but the fantastic possibility of three or four; "reduce" invites your best guess at meaning but refuses to confirm it; and "periodical tongue exercise" is linguistically eccentric beyond anything the Devil himself had in mind.

The novella is unfinished; like her rage it was a work in progress, but it does end after a fashion with the critic's resolution to leave the profession (unaware that his fate is sealed by the Devil). A critic is "a complication of lies," Dudley decides with cavalier ventriloquism —"for I was merely a bastard you know, no fault of mine." Dudley reasons, "So I concluded they were *all* bastards, for no properly begat man would accept a post where lies and bribery were its sole basis."[73] The transparent pretext of fiction to cathart the author's prejudices, and bizarre constructions of extreme language and imagery, conjure the deranged camp of Amanda McKittrick Ros out of the black arts.

The language and vision of Edward D. Wood, Jr. tests this dysfunctional aesthetic in the 20th century. The world of Ed Wood leaves the classical gambits of Sacher-Masoch, Corelli and Ros far behind. Wood's misadventure in camp expresses the pulp fiction, exploitation, cinematic imagery and cartoon strips of a generation immersed in popular culture. Historically, Wood's extraordinary literature shares a shelf with those flamboyant generations of camp authors who knew what they were doing. A legacy of camp by misadventure, there is a camp style that fashions the hybrid aesthetic consciously, expanding the artifice to trespass on the aesthtics of distortion. We find it in the sublime estrangement of Chloe Poems, and it addresses the question of how a frivolous aesthetic that was devastated by two World Wars can respond to the 21st century. And so Ed Wood takes his chronological place in Part Two, where six paragons of style develop the literary potential of camp from the last decades of the 1800s to the turn of the 21st century, with seemingly no effort at all.

PART TWO

Oscar Wilde (1854–1900)

"All art is at once surface and symbol."
— Preface, *The Picture of Dorian Gray,* 1890

Even in sweeping statements that court controversy and bask in outrage, camp never strains to make a point: that would be ungainly, and so
the author lets the reader construe "surface and symbol" as superficial if he
wishes. Wilde leaves it to Max Beerbohm, in an essay on artifice four years
after *The Picture of Dorian Gray,* to refute "the trustful confusion man has
made of soul and surface." Beerbohm questions exclusive thinking whereby
"man has come to think of surface even as the reverse of soul. He seems to
suppose that every clown beneath his paint and lip-salve is moribund and
knows it (though in verity, I am told, clowns are as cheerful a class of men
as any other)...."[1] Beerbohm proposes and Wilde illustrates a theme of this
book, the value of surface aesthetics that reveals not depths but reflections.
"I would like to protest against the statement that I have ever called a spade
a spade," Wilde said in 1892. "The man who did so should be condemned
to use one."[2] His protest against literal or functional use of language is an
aesthete's objection to the cultural dominance of content in communication and to the work ethic too; Wilde is promoting the aloof aesthetics of
seeming effortlessness and decoration.

Oscar Wilde was so charmed by style over content that he began his
projects with the book cover design. Yet the Preface of *The Picture of Dorian
Gray* responds to criticism of the tale as it first appeared in *Lippincott's
Monthly Magazine,* criticism that was moral censure masquerading as aesthetic objections. In Part One, Mario Praz invoked terms like "lack of seriousness ... conscience ... greedy ... irresponsible...." to impeach *The Picture
of Dorian Gray:* meaningless criticism to Oscar Wilde. The Preface was also
a literal exposition of the story, a tale of the symbol as the signified: the

dynamic painting that assumes the metaphysical likeness of its subject to leave its subject playing the artifact. It is an epigrammatic position statement on camp aesthetics. "It is the spectator, and not life, that art really mirrors," a witnessing consciousness that may be Buddhist or narcissistic, depending on your point of view. "There is no such thing as a moral or an immoral book," and, "All art is quite useless," justifies aesthetics as an end in itself without a political or ethical agenda. This is Susan Sontag's position in "Notes on Camp," but Wilde adds, "The moral life of a man forms part of the subject-matter of the artist." There are frequent moral sentiments of forgiveness and compassion in his work but no commitment, no reformist zeal: Wilde is not Dickensian, and aloofness prevails. Those forays into morality, in his fairy tales and some dramatic passages, foreshadowing his religious persuasion, are his weakest output, from a camp perspective.

George Woodcock[3] sees "a powerful element of social criticism" in Wilde's work but overstates the case by overlooking his aloof tone. Woodcock cites Lord Goring in *An Ideal Husband*, "My dear father, only people who look dull ever get into the House of Commons, and only people who are dull ever succeed there," but this droll remark that speaks for the author is, rather, unilaterally disinterested in political argument. Wilde's art at its best was purist, where purist and decadent paradoxically signify the same aesthetic. "Fired by his fervid words," Beerbohm credits Wilde as the aesthete of his day. "Dados arose upon every wall, sunflowers and the feathers of peacocks curved in every corner, tea grew quite cold while the guests were praising the Willow Pattern of its cup," a quaint example of decoration over function worthy of Saki's drawing-room, I feel.[4]

As Decadence waned, after Wilde and Beardsley and Huysmans' late conversions to Catholicism, the succeeding Symbolist movement toned down Decadent perversion and sensual indulgence but maintained the primacy of imagination inherent in Wilde's remark, "All art is at once surface and symbol."

Wilde contravenes his aesthetic when he adds, "To reveal art and conceal the artist is art's aim." Exposing his artistry is a camp presentation but disguise of the artist recalls the crafted guile of conventional aesthetics, and on these terms, Wilde, with his accustomed exhibitionism, is a misfit. Wilde also crafted his persona as art, a case of author-as-exhibit that Beerbohm celebrated as dandyism and Crisp paraded to the end of the next century. In "De Profundis," Wilde laments his internment in Reading Gaol, "Everything about my tragedy has been hideous, mean, repellent, lacking in style; our very dress makes us grotesque. We are the zanies of sorrow. We are clowns whose hearts are broken." Yet he recovers the camp aesthetic, beautifully, when he plays the tragedian with an actor's egoism and purples his pathos. In his descent from "pedestal" to "pillory," "De Profundis" puts the pillory on a pedestal. "There is only one thing for me now, absolute humility." Camp finds excess even here, where Wilde poses humility as a poetic aesthetic, "hidden away in my nature like a treasure in a field." Coy, yet flamboyant as ever.

Noël Coward calls "De Profundis" "one long wail of self-pity." He echoes the reservations of Quentin Crisp on Wilde, but without his Edwardian reserve. Acknowledging only *The Importance of Being Earnest,* Coward stages his objection with his own camp leanings, as bitchy as a queen himself: "It is extraordinary indeed that such a posing, artificial old queen should have written one of the greatest comedies in the English language." Coward is not enamored with Wilde's aesthetics: "The trouble with him was that he was a 'beauty-lover.'"[5] Coward's *Bitter Sweet* satirizes the Symbolist movement, heir to Wilde and Decadence. "Though we are languid in appearance," the elite "Exquisites" sing the Chorus that defines "The cause of Art," and dissuades striplings from liking Kipling instead of Wilde. This "charming frolic with the symbolic" reflects the amoral and aloof exhibitionism that Coward couldn't countenance yet that he too exhibited.[6]

Oscar Wilde's account is necessarily self-aggrandizing as he makes art of the self even in disgrace. E.F. Benson is kindly disposed to Wilde and his art. He knew Wilde and knew that tribulation could not alter his fanciful tastes: martyrdom was an aesthetic notion in "De Profundis." "It was the passion for writing a fairy tale, and not for living it which possessed him."[7] Richard Le Gallienne, another friend, suspected Wilde's psyche played his tragedy as theater — as he had played his trial — and "De Profundis" can be read that way. Grieving his mother's death, yet Wilde's consciousness of self is never far from his fey and swooning penmanship, with purple prose even when Wilde has no words:

> ... I, once a lord of language, have no words in which to express my anguish and my shame. Never even in the most perfect days of my development as an artist could I have found words fit to bear so august a burden; or to move with sufficient stateliness of music through the purple pageant of my incommunicable woe.[8]

Humility merely made Wilde bombastic, until his release and exile in France, where he reprised his aloof and epigrammatic style: "If England treats her criminals the way she treated me, she doesn't deserve to have any."[9]

His ensembles transparently disclose the author in pithy dialogue, while quotation marks distance the dogma of Wilde's generalizations. Languishing in Reading Gaol, he recognized Dorian Gray as foreshadowing his downfall. Wilde is an ambiguous hybrid of the artist who paints Dorian Gray and the model himself "who could be fashioned into a marvelous type,"[10] between artistic consciousness and cosmetic persona. The year before, Wilde wrote, "In point of fact what is interesting about people in good society ... is the mask that each one of them wears, not the reality that lies behind the mask,"[11] which sounds narcissistic indeed when each character reflects the author, loyal to surface aesthetics with barely a masquerade of the characters' idiosyncrasies. He revealed in a letter to Ralph Payne, "Basil Hallward is what I think I am: Lord Henry what the world thinks me: Dorian is what I would like to be in other ages, perhaps."[12]

Quentin Crisp finds himself in praise of narcissism but disdainful of the example. "One might describe Mr. Wilde as someone who used a very considerable literary talent as a trellis on which to trail an almost overwhelming personality." This is at least partly true of Crisp too, whose every written word augments his effeminate persona. Crisp equates lifestyle with dramaturgy and recommends that we "regard any incident as a kind of play, and this is what the ideal raconteur does."[13] Wilde went further, populating his plays with raconteurs, with characteristic pithy and paradoxical persiflage that makes so many Wilde characters, men and women, sound just like Oscar Wilde. "'I adore simple pleasures,' said Lord Henry. 'They are the last refuge of the complex.'"[14] When Lord Goring says in *An Ideal Husband*, "Everybody one meets is a paradox nowadays. It is a great bore. It makes society so obvious,"[15] I wonder if the author knew how pertinent Lord Goring was. Perhaps he did: by 1895 Wilde had set an urbane fashion for the blithe paradox, and his work finally caricatured all concerned, including the author, in self-reflective style. Lady Bracknell in *The Importance of Being Earnest* could be Wilde in drag. (On stage, Quentin Crisp would play Lady Bracknell, one of his many reluctant connections to Wilde.) In a section of Act III of *Lady Windermere's Fan*, dialogue is the pretext not for searching exchange between characters or plot development but for a fusillade of the author's witticisms in his accustomed offhand delivery. Characters are posed as artifacts on stage, modeling the art of lifestyle. Yes, but their dialogue is not driven by character as in realism: characters here serve one-liners that are themselves presented as *objects d'art*, conversation pieces. Lord Windermere sets up Cecil Graham, "What is the difference between scandal and gossip?" and Graham obliges, "Oh! Gossip is charming! History is merely gossip. But scandal is gossip made tedious by morality." Cecil Graham sets up Lord Darlington, "What is a cynic?" and Darlington obliges, "A man who knows the price of everything and the value of nothing," only to be topped by Cecil Graham, "And a sentimentalist, my dear Darlington, is a man who sees an absurd value in everything, and doesn't know the market price of any single thing"; and Dumby chips in, "Experience is the name everyone gives to their mistakes" ...a monologue call-and-response by Wilde. "The author people's his play with male and female versions of himself," the *Daily Telegraph* (22 February 1892) reviewed *Lady Winderemere's Fan,* and decided, "The play is a bad one."

The spirit of the author looms larger than his characters. Quentin Crisp, into his twenties, regarded other people "only as reflections of my own existence,"[16] and Wilde blithely projects this narcissism into his work, beyond his twenties. Camp is not shy of the footlights. Wilde wrote about *The Picture of Dorian Gray* to friend and writer Beatrice Allhusen, in 1890, "I am afraid it is rather like my own life — all conversation and no action. I can't describe action: my people sit on chairs and chatter."[17] The concession is rather disingenuous, for banter over plot and repose over labor is every aesthete's preference. Wilde's blithe epigrams influenced the droll dialogue of Saki and Coward and the monologues of Crisp, for better and for worse.

The Picture of Dorian Gray investigates the transcendent power of art (with a gothic take on the "Stendhal Syndrome," the psychotic identification with painted subjects) even as it examines Wilde's zeitgeist. The intrigue of the novel lies in Wilde's ambivalence where the direction of his aesthetic diverges from the undertow of his morality. Crisp concluded that Wilde's amorality was an act, style without sincerity, a sophist's delight in upending ethics with paradoxes while in reality, "He believed as firmly as Queen Victoria in good and evil."[18] Some of Wilde's stories and plays are Christian moral fables like the sermonizing short story "Lord Arthur Savile's Crime" (1887). Fantasies like "The Selfish Giant" and "The Happy Prince" and "The Star Child," drenched in pathos, lose the domestic-fantastic dichotomy of the camp fairy tale: so sentimental in their morality that even in fantasy they are bogged down by mediocrity, the scourge of camp. Children's fables also strip Wilde's baroque flair down to conscientious narratives of penance and forgiveness. His mature tales are less didactic, more ambivalent.

In *Lady Windermere's Fan,* the remarkable Mrs. Erlynne is a New Woman and anti-heroine. She claims the right to be decadent in the modern age and to flaunt it in camp style. "No— what consoles me nowadays is not repentance, but pleasure. Repentance is quite out of date. And besides, if a woman really repents, she has to go to a bad dress-maker, otherwise no one believes in her."[19] Dramatizing the excesses of the discrepancy, between the Christian moral imperative and the Decadent aesthetic, at least *The Picture of Dorian Gray* poses an intriguing dilemma for the reader. The novel is poised, like "The Fisherman and His Soul" of the same period, between

the cosmetic aesthetic of "The Decay of Lying" in 1889 and a Christian pre-
monition of "De Profundis" in 1896, like a backstage whisper, "Still, I am
conscious now that behind all this beauty, satisfying though it may be, there
is some spirit hidden of which the painted forms and shapes are but modes
of manifestation, and it is with this spirit that I desire to become in harmony."[20] Ambiguity in Wilde's philosophy inclines more to paradox than
conviction.

Wilde seeks the universal in masquerade (or characterization) beyond
the particularities of identity. *The Picture of Dorian Gray* uses mirror
imagery to pose the paradox. Eric Bentley[21] says, "Bohemianism was for
Wilde a mask. To wear masks was Wilde's personal adjustment to modern
life, as it was in Nietzsche's." Lord Berners too, says Mark Amory.[22] Masquerade is another presentation of artifice and distance as catalysts to revelation. Masquerade dramatizes the distance between role and consciousness,
and exposes the myth of the monolithic personality by revealing the guises
of our subpersonalities. "Is insincerity such a terrible thing? I think not. It
is merely a method by which we can multiply our personalities."[23] Wilde
said this with a skeptical take on the cult of analysis before it became embed-
ded in the 20th century psyche. Camp has no affiliation to the cult of explanation applied to orthodox evaluations of literature. Analysis is an
accomplice to seriousness, and not at all understanding of camp consciousness and its surface reflections.

Wilde's advocacy of insincerity as masquerade draws criticism from
Crisp and others who see masquerade as a way of being, while Wilde — so
the common criticism goes — made a disguise of style. Alan Bennett paraphrases the point in *An Englishman Abroad*, where Burgess disclaims a comparison to Wilde, "Though he was a performer. And I was a performer.
Both vain. But I never pretended. If I wore a mask it was to be exactly what
I seemed."[24] (I resist such moral literary criticism that employs masquerade in name only while enforcing a uniform way of being. It seems a paradox too far even for Wilde.)

St. John Hankin[25] wonders how Wilde failed to draw depth in his characters, "Possibly it was from mere indolence, because he was not sufficiently
interested." This is a perspective from the divan, disdainful of the equation
of seriousness or depth with truth. It may also suggest that Wilde wouldn't
take the ego seriously enough to find depth in the dramatic personae.
Hollinghurst finds in Firbank too "that the major characters in Firbank's
novels are perhaps only minor characters in them."[26] Camp characters are
seldom heavy but the best portrayals are polymorphously ambiguous, which
Wilde achieves through paradox. Noël Coward does not possess Wilde's
gift for paradox and may, on occasion, disown his camp portraits via other

characters. And so in *Quadrille,* Charlotte comes to a conclusion about Hubert, "You have wit and charm and a noble heritage indeed; but your character is watery."[27]

In the masquerade of *An Ideal Husband,* being natural "is such a very difficult pose to keep up."[28] Mrs. Cheveley is *"a work of art, on the whole, but showing the influence of too many schools."* In this play from 1895, portraiture frames the artifice of character and flouts realism: Sir Robert is likened to a Vandyck portrait; Mabel Chiltern is a Tanagra statuette; Lady Basildon and Mrs. Marchment are subjects fit for Watteau to paint; and Lord Caversham could be a portrait by Lawrence.[29] A tapestry of "The Triumph of Love" adorns the themes of the play, a spotlit backdrop in the décor advised by the stage directions. Saki takes up the notion of the persona as art that also enchanted Beerbohm and Crisp, but Saki projects the aesthetic onto fictional characters: Youghal in *The Unbearable Bassington* and Cicely in *When William Came* and René in *The Watched Pot* appreciate their reflection as art and not, Saki wants you to know, as mere vanity. Elaine in *The Unbearable Bassington* and Cicely in *When William Came* are figurative art critics in their studious appraisal of male poise and handsome highlights.

In *The Picture of Dorian Gray,* portraiture frames masquerade metaphysically. Lord Henry stands accused of a charge familiar to Wilde, "'Your cynicism is simply a pose.'" as self-portraiture extends beyond the frame and the subject of Dorian Gray. Camp finds paradoxical meaning in the narcissistic image, for narcissism too is a masquerade.[30] Lord Henry echoes Mrs. Cheveley (Wilde could never resist a retort), "'Being natural is simply a pose, and the most irritating pose I know.'" The bad publicity of narcissism assumes that it excludes everything but the viewer, when in fact the mirror implicates us all, or at least, everybody but the subject. The subject, in the final analysis, disappears, like a moment in eternity, which is the transcendental revelation of the universal at the heart of the particular narcissist. The priest in Wilde's short story "The Fisherman and His Soul" advises, "There is no god but this mirror that thou seest, for this is the mirror of Wisdom. And it reflecteth all things that are in heaven and earth, save only the face of him who looketh into it. This it reflecteth not, so that he who looketh into it may be wise."[31]

The portrait of Dorian Gray also sublimates the painter's infatuation into kinky art, a high camp elevation of low camp innuendo, a double entendre in oils. "There was nothing that one could not do with him. He could be made into a Titian or a toy."[32] Wilde makes another high camp translation of outlawed homoeroticism when Dorian falls in love with Sybil during her stage appearance in boy's clothes in *As You Like It.* But then love is a narcissistic projection of self, homoerotic or not: Wilde says so in a prose poem in 1893, "The Disciple." The portrait is now an idealized projection of the artist, his anima, a subpersonality coming to the painterly surface. Lord Henry tells the painter, "'Upon my word, Basil, I didn't know you were so vain, and I really can't see any resemblance between you, with your rugged strong face and your coal-black hair, and this young Adonis, who looks as if he was made out of ivory and rose-leaves. Why, my dear Basil, he is a Narcissus....'" Proscenium phrases "Upon my word, Basil," and "Why, my dear Basil," stage the familiar droll and aloof drawing-room tones, and the art nouveau Narcissus in ivory and rose-leaves is supremely camp. Florid and frivolous imagery weaves through the book in quiffs of smoke and fireside flames and alluring trails of exotic perfume to blend the subpersonalities of Lord Henry, the painter and his subject, and by reflection, the author. Art nouveau entwines around Lord Henry in the same passage, with a tincture of Decadence:

> Lord Henry elevated his eyebrows, and looked at him in amazement through the thin blue wreaths of smoke that curled up in such fanciful whirls from his heavy opium-tainted cigarette.[33]

I love the aggrandized gesture that didn't merely raise but "elevated" that theatrical brow, elevated again by Mrs. Cheveley in *An Ideal Husband*. Ronald Firbank negotiated the gesture to signal a forthcoming facial expression in *Concerning the Eccentricities of Cardinal Pirelli*, "The Cardinal sent up his brows a little."[34] In a Saki story, the camp protagonist is ushered from a garden party before a sea-mist sweeps inland: "I knew that the elaborate curl over his right eyebrow was not guaranteed to survive a sea-mist."[35] In Crisp's novel *Love Made Easy,* when a girl enquires the price of an antique, "With one magnificent eyebrow Roofingfelt added his query to hers."[36] And recalling his own response to a question from the audience at Quentin Crisp's one-man show, "I tilted a neatly penciled eyebrow in surprise."[37] A husband broaches a subject in order to rebuke *Delicia* in Marie Corelli's novel: "'It concerns you, and I should like to speak to you about it.'" Delicia remains self-composed: she has already reserved a place on the moral high ground, secretly... "'Yes,' said Delicia, with the very slightest lifting of her delicate eyebrows."[38] It's remarkable how kitsch such a slight gesture can read, but there is an extreme close-up in that excessive superlative "very slightest," and the expression "lifting of" reads like block and tackle for a gesture that is still under construction while posing ever so delicately. It's another instance of Corelli's elevation of the feminine ideal that adapts Wilde's ultimate artistic statement of personality as art, a distinction which she must share with Leopold von Sacher-Masoch and Ed Wood. And it is worth waiting to find out what Ed Wood does with eyebrows.

The singular arched brow puts wry distance from the regarded subject but also from the expression itself, subtle and aloof in not committing the face to align itself with the sentiment. Its asymmetrical curlicue arch is also rather art nouveau.

Emily Apter[39] describes art nouveau as "the decadent design fashion par excellence" and proposes Octave Mirbeau as literary exponent of its "panfeminine decorative forms." I suggest the camp aesthetic assumes more promiscuous relations with art nouveau, particularly Wilde in *The Picture of Dorian Gray* as Mirbeau went to press with *The Diary of a Chambermaid*. Tendrils weave relations between Wilde's characters, infiltrating the artist's studio:

> From the corner of the divan of Persian saddle-bags on which he was lying, smoking as was his custom, innumerable cigarettes, Lord Henry Wotton could just catch the gleam of the honey-sweet and honey-colored blossoms of a laburnum, whose tremulous branches seemed hardly able to bear the burden of a beauty so flame-like as theirs; and now and then the fantastic shadows of birds in flight flitted across the long tussore-silk curtains that were stretched in front of the large window, producing a kind of momentary Japanese effect....

...and so runs the eternal sentence. Wilde trails the capricious scents of the garden and transports the character's contemplations beyond causal time to where the moment is all, immediacy as gateway to eternity — and eternity is the ultimate excess. Exotic tussore-silk curtains stage the luxurious "momentary Japanese effect" that transports us beyond considerations of plot, time and space. This static art that poses motion, this incongruous interpolation between cause and effect, summons the fantastic in a domestic detail. It demonstrates the ideal of "De Profundis," which became Symbolism, "Time and space, succession and extension, are merely accidental conditions of thought; the imagination can transcend them and move in a free sphere of ideal existences."[40]

Ennui exists in that opiated state of slow motion, without losing urbane composure, the perennial camp temperament. And so, in "The Decay of Lying," Vivian belongs to a tongue in cheek sect of "'The Tired Hedonists'.... We are supposed to wear faded roses in our buttonholes when we meet...."[41] The jaded afterglow of blossoming, feminine and fanciful and effete, is an emblem of ennui, especially when "supposed to" implies that members can seldom be bothered to observe the propriety. Camp may *act* as if ennui is a state of dramatic sufferance, and often conflated with boredom — Quentin Crisp reviews *My Dinner with Andre* and sighs, the film "alas, was as boring as being alive"[42] — yet ennui is a lethargic graduation, the rarefied difference between a sigh and a yawn. And so "Elizabeth assayed a tired greatness" in Crisp's novel *Love Made Easy*.[43] Camp ennui, a tad postcoital, escapes the seasonal malaise of *Against Nature:* even with the aloof accessory of a cigarette, Des Esseintes has no distance from Decadence; in "delicious reverie, his mind was going full tilt in pursuit of recollections."[44] Boredom spurs a cycle of dissatisfaction-and-desire-and-satiety-and-dissatisfaction ... while ennui spurns it, by my distinction, resigning the chase to make a fey mantra of the sigh in the moment of fulfilment and reflection. Art and the camp pose make eternity of that moment. The "Ahh" effect achieves alienation in that sigh. We find it in the luxuriant posing of Wanda on the ottoman in *Venus in Furs,* contraposed with Severin's Decadent quest to saturate his angst in masochism. We find it in Corelli's heroines, in Princess Ziska on the divan, "half-closing her eyes, and regarding him languorously through her silky black lashes."[45]

"Languid" is the blasé camp term that attaches itself to Dorian Gray[46] before angst sets in, and to Lady Basildon and Mrs. Cheveley in *An Ideal Husband.*[47] Ronald Firbank captures the indulgent complacency of the term in *The New Rythum:* "She smiled, transported by a sudden idea, her physiognomy passing from languor to languor,"[48] so languid that the lolling alliteration leans on repetition. Saki's first sentence spells it out in "Reginald's First Drama," "Reginald closed his eyes with the elaborate weariness of one who has rather nice eyelashes and thinks it useless to conceal the fact."[49] Saki makes camp of Lewis Carroll's wonderland in *The Westminster Alice* in 1902: the cat introduces Alice to Ineptitude but, inconsequentially, forgets whether its function is to unravel what people believe or don't believe — but in any case, "'It really doesn't matter which,' said the Ineptitude with languid interest."[50] Languour often accompanies a snide and superior remark to distance the speaker from the intent and the target, and so the languorous Princess Ziska can make a colossal and rather bitter generalization, courtesy of Corelli, without any effort at all as she tells the flawed hero, "'It is the mistake all men make with all women — to judge them always as being of the same base material as themselves.'"[51] *Ardath* is positively complacent with lofty languid gestures, and the "languid indifference" of aloof Lady Sybil in Corelli's *The Sorrow of Satan,* "waving her fan indolently to and fro," was in 1895 a signal of sophistication but now reads theatrically and laughably mannered.[52] Wilde played quite a role in making these gestures and attitudes at once fashionable (and so now dated) and theatrical. Languorous ennui is a pose against the inconsequence of toil — in work, dogma, passion, or education — and so, in Saki's *The Watched Pot,* René echoes Ineptitude when he half-heartedly tries to recall a cousin: "A Canon, somewhere in the Midlands; he's got peculiar views— he believes in a future life, or else he doesn't, I forget which."[53] What does it matter? Energy, to the camp aesthetic, is potentially vulgar. And so in the same Saki play,

Ludovic disdains a woman's wedding prospects: "You have too much dash and go and — in — indefinable — characteristics. I don't know if you've noticed it, but in Somersetshire we don't dash." Here Saki spells out ennui in punctuation: Ludovic pauses and half-heartedly tries to define her objectionable traits before taking the path of least resistance and pronouncing them indefinable. Faced with the woman's indignation, Ludovic responds blithely, modeling the camp temperament to the last Act, "You're flying into something very like a rage. In Somersetshire we never fly into a rage. We walk into one, and when necessary we stay there for weeks, perhaps for years."[54] *The Watched Pot* never boils, the title domesticates the point, and the camp aesthetic and the camp temperament is always observed by its own reflection. Ennui is endemic in the play: marriage is proposed on a whim and instant refusal is accepted nonchalantly; René responds to his mother's dramatic disappearance with frivolous languor; and Trevor, an eligible bachelor, falls asleep as he is wooed. Ennui is what happens after Decadence, in trailing wisps of tobacco and opium, "that ennui, that terrible *taedium vitae,* that comes on those to whom life denies nothing."[55] Brigid Brophy is defining the "ambivalence" of baroque style when she speaks of "the baroque death of desire in the orgasm that satisfies it,"[56] a sweet evocation of camp ennui. In the climax of *Santal,* a Romantic investigation into spiritual contentment that reads like Herman Hesse in pink, Firbank eulogizes the spirit of ennui as "a great resignation."[57] Lord Henry Wotton's accustomed state of mind, ennui signals detachment from desire and ego. Like art nouveau, it is a *decorative* mood, ethereal, disengaged from motivation and labor as art nouveau snubs function. Beerbohm's essay on artifice portrays women as the supine sex but, in camp, aloof disposition is androgynously expressed by many a male hero. Basking in a surfeit of luxury on a divan, in the Decadent saturation of the moment, noticing "tremulous branches ... hardly able to bear the burden" of such beauty, this is as camp as it gets. "All art is tiring," Alan Bennett tells his diary in 1996 after wandering through Tate Gallery.[58]

By the time they weave their way back to the picture of Dorian Gray, those tendrils fashion gothic art nouveau from his features. See the twisted art nouveau in "Lord Arthur Savile's Crime": "The silent roadway looked like a long riband of polished silver, flecked here and there by the dark arabesques of waving shadows."[59] Despite Lord Henry's glib observation in *The Picture of Dorian Gray* that "Conscience makes egotists of us all."[60] morality's material effects are underestimated by its dismissal as a dispensable construct. Gnarling "the hideous lines that seared the wrinkling forehead, or crawled around the heavy sensual mouth,"[61] these gothic twists reflect Dorian's psyche, as Wilde investigates the consequences of Decadence —

and of time. Dorian Gray is locked in suspended animation, not in the eternal moment of Wilde's ideal aesthetic but in the purgatory of a dilemma where moral philosophy encroaches, uninvited, on aesthetics. The camp aesthetic is beyond the continuity of temporal consequences, while in life we must face the uncouth effects of our past, a karmic complication in Wilde's ideal of the self as art that compromises his decadent taste. And so the narrative gradually becomes less camp, more gothic.

Yet all the stylized traits are there. A camp collage of the morning post for young dandy Dorian Gray: a flourishing personal signature of popularity and celebrity simply too *too* obligatory, headlining art fashion and French dressing and invitations to premiers, all punctuated by a droll epigram that sounds truer to my ear today than for society a century ago, that "we live in an age when unnecessary things are our only necessities...."[62]

There's more, of course. Lord Henry's library in *The Picture of Dorian Gray* reads like the decadence of Lord Berners' library in *First Childhood:* ornate and exotic and floral, all gilt and china and French dressing and apricot lighting....[63] You can see Huysmans' influence on Wilde in his lush design of the library in *Against Nature,* six years before *The Picture of Dorian Gray.* It suggests a view of Decadence as a strain of camp. Camper than Wilde and too flamboyant to recount in detail, presenting the library décor as more important than the books, Huysmans' walls are bound like books in crusted morocco, and, amid the orange, "a piece of royal-blue silk from an ancient cope on which silver seraphim had been depicted in angelic flight by the weavers' guild of Cologne."[64]

Huysmans so prefers Art over Nature that his hero designs a living space inside a book. Decadent and camp aesthetics prefer art over plot. This seems cavalier and gratuitous (and so it is) to orthodox aesthetics and its cultural heritage of penance and toil and suppression of subjectivity. Edouard Roditi[65] complains of *The Picture of Dorian Gray,* "The thread of its narrative is too frequently interrupted by Wilde's aesthetic preaching, by useless displays of aesthetic erudition, by unnecessary descriptions of works of art and by paradoxical table-talk which have little bearing on the plot.... The conversation, at times, even distorts the plot. It allows a vague number of duchesses and other characters, doomed to vanish almost immediately after their first appearance...." Camp simply appreciates the entrances and exits, narrative notwithstanding, and so Exit the Duchess, "Looking like a bird of paradise that had been out all night in the rain, she flitted out of the room, leaving a faint odor of frangipani."[66] These same pejoratives in Roditi's essay, "useless displays ... unnecessary ... little bearing on the plot...." were commonly aimed at Huysmans too. By camp values, I suggest *The Picture of Dorian Gray* is not cavalier enough in its relegation of plot and suffers from mainstream concessions to genre convention.

I have put the case for another cause of neglect of camp literature: commentators ascribe aspects of camp to the Decadent movement, though camp predates Decadence and plays on a bigger stage, more aloof and thereby reflective, less intoxicated by its excess. *Against Nature* achieves critical distance through retrospection and intellectual exposition — but not incongruously, not via oblique juxtaposition, not with ironic distance from the integrity of Naturalism that still impresses Huysmans even after renouncing the movement. In *Down There,* another Huysmans alter ego is writing the ferocious history of Gilles de Rais: this book within a book gains intellectual distance from the outrages disclosed, but no ironic distance from narrative detail or the practise of narration itself. Octave Mirbeau's *Torture Garden* (1899) is a Decadent classic, indulging torture as an art form. Its floral symbolism, narcissism, extreme contrasts, excess, assertive women and malleable men, and its amorality, recur in camp — yet *Torture Garden* has no distance from its lust and fascination. Its searching seriousness is caught up in the nature of sadism, as intense as Sade's Decadence, and demonstrably not camp.

Even with Decadent affiliations, even as Dorian Gray is influenced by *Against Nature* (the book is alluded to, and finally identified by Wilde in the Queensberry trial), Wilde shows the difference in his work. The subplot, Dorian's destructive love-affair with Sybil Vane, and her brother's vengeance, is not in the story's original instalment, it is a heterosexual concession to convention for book publication. Wilde makes no effort to nest the subplot artfully in narrative but highlights the artifice. Sybil tells her brother, "'You are like one of the heroes of those silly melodramas'" in his vow to kill any man who breaks her heart. His overreaction is an obvious foreshadowing that tips the writer's hand, since her brother had no occasion to suspect any such thing: there is no preparatory history in the narrative. Herself an actress, "The exaggerated folly of the threat, the passionate gesture that accompanied it, the mad melodramatic words, made life seem more vivid to her."[67] And to conventional expectations of mainstream readers, perhaps. The novel was written off the cuff so quickly that the process too may show Wilde's disdain.

As Mrs. Cheveley prepares to bribe and blackmail Sir Robert with unscrupulous revelations in *An Ideal Husband,* a stage direction advises her, "[*in the most nonchalant manner*]." Theater becomes pantomime when Wilde endorses the camp affiliation to fairy tales. Mrs. Cheveley makes a wonderful Wicked Queen at the close of Act III. Stage directions play up her latest triumph with no apologies to realism: "[*Her face is illumined with*

evil triumph. There is joy in her eyes. Youth seems to have come back to her].”[68]
St. John Hankin[69] notes the strong curtain of Wilde's plays and vents the
usual orthodox reservations about his theatricality — “a purely theatrical
device only worthy of a popular melodrama” in *An Ideal Husband* — and
“the long soliloquy which opens the third act of *Lady Windermere's Fan* with
such appalling staginess.” He notes the atypical curtains of *The Importance
of Being Earnest*, “Act I and II end in the casual, go-as-you-please fashion
of the ultra-naturalistic school,” but camp sensibility would appreciate this
droll equation of drama and life.

Theatricality swans across the pages as Wilde celebrates the artifice of
form and spurns the culture of guile. The tell-tale broach in *An Ideal Husband,* and the device of confidential letters to set up intrigue and revelation, is unashamedly stagey even for a century ago. The confidential artifact
in *The Picture of Dorian Gray* is the hidden portrait itself. The fan is a customary camp accoutrement, adorning the artifice of personality and useful for brushing aside serious analysis. A more self-conscious 19th century
fashion than in Elizabethan theater, it is a character signifier in *Lady Windermere's Fan* in 1892. Isherwood tips his hat to Wilde in *Goodbye to Berlin:*
The Lady Windermere is where Sally Bowles sings, and the iconic fan looms
over the bar. Obligatory for matriarchal Wilde women, the fan ventilates
intrigue, innuendo, and inflammable gossip. If intrigue cannot be promoted by that other favored device, the confidential letter, then it must be
fanned by inflammable gossip. Like the cigarette, it is an accessory to finesse
and aloof poise. The fan presents the eyes in a flirtatious disclosure of the
masquerade of persona. “The Princess has hidden her face behind her fan!”
the Young Syrian observes of *Salome*, where characters *perform* their actions
and intentions in decadent pose and dialogue, and dialogue is often explicit
stage direction, making stylized drama of religious history.[70] The fan is
plumage to the narcissistic pose, as Beardsley's cantatrice fans herself in
“The Three Musicians.” The fan entails a fickle gesturing, flaunted by Corelli
in a rare flippant portrait that owes something to Wilde's fashion, I feel:

> Lady Fulkeward unfurled her fan and swayed it to and fro with an elegant lan-
> guor.
>   “How delightful that would be,” she sighed. “So romantic and solemn — all
> those dear old cities with those marvelous figures of the Egyptians carved and
> painted on the stones! And Rameses — dear Rameses! He really has good legs
> everywhere!”[71]

Coy yet ostentatious, the fan also masks character and motivation —
and the mannered manipulations of the author too. Wilde flirts with his
audience in self-consciously poetic form in *Salome*. Herodias too fans herself in decadent indifference to her daughter's blasphemy. This bourgeois

drawing-room talisman conjures masculine authority behind feminine reserve. Mrs. Cheveley flouts patriarchy and browbeats Sir Robert like a dominatrix in *An Ideal Husband:* "For the moment I am your enemy. I admit it! And I am much stronger than you are." She is one of many Wilde women who binds feminine and masculine traits assertively. A stage direction juxtaposes femininity with the assertion of a *femme fatale* who holds Sir Robert's masculine energy and his fate in check, as Mrs. Cheveley *"detains him by touching his arm with her fan, and keeping it there while she is talking."*[72]

I sense the dramatist treading the boards and performing his stage directions, pausing to admire their dramatic effect, not at all stage shy. Look at Lady Chiltern's reaction to her husband's fraudulent past, not so aggrieved that she overlooks an opportunity for peremptory scene-stealing and a dramatic refrain to aggrandize her grief: "[*thrusting him back with outstretched hands*]: No, don't speak! Say nothing! Your voice wakes terrible memories — memories of things that made me love you — memories of words that made me love you — memories that are horrible to me. And how I worshipped you!" (Such archetypal histrionics are satirized beautifully on film by Dianne Wiest in *Bullets Over Broadway* (1994) — and taken perfectly seriously, of course, by Marie Corelli.) Wilde shows his melodramatic sensibility in a final stage direction,

[*She sways like a plant in the water. Her hands, outstretched, seem to tremble in the air like blossoms in the wind. Then she flings herself down beside the sofa and buries her face.*][73]

Of course she does: Wilde's ensembles always do that, in public displays of despair and ennui and petulant frustration: their public expects it of them, and like the dramatist, they are always implicitly aware of their audience.

In *The Picture of Dorian Gray,* Sybil Vane provokes the theatrical perspective of camp with unfeasible overacting. Dorian falls in love witnessing Sybil's Shakespearean performance as Rosalind and he rejects her love the moment he rejects her stagey appearance as Juliet. His sensational lurch from adoration to bitterness is too sudden and trivial for realism, but it is high melodrama. Lord Wotton's commentary on life from the wings achieves an intellectual theatricality. When he "plucked a pink-petalled daisy from the grass, and examined it,"[74] his detachment is camp, so is the floral symbolism, and the contemplation gives the Bigger Picture on personal circumstance that oversees plot and motivation. Dorian Gray's nonchalant pose of spectatorship even in a moment of dramatic revelation in the novel, smelling his buttonhole flower "or pretending to do so," encourages reflection rather than compelling our intrigue in the narrative. His painter confronts the supernatural painting that now has a gothic life of its own, as "the lamp cast fantastic shadows on the wall and staircase" in one of several caricature vignettes of Poe. Dorian makes gothic melodrama of the unveiling, tearing down the curtain, yet he is his own detached spectator, watching "with that strange expression that one sees on the faces of those who are absorbed in a play when some great artist is acting."[75]

Wilde's reflections on the art of aloof temperament in *The Picture of Dorian Gray,* a seeming preoccupation with surface, makes aesthetic and philosophic ripples that Buddhism has contemplated for thousands of years. "It is said that passion makes one think in a circle," Wilde invokes the karmic wheel, and Dorian Gray's final, total indulgence in desire is depicted as enslavement to impulse.[76] His spectatorship at the revelation of his portrait yields to frenzied murder of the painter, without reflection.

Dorian's initial development is inspired by Lord Wotton to make transcendental connections from lush aesthetics—"Old brocades, green bronzes, lacquer-work, carved ivories, exquisite surroundings, luxury, pomp...." to the witnessing consciousness that rises above the gravitational pull of ego and will-power, just as camp aesthetics disengage from plot: "'But the artistic temperament that they create, or at any rate reveal, is still more to me. To become the spectator of one's own life, as Harry says, is to escape the suffering of life.'" Like the disowning separation of action and consequence between his portrait and his self, Dorian's disengagement is psychopathic and distracted, not reflective, for it does not control or inform his actions. "'It seems to me to be simply a wonderful ending to a wonderful play.'" Dorian says of Sybil Vane's suicide, never a believable actress. "'It has all the terrible beauty of a Greek tragedy, a tragedy in which I took part, but by which I have not been wounded.'"[77] And so Susan Sontag asserts that camp is "irony over tragedy."[78] Tragedy mourns its fate in bleak emotional immersion; camp, more fatalistic, shows awareness of the masquerade of ego and its dynamo, will-power. Dorian Gray ceases to be camp when his driven actions betray that poise and with it the pose of lifestyle as art. His portrait decays as he abandons those cardinal camp values, but every contact with his portrait sparks self-awareness. "It had made him conscious how unjust, how cruel, he had been to Sibyl Vane."[79] A moral message or the magical oracle of fairy tales, an animate looking glass that simply reflects all it sees? From his first encounter with his portrait that birthed his awareness of his mortality, cosmetic aesthetics is Dorian's only catalyst to reflection.

Critics infantilize the sense of wonder of camp aesthetics as trite escapism, a frivolous flight from reality. The domestic-fantastic conceit tests the boundaries of reality with horizons beyond the definition and potentiality of realism. Realism, or Naturalism, doesn't dream, it grounds awareness in empirical detail. Realism does not speculate beyond the perceptible horizon; reality, however, includes possibilities beyond today's experience. Camp courts those fantastic dimensions in theatrical vocabulary and a view from the wings.

The aesthetic and philosophic virtue of reflection prompts Vivian to propose, in "The Decay of Lying," "Art takes life as part of her rough material, recreates it, and refashions it in fresh forms, is absolutely indifferent to fact, invents, imagines, dreams, and keeps between herself and reality the impenetrable barrier of beautiful style, of decorative or ideal treatment."[80] "Life" in this treatment means our active and egoistic engagement with the process of living; "art" brings reflection by standing off its effects. Reflection requires distance, at least the focal length of a mirror. Irony generates distance by inserting incongruence between cause and effect. Camp prefers theatrical irony in overtly artificial representations. It distances consciousness from ego by playing character larger than life, performing one's identity.

In *Quadrille,* Noël Coward voiced a common objection to camp, leveled at the frivolous aristocrat Hubert, "Your phrases are so extravagant, so fanciful. Do they spring from your depths, these highly colored words you use, or are they merely decoration...?"[81] They are decoration, Coward reveals. Accused of cynicism, Hubert responds, "It is a matter of self- preservation."

Camp fashioning of distance is often interpreted as cynicism or defensive insulation from the crude consequences of life and social injustice. Wilde's paradoxical aphorisms seem indifferent to any such interpretation. Coward encourages the view with his portrayal of the writer Quinn in a not very camp play, after all, *Point Valaine.* Quinn saves the psychoanalytic critic some time with this self-diagnosis: "My role in life is so clearly marked. Cynical, detached, unscrupulous, an ironic observer and recorder of other people's passions. It is a nice façade to sit behind, but a trifle bleak." He muses, "Perhaps I have suffered a great deal and am really a very lonely, loving spirit."[82] Quinn is not the personification of camp, I suggest: camp does not deign to "despise" and is not "cynical" in its detachment. Quinn is a maladaptation of the camp persona and therefore a suitable subject for pathology ... but critics have said the same about Berners and Firbank and Saki too. In her critical study of Firbank,[83] Brigid Brophy notes his famous shyness (but not the paradox), "He was incapable of intimacy," and forges a psychoanalysis of his art. In keeping with camp at least, Ifan Kyrle Fletcher manages at once to pathologize and romanticize his detachment: "Like the Sleeping Beauty, he lived in a shadowy haven of retreat, secure from the world behind an impenetrable barrier of briars."[84]

Mark Amory[85] depicts Lord Berners "as though he was engaged in keeping life at arm's length," prompting speculation that Berners was "wounded" early in life. J.W. Lambert on Saki: "A basic detachment informs all his best writing as well as what little is known of him as a man: detachment possibly formed in early childhood as a defense against his sister's emotional cannibalism, and which made it impossible for him to form a close bond with another human being."[86] The fatalistic tone of Bennett and Crisp buffers society's shocking decline in decorum and sensitivity. Deft in the art of detachment in demeanor and literature, Crisp himself says, "Aloofness is the posture of self-defense." Crisp remained aloof even from misanthropy, though it tempts his observations in a bullying society. He also says, "Romance is that enchantment that distance lends to things...."[87]

Max Beerbohm credits the philosophical development of aloof disposition to the highest spire in higher education: Oxford, "that playful and caressing suavity of manner which comes of a conviction that nothing matters, except ideas, and that not even ideas are worth dying for...."[88] This passage, written three years before World War I, values witnessing consciousness, not will-power; such narratives are not plot-driven. The aloof and dandy Duke in *Zuleika Dobson* falls in love quite out of character, "For in him the dandiacal temper had been absolute hitherto, quite untainted and unruffled." But here Beerbohm characterizes distance from the outside world as egoistic. Profiles of the aloof temperament are often ambivalent, and the nature of the temperament itself is noncommittal — engaged enough to weave a narrative yet detached enough to observe and dissociate.

There is surely an insulating value in aloof aesthetics, a buffer against banality and trauma, but commentators who pathologize the pose as defensive and post-traumatic curtail an assessment of the author's art: their investigations into the cultural effects of mannered distance go no further, taking the psychoanalytic view that formative childhood is the last word in (arrested) development. They ignore those philosophic realities revealed by ironic distance. So does Dorian Gray: when he aspires "to escape the suffering of life," he means to disown the consequences of his actions, which undermines his capacity for reflection.

Edouard Roditi[89] distinguishes Dorian Gray's corruption, which he defines as egoistic absorption, from Lord Henry Wotton's "philosophy of inaction: beyond good and evil." Lord Wotton's and Wilde's paradoxes "only illustrate the Taoist identity of contraries where both conscience and temptation are placed on the same footing but then transcended." Roditi concludes, "Lord Henry never acts and never falls." (The expedient actions of Dorian Gray drive events for the sake of a plot to appease genre conventions.) It could follow that Lord Wotton never risks or invests in life and his aloof poise insulates him from consequence, the criticism that "Your cynicism is simply a pose." But camp performance is never so paralysed or mean-spirited in its larger than life perspective. Lord Wotton's revelation of Naturalism as another pose merits a reconsideration of "surface" aesthetics.

Wilde gives a minor character, Mrs. Erskine, a major epigram:

> "Well, the way of paradoxes is the way of truth. To test Reality we must see it on the tight-rope. When the Verities become acrobats we can judge them."[90]

Whimsical, yet the poise in the statement is never unbalanced by bias, under no obligation to seriousness, politics or morality.

In the drawing-rooms of Wilde's plays and tales, the divan symbolizes the detached equilibrium of ennui and the poise of the paradox, aloof from bias and pleasingly symmetrical, a philosophical touchstone for Wilde's ensembles, that is, a matter of style. "Lord Arthur Savile's Crime": "After breakfast, he flung himself down on a divan and lit a cigarette."[91] The protagonist of *The Model Millionaire* "found himself a comfortable seat on a divan" within two pages of Wilde's short story. "A delightful, ineffectual young man with a perfect profile and no profession," an effeminate in a masculine world, like Quentin Crisp he makes a virtue of uselessness.[92] He entertains the whimsy of modeling as the most natural and artificial expression of style over content and being as performance ... like the acrobatic analogy of Mrs. Erskine's paradox, whose poise stays aloof from the gravitational pull of opinion and, frivolously, from gravitas, an aesthetic assurance of vision unblemished by egoistic interest. This is the virtue of incongruous juxtaposition, whose contrasts defy gravitas. In Wilde's world,

> Gorgeous peeresses chatted affably to violent Radicals, popular preachers brushed coat-tails with eminent skeptics, a perfect bevy of bishops kept following a stout prima-donna from room to room, on the staircase stood several Royal Academicians, disguised as artists, and it was said that at one time the supper-room was absolutely crammed with geniuses.[93]

Wilde's ecclesiastical camp borders on Bunuel with a bevy of bishops in pursuit of a portly prima-donna. Even Royal Academicians and the orthodox culture of clever disguise is unmasked with beautiful irony in this tongue cheek tour de force masquerade.

For all his frivolity, Oscar Wilde is a classic example of intellectual camp, not weighted by ideology, unpossessive in its lateral concentration. His intellectualism is tongue in cheek, picturesque, lush, fanciful. Follow the sweeping strokes of Romanticism, the ivy art nouveau and profligate alliteration as Lord Henry muses:

He played with the idea, and grew wilful; tossed it into the air and transformed it; let it escape and recaptured it; made it iridescent with fancy, and
winged it with paradox.[94]

Philosophy is feminized as a whimsical nymph: "Facts fled before her
like frightened forest things." Poetic license would never sanction the decadent personification of Philosophy as a nymph soused with wine, nor pass
the excessive alliteration, though it makes elegiac sense to me. Camp gives
the writer carte blanche to flout convention. Indeed, it is obligatory.

Over a century after Wilde, Will Self wrote *Dorian* and ushered the
cinematic convention of the remake into literature. Self updated the characters and themes of *The Picture of Dorian Gray*, and their intriguing stylistic differences illuminate the camp aesthetic. *Dorian* questions whether
camp can address life in contemporary society with any significance. Self
references Wilde's blueprint and makes camp of the anachronistic
reflections, but his prose is more direct and realist and vulgar than Wilde
would countenance. Wilde keeps his distance but Self is partisan in prose
whose every sentence is the last word on the subject. Wilde's angular takes
were expedient in a society that outlawed homosexuality, whereas Self is
brazen about buggery; a permissive age renders lewd *double entendres*
redundant. Self does not leave ambiguity ambiguous. "Helen was so fucking tired she didn't notice the anachronism that was Dorian."[95]

Self preserves the camp persona of Henry Wotton, "supremely mannered," but in defining his traits so elementally his style assumes none of
the camp of the character:

A collector of *bons mots* and aperçus and apophthegms, an alfresco rehearser
of the next impassioned, extempore rodomontade, whose greatest fear in life
was inarticulacy, or worse, *esprit de l'escalier*. Henry Wotton might have pro-
fessed an indifference about his position in society, but in truth, like all those
who have ascended too high and too fast, he had failed to acclimatize, so he
grasped desperately for the next inspirational acknowledgement that he existed
at all.[96]

Self pulls back the curtain of Wotton's act to reveal an existential motivation — altogether too clinical and judgemental for camp — and in the process,
"in truth," imputes the camp demeanor as fraudulent. Self does not fashion
the ironic inflection between masquerade and the actor. The rhetoric is
straight-ahead, without Wilde's kinks. Still, in this passage, you hear the author
rolling exotic syllables and a soupçon on his tongue like mulled and rather
fruity wine: "*aperçus* and apophthegms ... extempore rodomontade...." Self
perceives the camp constituents of the character, his lofty manner, stylized
theatricality, verbal showmanship and his apparent indifference in this passage that glitters with esoteric touches like the obligatory French term.

Self fashions his epigrams after Wilde — "We are in an age when appearances matter more and more. Only the shallowest of people won't judge by them"[97] — but while Wilde fashioned persona and lifestyle as art, Self deconstructs those presentations and finds sophistry and nihilism. Masquerade is not artistic and radical but insidiously colluding in the corruption and emptiness of mainstream culture. Let's compare the motif of cigarette smoking, art nouveau and effete in its wispy dissipation over the heads of drawing-room conversationalists, in *The Picture of Dorian Gray* and *Dorian*. First, survey the context. The cigarette is a popular performance accessory to the aloof poise of the camp perspective. As camp rises above dogma, the cigarette (from the poise in the wrist to the ethereal firmament of smoky curlicues) exudes that meditative detachment, a leveler of frivolity and high seriousness. Firbank writes in *The Flower Beneath the Foot,* "Musingly he lit a cigarette. Through the open window a bee droned in on the blue air of evening. Closing his eyes he fell to considering whether the bee of one country would understand the remarks of that of another."[98]

Harold Nicolson wrote a fictionalized portrait of Firbank, recalling the man as if indeed he were an imaginative invention — which indeed, like Quentin Crisp, perhaps he was. Beside his grandstanding diction and famous undulating gait, "He held his cigarette between the index and the middle fingers, keeping them outstretched together with the gesture of a male impersonator puffing at a cigar."[99] This theatrical prop was a very male signifier at the time: Firbank is performing "maleness" in a way that highlights the construct as artificial, just as Nicolson says. He could glory in the paradox that in the male appropriation of smoking, the cigarette, like the fan, is an ephemeral accessory to the feminine dexterity of the wrist. To Max Beerbohm, it signals unparalleled poise: "In the art of taking and lighting a cigarette, there was one man who had no rival in Europe."[100] Saki stages the sharing of a cigarette as grandstanding self-sacrifice in *The Unbearable Bassington;* and in *When William Came,* we indulge the suspended moment of a dandy enjoying a smoke, "whose soul for the moment seemed to be in his cigarette."[101] When someone asks if there are any objections to smoking in *The Watched Pot,* a senior camp character makes the association between smoking and not-doing: "Not in the least. I like seeing people idle when I'm occupied. It gives me the impression that I'm working so much harder than I am."[102] His camp protégé in the play is René, whose key stage props are the mirror and the cigarette.

In Mr. *Norris Changes* Trains, Christopher Isherwood signals his camp protagonist with the camp accessory: "He puffed at his cigarette with exaggerated nonchalance,"[103] an accessory to equanimity, an attitude itself made aesthetic by camp. John van Druten's adaptation, *I Am a Camera,* extends the accessory as Sally Bowles takes a smoke: "Do you ever smoke any of Fritz's cigarettes? [*Takes holder from her handbag, fits cigarette into it and lights it.*] They're absolutely devastating. I'm sure they're full of opium or something. They always make me feel terribly sensual."[104]

The opium cigarette has exotic *fin de siècle* associations with Decadence, imbibed on a divan by Kate Chopin's protagonist in "An Egyptian Cigarette" (1900). Another female author of the Decadent period, George Egerton, lights a cigarette for her assertive female protagonist in her short story "A Cross Line" (1893). With theatrical whimsy, with her lover, "She smokes and watches him, diverting herself by imagining him in the hats of different periods." The cigarette offers a reflective release from the corruption of conviction (which leans on truth with vested interest), "a cigarette poised between the first and second fingers, idly pleased with its beauty of form and delicate slightness. One speculation chases the other in her quick brain; odd questions as to race arise; she dives into theories as to the why and wherefore of their distinctive natures, and holds a mental debate in which she takes both sides of the question impartially."[105] Cigarettes dissipate the narratives of persuasion and motivation; smoke drifts and trails its freethinking metaphor over the positions of the players.

Ed Wood also lit this iconic accessory to dégagé sophistication. He often tried to capture its smoky charisma on the page. The death-row convict in *Death of a Transvestite* smokes a last cigarette as he responds to a ridiculous enquiry about his evening. "He let the smoke drift up around his head. 'Want me to say fine, the hotel service is great?'"[106] Glen performs his death scene in drag: "She took the burning cigarette from her lips and her eyes grew bright at seeing the smear of fresh lipstick on the end. Such a small thing, but so powerful in its meaning during the last few minutes." Wood was never one to let symbolism speak for itself. Characters let smoke drift around their heads and reach for that ethereal blasé disposition, like Adam on a divan, but not so Michelangelo in the hands of Ed Wood. Accompanying dialogue and narrative is heavier than smoke. A pornographic actor named Studd in *Hell Chicks* is entirely complacent about his sexual endurance: "Studd let the smoke drift up around his head in a great grey cloud and his overtly confident grin matched his words. 'You ready for another go, leader broad?'"[107] This American pulp caricature feels a long way from Wilde's brand of camp, but both authors make a camp motif of the cigarette.

Oscar Wilde presents a blasé first impression of Lord Wotton, "From the corner of the divan of Persian saddle-bags on which he was lying, smoking, as was his custom, innumerable cigarettes...." trailing a decadent paradox:—"A cigarette is the perfect type of pleasure. It is exquisite, and it leaves one unsatisfied. What more can one want?" The answer is implicit in the smoking experience, "More of the same." A fully satisfying experience would leave us burned out, unable to indulge desire again, but while the cigarette is fulfilling in the ephemeral yet eternal moment, its embers burn out before it can satiate or anticipate the next instant. Victoria Cross relates pure pleasure to aesthetics in the decadent indulgence of the moment in "Theodora: A Fragment" (1895). Late in Wilde's tale, signaling Dorian Gray's moral and aesthetic decline as he loses his poise, displaced, exiled from the moment, "he lit a cigarette and then threw it away."[108] So it is understandable when, in *The Importance of Being Earnest,* Jack is put out at the loss of his cigarette case, "I have been writing frantic letters to Scotland Yard about it."[109]

Exploding the character's poise, Will Self subverts the camp motif with a public health warning — "'Gaaa...! Christ — Christ!' Wotton fought for breath while lighting an outsize filterless Virginia cigarette."—followed by a stark revelation of uncouth realities behind the marketing image of Turkish State Monopoly cigarettes: "'the most morally costly tobacco in the world. Every time you light one up — a Kurd dies.'" Symbols are a sign of the times in Self's political vision. The slow motion of smoking breaks the causal chain of time and plot in the camp aesthetic to fathom eternity in the defining, inert moment. When Wilde's characters light up, plot is the last thing on their minds. To Self, smoking symbolizes creeping karmic consequences of time and corruption. Smoking is a cancerous symbol of social, moral and physical dissolution. He spells out the cost of decadence, dispensing with allusion, "He paused, groping for his cigarettes '... I shall be compelled by ennui to kill another Kurd.'"[110] Wilde's Wotton would never "grope," and the blunt politics seems stark to the camp aesthetic, though contrast of leisurely ennui with suffering is deliciously decadent. Ironic tension stresses our enjoyment of the contrast at the expense of a harsh political reality, a rare and modern instance of kinky camp in Self's novel, even as Self satirizes the amoral aesthete.

In an age where image matters most Self summons a different aesthetic. He takes a Wilde exemplar of urbanity and evicts him from his drawing-room, depicting his anachronistic and vulnerable state — diminished by realism — in the cruelty and banality of the outside world where Wilde's characters ventured so rarely. The disillusioned narrative no longer believes in the integrity of image, and nor does its emblematic character Wotton: "Style — the very word could trigger the telling of another hundred decades on his internal rosary of contempt." This is a society where political representation, the news media and the economy have converged in centralized collusion, the antithesis of Wilde's ideal in "The Soul of Man Under Socialism." Truth, which Wilde found in the surface of the stylized image, is spin-doctored in modern politics and commerce. Narcissism is no longer outrageous or arty but a respectable consumer motivator manipulated by marketing. Multiple images of the video installation of the new Dorian Gray highlight the cult of celebrity that has demeaned Oscar Wilde's ideal of the art of self. With a heavier hand than Wilde's feminine finesse, Will Self hones a confrontational style for the 21st century to face the uncouth consequences of such a commercial and vacuous fabrication of meaning. Irony is too close to sophistry to serve his social purpose. As Wilde has been absorbed into classic literature, *Dorian* is counterculture; Self is challenging mainstream representation to expose its consequences, ruthlessly.

In Wilde's day, camp reveled in artifice. A century on, politics and commerce sell the façade as reality and "backstage" is off-limits. Now, surface and image is projected as depth, manufactured sincerity. Surface aesthetics cultivates the view from the wings to show life is play and depth is nothing but a backdrop: camp unmasks the symbol to expose seriousness and the cult of meaning as a sham. The unconvincing inadequacy of manufactured meaning leaves us impoverished and needy of more convincing delusions, but camp keeps aloof from the search, content to present the masquerade of all such representations of "reality" and "being" in quotation marks. Orthodox aesthetics of disguise, the culture of guile, the academic ethos of seriousness, is implicated in the meaningless charade of the manipulated image, the 20th century corruption of artifice.

Wilde's surface aesthetic is not the modern commercial and political manipulation of image. Camp and Wilde flee the democratic dogma of the common denominator with flourishes of theater and fancy. Wilde, and camp, is reflective, witnessing and revealing as well as fashioning the process. Modern "spin" masks the insidious manipulation, deterring skepticism by anaesthetizing awareness. From the subliminal message to the hard-sell and the showbusiness of broadcast news, media projections strive to convince, while Wilde's paradoxes bamboozle conviction, and there is parody in his irony. The epigrammatic *bon mot* has become the soundbite; the paradox is now the Lie. Modern projections of surface — in journalism, advertizing, corporate identity, in mainstream culture altogether, and especially politics — depend on loyal commitment to the Lie, aided, profoundly, by seriousness. Integrity is measured by dedication to the Lie. Wilde's transparent and frivolous manipulation of the Art of Lying is treacherous to the great Lie that is modern politics and media management. Camp can expose the Emperor's New Clothes in a *double entendre.* Ironic, isn't it, given the apolitical aesthetic and its surface gloss: in the revelation of artifice, at the click of a finger, camp now carries the subversive potential to expose a society driven, as in a state of mass hypnosis and diminished responsibility, by image.

Ronald Firbank (1886–1926)

"But never forget this, dear, I will walk with you
to the last under the same parasol."
—*The Artificial Princess,* posthumous, 1934

After the demise of Oscar Wilde, Ronald Firbank took his pen and picked up the legacy of literary camp ... and dropped it. Camp was heavy with aesthetic rumination after Wilde, so Firbank took Wilde at his word and made camp all surface and symbol. While E.F. Benson did write the occasional serious novel (though it didn't take) Firbank remained faithfully frivolous.

Ifan Kyrle Fletcher remembers Firbank's esoteric personality: "While others thought of vice and virtue, he was concerned about vulgarity and elegance. There are so few people in the world who will not read a book because its cover is ugly, and who build up friendships on the nicest subtleties of unspoken intimacies. And in the end, morality and immorality are both just a little tedious." In correspondence, Firbank passes judgment on his latest publication, though we can only assume he was satisfied with the actual writing: "The 'crocodile paper' would be very effective with a dull silver label edged with blue—turquoise—and palm or emerald green top. The silver should be quite dead, almost oxydized and subservient to the gold—and in any case the blue border would relieve a too sharp contrast."[1] I recall the childhood library of Lord Berners or Lord Henry's library in the *Picture of Dorian Gray,* where décor effaces the book titles. And so too, under the spell of ennui, Lady Agnes judges a book by its cover in "A Study In Temperament": "She got up and went to a little table covered with books, and picked up a small volume bound in grey. 'A touch of grey will improve my dress....'"[2] Still, Firbank plants "one of Materlinck's plays" according to his own Decadent taste, just as Wilde planted Huysmans in *The Picture of Dorian Gray.*

Formatively influenced by Wilde — his early play *The Mauve Tower*
doffs its plumed hat to *Salome* — yet Firbank had no inclination to intellectualize camp. He demonstrated a flair for flamboyance without ever
expounding camp aesthetics, with less regard for plot and depth than Wilde
and less egoism in his writing. His own characters disparage his work, "'But
this Ronald Firbank I can't take to at all. *Valmouth!* Was there ever a novel
more coarse. I assure you I hadn't gone very far when I had to put it down.'"[3]
(In Max Beerbohm's novel, the Duke highlights the artifice of his author's
dialogue, specifically, "the literary flavor" of Zuleika Dobson's speech. She
responds, "'Ah, that is an unfortunate trick which I caught from a writer,
a Mr. Beerbohm, who once sat next to me at dinner somewhere.'"[4])

The New Statesman (3 March 1923) reviewed *The Flower Beneath the
Foot*, "A fantasy of fluttering, delicate, drooping creatures who have scarcely
strength to finish their sentences or drop on to a convenient throne." The
book was inspired by the characters, or at least the phrases, "Her Dreaminess, the Queen" and "His Weariness, the Prince," and before long we read,
"She found her sovereign supine on a couch piled with long Tunisian cushions." So *supine* that the word reclines on *her sovereign* without an attendant verb. His Weariness the Prince "murmured in a voice extinct with
boredom," while "The English Ambassadress plied her fan," and even more
royally steeped in ennui, "Miss Montgomery took a deep-drawn breath of
languor." The landscape too conspires to detain the narrative as description captures the moment in its glorious inconsequence, unmoved by the
manipulation of textbook cause-effect that plots novels.

> The bitter odor of the oleander flowers outside oppressed the breathless air
> and filled the room as with a faint funereal music. So still a day. Tending the
> drooping sun-saturated flowers, a gardener with long ivory arms alone seemed
> animate.[5]

And seeming animation is merely a trick of the floral background. This
was the ennui that sighed over the *fin de siècle* generation but now without
Wilde's ideological structure to underpin its reclining pose — and frankly,
The New Statesman was tired of it by 1923.

The Times Literary Supplement (21 March 1929) reviewed its attitude
on Firbank and decided, "A golden tongue is worthless to the man who has
nothing to say." Many a preening skylark would disagree. Camp disinclination to enquiry and argument is what we call flippant or frivolous. Firbank would gladly accept the adjectives but fail to note them as pejorative.
Brophy describes Firbank's writing as "pioneering backwards," reviving
18th century aesthetics as Wilde did at his best.[6] Let's call him a recidivist
revisionist.

His lightness and baroque embellishments makes a gendered contrast with the intensity of D.H. Lawrence. Lawrence is keen to get his fingers dirty and dig deep into fecund forbidden territory, at his most poetic when he's lusty. Short story "Lady Appledore's Mesalliance," from Firbank's juvenilia, is the nearest that camp gets to *Lady Chatterley's Lover.* Firbank got there first but left no tracks across the garden. Lady Chatterley's gardener in Lawrence's tale, written two years after Firbank's death, summons earthy animal passion, the stuff of life girdled in his loins, transgressing taboos of class and sexuality. *Lady Appledore's* gardener evokes flowers. "He dreamt of peach stones, and a lady with a lace parasol, whose face he could not see." He feels "languid" and speaks French, hardly Lady Chatterley's "bit of rough." Lady Appledore's gardener is actually an aristocrat in disguise, and so as they fall in love, no social taboo is transgressed, and anyway, before the implicit romance gets explicit, the gardener leaves.

> "My dear lady," he said, "I am sorry to have to leave you. I have been so happy at Wiston, I am afraid I shall never be as happy again, unless—" he broke off— "Oh promise to write and tell me all about the herbaceous borders, and whether old Bartholomew succeeds in inventing a grey Geranium!"[7]

In an anecdotal coda to this gentle satire on heterosexual romance, with a token gesture to sentimental expectations and the reduction of plot to gossip, we find out they did marry.

His style is just as contrary to the diligent, flattened, and doctrinaire writing of George Orwell that would ration the tone and tighten the structure a generation and a world war after Firbank. As World War I raged, Firbank wrote *Caprice,* where an actress visits "the most histrionic couple in the land" to audition at a reading: "Miss Sinquier lodged a complaint.

> "How can I when I don't know the plot?"
> "What does it matter — the plot?"[8]

A chorus of camp writers would cheer the sentiment, but many a critic would heckle the narrative. (Jon van Druten dismisses the fixation on plots that resisted staging his play *I Am a Camera,* which was criticized as "plotless." In the "Notes to Producers" he says, "I have done my best work always without them.")

In his biographical portrait, Fletcher[9] describes Firbank in picturesque conversation, but it just as easily applies to Firbank as narrator: "He seldom directed the conversation, but added to its piquancy by a well-timed anecdote. Frequently his stories were unfinished." In his conversational writing style, he often lost the plot behind the baroquery, and whenever it had the temerity to return, the plot became the digression. Fletcher cites a bookseller in Charing Cross Road who remembers Firbank as a customer.

As the bookseller talks of Firbank, it occurs to me that the loose narrative structure of his work is physiologically indigenous to the man: "All his joints seemed to be loosely attached, like those of a marionette, and his movements in fact closely resembled those of a marionette, the controlling threads of which had been slackened. In short, he was a decidedly limp specimen of mankind." Limp, loose, effete — define it not as lack of masculinity (or the absence of structure in his camp narrative) but a persuasive effeminate way of being and writing. This essential camp aspect would wait another half century to "come out" in literature with the autobiographies of Crisp and with Poems' work such as "The Effeminate." Firbank was not interested in the reflections of Wilde and not ready for the political assertion of Chloe Poems: Firbank simply promenaded his paragraphs like a boulevardier.

Crisp wanted a stylized world "where all speech will be a kind of literature, every movement a form of dance."[10] Firbank's novels come close to the ideal, as far from realism as a daydream.

Brigid Brophy notes that Firbank often wrote his tales in purple ink on blue postcards, surface and color being everything to camp. Brophy reveals that she too wrote her critical biography of the man in purple ink. My working copy of Brophy's book is on loan from Manchester University's library. At this purple confession on page 173, a university student, doubtless heading for ordination — graduation, I mean — has written this response in the margin (in blue ink): "are you really as besotted as *this*? If so, we don't want to know — at least maintain a pretense at objectivity please." This student is schooled in the scientific application of self-effacing objectivity to aesthetics. S/he represents an impressive and pole-faced scholarly assembly, a masculine multitude of mortar boards that is always going to be exasperated and offended by camp.

John Gross[11] echoes the academic dismissal of Firbank in 1969: "The idea of a graduate seminar on Ronald Firbank would be Firbankian." The application of academic gravitas to fathom such a frivolous writer — the test of high seriousness, of analysis and historical comparison and a line of enquiry that presumes a layering of themes and symbology primed for revelation — does seem paradoxical. The omission of a whole genre of literature from the canon follows from such peremptory dismissals. And so Alan Hollinghurst,[12] in his Introduction to Firbank in 2000, regrets the likes of James Joyce and Virginia Woolf "crowd him out of histories of modernism in English." Perhaps academia should lighten its tone, its genre language, its classical frames of reference and its deconstructing analysis that finds merit in depth and guile, to admit a literary remit of flouting the valuation of seriousness, so that we may admire the blithe artistry required to dance on the surface of text for the length of a novel without ever once sinking into profundity. Yet the prose remains reflective.

Even Brigid Brophy used psychoanalytic interpretation to extend her portrayal of Firbank and his work, the least convincing aspect of *Prancing Novelist*. Psychoanalytic technique investigates hidden meaning in the legerdemain of the artful unconscious. Ronald Firbank doesn't have an unconscious. He writes without one. Anthony Powell doesn't find one in Firbank's books: "They are little more than bursts of description and dialogue linked together. There is no shape, no story and only a vague suggestion of character," as far as Powell could see in *Punch* (15 August 1956). His assessment put him on the spot five years later when Powell was asked to write an Introduction for a Firbank anthology. "What then is the point of Ronald Firbank's writing?" he pondered, under some pressure to find one in an aesthetic supremely disinterested in the search. With no content to go on, Powell tentatively affirmed his stylistic technique and, secondly, he proposed, "his daydream is a more popular one than might on the surface be expected."[13] Yet on the surface is where we find it.

Santal reads like a daydream from cover to cover. *The Mauve Tower: A Dream Play in VII Scenes* has the wistful and exotic and fanciful aura of a timeless daydream, lush and ethereal and theatrical in décor and costume and atmosphere and dialogue and stage directions:

All the air smells of roses, and about the trunks of the palm trees cling mysterious-looking orchids. INGRIA *walks as in a dream, her eyes fixed upon the mauve tower, at the foot of the tower she stops. A purple curtain hangs across the door, the curtain is embroidered with sunflowers, prophets, and strange birds.*[14]

The purple curtain on stage, ready to draw back onto another world, makes for a theatrical revelation. A friend of Firbank and the son of Oscar Wilde, Vyvyan Holland[15] finds that Firbank writes "in that nebulous state of mind one is in just before fully regaining consciousness, while the dream still holds one in its spell, and its improbability and absurdity are not yet apparent." It is the creative state of mind before ego, social norms and analysis take hold, the naive sense of wonder that he shares with Berners and Wood and Poems and indeed most camp writers, yet so few adults.

Brigid Brophy[16] finds Firbank in a daydream too, but she allows a psychoanalytic diminution of daydreaming as regressive, a masturbatory fantasy, childish compensation for ineffectual relations. Sigmund Freud, who made a profession out of double entendres, interpreted an underlying meaning behind ulterior intentions, a deeper, unconscious significance in a culture of guile. The psychoanalytic view was preceded by an early 19th century shaming of fiction as "lies." Cultural prejudice against camp was set by the time Firbank came of age. Revision of its merit must depreciate seriousness to let narrative daydreaming rise to the surface. Brophy attributes the author's painterly technique of "isolating a single image in space," an aspect of his "aerated" style, to the line drawings of Aubrey Beardsley. Beardsley framed images by lines or art nouveau motifs, in turn influenced by the isolated images in Japanese prints and Japanese poetry. Again, she notes, incongruous juxtapositions of images space them apart on Firbank's pages. "The image is displayed in its importance during the pause the reader is forced to make as he negotiates its unpredictable relation to the image before it." This dissociation of narrative time and distancing from content, suspending plot to crystallize a moment, a look, a style, reveals the author plying his craft behind the scenes. He sets the scene in *The Flower Beneath the Foot*[17] with a style as momentary (if not as disciplined) as haiku:

> Swans and sunlight. A little fishing boat with coral sails. A lake all grey and green. Beatitude intense. Consummate calm.

Minimal, simplistic as Japanese brush-strokes, yet lush and dreamy: "Beatitude intense" and "Consummate calm" are saturated in luxury and fantasy. Decadent literature indulges stasis and retards plot in stagnation and malaise. In camp — and particularly Firbank — the moment is a blossoming. In a royal procession at the end of the *Flower Beneath the Foot,* a pause becomes eternal as Firbank slows, stops the story to take a photograph, so to speak, a souvenir of his novel.

> In the intense meridian glare the thronged street seemed even as though half-hypnotized; occasionally only the angle of a parasol would change, or some bored soldier's legs would give a little.

Even military masculinity is affected by ennui, becalmed. The dreamy spell is broken by Cathedral bells that could be a Zen call to tea after contemplation.

Bertolt Brecht idealized self-contained scenes, as disdainful as camp of enslavement to plot, and as keen to promote distance from the content and the medium. Any moment can be catalytic and any scene is representative: this became a socialist idea for Brecht. For all Firbank's pageantry of color and costume, he shares an aesthetic effect with Bertolt Brecht without ever considering politics. Firbank's daydreamy tone glosses the surface majestically, poetically. When not concocting hybrid haikus in prose, he indulges lush alliteration and fabulous similes (in purple ink on blue card), in meandering sentences untroubled by any thread of an argument, to ease his whimsical progress. *The Artificial Princess,* unhurried by full stops, trails clauses as capriciously as the riband simile, set up by exclamation and dramatic rhetoric to subside wistfully into picturesque reverie:

Who could have guessed that behind the swaying curtain of the trees, stood the curly wrought-iron gates, with prowling Sentinels in gay plumed hats, and sun-fired swords; while beyond, the white town, with its countless Spires and gold domed Opera House, its Theaters and spacious streets, its Cafes, from whence, sometimes, on still nights, you might hear the sound of violins, trailing capriciously, like a riband, upon the wind.[18]

A rhapsodic refrain, "What an elegant view! What deceptive expanse!" book-ends the passage, but the writing is pleased with its artifice and the exclamations rather congratulatory. Firbank concludes, "So much, contained on so little, suggested a landscape painted delicately upon a porcelain cup or saucer, or upon the silken panel of a fan." The domestic touch that puts a landscape on a cup and saucer is the scope of camp that plays epic grandeur against an incongruous and unassuming backdrop. As prose "bubbled heedlessly" without urgency, indifferent to the rigors of structure, Firbank invites our admiration at his romantic, detached vision of a town as free from banality as a film set. The metaphor that sways a curtain of trees makes theater of nature. Wrought-iron draws the obligatory arabesques of art nouveau, a heritage of his lifelong enthusiasm for the literature of the 1890s. Military masculinity is subverted by gay plumed hats, and the enchanted tone as well as the pretty detail is eminently feminine. The painterly writing isn't looking to engrave tablets of stone, nothing so monumental: painted on a fan will do nicely. The passage encapsulates the ephemeral narrative of his novel, so much, contained in so little, and vice versa.

Firbank skimmed the surface weightlessly throughout his career with agile and flamboyant and meaningless figurative poses like an ice-skater. *The New Rythum* is his final novel, unfinished and posthumously published, the most camp book of his life: all choreography and no plot.

Speeding along in her cosy car, the utter hush of luxury, Mrs. Rosemerchant abandoned herself to reverie.

All a-shimmer in the early dusk, Croton Reservoir surpassed in exuberance the costliest Tiffany tiara, set in the emerald meadows beyond. Calcined against its glitter, she caught the laughing silhouette of Laura Shymoon of the Ziegfield Follies trotting her notorious pink-nosed ponies and, flitting on, glimpsed the purpurine plague of Harlem Mere.[19]

"The utter hush of luxury," effete yet emphatic, sighs and reminds us that ennui can be blissful rather than labored. The dazzling simile that crowns the distant Reservoir bestows on banality a royal patronage that surpasses itself quite unnecessarily. Firbank's style is interchangeably called by critics *baroque* or *rococo*. Baroque is whimsically ornamental and rococo even more wanton in cavalier disregard for structure or consistency, then his prose is baroque, his symbolism is asymmetrical yet not so inconsistent as rococo and his narrative voice more refined.

Never really nightfall and clearly not real, the impressionist dusk of the passage basks in being picturesque: photographically lit, Firbank's arc lamps cast silhouettes and polish water and highlight pinky purples. His writing becomes quite prismatic at dusk, his sensitivity to hues, at least, critically acclaimed. The discernment is particular to female writers, Robin Lakoff has already observed, but Firbank leads those male writers whose effeminate styles preen their attention to color and couture. An extravagant stage direction from *The Mauve Tower*: "*The lake changes to the color of the sky—orange and red,*" and later, "*As the scene progresses the palm trees turn from green to blue, from blue to violet, from violet to black.*"[20] Over fifty years on, Noël Coward is indebted to the same electrician to illuminate his sunset, in "Vista-Vision," in his novel *Pomp and Circumstance,* where the sky changed "from pale yellow to pink, from pink to mauve and from mauve to deep blue as though it were being controlled by an over-enthusiastic chief electrician from some celestial switchboard."[21]

Names like Laura Shymoon in Firbank are always shamelessly emblematic of frivolous characterization, as with friend and author Lord Berners. Exotic and alliterative phrases like "purpurine plague" make decorative sentences bluff the semblance of greater import than their content. Anthony Powell recalls the early ornate style of James Joyce and *A Portrait of the Artist as a Young Man.* Powell overreaches, compensating Firbank's lack of substance, I think, in claiming a foreshadowing of *Finnegans Wake* in *The Flower Beneath the Foot*[22]—but Firbank is as self-consciously poetic and modernist as Chapter One, at least, of *Ulysses,* though never so earnest or loquacious.

"Flitting" and "glimpsed" don't allow *The New Rythum* passage to settle or focus with any gravity. Firbank's elegant glide across the surface requires fleet of foot, not sleight of hand. Distracted by appearances, clauses digress capriciously in peripheral attention to signature detail, easy on the eyeline, seldom laden with premises and conditional structures, extending rather than qualifying with camp inclination to excess.

"There was an intriguing irrelevance, a delightful, fantastic silliness in all he said or did," friend Lord Berners remembers.[23] Firbank testifies to Lord Henry's observation in *The Picture of Dorian Gray,* "'The only difference between a caprice and a lifelong passion is that the caprice lasts a little longer.'"[24] Like Eddy Monteith in *The Flower Beneath the Foot,* "Attached first to one thing and then another, without ever being attached to any,"[25] Firbank's weightless oeuvre compiles caprices, but each morocco-bound fancy remains in print long after the author's last sigh. The narrative sequence of events is ineffectual happenstance, "So the days slipped by quietly as on silver wings,"[26] and consequence — the import of one moment on another that customarily drives plot — is subverted with photographic time lapses for a poetic turn of phrase and a flash of color and a vision of effeminate flamboyance, fleeting yet memorable. A common critical question in writers' classes and groups, nested in priorities of plot and a congregational need for determinism, and impatient for the next narrative event to transform character and advance the story, is, "Where is this going?" Firbank could not hope to satisfy the question, since he was not the least interested in the answer. His compass points not necessarily north but wherever the wind blows.

Every year, Firbank journeyed Europe and the East, and traveled light: his frivolous travels chart no philosophical quest. His flights of fancy enhance his exotic and escapist visions. His novels venture well beyond the English drawing-rooms of Wilde's world, but characters maintain their divan demeanor even on the high seas, insulated from uncouth elements: "'I hope the sea'll be level, dear. I can't endure it rough.'"[27] Alan Hollinghurst notes "a British West Indian idiom cheerfully at odds with the Hispanic society" in *Prancing Nigger*.[28] *Santal* brings decadence to Islam and finds Moslems quite as capable as westerners of "a sardonic sidelong smile." *Santal* bequeaths on a Moslem woman the urbanity and feminine-masculine confluence of camp, at the expense of some authenticity, and into the bargain evokes this sacrilegious juxtaposition of the domestic-fantastic: "'There is nothing to absorb a woman much in the Koran,' Amoucha agreed. 'Given in at Mecca'; 'Handed in at Mecca'; it reminds one, doesn't it, of the Post Office?'"[29]

"Ah, the East...." Firbank sighs in 1924, "I propose to return there, some day, when I write about New York."[30] In *The New Rythum*, finally, he did write about New York, without ever visiting there, eluding any trace of banal realism: and so the first paragraph sets another roving panorama on a "pink and elusive evening" as dreamy as the gleaming never-land we spied in *The Artificial Princess*:

> Zephyrs and Flora caressed New York, yearned above her glimmering parks and gardens, brooded above her budding avenues (awakening young chestnut-leaf and drowsy lilac), rippled that way, this way, all caprice, eventually cutting an elfin caper with the night above the aloof façade of Mr. Harry Rosemerchant's residence on Riverside.[31]

An elfin caper describes the fantastical whimsy of the feminine narrative that blows the breeze over conversational commas, floral highlights and an aloof façade, a camp attention to surface and overview, yet not at all nondescript and god forbid banal. *The Mauve Tower*, emulating *Salome*, is rhapsodic with superlatives and operatic gestures:

LIERIES [*stretching out her arms in ecstasy towards the sun*]: Oh! the sun! the sun! This must be the country of the sun. The blue sea is turning yellow in the sun.[32]

His florid writing comes out in the sun. Firbank moves camp from an actorly to a painterly format. He is fond of the pink and violet refractions of dusk and dawn, but evening is elusive because literal nightfall is merely a metaphorical stage curtain in Firbank's books. Precious stones and saturation of light and color and improvements on nature catch the sun as a performer would seek the spotlight. In fact, Firbank was exempted from active service in World War I due to sunstroke.[33] From "Lady Appledore's Mésalliance":

The sunlight shining through the leaves was so beautiful that it seemed to him that each leaf must be an emerald, and the song of a thrush, just on a bough above, lulled him into entrancing drowsiness.[34]

He flouts the gravitas of darkness, though it catalyses the unconscious in classic literature and lore. The angst-driven metaphor of the dark night of the soul is put to bed with a hot toddy and a fairy tale. Nothing happens in the dark in Firbank's world, but come dawn, "the great round dome of St. Martin's Church looms like a ripe apricot against the sky."[35] Trivial visual images of manicured landscapes are whimsically surreal and resplendent in their iconic form: he powders the sky with *poudre de riz* in *The Artificial Princess* and coifs his misty mountains all the time. E.F. Benson rarely assayed this domestic-fantastic landscape, and when he did he contextualized it, focalized through frivolous characters like Lucia — "The moon rose, like a gelatine lozenge," where that self-conscious comma momentously sets up the whimsical simile tongue in cheek[36]— but Firbank sees the world through these images. Mount Matmata in *Santal*: "Coiffed with clouds, it had the air of some fabulous mosque as it soared amid the sky."[37] Daylight is primordial, the stuff of daydreams, while the colorless night is no more significant than an interval, expedient for pacing and scene-shifting, that's all.

Firbank never shyed away from his shallowness, skimming the ripples in the wake of James Joyce's stream of consciousness. Joyce's celebrated abstractions are the prose exposure of the oblique *un*conscious, dense and obsessive, fashioning poetic associations from parapraxes that would have delighted Freud. Firbank's prose is a shallower lagoon that catches reflections, not depths. The narrative is too tongue in cheek and the characters too narcissistic to be unconscious of their effects, and so a Countess exchanges a glance "known in Court circles as her *tortured-animal* look."[38] Firbank's stream of consciousness encounters "a flash of inconsequent insight" after an ellipsis (ellipses feature in Firbank's style, especially in dialogue, to divert language and make meaning ... drift), and reflects on a precious concession, "what prurient persons might term, perhaps, a 'frolic.'"[39] Clauses murmur on the stream of reflections, dissuaded from coherent argument by commas and semi-colons and dashes and ellipses, eased by alliteration and paced by "ex-cathedra" exotica, with a fluency and style that doesn't relate to the likes of Lawrence or Orwell but will bear comparison to a more intellectual writer when we read Goytisolo.

Brigid Brophy[40] describes the ellipsis as ventilation in Firbank's "aerated" style. She suggests that his peppering of exclamations was inspired by the look of notes on the page in musical notation. Siegfried Sassoon recalled Firbank's facile conversation about style, his whimsical adoration of italics, in Part One, you remember. "Development ... of white space" suspends his images in narrative time for contemplation, Brophy is saying, not abstract but graphic. It's a beautiful observation. It enhances the poetic nature of his style, the design of space in his prose sometimes akin to poetic verse on the page. There is more whimsical graphic design in his celebrated dialogue —

"..........?"
"..........!" (*The Flower Beneath the Foot*[41])

Every dot of that style can be loaded like bullets for critics who deride the aesthetic as insubstantial. It's certainly facile. These surface aesthetics recall Oscar Wilde beginning a new book with the jacket design, and Quentin Crisp as book jacket designer before he became a writer — before he wrote a book on window-dressing. Firbank embodies a paradox that would have amused Wilde, minimalism in an aesthetic famed for excess. You wouldn't guess it from his flamboyance, but Firbank pruned his prose like roses.

Crisp has a simpler explanation for camp antipathy to plot: the camp antipathy to the work ethic. Writing books is harder than painting, he laments, because narrative proceeds in time, not space:

> For an artist to be able to appreciate the difficulties that beset authors, he would have to imagine designing a mural that continued from one room to another. Then he would be forever running from the end of his frieze to the beginning and back again to make sure that all the details contributed in the right measure to the final effect.[42]

Firbank disperses his aerated narrative in space instead. Perhaps those painterly visions that suspend time in text are borne of sheer, glorious lethargy; any relation to the philosophical Bigger Picture is purely incidental. This is, anyway, one reason why Poems writes poems and, if pushed, a short story and a play or two, rather than tomes, and it may explain why Wilde specialized in epigrams and not explanations. For another paradox, compare Firbank's rejection of banality with his bland dialogue; another fantastic juxtaposition resolves all that, the graphic presentation of droll dialogue in striking patterns of type and space, and too the creative incoherence of narrative that tunes in and out of reported speech whimsically.

Firbank's conversations are sometimes a polyphony of interruptions that break the linear structure of the novel and simulate simultaneity ... but the content is gossip. Punctuated by silence, incoherence, and deleted expletives, conversations occasionally read like transcripts from an eavesdropping microphone on a roving boom. Emulated in Brophy's fiction, Firbank is acclaimed for reproducing in speech the socialized aspects of stream of consciousness that James Joyce confined to introspection. He makes interior monologue come out in conversation, for sometimes exchanges are actually overlapping monologues, particularly in *The Flower Beneath the Foot*. Hollinghurst[43] recognizes Firbank's fashioning of "the shape of thoughts, the frail chains of ideas, the easy distractions of the suggestive mind," and although Hollinghurst particularly credits dialogue and focalization, I find this stream of consciousness most fluent in pentimento traces of the author's hand in third person narrative, such as the landscaping and lighting that we have already seen, improvizing his whimsical associations.

Take the sadomasochism that Joyce fashions between Bloom and Bella/Bello, the ringmistress in the most camp scene in *Ulysses*. Joyce exploits the dark intensity of taboo sexuality through the sadomasochistic (and highly camp) symbolism of horse-riding. Juxtaposition of the sweating animal bound and slaving under its elegant rider, who sits arrogantly controlling its exertions, is extreme subversion of masculine supremacy, as well as brazen innuendo of the pumping phallic symbol between the rider's legs. Freud used the equestrian analogy to recommend a dominant superego (rider) over the id,[44] as Jung likened horse and rider to higher consciousness and shadow.[45] Camp flaunts the irony that the rider, seemingly aloof and suppressing the animal's basic impulses, herself indulges the lusty decadence that Freud associated with the uncivilized id. In a society parade in *The Flower Beneath the Foot*,

> a "*screen artiste,*" on an Arab mare with powdered withers and eyes made up with kohl, was creating a sensation. Every time she used her whip the powder rose in clouds.[46]

(The actress reappears in her riding outfit at a party in *The Artificial Princess,* with a feather boa this time.) This camp and kinky and Beardsleyesque exhibition of feminine dominance over the masculine beast—

whipping as spectacle, powder puffing under each slap, the horse flaunted by the whip-handed actress as a fetish accessory, effeminized with her cosmetics — is frivolously free of the dark and guilty psyche of Joyce's sadomasochism.

James Joyce's stream of murmuring consciousness is as introvert as a Catholic confession, in prose driven by compulsion. Firbank's camp so postures its own reflection that there seems no unconscious for the critic to uncover — which many a critic cannot forgive. Brigid Brophy[47] cites *Vainglory*—

> Lady Barrow lolled languidly in her mouse-eaten library, a volume of medieval Tortures (with plates) propped up against her knee. In fancy, her husband was well pinned down and imploring for mercy at Figure 3.

— as an example of Firbank's sadomasochism, and so it is, but the Lady's leisurely domination, and unspeakable torture made innocuous by "Figure 3" with camp's ubiquitous use of "languid," beside the cavalier subversion of gender hierarchy, makes flippant camp of sadism and suffering. Sade, I maintain, is too lusty in his quest for such a feather-light touch of the quill. Concentration never dwells for more than a wry smile, and although teasing suggestions of flagellation recur in Firbank, they sting like a butterfly. Yet the striking image of the actress in procession, whipping the powder off her mount sensationally, sets itself indelibly on the page suspended from narrative time (compelling another citation from Brophy).

On the subject of browsing books — and sadomasochism — having browsed the libraries of Firbank and Wilde and Berners, here is Amanda McKittrick Ros and her character's recommendation in *Helen Huddleston*: "'Have you read *Barney Bloater, K.C.* by this eminent Author? She writes chiefly about lawyers, whipping them severely with the lash of truth, never ceasing to thrash them with the force of its thong....'"[48] Lustier than Firbank's flagellation, I fancy, but thanks to inadvertent irony more camp than Sade.

In *The Flower Beneath the Foot*, there is kinky innuendo in equestrian symbolism so theatrically presented. When a smitten lady desires to dance to the click of a rider's spurs, the preening gesture in the mirror that accompanies an aloof reply is a classic camp accessory to understatement:

> "You'd not be the first to, dear darling!" Mademoiselle de Lambese replied, adjusting her short shock of hair before a glass.[49]

Pause a moment before the mirror to underscore our observations of the self-image. Firbank catches the distance in the reflection of narcissism so ascribed to femininity. The woman's adjustment in the mirror, the consciousness that notices and "edits" the self-image, is as attentive and detached as an artist: she is model and sculptress both. Firbank her rejoinder synchronizes with her preening to catch the detachment in the *gestus,* as Bertolt Brecht would have it, the gist and gesture, the performance and the sub-text, which gives irony to both the throwaway remark and the gesture. This effeminate style of the character and the narrative diversifies the intensity of masculine energy just as Firbank dissipates the obsessive intensity of Joyce's idea of stream of consciousness. It seems to identify one meaning while subverting it with another, which is not possible without an aloof perspective. Again: aloof disposition is the measure of detachment required by irony to transcend singular focus and singular meaning. Camp can be aloof because this effeminate divergence removes itself from the force and friction of polarities, above the dynamic of opposition and contrast, much as Mademoiselle de Lambese oversees her mirror-image.

A tongue in cheek aside in *Santal,* punctuated by sighing commas, subverts the masculine notion of the hero astride his horse, so dominant in Romanticism, so lionized in Tennyson, so effeminate in Firbank: "And after riding many a day (sometimes sideways, to vary, however slightly, the tedium of his saddle)..." though Firbank himself was an accomplished rider.[50]

Reading is usually gloriously prurient in camp, and in *The Flower Beneath the Foot* the Queen reads about the society of Sodom and Gomorrah only that men rode side-saddle while women rode astride — which does suggest something about gender roles. A Prince recalls a splendid yet "sinister impression" of a Princess, as indelible as Jane Eyre's first impression of Rochester: out riding with the hounds, a huntress with a kinky detail of a man's felt-hat, her riding habit torn and her face smeared with fox blood.[51] Riding enforces masculine portrayals of women in camp, dramatically. In *The Princess Zoubaroff,* a Firbank play, the Princess enters "*glowing*" after "*a heavenly ride,*" wearing a riding habit and, "*In lieu of a riding crop, she holds a fan.*"[52] Whimsically kinky in its unlikely sadistic symbolism, adding a sting to the customary feminine accessory. Anticipated and overshadowed by Wilde's prolific bourgeois camp, without his intellectual perspicacity but with greater poetic fluency, Firbank could only take the motifs to excess. Wilde's Mrs. Cheveley strong-arms her victim with the touch of her fan in *An Ideal Husband,* so Firbank's Princess wields her fan like a riding crop. Lady Windermere's name adorns her fan, but a Firbank duchess is discovered in conversation, spreading the flamboyant wing-span of an ostrich fan.[53] Not to be outdone by associations of character with portraiture in *An Ideal Husband,* in *Lady Appledore's Mésalliance* we find "a small woman, faultlessly dressed in a linen gown by Worth, her pyramid of bright red hair was an exact match of the Water Naiad's in Henner's picture at the Luxembourg."[54]

Brophy deduces that Firbank learned from painting "the subordinate importance of subject-matter. Indeed a work's design can be its own subject-matter."[55] The same could be said for the self. In *The Flower Beneath the Foot,* Eddy Monteith contemplates his latest caprice, to join a Jesuit monastery: his first commitment to this new persona is his redefinition by portraiture. "Indeed he had already gone so far as to sit for an artist for his portrait in the habit of a monk, gazing ardently at what looked to be the Escurial itself, but in reality was nothing other than an 'impression' from the kitchen garden of Intriguer Park."[56] Already going "so far as to sit for a portrait" is whimsy: the gesture is as close to monastic transformation as he gets; and the exotic, immaculate conception of his pose is disrobed by the domestic detail that we find beside the fantastic in camp.

In *Concerning the Eccentricities of Cardinal Pirelli,* Count Cuenca is left unstrung by a woman "in a hat edged with white and yellow water-lilies."[57] So effete, his temperament is rattled by a camp hat, or else the hat is so ostentatious that it can make a man "a mass of foolish nerves," extremes of cause-effect pull both ways. Firbank is most ostentatious in his fanciful feminine costume designs, the emblem of narcissism, transfixing many a mirror gaze: "Garmented charmingly in a cornflower-blue frock with a black gauze turban trimmed with a forest of tinted leaves, she lingered, uplifted by her appearance, before the glass."[58] Like masquerade, camp dress sense transcends banality fantastically. Costume gives poetic prose a free and flourishing hand with designs like baroque architecture: a gown of

> kingfisher-tinted silk turning to turquoise, and stencilled in purple at the arms and neck with a crisp Greek-key design; while a voluminous violet veil, depending behind her to a point, half-concealed a tricorne turquoise toque from which arose a shaded lilac aigrette branching several ways.[59]

Layering sumptuous detail, the author admires his subjects and thereby admires his own style: the easy fluency of glib conversation but the pomp and contrivance of a royal investiture. Luxuriant prose wears phrases like costume accessories to match the flamboyant designs, as alliteration saturates the page. The palette of his rich coloring and his poetic syllables is deliciously sensual: succulent on the tongue and opulent before the mind's eye. Roll the syllables around on the palette like a mulled and rather fruity wine, which tends to provoke a wry smile. The subject is merely the bouquet. "Voluminous violet veil" and "a tricorne turquoise toque" tease the tongue deliciously ... tease, too, the principled restraint of orthodox aesthetics, which expects the point of the sentence (the argument or plot or character advancement) to lead the poeticism.

"Humming airily, she conceived a few fanciful designs, surpassing

Nature boldly in improvising venturesome festoons and falling streamers,"
in his last novel,[60] reads like the author's self-portrait in full flight with an
effeminate free hand, embellishing banality with flourishes of fancy. Aged
fourteen, Firbank was already dealing in characters who favored artifice
over naturalism: "'Besides the real country bores me so, I am only fond of
the country when I see it on the stage.'"[61] The character exaggerates Firbank's position, not anti-nature but so admiring of its colors and blossoms
that he flatters through imitation and embellishment, with the Decadent
philosophy that art improves upon nature, as theater embellishes social
behavior, so costume embellishes flora and fauna.

Before theater bowed to realism, camp dress code was a wanton accessory to histrionics: "She was looking unreckonably temperamental in a delicate mouseline dress, with a little veil like a sea-net, caught across the
eyes."[62] (The veiled reference to sea nymphs here had so enchanted *fin de
siècle* art.) The woman we read about in *Caprice* in turban trimmed with
tinted leaves is an actress, and her picturesque attire evokes not merely a
role but a whole scene: "The sober turban, no doubt, would suggest to Mrs.
Bromley Macbeth — the forest scene."[63] This fashioning of appearance is an
exposé of the pose as artifice — on stage, in society, in the mirror. The witnessing consciousness is always in the audience — the patron, the reader,
the artist, catching reflections of process. The exposé is revealed by contrived designs and lush eloquence.

Madame Poco is a spy who prepares to expose the corruption of Cardinal Pirelli, while the author recalls a *fin de siècle* camp specialism, the
femme fatale: "Since becoming the courted favorite of the chapter, she had
taken to strutting-and-languishing in private before her mirror, improvising occult dance-steps, semi-sacred in character, modeled on those of Felix
Ganay at white Easter, all in the flowery spring." Supremely narcissistic,
she rehearses the archetypal role that recalls Wilde's play and Beardsley's
illustrations, and she also plays audience to the theater of her mirror image.
Her generous histrionics anticipate Gloria Swanson's cinematic camp in
Sunset Boulevard a generation later: "Finger rigid, she would advance omi-
nously with slow, Salome-like liftings of the knees upon a phantom Cardinal: 'And thus I accuse thee!' or, 'I denounce thee, Don Alvaro, for, etc.'"[64]
Etcetera blithely disclaims the melodrama, in case we were getting involved,
though it is the nearest thing to a plot.

In an obscure one-act Firbank play, "A Discipline from the Country,"
Lady Seafairer remarks of an acquaintance, "One evening she came in from
riding in the sun and fainted. I never saw her look prettier; fainting suited
her. 'Do it again,' I said, 'do it again,' and she did it most beautifully."[65]
(Given the symbolism of riding, the horsewoman's swoon would seem an

ecstatic encore of overindulgence.) Narcissism follows naturally, rather than pathologically, from such reflective consciousness of pose and process. The actress in *Caprice* offers a backstage prayer on opening night: "'O dear God, help me. Hear me, Jesu. Hear me and forgive me and be offended not if what I ask is vain ... soften all hostile hearts and let them love me — adore me!'" Firbank, meanwhile, relishes the grandiose décor of the London theater. Esoteric, French, with fans and fantastic horses and feathers and flowers and precious stones and words unencountered before, details crafted to overwhelm the reader's everyday credulity in baroque prose laden with decadence and fantasy.[66] "Busts of players, busts of poets, busts of peris, interspersed by tall mirrors in gilt-bordered mouldings, smiled on her good day." You may feel such abundance should modestly decline the tall gilt mirrors that amplify the splendor, but that would be the penitent asceticism and exclusive logic and hushed communion of orthodox aesthetics, where less is more. The architecture of the passage enshrines escapism: theaters, like those glorious art deco cinemas of the 1930s, are exhibitionist interiors of the imagination, churches to the dreamer's sense of wonder, showing grander ways of being and dramatizing the human condition as play-acting according to camp. A garden or a drawing-room or a dressing-table or a book presents the same potential to the camp sense of wonder. In fact, costume, flowers and décor are exquisite pretexts for camp writers to preen the plumage of their elegant poetic prose.

From *The New Rythum:*

> Rising here in terraced slopes, nestling there beneath tall clumps of Indian palms and flame Flamboyants, growing in massed profusions everywhere, the brilliant blushing fruit had usurped the finest dance-floor in town.[67]

Even the finest dance-floor in town is swamped by florid detail: *Flame Flamboyants,* the most camp name for lush shrubbery — and this is an interior!

Exotic prose wafts the fey alliteration of "flaunting fan-palms" over a character, where the alliteration of her descent as she takes a seat, spreading over three words, "dropped daintily down," steps gradually out of sight behind all that foliage. The narrative refinement of nature in the fashionable "rhododendrons of a quite new and amazing mauve" proffers a whimsical cameo of Firbank's favorite color.

Sauntering in *The Flower Beneath the Foot,* the dilettante dalliance of a character, pausing to admire the writer's sunlit vision, obliges the writer's butterfly aesthetic that flits from one flamboyant detail to another, and often cites "here and there" or "this way and that" as a frame of reference as she pauses to pick flowers.[68] (And note a penchant for plays on words in

The Flower Beneath the Foot, a stage dancer called "April Showers," which does convey a colorful and exhibitionist and possibly salacious performer, escaped from an Ed Wood novel. Like most camp puns, facile and flagrant and hinting innuendo even when there is none, April Flowers borders on kitsch.)

Firbank is the patron saint of ecclesiastical camp. Skeptical yet attendant to orthodox ritual, his ecclesiastical-pagan incongruence is favored by camp authors, especially of a Catholic background that they can subvert but they can't quite shirk, and that leads them into temptation to court a boutade. Her Dreaminess in *The Flower Beneath the Foot* coaxes the Archbishop to give the "first act of *La Tosca* in the Blue Jesus."[69] *Concerning the Eccentricities of Cardinal Pirelli* is the cardinal example. The Cardinal's own prurient bedtime reading includes, "The Trial of Don Fernando de la Cerde, Bishop of Barcelona, defrocked for putting young men to improper uses; a treatise on the Value of Similes; an old volume of Songs, by Sa de Miranda; The Lives of Five Negro Saints, from which escaped a bookmark of a dancer in a manton." The Treatise on the Value of Similes is a nice touch, a wry affirmation of camp aesthetics that lavishes similes on any gesture. Like his sadomasochism, Firbank's wit stings like a butterfly, though his subjects are ridiculed even in *Concerning the Eccentricities of Cardinal Pirelli:* "Perhaps of the many charges brought against the Primate by his traducers, that of making the sign of the cross with his left foot at meals was the most utterly unfounded — looking for a foot-cushion would have been nearer the truth."[70]

Sample some gossip from "A Discipline from the Country": "People already talk of her as Saint Angelica; it will be her own fault if she doesn't marry at least a Bishop ... Stella is artistic, in a Cathedral she would find scope for her tastes."[71] What a whimsical motivation for marrying into clergy, yet camp's reverence for décor sanctifies the sentiment, whose grand, baroque aesthetic would not be overawed by the scale of a cathedral. Homely as a church, here is Firbank's directions for a domestic set decoration in "A Discipline from the Country," saturated in lush holiness, as asceticism goes to the wall:

> [*On the walls religious reproductions of early Flemish Masters, Statuettes of Saints and Martyrs arranged in sociable little groups and sets on the mantelpiece, a large China bird, possibly a woodpecker, in their midst, strikes a personal note all its own. A Bishop's miter, an embroidered cope, slung over a Louis Quinze screen, make a picturesque background for a luxurious-looking sofa...*]

Religion is theater: Firbank cultivates the analogy to decorate his play with holy trappings. Christianity seems off-duty in this "sociable little grouping." The Bishop's garb is presented as theatrical costume, disinvested of its iconic authority, unceremoniously "slung over" the screen, though conspicuously planted by the playwright as an ironic accessory to luxury: its informal assignation here enhances another appearance of the divan.

Concerning the Eccentricities of Cardinal Pirelli makes theater of church ritual: "Inclined to gesture, how many miles must his hands have moved in the course of the sermons that he had preached!"[72] — where the moral imperative of the Christian message is upstaged by style. *The Flower Beneath the Foot* seems to liken the Church to music-hall with a wry eulogy, "O, the charm, the flavor of the religious world! Where match it for interest or variety!" This coronation of exclamations crowns the previous extravagant sentence that indicted those Holy Church dignitaries who scamper at the high heels of high society, *à la fourchette.*[73] This high status sentence whose clauses mingle like articulate guests at a cocktail party, with lyrical fluency and beguiling turns of phrase, makes sure that the reader too feels some of the girl's bewilderment amid the pomp and circumstance. *Inclinations* puts it in a pert remark: "'After all,' she enquired, 'isn't heaven a sort of snobbism? A looking-up, a preference for the best hotel?'"[74]

Royalty and splendid palaces like cathedrals are his prolific variations on ecclesiastical pomp. Royalty is an element in Romanticism and *de rigueur* in fairy tales, two genres courted by camp. The most common occupation in Firbank's literature is being royal or a titled aristocrat, recalling the privileged camp lineage. Until we get to Chloe Poems, socialism does not strut in camp literature — even in Wilde, a self-declared socialist — and even Comrade Poems is a "royal watcher." Royal pageantry and personages, like high status clergymen, are emblematic of aloof poise, costume finery, and ennui (what do you get the Queen who has everything?), posing the camp preoccupation with being-as-a-role. The Queen is a Colonel "in several dashing regiments" in *The Artificial Princess,* authorized to give this reassurance to the military:

> "It is mortifying to be obliged to think constantly of expense, and to have to bargain, but now that the Army is being increased, and the uniforms have been changed from lemon and silver to periwinkle and violet, one must do what one can. But never forget this, dear, I will walk with you to the last under the same parasol."[75]

This frivolous pageantry could be the solution to end all wars, the promenade to end all marches.

In Firbank as it is in camp full-blown masculinity is uncouth and should be offset by irony or bent by femininity in masculine females and effeminate males or made reflectively narcissistic by homosexuality. Gender

too has costume and character traits to complement the socialized masquerade: camp reminds us of that by changing the prescribed gender
wardrobe and varying the traits.

Firbank's females, though not as abrasive as Wilde's women, can be
formidable: "She felt herself no mean match for any man," in *Caprice*,[76] is
echoed in *Santal*: "'I should like to meet the man,' Amoucha menaced,
'who'd repudiate me!'"[77]

Women assert their sexuality beyond the objects of male desire—just
barely sublimated in this artistic innuendo in a statuary in *Valmouth*:

> She was just passing a furtive hand over the promising feet and legs of a
> Discobulus, broken off, unfortunately, at the height of the loins, as Mrs.
> Thoroughfare entered.[78]

Given that camp always keeps some distance even as it courts decadence, this is a striking period moment of kinky female sexuality ... written by a man. The attraction of camp to exotica and ambiguity is eroticized
in gender and sexual diversions from social prescription. Gay/bi-sexuality
and masculine females and effeminate males are socially marginal, and so,
esoteric, and so, prolific in camp literature.

Firbank was nine when Oscar Wilde went to jail. Firbank carefully
courts homosexual tones, including Cardinal Pirelli's romanticized vision
of younger men, sublimated by another flirtation with art, "as naked as a
statue," yielding to bolder innuendo in the same paragraph with the familiar simile of swans' necks.[79] In the same novel, a Countess considers whether
a companion for a caged bird should be same sex, whereupon, "The priest
discreetly coughed." The King in *The Flower Beneath the Foot* seems to share
the Cardinal's tastes, admiring "a shapely page (of sixteen) with cheeks
fresher than milk."[80] As we find in Wilde, what makes these allusions camp
is their necessary innuendo in a homophobic society, extending the proscenium detachment of camp from its subject. Now it's out loud and proud
in an integrated culture, it may cease to be camp.

Costume adorns androgyny in *The Flower Beneath the Foot*, where one
could mistake a King for a Queen in the confusion as to "which was the
gentleman, or which the lady of the two. The king's beard long and blonde,
should have determined the matter outright, but on the other hand the
Queen's necklet of reeds and plumes was so very misleading...."[81] The
androgyny that Virginia Woolf first idealized as a transcendent writing style
is close to Firbank and to several of his characters. *The New Rythum* indulges
femininity yet not without intriguing masculine potential, where the camp
framing of persona as art, and the mirror image, can bend the rules of gender:

She surveyed seraphically her reflected image with half closed glittering eyes: the Cornabilt nose, piquant, devil-may-careish, and determined, slightly masculine lips and chin; the slim Madonna neck, supporting heavy gold-burnished locks, that seemed to shed, somehow, the halo of money. "Ah, darling." A tender sigh escaped her.[82]

Assertive and slightly masculine, yet the women remain ever so feminine, but then so do the men. Firbank's effeminate touch is reflected in flamboyant costumes; lavish décor; sensitivity to color; predominance of women; droll drawing-room dialogue associated with the domesticity of women in patriarchy; mirror images; the calming pace unhurried by "the art of persuasion"; deft and precious language that kid-gloves its subject; and on the zephyr of all those ennui sighs that "escape" from his characters, wafted by (hand-painted) fans, indifferent in the face of action —

ERIC [*to* Enid]: Shake me a cocktail, darling.
ENID: Oh, don't ask me to do anything so violent, Eric.[83]

— the closest Firbank gets to anticipating Noël Coward's droll tone. Angela Carter projects this droll ennui onto Firbank in her dramatized "artificial documentary" on the man, even reclining on his death-bed, "[*Sigh*] So there I was, you see: a 'spinster of fate' all alone in a hotel room — such dreadful wallpaper!"[84] Style over content even in a death scene.

We can distinguish between badinage and persiflage as two degrees of banter, like sadomasochistic complements, with persiflage as fey and lateral and softer banter, badinage being more biting and consequential. Let's refine our identification of tones of dialogue among camp specialists: Wilde inclines to badinage, like the barbed wit of Quentin Crisp, while Firbank, like Coward, frolics in persiflage. Badinage and persiflage might be projected along a masculine-feminine spectrum. It's all a matter of plumage: Firbank is a persifleur of a different feather, one of the most effeminate writers in the canon.

In *The Flower Beneath the Foot,* facilitated by another spiritual affirmation of ennui, watch Eddy Monteith in transgender transformation, at least metaphorically, with deft homosexual strokes:

Lying amid the dissolving bath crystals while his man-servant deftly bathed him, he fell into a sort of coma, sweet as a religious trance. Beneath the rhythmic sponge, perfumed with *Kiki,* he was St. Sebastian, and as the water became cloudier and the crystals evaporated amid the steam, he was Teresa ... and he would have been, most likely, the Blessed Virgin herself, but that the bath grew gradually cold.[85]

I read Aubrey Beardsley's influence in the decadent yet precious sensuality of "his man-servant deftly bathed him" with "rhythmic sponge." The "quasi-amorous functions" of bathers attend the hero in his camp master-piece *Under the Hill*, "The delicate attention they paid his loving parts aroused feelings within him almost amounting to gratitude...."[86] Beardsley's innuendo, which preciously alludes to sexual stimulation yet falls short of outright "gratitude," seems an expedient negotiation of obscenity laws but more than that it is an aesthetic style. More than Wilde, Beardsley's baroque and fantastical prose is a profound heritage behind Firbank's novels.

However, Ronald Firbank is not ready to follow Beardsley's forays into pornography and fetishism. Even if homosexuality had been legalized, just as Wilde's artistic sensibility forbad explicit sexuality that Will Self could indulge in *Dorian* and that future camp practitioners like Chloe Poems would enjoy (taking Decadence at its word), Firbank's precious and whimsical aesthetic prefers to alight deftly on allusion — as deft as Monteith's bathing — without laboring the point or the politics. Labor was never a virtue to Firbank, his effortless fluency and frivolous excess and flippant regard for research testifies to that. Shake you a cocktail? Darlings, don't ask him to do anything so violent.

Quentin Crisp (1908–1999)

"There I sat trying to look like a Twenties
academician's illustration of a poem by
Tennyson— languid, mournful, effete."
—Resident Alien, 1994

Quentin Crisp turned his hand to writing before becoming famous, but it wasn't as rewarding as prostitution. He wrote a book on calligraphy in 1936 and another on window dressing in 1938 and an article on life modeling in 1949, all about surface, and he wrote a limerick narrative in 1943, published modestly. In between book jacket designing and modeling, he wrote tales and poems and plays and libretti, all unpublished. The media brought him out of his bedsit and into the outer world at sixty years of age: his first autobiography in 1968 made him a famous personality, a televisual raconteur. It took half a lifetime to move English camp on to its most significant development since Firbank— Crisp had been ready for some time, but society, and its publishers, lagged half a lifetime behind. When a publisher did court him for a memoir, "Even a little of my life proved too much for Mr. Kimber."[1] Camp excess is always a problem for the aesthetic equivalent of Whitehall (a locus yet to agree on a building).

His life span and his reflective tone in the memoir genre cast a historic perspective on *The Naked Civil Servant*. Effeminates and homosexuals were ostracized until the time of writing, and Crisp represents a missing link in pre- and post-war Britain, a sociological litmus to measure cultural change. Crisp isn't the late bloomer: society is. From decades of repression to the social transformation of the 1960s, "By wearing bright colors and growing my hair long I had by mistake become the oldest teenager in the business." *The Naked Civil Servant* has not been considered historically or academically, you might have guessed, because here is another camp writer who hangs his prose on style rather than plot — and historians, like conventional novelists, are driven by plot, whose contrivance is called a *thesis*. Crisp too dethrones the cult of seriousness. Crisp heroically upheld the heritage of the aesthetes and the Edwardians after Wilde, Beardsley, Saki, Berners, Firbank, and Benson were gone. Wartime England with Nazis overhead offers a theatrical analogy to Quentin Crisp, the pantomime rehearsal of air-raid drills and gas attacks.

While Juan Goytisolo relishes a mustachioed penchant for homoerotic military masculinity, Quentin Crisp tips his fedora to effeminate poses of wartime G.I.s, "packed in uniforms so tight that in them their owners could fight for nothing but their honor." Not depicted in battlefield maneuvers as historians and newsreels would have it but in gloriously languid postures, making innuendos on "Shaftsbury Avenue," irreverent in the face of the repressed British stiff upper lip, "these 'bundles of Britain' leaned against the lamp-posts of Shaftsbury Avenue or lolled on the steps of thin-lipped statues of dead English statesmen." Crisp valiantly concludes, "Never in the history of sex was so much offered to so many by so few." Moving from World War II to the Cuban crisis, even a death wish sounds camp: "When the war threw me over, I took up with the atom bomb. We were to be married in the spring of 1963."[2] Ghoulish surrealism fantastically posed against the pun of a war bride in black humor, yet the droll tone is as frivolous as Firbank. In later memoirs, he posed as the Statue of Liberty.

He used his belated celebrity to publish a novel that had languished under his bed for twenty-five years, *Love Made Easy,* but his resurgent literary catalogue, another novel, memoirs and film and book reviews, is viewed, I fear, as fetching window dressing to his public persona, a camp *object.* To contain his literary reputation to "humorist" is no truer of Crisp than it is of Wilde: there is far more to see on the surface. With cultivated humility, Crisp encourages his own dismissal, "If I have any talent at all, it is not for doing but for being."[3] It's a decadent thing to say, as Crisp becomes next in line to flout the work ethic and adopt the divan perspective. His books embody such ironic personality and idiosyncratic figures of speech that Crisp himself was reinvented by them, I suggest; he became an open book — "literally."[4]

He dressed as an effeminate dandy, not as a woman, because a fully transvestite appearance would contrarily magnify his masculinity. Instead, his dandiness in male clothes highlighted his femininity. His sartorial prose is cut to this philosophy. The text seems penned with a quill, scratching the parchment with barbed wit and a feathered arabesque. Often assertive, terse, even dogmatic, yet the signature of his style is an aloof and effeminate flourish. His Edwardian fantasy *Chog* is mostly idiosyncratic third person narrative with little dialogue, flouting the banal injunction, "Show, Don't Tell"; in fact, Crisp is showing his panache as an anecdotal raconteur with a penchant for exhibitionism. Storytelling by reflective narrative is passé but in keeping with this anachronistic boulevardier, who writes prose less to convey meaning than to be seen.

Love Made Easy has more dialogue and focalization but, like Wilde, out of the mouths of characters come *aperçus* of the author: "'My experience is that love makes people *un*happy.'" Sir Walter approximates the author's philosophy of distance as a civilizing influence and emotion as a legacy of barbarism. Contemplating the organized promotion of culture, "Miss Phipps could think of nothing worse."[5] Neither could our skeptical author, especially when it was called art. Camp relishes coming out; no such author will subscribe to the retiring aesthetic that prefers novels to speak for themselves in quotations and novelists to be sedated. "Lady Drea flung off her coat with a movement that would have flummoxed a Spanish bull" in *Love Made Easy*, and when desperate Mrs. Hashett is offered a ride, "She tottered toward him with one hand outstretched like a desert nomad in search of an oasis." How flagrantly extravagant—yet urbanely succinct. Embellishments ripple his understated simplicity; the sun doesn't shine on his prose as it does on Firbank, his fatalism mutes his colors. Far from Firbank's romantic fantasies, and far from the sentimental moralism of Wilde's fairy tales that Crisp found mawkish, *Chog* is close to the grotesquerie of Beardsley's fantasy *Under the Hill*, but darker, closer to the gothic atmosphere of Ed Wood's horror tales. In fact, in its bestial grotesquerie, patches of *Chog* approach the kitsch impact of horror that Wood foregrounds without reserve.

Like Wood, this effeminate author does enjoy feminine detail, lingering on precious and aloof refinement, "She was just drifting into a slightly *retroussé* reverie when Paul telephoned her," (Miss Cohen was, of course, an actress) and painting up the prose in thick foundation, "Then she leaned towards her companion a heavily bejeweled ear in perfunctory valediction,"[6] rather like the author's hand in memoir, "weighed down with coral and turquoise."[7]

Crisp's ironic effects often depend on the rhetoric of contrast, made pithy and dramatic by his blithe lack of qualification. Although his antipathy to Oscar Wilde is a matter of record, his style is most resonant of Wilde's dégagé epigrams. He would sound positively antagonistic if only he could be bothered. Raw material for his ironic contrapositions are: domestic-fantastic; past-present; gay-straight; work-leisure; England-America.

> In England, the people are hostile to a man but the system is compassionate. The very old, the very young and the ill-equipped-to-live will always be looked after. In America everyone is friendly—almost doggie-like—but the system is ruthless. Once you can be pronounced unproductive, you've had it.[8]

What a wonderfully dry, droll and fatalistic final note.

A typical rhetorical contrast opposes fantasy and reality to dramatic effect, "In the one I was a woman, exotic, disdainful; in the other I was a boy. The chasm between the two states of being never narrowed."[9] But they *did* come together in his writing. Crisp stylized the literary androgyny envisioned by Virginia Woolf: masculine in direct, oppositional assertions and stoic endurance, and feminized in his passive personification and attention to the cosmetics of style and the occasional refrain, "I had a good cry."[10] Even in autobiography, his wide open first person disclosures project third person distance, self-effacing yet never nondescript. In his anecdotal writing, events *happen to* the author; his antipathies are passive-aggressive; and his extraordinary courage to go against the grain of oppressive society is passive resistance rather than a combatant stance, which he distances from heroism in self-deprecating yet dégagé style: "Even if you only lean limply against a wall and you happen to live a very long time, gradually it will begin to give way."[11] Even sweeping generalizations are a matter of cavalier style. Whimsically or sensationally, camp may court controversy to upstage mundane propriety, and unqualified assertion is just the ticket. A raconteur's rhetoric is tidier and more engaging without the clutter of clauses, and Crisp is the most accomplished raconteur since Wilde. "She was the richest and noisiest girl in the world," he gaily proclaims of a neighbor.[12] His blithe spirit does not hesitate to sum up a nation and in the process feminize one of the most masculine cultures in the west: "Australians are a nation of Madam Butterflies. They are forever standing on the shore watching for that wisp of Heaven-knows-what that will appear on the horizon one fine day."[13]

The literal construction of his sentences models the propriety and the diplomatic precision of a statesman, a tad Beerbohm. This is the studied formal phrasing that Ed Wood fumbled self-consciously in his writing. It articulates his ubiquitous good manners as a matter of fundamental aesthetics applied to lifestyle, so that, even in a routine film review for *Christopher Street* magazine, "I saw *Betrayal* at Cinema 2 on Third Avenue, where I would like to report that the staff is exceptionally courteous."[14] Crisp's gloved handling of semantics, even when dogmatic, poses precious distance from both the subject and the text itself. His formal address of celebrity and sundry alike in his memoirs, including "Mister Sting" and "Mister Claus," is whimsically mannered. "I began to lose my grip on culture with the poems of Mr. Eliot, the plays of Mr. Beckett, and the novels of Mr. Joyce."[15] Anachronistic by the time of writing in the informal late 1960s, this formal Edwardian contrast with his leisurely pace and colloquial, homely figures of speech is a mark of his style.

His first page of autobiography establishes the author's accustomed abdication of preferences, attaining the blithe spirit that eludes Decadent ennui. Disdaining romanticism, Crisp explains that his detachment is an absence of choice as an outcast. Expediency sets up his passive response to a hostile environment — though it reads like innate temperament to me. After all, this nonconformist is known for his passive resistance. His natural effeminacy inclines to passivity and his philosophical fatalism ordains it. He does not manipulate events in his life or in his memoirs, he is merely witness to the proceedings; this is his variation on flouting plot. "Life was a funny thing that happened to me on the way to the grave" describes his fatalism, and for his saintly elevation of masochism, yielding to the inevitable with good grace, turn to the end of *The Naked Civil Servant*: "I stumble towards my grave confused and hurt and hungry...."

He carries the sanctified air of Joan of Arc — her suffering, endurance and martyrdom, anyway, though not her masculinity. He models Michelangelo's masochism, and as a model, "I was determined to be as Sistine as hell."[16] He modeled "morning, nude and night," one of many, many puns in the Crisp canon. Ecclesiastical camp takes another kinky turn. He stylizes masochism as a slave to style, impeccably submissive, like a butler in a Noël Coward play. The last chapter of *How to Become a Virgin* marks the transition from obscurity to celebrity, from Soho to New York, with one last engagement as a model at a College of Art, where puritanical self-denial takes center stage. Awaiting a class of housewives, posing on his dais, as the first arrival engages his menial conversation:

"So you've come back to us."
"Yes, madam."
"You *were* a nine days' wonder, weren't you?"
"Yes, madam."
"In quite a long time this was the most coolly bitchy — the most English — remark that had been flung at me. Malice is in no way redeemed by being true."[17]

His celebrity lasted the rest of his life, in fact. The college engagement was no more than a coda: his dramatic emigration to America was imminent, not only turning the other cheek but turning his back on English persecution, forever. (When he died in England, his ashes were scattered in New York.) However, his peerless humility treats fame and anonymity just the same. And just as Crisp admired Miss Phipps' devastating capacity for calculated revenge in *Love Made Easy,* do I detect a certain relish in our housewife's choice, submitting to her barbed remark? set upon a dais as a helpless target, modeling his narcissistic masochism as art, playing off her sadism. Like a Noël Coward maid, his deferential laconicism seems to curtsy to madam's curt and spiked prompting. It is a rare passage when Crisp suspends narrative to feature dialogue and let the scene play. There is perhaps secret appreciation of his partner in this theatrical set piece, like a sneaking admiration for Bette Davis. Admiring one's enemy is such a supreme expression of equanimity.

In autobiography he drifts in and out of employment in decorative professions, accepting the vicissitudes of his hirings and firings just the same, lightening the fatalism. After lettering film credits, after working as a commercial artist, at the bidding of a man with "a delicatessen accent," he drifts into scenery. "I had never painted scenery in my life, but I said I would if he would tell me what I was to do."[18] Penchants without passion, at your service. (Yes, and if "delicatessen accent" conjures no particular accent for you, you may find the delicious sound of the term itself sufficient dessert.)

In his one-man stage show, his description of music as "a mistake" underscores his deadpan tone:

> Everything that has gone wrong with the world since the place was opened is due to music. Music is an insistent beat slightly more repeated than the heart and is accompanied by a few phrases repeated over and over and over till the entire tribe notices. Its purpose is to unite and arouse the male population, in years past usually for a waltz. Now you have no waltz, so you have a united and aroused male population with nothing to do.[19]

How detached his perspective becomes: "you" refers to humanity. His prose, like his speech, carries the unruffled meter of a reclining heartbeat and the factual tone of an imperturbably rational observer. Whimsical informalities like "ever since the place was opened," a gloriously theatrical and irreverent figure of speech for the creation of the world and the beginnings of civilization, untouched by anything so excitable as awe or romance, transfer easily to his writing.

In an impassive article for *New York* magazine, "I Visit the Colonies," Crisp satirizes his own blithe inclination to generalize and dispense with untidy qualifiers—and through his modeling, inconspicuously, mocks the whole of society's tendency to do this. His first visit to New York, after a first impression of "transatlantic kindness," models his detached equanimity at the dramatic extremes of society and the fickle fancies of fate that so complements the urbanity of New Yorkers:

> The day after we arrived, there was a robbery; the following afternoon, a fire. The inmates brought their cats downstairs and sat in the hideous lobby talking airily of this and that without so much as a mention of the flames. Thirty-six hours later there was a murder.[20]

Key to the impassive tone of Crisp in fact or fiction is his philosophy of equivalence. Survival or suicide, it's all the same to Quentin Crisp. Natural selection is, like fairness, an artificial construct; in reality, there are simply events of equal (in)significance under no obligation to our egos and ethics and orderly intellects. In *Love Made Easy,* the busy detail of "people who hurried through the streets on urgent business or loitered about them on equally urgent business"[21] equates respectable trading with whoring, one way or another, and *Chog* restates the equation. This philosophy bestows a pleasing symmetry to his sentences as in a Wilde paradox.

In a world of style over content, where appearances are sacrosanct, manners are the new morality. Hypocrisy being the better part of discretion, Crisp cultivates a vocabulary of synonyms and euphemisms to address two types of language: one spoken in earshot of the subject (say, Junoesque) and another uttered behind his back (obese). *Manners from Heaven* is the ethics of stylized comportment, as reasoned as John Stuart Mill could wish for, more rational and practical than the etiquette of Confucius but every bit as concerned with seemliness. It's the same domestic equation of decorum and righteousness that Noël Coward conveys in *Blithe Spirit* when he gives Charles this line about his ex-wife: "I remember how morally untidy she was."[22]

Crisp's domestic solution to man's inhumanity to man adapts a familiar metaphor to English camp, taking tea in indecorous circumstances (see Part One: "Saki's Cat" and "Shakespeare's Sister"). In his conscientious philosophy of equivalence that treats all eventualities just the same, comportment remains important even on doomsday: "The fact that someone may drop the Bomb in the middle of our mad tea party should in no way deter us from serving the best tea and the best conversation in our best manner — for ever."[23] In the Lewis Carroll politics of nuclear brinksmanship, observing decorum while taking tea on doomsday makes as much sense as anything else.

In his novels and memoirs, morality is relative; protagonists do not enjoy special privileges in their destiny; death is an inconsequential fact of life. It is not a matter for tragedy and the reader's grief is not solicited. Death is an occasion for slapstick in *Chog,* and in *Love Made Easy,* when a character is struck dead by the falling Statue of Happiness, the author finds an epitaph: "His problem of how to fill in the time between now and the grave was solved."[24] As understated as an undertaker, both novels exhibit the irreverent solemnity of black humor that was popular, at the time of writing *Love Made Easy,* at Ealing Studios. Even as an extraordinary exile, Crisp remains recognisably English in his eccentricity.

The author's status as protagonist of his memoirs is prone to the same fatalism: "I was asked if I was worried by the idea of mortality. I replied that I was not and added that next Tuesday would do fine for my own demise."[25] Suicide is not an option because it exercises volition and robs fatalism of its whimsical turns of events, and so Crisp goes public with that masochistic and saintly forbearance to fate: "It was not so much that I longed for death as that I didn't long for life. Emptiness, though, was not a sufficiently definite feeling to lead to a violent act."[26] Crisp leans on resignation, triumphantly. When this answer fails to please, as the years go by, always obliging, the author pacifies his critics with an alternative take: "The answer is that I'm a sissy."[27] His enlightened ennui is Taoist in obliging the force of opposition.

Willpower, the masculine assertion of ego, is subsumed by the womanly wiles of fate. Our egos are not nearly so distinctive as they like to think. A description of the servant protagonist in *Chog* makes an artifact of his character, recalling Beardsley's delicate prose portraits—and Beardlsey's art—of Venus's head and shoulders "wonderfully drawn" and an effete hero in *Under the Hill*, "His hand, slim and gracious as La Marquise du Deffand's in the drawing by Carmontelle."[28] Crisp makes a metaphor of artifice:

> Davies was like a pencil-drawing of his master, executed on parchment by an indifferent artist.[29]

Crisp is the artist, indifferent to character development and convention. Dogs have as much significance as human beings in this gothic fantasy. The servant is chaperone to his dog, which enjoys sex with a prostitute until she gives birth to a child-dog, *Chog*.

> None of the participants in this scene thought that what they were doing was a sin. Sin is an idea that has to be redefined by each god as he is voted into power.[30]

Even Deities are interchangeable; opinions too, in the final analysis. Donald Carroll[31] once asked his guest to answer the phone and tell the caller that Carroll was out. "Quentin nodded, and then spoke soothingly into the telephone: 'I'm afraid Mr. Carroll can't come to the phone at the moment, but if you are willing to talk to me I will say exactly what he would have said.'" Crisp is a vessel for equivalence. When publishers send him manuscripts for recommendation, "To these I always reply, 'Please feel free to quote me as saying anything that will promote sales of this excellent work.'" He adds, "One firm quoted the whole line which I thought really daring and funny."[32] An editor's sensibility is as good as his own, and his own opinion is ultimately of no consequence anyway, and so "If, once I've written something and an editor says he's got to change it, say it the other way round, I say fine."[33]

Paradox makes a mockery of position statements. This philosophy equalizes his response to narrative events, his insouciant fatalism and deadpan irony. His exile and contemplative age by the time of his writing career adds distance, wryly: homely and dry, "sitting in front of a metaphorical fireplace in calm reflection of the slapstick tragedy of human life, even the story of *Othello* seems ironic. All that fuss over a handkerchief. And a woman."[34] Even his disdain is reflective, arching over a pause like an afterthought. His narrative propriety has no use for exclamation marks or swearing. "As someone who no longer wrestles with the winking Cyclops-of-sex, or need worry about things that go hump in the night, my life is now one long sigh of relief."[35] And resignation. A comma away from a sigh, the rhythm of his late bloom is content to wait another sentence or two before accounting for the following refutation in *Chog*:

> Presumably patients are always made to wait for hours in hospital because it is hoped that, after a while, their fatigue will become harder to bear than the pains of their illness and they will go away again.

In the case of Mrs. Davies, however,

> A social superior had given her a letter to deliver. This was a mission that only death could prevent her from carrying out.[36]

You can hear the dry, fatalistic monotone draw breath between inevitable statements in this satirical explication of the inviolable British class system. Again, snubbing the maxim "Show, Don't Tell," Crisp relies entirely on his distinctive narrative voice to convey character, mood and situation. "I do feel that the weakness of my writing is that I do always write in the same way."[37] His philosophy of equivalence rises above reaction and concessions to mood and pace. It's a striking contrast with the high energy of Ed Wood and Chloe Poems.

Camp is reflective more than reactive, refined, not instinctive. The distance and the revealed artifice catalyse the Alienation Effect, which in camp means aloofness. "Wherever I am on this earth, I am and shall always be only a resident alien," he reflects on his "alien" U.S. status and exile from England in 1981 and, moreso, the philosophical detachment that informs his world-view. His alien status is not a position statement, *How to Become a Virgin* puts us straight: "I am not a drop-out. I was never in." In the scheme of things, alienation isn't where the deprivation lies: "The truth is that the people on the inside are trying to get out."[38]

The most iconic outcast in England offers the most alien perspective on society:

> I was staring aimlessly at my feet which were sitting in the chair opposite me when the front door bell rang. No one was expected but I took this sign from the outer world calmly.[39]

So begins another camp anecdote grounded in domesticity yet eccentrically depicted. The indolence of the moment displaces time (that phenomenon by which we clock everyday life), and Crisp is so detached in vacuous contemplation that his own feet are related as disembodied and autonomous companions. The domestic occasion of a door bell rings an intriguing association with "the outer world," which attains mythic status. "The outer world" is a wry introspective refrain throughout Crisp's work, a measure of the distance between his flamboyant effeminate persona and the repressive society that shunned him for sixty years then embraced him as a celebrity. Crisp remains whimsically aloof: "I will not be nudged into a quarrel with the human race. Now that we've finally met, I love it."[40]

His disclosures are unequivocally honest, intimate but not immediate. His ironic distance from society—even from the incidental leading part played by his ego—spans his autobiography. Phases of his life are "Acts," and "My whole life was an unsympathetic part played to a hostile audience." Just like Brecht, he spurns sympathetic identification.

In such a prejudiced and brutish society, school is harrowing for any effeminate child—for Lord Berners in his autobiographies and Poems in "The Effeminate"— and Crisp is open about the misery. Yes, but look at the perspective he gets, up on the moral highground, over his public school: "This school was on the top of a hill so that God could see everything that went on. It looked like a cross between a prison and a church and it was."[41]

Throwaway delivery dispenses unequivocally with commas to declare the school was exactly the metaphor it appeared to be. An irreverent pun on "cross" follows an ironically skeptical sentence that poses the perspective of the Eye of God. It flouts any earthly authority and is poised even above the heavenly equivalent that is preached in assembly halls across the country.

Alienation translates to skeptical commentary in his fiction. His narrative makes no disguise of omniscience larger than objective journalism: "He really believed that he could form an unbiased and detached opinion of the outer world merely by reading a daily paper from cover to cover."[42]

Anachronistic Edwardian phrasing, on occasion, keeps the subject at arm's length. Wilde demonstrated how faint authorial intonations somewhat draw on ennui and the urbane dandy's reserve. Crisp articulates precious effeminacy aloof from force and, too, cultural, philosophical and emotional detachment that is not enervated, only alienated, the sound of distance. The Alienation Effect is so extreme it barely participates in the human race except to cut a dash in the slipstream.

It surely doesn't inspire the political activism of Mister Brecht. His fatalism doesn't allow it. Politics is "the art of making the inevitable appear to be a matter of wise human choice."[43] He never voted. "Just as religion is for evangelists, not for congregations and education is for teachers, not for students, so politics are for politicians, not for voters."[44] It all leaves this most obliging of men who stands at your service, whomsoever you may be, impeccably redundant, with nothing to do but to be. It's a particularly camp way of being. (Performance artist The Divine David was asked what he was doing these days after his television success. He replied genuinely, if languidly, that he was occupied in looking after his neighbor's cat.) Even when Crisp takes full-time employment, "for me no job could ever be more than a seaside romance with respectability."[45] What a whimsically decadent figure of speech, as deft as taffeta.

"Though I would prefer to do absolutely nothing at all, I do not dislike composing pieces of prose if they are short."[46] "I do not dislike" typifies his precious disinclination for inclinations. Impassive and epigrammatic style and those flagrant generalizations that really can't be bothered with banal qualifying clauses speak of the oral and theatrical tradition of camp: in prose or in person, he is a raconteur. Aside from the occasional precious double-negative, as insouciant as his attitude, his fluent prose takes the path of least resistance. Crisp warns the apprentice writer against "grammar and syntax far more complicated than he would ever use when speaking." His own phrasing is Edwardian at times but he *speaks* that way, and, like Wilde, his conversation is refined by rehearsal and repeat performances. Question and answer sessions at his one-man shows testify to his literal way of speaking and oratorical way of writing: transcripts of these shows—in *The Wit and Wisdom of Quentin Crisp*—quote his books but his books are equally informed by his addresses and chats and monotone intonation that define his impassive authorial voice. His prose affirms an oral tradition that Goytisolo and Poems promote in the 21st century and which Wilde traces to Greek classic culture. In 1890, in "The True Function and Value of Criticism," Wilde recommended the ear as the arbiter of good writing, listening for metrical and musical tones.

His lifestyle is another indictment of the work ethic, another recommendation of style over content. It takes the form of decorum over sincerity in *Manners from Heaven*, but it also applies to literature when style is overrun by busy plots: "The busier you are the more your manners will decline, and then you will excuse yourself by saying that you haven't got time for Crispian flourishes and that people will just have to understand if you take short cuts in courtesy,"[47] he says in a final chapter called "Designs for Living," echoing Noël Coward's play *Design for Living*. Crisp and Coward share an English conservatism. We find lines like these in Coward's *Relative Values* in 1949: "Dearest Cynthia. You really must not let righteous indignation play such hell with your syntax," and, "One of the worst aspects of modern English life is that so many of one's friends have to work and they're so bad at it," and, "Comedies of manners swiftly become obsolete when there are no longer any manners," Crispian sentiments, all, and Crisp could join Coward's final toast in Part One to the demise of social equality.[48]

Deadpan Crispian monotone inclines ironically to cynicism and dégagé acceptance of doom. It makes a sentence like "Peace broke out"[49] peal like a death knell. Orally he intoned doomsday in his televized Alternative Queen's Speech to the nation, when he warned us all to get out of England, now, while there was still time. There is a bitter, misanthropic subtext that is black comedy in his sweeping generalizations, ironic in his book on good manners with a brusque insult to mankind that is yet, in accord with his philosophy of equivalence, entirely egalitarian: "We are all horrible the way we are, and no one should be asked to put up with our *natural* selves or see us as we really are, ever."[50]

Artifice is a civilizing influence. "I was trying never to close my hand against anyone unlovable (in dealing with whom I was having a great deal of practice),"[51] with only parenthesis to signal his distaste for the inhumanity of mankind. And in 1991 he writes, "I answer almost all correspondence — even the most hostile."[52] His philanthropy is, like his misanthropy, egalitarian, and his egalitarianism is, like his masochism, exhibitionist. His polite prose is always mindful of his readers, as an engaging conversationalist should be, "but we must never forget that politeness is a way of dealing with people whom you do not like."[53]

Yet Crisp has many readers, gay and straight men and women who relate closely and warmly to his books. His style is stately yet homely. The effeminate, domestic tone foregrounded in all his work is accessible to all, a foil to his eccentricity that makes Quentin Crisp a master of domestic-fantastic juxtaposition, fedora and shoulders above his camp peers. "I certainly felt that my life in England fulfilled the basic definition of surrealism: the absurd juxtaposition of two objects not normally found together."[54] The domestic grounding of his fanciful flights is classic camp, like taking tea on doomsday. His inverted interpretation of *Othello* reduces a monumental Shakespearean tragedy to all that fuss over a handkerchief and a woman. Part One of this book cites another Crisperanto example of domestic literary criticism: the masculine prowess of D.H. Lawrence shown as the compensation of a domesticated husband.

Crisp's publisher Donald Carroll credits his "almost alchemical wizardry in converting seemingly lacklustre truths into lustrous *aperçus*"[55] — and vice versa, I want to add. His historic perspective on the Medici family is "those darlings of the color supplements." His mission, had he chosen to accept it, would have been the splendid embellishment of banality. *Chog* reflects on the amoral prostitute, "Raina's lifestyle challenged the fundamental mathematical tables by which society calculates its degrees of respectability. She was to ethics what Mr. Einstein would one day be to physics."[56] His resistance to realism is just this, and so he can't understand director Ken Loach: "He is on record as having said that he wants television plays to look like the news. What a poor wingless creature he must be! Why does he not want the news to be as well acted as a play?"[57] One might interpret this as a bid to make social realism theatrical. Alternatively, camp *perceives* the essential theatricality of social realism and performs it: surrealism within the domestic-fantastic dynamic is no more than revelation of what is latently there.

I call his style *domestique:* domestic with an esoteric flourish. His tonal range is domestic, from bland to deadpan, a grounding counterpoint to his sweeping generalizations, his flourishing eccentricity, and his extraordinary narrative turns of fortune. His autobiographies encounter homely surrealism at every turn. His flamboyant appearance draws eccentricity out of the shadows, yet his passive temperament and impassive narrative depict his own character as the domestic counterpart to fantastic events that *happen to* him. His effeminacy catalyses the latent homosexuality and eccentricity of repressed psyches in a society made mediocre by denial and oppression. (Chloe Poems satirizes the phenomenon in "Some of My Best Friends are Straight" and "The Effeminate.") In this respect, Crisp is the fantastic element in his domestic-fantastic juxtapositions. Then again, what could be more surreal than World War? Crisp is a pacifist navigating a local landscape rendered surreal by the Blitz: "When I asked an invisible passerby where I was, he kissed me on the lips, told me I was in Newport Street and walked on."[58]

His philosophy of equivalence remains matter of fact, equating the domestic and fantastic just the same, domestique. He plays the contrast merely for rhetorical effect on the page.

Domestic-fantastic contrivances tease his similes with bathos. Long after leaving a job in the city, he reflects that the building itself has now been "removed—carefully, like a slice of cake. Weeds grow where once I stood."[59] Homely analogies of confection and horticulture and allegories of life and death summon apparitions of time past and former roles. The historic and philosophic range of his lifetime as a senior writer is the *fantastic* tangent in all this. Relating the exotic flora and fauna and birdlife of Los Angeles, Crisp alights on swallowtail butterflies, "which in England are as rare as number fourteen buses."[60] Running to fetch a tape-recorder to capture

Crisp's every word, a man returns "with a contraption as big as a gas meter,"[61] mundane yet formidable — and appropriate to the scale of his generalizations and his caricature of himself as a gasbag.

On stage, he talks about God in his literal way that recalls his oratorical style of writing: "I am unable to believe in a God susceptible to prayer as petition. It does not seem to me to be sufficiently humble to imagine that whatever force keeps the planets turning in the heavens is going to stop what it's doing to give me a bicycle with three speeds."[62] The cosmic absurdity of the proposition highlights the speaker/author's impassively rational vision and tone.

Even grotesque fantasy *Chog* is a domestic affair. Domestic servants parody the author's obliging deference: Mrs. Davies is conditioned to servility and guilt by her status and a career of domestic mishaps. When she anticipates police questioning, the drama of a sensational killing is snubbed on a whim.

> Now someone she had never seen had died in a street along which she had never walked and people were going to ask her to account for it. Would the cost of this tragedy also be deducted from her wages?[63]

The irony that intones the "tragedy" stays wryly aloof from any such gravity.

When Mr. Davies takes clandestine visits to the local prostitute, he is servant to the desires of the aristocratic dog in his care. It is Fido who has congress with the prostitute; Davies is the voyeur. This satirizes Britain's dog-walkers on the leash of domestic routine in service to their dogs. When Mrs. Davies suspects his perverted evening walks and confronts her husband, the pedestrian picture of walking the dog is incriminated and sensationalized, and the man is caricatured in a photographic moment of passivity: "Davies stood before her with his mouth open, one hand holding the dog's chain and the other in the sleeve of his mackintosh."[64]

The prostitute gives birth to the dog-child, Chog. "Taking an occasional stroll along the pavement with her new perambulator," she attracts womanly curiosity over the baby-puppy's strange development as "the chuppy was fast becoming a chog." And so the pedestrian act of pushing a baby-carriage, like the pedestrian ritual of walking a dog, becomes a memorable domestic-fantastic oddity. Domesticity dominates so much of our lives, our imagination is leashed to mundane routine, but Crisp transforms banality brilliantly in juxtapositions like this.

His 1949 article, "The Declining Nude," describes how unglamorous modeling can be. "In a gallant effort to counteract boredom, the artist or art master always praises the model on the same principle as that which urges you to praise your charwoman. 'No one can get the sink as clean as you can, Mrs. Phipps.'"[65] His domestic analogy puts ironic distance between how we might imagine the artist's finished portrait — intensely seeking the essence of the person in that moment — and the unromantic reality of posing in that moment for an hour.

He penned *All This and Bevin Too* in 1943. With fantastical illustrations, this narrative limerick relates the ostracism of an anthropomorphic kangaroo — our effeminate author was himself as exotic as a talking kangaroo to 'forties Britain. Rejected even by the zoo, the kangaroo returns to his room — (O Bloomsbury where is thy bloom?) — and lights a candle to make it "dramatic."[66]

Banality begins at home. Crisp is famous for living in one dingy room —"I like living in one room and have never known what people do with the room they are not in"[67] — but here dramatizes the meager lifestyle simply and overtly with theatrical lighting ... and a talking kangaroo. The fey and florid reference to Bloomsbury is an arty camp aside. When he famously declares it unnecessary to clean one's home because the dirt doesn't thicken after four years, he adds "It's just a question of not losing your nerve," making melodramatic suspense of the most domestic subject. He drew this distinction between his own artifice and Oscar Wilde's: for Wilde, artifice was an adornment and "never a part of him," while Crisp advocates style as a way of being.[68] Crisp modeled his aphorisms: by all accounts, his flat really did test the theory. Where lifestyle is art, the sitting room is our stage.

In 2004, David Hoyle returned to performance art, after retiring his theatrical persona "The Divine David," by transplanting his sitting room to an exhibition space. There, all day, he could be found sitting under a lampshade, or painting canvas walls or canvas floorspace, or playing records, receiving visitors. This stylized, exhibitionistic installation of domesticity extended the fantastic banality that Crisp was such an exponent of. In his meager wartime flat, Quentin Crisp wryly describes "the early Caledonian Market furnishings of my room," where "Caledonian" plays like a European art period rather than his local London market, making Bohemia of banality. Conversely, Crisp defrocks pretentiousness with an exposé on bedsits that are so sparse and "so lavishly unkempt that their occupants feel the only thing to do is call them studios."[69] ("Lavishly" becomes a camp adverb when applied to "unkempt.") He calls his own unassuming flat "my dressing room."[70] Finally in 1968, fantasy camps in the hearth of bedsit domesticity when Granada Television comes to call on Crisp, the subject of a documentary:

Sheets of pink acetate were fixed over the windows of my room and for four days as though lit by the dawn of a new Doris Day, I walked about, sat in my chair or rolled on my bed droning on about eternal things.[71]

Doris Day is a familiar nod to her iconic status in gay culture. Crisp ushers in occasional Hollywood golden age references to glamorize banality or feminize force.

Naturally, New York, New York beckoned. His lone emigration as a senior citizen is another act of courage, but how could he resist? He was moving into the movies. "Every street along which we drove brought back the memory of some long dead movie seen when life was dreary and only the world of celluloid was rich and full." New Yorkers, you see, "resist all tendencies to reduce people and events to their lowest common factor."[72] *Resident Alien* records inclement weather in Boston, "the only thing lacking from the scene was a glimpse of Miss Lamour, in a wringing wet sarong, clinging to a bent palm tree."[73] In a recording studio, a madcap film metaphor conveys his anachronistic alienation: "In one part there is an instrument panel as complicated as that which bewildered Miss Doris Day when she was required to land an air liner aided only by instructions from the control tower."[74]

"When I was young and thought that going to the theater would make me seem to be an aesthete, most drama, other than the classics, was domestic and was played in front of what that formidable iconoclast, Joan Littlewood, called 'those bloody French windows.'"[75] Crisp couldn't afford those bloody French windows and re-styled the drawing-room demeanor of Wilde and Coward to the bedsit comportment of a self-effacing narcissist, simplifying drama to self-contained memoir. He adapts the "kitchen sink" context of the "kitchen sink drama," popularized by gritty northern working-class plays and films of the late 1950s-early '60s, but he pulls the plug on the attendant emotional crises. From the kitchen sink crockery of yesterday's events in *The Naked Civil Servant*, chapter endings are soap opera hooks to the next episode. Teasing understatement preserves narrative equanimity at those twists of fate in chapter codas.

Love Made Easy reflects on the makeshift clerical jobs of an ex-art student. "Occasionally, when she beheld a pound of liver on a crumpled newspaper or some dirty crocks in a basin, she felt that resurgence of aesthetic longing which, in a student of a former generation, would have been brought on by a sunset or a thatched cottage..."[76] a rather satirical collage of domestic aesthetics. From his bedsit to Bohemia was a short walk, even at a saunter. "Flamboyant Street" in *Love Made Easy* stands in for the author's local fringe hangout, where he enjoyed the bonhomie of fellow Bohemian fantasists—"In the good old days Charlotte Street was full of people who were nearly on the stage or were just about to write a play."[77] Charlotte Street nurtured artifice on a whim and a shoestring.

In the next decade, make-believe transformed his horizons—from a bedsit in Soho to a bedsit in New York. Living under an assumed name (he was christened "Denis") and an assumed personality for all his adult life, Crisp demonstrates that today's fantasy inspires tomorrow's reality: the better way of being projected by cinema became his future lifestyle on the impressive backlot that is Manhattan. "My life has become an MGM musical full of singing, dancing and love."[78] His film review of *The Cotton Club* (1984) celebrates the artifice of his adopted town and his natural style:

> As the lovers leave the city, their departure is intercut with — nay, becomes the same thing as— a cabaret act in the club, performed by dancers dressed as railway porters and carrying suitcases. It is impossible to discern whether Grand Central Station is a building or a backdrop — whether the participants in the scene are acting living or acting acting. This catches the very essence of Manhattan. It may not be the "gayest" city in the world but it is certainly the campiest.[79]

Critics indulge the same speculation over acting living or acting acting about the memoirs of Quentin Crisp, which his paradoxes tease.

The aesthete's perspective reveals artifice in every event, above the conflict that clogged up "kitchen sink drama." It informs his taste in films, which inspires his writing.

> If drama was what was hoped for, Paul's appearance was the answer.

Here, the narrative is commenting on Paul's entrance as an expedient device, distancing the dramatic value. *Love Made Easy* satirizes the conventions of pulp fiction that Ed Wood courted so sincerely. The narrative plays Russian roulette with a pistol as a portent, passing it from one character to another to keep us guessing who would get shot and who would do the shooting ... until Paul, a writer, shoots a critic of his script. Disdainfully, the narrative obliges convention while disowning it: "Influenced by second-rate films he had seen and the third-rate one he was writing, Paul decided he must conceal the body." Neither will Crisp be enslaved by the obligatory profundity of death. Mr. Roofingfelt (like Firbank — and like Amanda McKittrick Ros, strangely — Crisp conveys the artifice of personhood through improbable and punning names of characters like Mr. Bottle-Green, Cyril Hardness, Sir Walter Cunningham-Bilge, and Mr. Roofingfelt) criticizes Paul's inaccurate crime script and, borrowing the gun, attempts to show the author how it is used ... and accidentally shoots him dead. When the secretary enters, all she can say is, "'Was his script that bad?'" It was, in point of fact. Anger is processed as film stock: "His rage, which had until now been in monochrome, flared up into technicolor."[80]

"I like movies about movies," Crisp explains. "Usually they provide actresses with the opportunity to play actresses, which they do with special relish."[81]

Enter Bette Davis:

> After many long years, Miss Bette Davis was finally given the part of Regina in *The Little Foxes*. This gave her the chance to say, "Very well, then, die. I'll be waiting for you to die." We could tell from the glaring eyes and the mouth worn upside down that this was what she had been waiting to say for years.[82]

And Crisp had been longing to hear it, relishing the melodrama as much as Miss Davis, the clipped, sophisticated bitchcraft, the stylized catharsis of passive-aggression that simmered in understatements like theatrical asides beneath his Edwardian surface after so many years of persecution. You can't say "for years" without baring your teeth — and turning your mouth upside down. *How to Have a Lifestyle* is punctuated with iconic exemplars of womanly style in cinema, his formative inspiration.

Alan Bennett's fatalism recalls this voice but usually without Crisp's whimsical exhibitionism. Bennett does match the pleasing symmetry of Crisp's philosophy of equivalence. In his 1999 diary, Bennett notes a news story about falling education standards, wryly: "I am pictured, though whether as evidence of decline or hope for the future I can't make out. Either would please me."[83] When Bennett does get fantastical their kinship is clearer. In memoir, after a harrowing sketch of the psychiatric ward where his mother was kept, Bennett parodies his culture shock on his first visit: "Obviously, I thought, we have strayed into the wrong ward, much as Elizabeth Taylor did in the film of *Suddenly Last Summer*." Acclimatizing to a dementia ward as his mother ages, cinema reframes his unflinching and poignant and, to my view, urgent observations on the institutionalized and undignified side of life. As nurses come and go, "They know they are in a 'Carry On' film. I am playing it like it's *Brief Encounter*."[84]

"The world is pining for a steady diet of celluloid; it desperately needs an alternative life to that through which it drags itself at the office or, even worse, at home," Crisp introduces a collection of film reviews. Bloomsbury where is thy bloom. "Something went wrong with the notion of victory through cosmetics, and some twenty-five years ago, women abandoned the idea, adopting instead the strategy of victory through work, which they called liberation. This was the final nail hammered into the coffin of stardom."[85] He cannot be accused of male chauvinism, readers: Crisp himself models his cosmetic ideal of femininity. The cinema of his youth replenished an impoverished imagination as Greta Garbo and Marlene Dietrich transcended drab industrial labor, economic depression and wartime rationing. He adds, "Only prostitutes at that social level wore vermilion hair, gold eyelids and green fingernails."[86] Like Ed Wood, Crisp featured a prostitute as protagonist: as Cynthia is a strong prostitute in *Death of a Transvestite* and Sandra dominates in "Gore in the Alley," so Crisp features Raina in *Chog* and himself in autobiography. Like Wood, Crisp found his inspiration somewhere between Hollywood and the red light district, and before long he is able to refer to "the architecture of my coiffeur."[87]

Chloe Poems celebrates the city's oldest profession in "The Cocktail Hour" and raises the ladies of the night above their unlikely regal counterparts, the royal family, in "Whore." Edwardian intonations announce the Madame of the Buckingham whorehouse, the Queen Mother, sardonically, rolling the ostentatious trappings of both decadent professions around on the tongue, in his cheek:

> But for personal services
> At her palatial bordellos
> Oh my dear fellows
> You must pay more.[88]

"Whore" finds royalty an insidious corruption of prostitution without its honesty: the royal Madame carries "The attributes of a prostitute /Without the dignity of a whore." The sensational antipathy is two generations too radical for Crisp, and yet whores are heroic figures in the work of both Poems and Crisp, having both been prostitutes themselves. We saw *Love Made Easy* acknowledge the business of streetwalking as urgently as anybody else's business. Crisp finds a realist heroine in his fantasy *Chog*: "Lacking in maternal instinct and with very little capacity for tenderness," still, he reminds us, overtly, "prostitutes spend much of their time alone with men whose appearance or whose sexual habits are so repellent and so frightening that they dare not try foist themselves upon women whom they know socially. Raina was truly a heroine."[89]

Those gay male prostitutes gifted with Irish lyricism to importune rich clients run "up and down the scales of flattery without a hint of pianissimo."[90] The Liberace flourish is both the author's and the prostitutes.' Prostitutes are actresses too, you know, and camp celebrates luvvies of all denominations for their embargo on banality, their mediation of the mediocrity of marriage. Closer to kitsch than to camp, perhaps, yet prostitution, like theater, is an essentially exhibitionist masquerade, and its denizens pose like boulevardiers. They may even showcase their talent in windows, ready to be defenestrated, just as Crisp frequented the window seat of a Lower East Side restaurant as a dandy raconteur: "I used to sit on exhibition like a Dutch prostitute."[91] Crisp recalls nocturnal gay friends and

whores who transcended "humdrum" daytime jobs.[92] In *Chog*, "To the people who lived opposite to her, Raina's life had been like a serial story in a
woman's magazine. Each instalment had been more exciting than the last."[93]
And so "the idea of the orchidaceous woman" is superimposed over the
scarlet woman to inform Crisp's effeminate appearance and his language,
as his plumage rises above mediocrity, not always in terms of content but
always in style.

Conformity to mediocrity is a most virulent social disease, spread by
peer pressure and the tyranny of labor. Individuals "are exhorted to be no
more than reasonable; that is to say they are asked to allow their behavior
to be governed by other people's logic. They are urged to think construc-
tively; this means to employ their own energies to build other men's
edifices." The urbane manual *How to Have a Lifestyle* will set you free, and
as a bonus, in this stultifying culture, it will also make you unemployable.
The domestic-fantastic genius of this artist is not to deny banality but to
stylize it. You may be ordinary,

> but you must be so ordinary that you can imagine someone saying, "Come to
> my party and bring your humdrum friend," and everyone knowing he meant
> you.[94]

This is as far as he goes toward what playwrights and novelists call
character development, but Crisp is dealing in signatures, not detail. *How
to Have a Lifestyle* models his fundamental rule of style: "That which cannot be wholly concealed should be deliberately displayed." Crisp modeled
the principle impeccably when he was arrested for homosexual soliciting
in the 1940s.

The trial became a dramatic highlight of *The Naked Civil Servant* that
superbly demonstrates life as theater. "Of all the professions the one that
offers the most direct route to self-realization is the stage," and indeed,
"Soon there will be very few professions that are not also the profession of
acting," he prophesies in 1975. He professes that you can make anywhere
your stage and any action your performance, "the dextrous use of a carefully selected and patiently rehearsed set of mannerisms,"[95] which extends
to his deliberate and reflective prose. "Muddled syntax is the outward and
audible sign of confused minds, and the misuse of grammar the result of
illogical thinking," he says in *Resident Alien*.[96] Now, Ed Wood stylized this
very symptom, in accord with Crisp's expedient recommendation to promenade that which cannot be concealed, over-reaching his genres and stretching syntax in fantastic expressions that prompted the title of one book about
Wood's oblivious genius, *Muddled Mind*. However, Quentin Crisp spurns
spontaneity to rehearse his clarity, precision and supercilious humility —

even when the culture of perfection leads to refined repetition in his books and in his appearances.

If "Style, in its broadest sense of all, is consciousness,"[97] then self-definition leads to self-realization, the stylized creation of personhood. Very well. Here was his chance, in the 1940s, with a potentially devastating appearance in court.

The authorities played into his penchant for saintly public masochism, his theatrical talent for exhibitionism. The trial demonstrates his extraordinary courage, but Crisp underplays the heroism and the drama by playing it *as* melodrama — and comedy, quite a contrast with the tragedy of Oscar Wilde's ruinous trial. On the eve of his court appearance, Crisp offered "speaking parts to friends of long standing who could act as character witnesses, and others to people who might like to appear as crowd artists." He defended himself, a martyr to the truth with a starring role at last. He decided to play his big scene "dead straight like Imogen in *Cymbeline.*"[98] He was acquitted, he says, on a euphemism for manufactured evidence, "insufficient evidence." Crisp analyzes the feasibility and motivation of the charges with lucid, flawless logic, an acute intellectual capacity aided by his transcendence (or suppression) of emotion that really does promote style as a form of consciousness. He conscientiously applied the same awareness to street mobs that bullied him.[99] He doesn't convey the force of their violence as Goytisolo would do in homophobic beatings in *A Cock-Eyed Comedy*, for instance; his prose remains as aloof from physicality as the Apostles.

Finally, in the aftermath of his encounter with the law, "In the last analysis I cannot say that I have ever refrained from taking any course of action on the ground that it was wrong or illegal or immoral." Even freedom and action sound passive in his customary style, "I cannot say that I have ever refrained...." but he expresses the amorality of camp aesthetics, alien from the mores of society and establishment. Criminalized by his sexuality, society's definition of right and wrong becomes alien to his way of being. His literary account of the court proceedings, portraying himself and his predicament with absurdity, declines the mantle of hero for the crown of drama queen — but any reader with an understanding of the awesome social pressure that Crisp resisted so publicly that day will recognize that he merits both accolades. The trial was a defining moment for Crisp and for all effeminate homosexuals who are disenfranchised and looking for inspiration, and so the art school model, who lived his life as a poseur, became a role model. Crisp demonstrated that effeminacy, pretty and precious as it is, can be admirably courageous and resilient, and the same could be said for his camp prose.

Crisperanto, those courtly flourishes of rhetoric and arched irony against a contrapuntal deadpan tone, is "the art of speaking with such guile, subtlety and duplicity that an opponent never knows what seduced him."[100] *The art of speaking* in his writing articulates the matter of fact cadence and barbed wit so audible in his droll, monotone intonations and clipped pronunciation. The notion of *opposition* is prevalent in classical rhetoric that poses distinction by contraposition. Crisperanto may be driven to innuendo and sophistry under society's oppression: politicized studies often depict camp as the deflected symbology of gay culture, too disenfranchised to express itself directly. Like Wilde, Crisp advocated the art of lying, but characterizing Crisperanto as duplicitous plays into common criticism of camp as deceitful because it flouts seriousness—a criticism depending on a linear, analytic and humorless notion of integrity that does not tolerate paradox.

Crisp demonstrates disarming honesty in his autobiographies. His effeminate manner of speaking is diplomatic in the face of confrontation with seductive ornate eloquence, yes, but his fluent prose feels natural to my reading, at ease with itself to the point of complacency, even despite the author's introjected pathology of his sexuality. This most obliging of nonconformists finds his voice and his innate predisposition in spite of oppression, self-effacing but never nondescript, *domestique*. His publications journey toward social acceptance on his own eccentric terms, and his writing was part of the process. This spirit of affirmation can be read in his work, rising above repression and, what amounts to the same thing, banality.

This is the spirit that "The Effeminate" celebrates, which, in 1999, Chloe Poems was due to perform by way of a stage introduction to Quentin Crisp at the Green Room Theater, in my godforsaken city of Manchester. It became a tribute when Crisp died on the eve of the premier. On stage, under a spotlight: the famous fedora, dandy icon of his book covers, served as a prop, lending a touch of panache to a hat-stand. This was nice symbolism, a tad Magritte, and as creative as the real thing in the interchangeable scheme of things, in Crisp's equivalent philosophy of life and death and artifice and earth. The absence of the author, which could not be concealed, was deliberately displayed. Crisp would have been proud of the dégagé hat-stand, which upstaged his absence and won a standing ovation.

Edward D. Wood, Jr.
(1924–1978)

"Nothing is stranger than the strange itself."
— *Hollywood Rat Race* (posthumous, circa 1960s).

"... *stranger than the strange itself....*" That tautology touches the abstraction of conceptual art — and recoils — made all the more creative by not quite making sense. The ironic art of camp, its mirroring images, its decorative flourishes and profligate asides, its proscenium temperament and ironic resonance from the wings to the balcony, is a posthumous legacy in this chapter. Over Wood's dead body, time sounds out the resonance, we provide the irony.

The name of Edward D. Wood, Jr. lives on, thanks to polls for the worst director of all time. Camp is the art of superlatives, and if the artist cannot be the best, he can surely be the worst of all, and, as Juan Goytisolo says, via Karl Marx, "as the end sanctifies the means, the worst must be the best!"[1] Wood's filmography and biography triumph over banality, against the odds, attesting to the beauty of naiveté, the power of enthusiasm, and the endurance of the human spirit, on the rocks. Ed Wood is a winner with a losing streak: he made a meager living but he made it putting his dreams in the public arena and he made it against the odds fixed by corporate America and the condescending cognsoscenti. Tim Burton evoked this entrepreneur on film in *Ed Wood* (1994), but there was another side to Ed Wood's art that should not escape public awareness, that cultural historians must not be *allowed* to avoid: Ed Wood the writer, the novelist.

His "Lights, Camera, Action!" enthusiasm staged a production number out of every sentence he wrote. He was a prolific novelist, wrote over a hundred screenplays, hundreds of short stories and articles. He wrote

"Captain Fellatio Hornblower" and *The Drag Trade*. He also assayed a memoir, unpublished, which he sent to Bela Lugosi Junior. He wrote the horror story, "Scream Your Bloody Head Off." Sometimes the title is all you need to know. "Missionary Position Impossible" is camp beyond 1960s T.V. espionage: camp makes decadent theater of sex, subverting banality with kinky and incongruous juxtapositions like outlaw gay sex, S and M, transvestism, exhibitionism ... opposed to that most banal of sexual poses, the blanket expression of sanitized sex that is straight and vanilla and quite out of the question, the missionary position.

Wood was more prolific than Kilgore Trout. He had to be to pay the bills because his work sold for peanuts. He wrote at least eight books in 1967 alone — and David C. Hayes and Hayden Davis put the toll even higher in their anthology of the man's work. The next year he wrote eight more novels and four sensationalized "studies" of sexual perversion too tactless for *The National* Enquirer. Third wife Kathy Wood pictures the process, "When Eddie was thinking, writing, composing, he walked round and round, back and forth, clenching and unclenching his right hand." This unstoppable author compiled magazines autonomously on occasion, and assumed several pseudonyms to suggest other contributors. And so the detective inventory of Ed Wood's oeuvre is ongoing. Rudolph Grey documented his life and times and does not flinch from the truth: "It is conceivable that Ed Wood wrote as many as seventy-five books."[2]

And Hayes and Davis put the toll higher.

There is no truer witness to the reality of the First Amendment to the Constitution of the United States than the uncritical expression and publication of Edward D. Wood. In the words of the novelist,

> When I see a character like this so-called God, Swahili, I can only remember the words of a really great American, and then I get chills all over, thinking that the freedom of speech could so be used for the blasphemy this man has used it.[3]

This peculiar literary kudos germinated in active service in World War II. Our war hero won a medal for valor and Roosevelt awarded him another one as "the fastest typist in the marines." A publisher declared, "He was the most prolific writer I've ever seen, and the fastest." Faster than Mickey Spillane, more rhetorical than a runaway sermon, able to stretch the boundaries of the simile in a single leap of the imagination, it's true, Ed Wood could answer the telephone, watch television, welcome visitors and complete a novel at his typewriter all in a single sitting.[4] His indefatigable spirit in the face of rejection is a lesson to us all. After nine novels, an editor at his usual publishing house didn't believe Wood was on the books. Wood had difficulty proving to the fresh editor that he was not a beginner. When he did, he was commissioned for a novel:

> It was a simple novel, but it took me a little more than a month. My original editor returned from his leave and rejected it. Not suitable. There went more than a month of work down the drain — a month I could have devoted my attention to things that would have paid off.[5]

He demonstrates no sense of irony in that indignant anecdote, in the uphill task of convincing his own publisher that he was not a beginner and then lamenting as an epic lapse the passing of a month to write a whole novel. He could not know at the time of writing that even this account would only be published twenty years posthumously, yet *Hollywood Rat Race* is a misfit masterpiece.

"Here you are in Hollywood. And Hollywood is damn well going to know about it." Picture the reader, standing at the crossroads with a single valise, green and stage-struck yet feisty like Judy Garland or Shirley MacLaine, all set to burst into song. Partly a pep talk to an entirely imaginary, gullible and zealous college readership to prepare them for imminent movie stardom, partly a demoralizing grounding in the mercenary practicalities of Hollywood, *Hollywood Rat Race* suddenly changes course to address all those budding writers out there. It's one of those delusional, disorienting lurches between genres and moods and imagery that skews and patents his uncanny style, reminding the reader that this is an Ed Wood book, none other and nothing less. Another sensational lurch from paternal advice into sexual fantasy warns of sleazy producers—"And more than a few of them will be undressed and into your dress or sweater and skirt, almost before you've got them off"—an extraordinary fusion of self-revelation and damning dissociation in a single sentence. He distinguishes himself as "an independent producer" but his warning is conspicuously detailed. His irrepressible honesty and a compelling personal fetish take over: "Strange as it may seem, a few of these characters will let you just stay on your back, nude, while they try on your clothes. Your panties, warm with the heat of your body, your sweater of an expensive and, usually, a furry nature are hot items to these characters."[6] Transvestism is a subject that we will revisit, obsessively.

Wood's distinctive writing style is the conspicuous expression of *writerly behavior,* the writer *acting* as wordsmith. In *Death of a Transvestite,* "The Killer slopped a good portion of the Martini over the table as he traveled it toward his lips," such a peculiar conveyance, normally reserved for long distances and material transport, that we are supremely aware of the author *writing* the motion, as was the author, methinks. His unique, accident-prone narrative presents the wording itself as the happening to the modern reader, not plot. In the opening sentence of *Death of a Transvestite,* despite the documentary precision of "seven-thirty p.m." and the realism of bars and cement, something artificial intrudes on the narrative: "We entered Glen Marker's cell, a bleak, cold arrangement of bars and solid cement, at seven-thirty p.m."[7]

The defeating contrivance of bars and cement conveys not solidity but an abstracted index to the writing process: a figurative "arrangement" of words on the page. Too precious for prison material, more peacock than jailbird, the wording haplessly refers back to itself, stylized by misadventure. In this prologue chapter to *Death of a Transvestite,* a wisecrack is pointedly, bluntly, self-referential and preened with self-congratulations. The convict, awaiting execution and about to narrate his memoirs, asks how much time he has left. Three hours: "'Just about time enough to read a novel,' Glen grinned. 'That is if one reads fast enough.'" The pronoun is too formal and affected for the genre but not for a precious transvestite like Glen — or Ed — whose royal detachment from incarceration surpasses Oscar Wilde. It is intended that we read pulp fiction quickly — dialogue is throwaway and prose stalks the plot doggedly to the end — but Wood's style constantly derails the genre by showing its artifice so that we pause to savor those beautiful and hilarious accidents and to recover what the writer *means* to say. This example wants to be a hard-boiled wisecrack according to its genre, but he flags the quip and salutes it to take full credit for crafting it. The flag is the remark on the novel, the salute is the addendum on reading fast enough, and the grin, goofy with alliteration, is the author's mask, altogether pleased with himself.

He sounds like a rejected caricature from Beerbohm's book of fictional auteurs and aesthetes with no taste, *Seven Men:* too risky for publication but somewhat like Beerbohm's seeming biographical study of "Savonarola Brown." The difference is that Ed Wood is a more vivid character than Beerbohm himself. No stereotype, he had the complexity of an artist, if not the actual artistry. His pastoral tone may surprise you, an ecclesiast's sense of responsibility in his writer's role, despite his subject matter. His sense of wonder at the process of publication, his reverence for setting the imagination in type, makes every word conspicuous, awed by the pulp medium. What to tell the multitudes? He inspires his flock with a variation on Ralph Waldo Emerson's famous maxim, "Hitch your wagon to a star," but, though the diligent reader may try to stay with him, his analogy goes off the rails and takes us into orbit, distracted by his favorite genre, science fiction, via a misguided lesson in astronomy:

Aim for the stars and if, at the end of your life, you've only reached Mars, remember one thing. Stars flicker in and flash out. Mars is a planet. A constant light. A stable entry that will be here as long as life itself.
A character even in our own solar system![8]

I find a strange and moving beauty in Ed Wood's work that renews my faith in humanity. Wood has rare credibility — not in his narrative but in his conviction in his art, his sense of wonder, and in the integrity of his naiveté. He was also opportunist, competing in commercial markets in '60s America and exploiting sensationalism, kinky sexuality and carnivalesque curiosity. But then, Venus fucks her pet unicorn in Beardsley's *Under the Hill* in 1897, so let's not spill our tea over it. Never far from destitution, Wood's sensational sleaze shows the reality of skid-row neighborhoods close to the author's residence and a long way from the aristocratic ancestry of camp. Wood was never reticent about the underside of existence so foreign to Firbank and Berners and Saki and often consigned to lowbrow genres as bad taste in the repression that disowns our primal instincts. Bad taste is one definition of kitsch.

Oblivious of his ironic effect, not modern and not postmodern either, yet he conveys the iconic and unique style of an auteur. His narrative contrivances to compel the reader backfire, beautifully. He fashions his material as do all artists and writers; the question is whether the artifact must match the intention to win artistic merit ... and that depends on the particular aesthetic. I contend that his oeuvre has equal value, in effect, to the collected works of Oscar Wilde — and just as enlightening on process. Ed Wood profiles the camp *object* that is not conscious of itself. He was simply too *fast* to be self-conscious. And, possibly, too drunk: he had Eugene O'Neill's reputation for hard drinking, which gives an intoxicating shot of this-is-the-greatest-thing-I've-ever-written to everything he wrote. Susan Sontag defines this camp type as "naïve, or pure ... the essential element is seriousness that fails," but it requires "the proper mixture of the exaggerated, the fantastic, the passionate, and the naïve." Although she divorces kitsch from camp in a loveless separation, what Sontag describes as the naïve camp object identifies the kitsch of Ed Wood. "When something is just bad (rather than Camp), it's often because it is too mediocre in its ambition. The artist hasn't attempted to do anything really outlandish."[9] Wood never lost his outlandish ambition — at least, not until he was evicted from skid-row for the last time.

Milan Kundera[10] uses "kitsch" as a pejorative value judgement on bad art, a product of mass consumption and production whose cheap plasticity can be replicated. Rosie Lugosi approaches kitsch by adapting the meters of music-hall and popular song and even opera, but then, even a sonnet or a haiku is a moulding of scansion and perhaps of patterns of thinking too. Yes, and like Wood's artiste associate Vampira, Lugosi embraces imagery from a lowbrow genre in a mass-produced medium. By this measure, most of popular culture is kitsch. Wood was certainly mass-producing an oeuvre for transient consumers. Yet he was not kitsch in Kundera's implication of undistinguished, faceless mass appeal. Just as Rosie Lugosi teases taboos and braves non-conformism, Wood and his work showed extraordinary character that stood out from his genre, however mistakenly, unmistakably. Kundera's stimulating observations make a better description than a definition — the delineations of a good definition seem faint here, making kitsch candidacy ambiguous. Its mass stereotyping and false consciousness oppose truth and individualism, says Kundera — which would not then include such a distinguished eccentric as Ed Wood, even though he tries to conform to every genre rule in the book. "The true opponent of totalitarian kitsch is the person who asks questions.... A question is like a knife that slices through the stage backdrop and gives us a look at what lies hidden behind it."[11] Camp too peeks behind the scenes — though the figurative knife (and Wood wields a few in his horror tales) turns out to be a stage prop, naturally. Kundera didn't consider the reflective capacity of camp and kitsch, in their larger than life represenations. Ed Wood and Chloe Poems come closest to kitsch in our camp ensemble, and both plant questions conspicuously, though often rhetorical. Wood intrigues the reader with question marks peppered like ellipses —

> He didn't give a good goddamn.
>   Or did he?[12]

— while Poems inspires revisionist thinking, although the rhetorical questions occasionally recall the Woody double-take of incoherence:

> If we've fucked up where we're going
>   How did we ever know where we were?[13]

Wood makes a rhetorical convention outlandish: the lurch from emphatic closure of his subject, compounded by "give a good goddamn" alliteration, only to be followed by a nagging afterthought that opens the subject and blows the convention, is peerless. Wood's questioning is intent on creating suspense. Or is it?

> The fog seems to cut through me. Could it be the Banshee? Could it be she? The reason for my return? It must be. She has to be the reason. She is calling me, but why?[14]

So overplayed, it becomes stylized. Pulp crime fiction and the horror genre — which Kundera might term kitsch — depend not on stylized individuality but narrative hooks, page-turners to keep the reader fixated on storyline. Ed Wood plants questions to make his reader want to know, what's on the other side of that page? But he does it so blatantly and melodramatically that the reader may be loath to turn the page before appreciating fully, like a fine wine from Mars, the fantastic rhetoric. The questioning reveals the genre device like a knife that slices through the stage backdrop and gives us a look at what lies behind it — a writer hitting keys like Liberace. *Hell Chicks* literally beggars belief when biker girls raid an army camp: "Who in hell could, in those first moments, believe that twelve bare-assed, leather topped broads would go screaming, tearing through the bivouac area and scoop — literally scoop them up on the cycles and speed back off into the darkness again before anyone could do anything about the situation."[15] It's a rhetorical question: we are *supposed* to believe it: the author believes it — so committed to his vision that he doesn't notice the incredulity of his readership as we wonder who indeed could believe it for a moment.

Behind the scenes of the writing process, an author's questions are private musings over plot and motivation to find narrative direction. Max Beerbohm gives a glimpse into his first attempts at writing a short story after witnessing a real altercation: "Who were they, those two of whom that one strange glimpse had befallen me? What, I wondered, was the previous history of each? What, in particular, had all that tragic pother been about?"[16] But Beerbohm recounts this struggle over plot in an article: he never did weave an answer to his embryonic questioning over plot and so the story was unfinished and never published. Ed Wood wonders aloud in a short story about two deadbeats who talk about killing for kicks, "Now, just what in hell could anybody be doing just sitting on the curb, in the dark, minding their own business?"[17] The answer, in the absence of a plot, is nothing. The story seems inspired simply by the pun in the title, "To Kill a Saturday Night," and beyond the title the author never gets past that narrative question: after talking of killing, the deadbeats fall asleep: The End. (Postmodernists can at least applaud the sentiment: Beckett with talk of murder instead of Godot.) A stalled story is no hindrance to finishing and going to press with Wood's original question to kick-start a plot for all to see on the first page.

In Quentin Crisp's early novel *Chog*, self-consciousness sometimes inhibits fluency so that, when "a noise like a wasp wrapped in tissue paper" issued from an intercom, "Someone accustomed to this phenomenon could distinguish it as the voice of Mrs. Hashett," a speculative contrivance, transparently trying to identify the speaker within local knowledge but, with no such someone at hand, the author names her anyway. A mature Crisp would flout such loyalty to realism and play the artifice confidently as a matter of style. When a G.I. "flung a note on to the floor as though it were a grenade,"[18] even if in keeping with the character it is, like his fake American pulp fiction accent, uncharacteristically indecorous for Crisp and more in keeping with Wood. Crisp grew beyond uncouth phrasing even during the progress of this novel. Wood made such touches the identifiable lifelong signature of his work.

Anachronisms may become camp by misadventure, upstaging history. In a short story attributed to Wood pseudonymously, incongruity sabotages the author's committed engagement with his narrative: the reader provides ironic distance when the archetypal Ayesha-like *femme fatale,* on the verge of a pagan supernatural ritual, commands: "'Begin the feast of earthly delights right here.'"[19]

"Right here" scrambles ancient Eastern ceremony and modern American city-slick culture that upstages the narrative and blows some surprisingly realistic dialogue. Any such incongruity, conscious or not, breaks the narrative spell, a facility of camp. "Final Curtain" is a gothic short story that opens after the last night of a stage play, when the protagonist is left alone in the theater. Wood exposes conventions of the horror genre by overplaying those breathless pauses and gothic symbols and suspenseful dashes and fearful questions — "What is this — this blackness I face here in the theater, long after all others have gone?" — the alarming exclamations a touch hysterical! It's all too stagey to allow us to forget for a moment that this is an Ed Wood story, but the venue is perfect. Empty theaters are famous haunts of old ghosts, and Wood indulges that intriguing cliché for a page or two ... but then follows his distractions with the spontaneity of an inspired lack of planning or revision, as foresight and hindsight go to the wall. There is no telling what is round the corner because the author himself is not sure where this is going. This is a theater story of the temptations of transformation as the protagonist actor is compelled to explore backstage rooms for no clear reason, unless the reader knows the author's transvestite inclinations, "All the rooms where one may change his appearance to any character nameable — and in many cases — unnameable."[20] "Nameable" is a clumsy contrivance that is redundant except as a rhetorical device to set up its opposite (in lights, thanks to overt signaling of the contrivance) and imply a taboo to intrigue the reader. A smoother posing of these rhetorical opposites would hook our interest in the next sentence. Here, the writing is so conspicuously misfit that every sentence upstages the suspense, captivating the reader unconditionally in the process itself: "the nameable" is more incredible than the unnameable.

Kitsch "represents an unwitting failure on a massive scale," says Mark Booth[21] — a quality that Wood turned paradoxically triumphant: he succeeded, literally if posthumously, beyond his wildest imagination. Andrew Ross[22] defines kitsch as "gracelessly sincere," not so skewed by irony and more a product of American culture than the camp of British reserve and the class consciousness of camp's history — though I classify the oblivious camp of Victorians Corelli and Ros as kitsch too. Camp and kitsch are cosmetic, but I imagine camp as an attitude and kitsch as an artifact, where consciousness makes all the difference. The dichotomy isn't so clear-cut if I take Kundera's point that kitsch may also describe attitude and behavior; perhaps kitsch is attitude without reflection, unenlightened behavior. Camp has a deft or spiked touch, detached from the sweeping gesture, but kitsch impact requires more force. Kitsch describes the uncritical commitment of Ed Wood. "The realization hit me as if it had been the fist of a two hundred pound man."[23] *Blam!* with the physicality of sports writing, comparisons clash and rhetoric clatters as phrasing tackles a simile. A newspaper seems made of plywood: "Glen turned the page. His eyes opened wide. He slammed the page shut."[24] Camp is aware of the boundary where enough becomes too much — and may even signify it with a mannered pause — but blithely goes beyond anyway; kitsch is oblivious and proceeds without hesitation, losing its bid for pulp impact in our awareness of its overstatement. A wife walks out on Wood's protagonist in the short story "Gemeni": "It was a tremendous kick in the face; a slap to the teeth; a smash below the belt." *Blam!* pop art meets pulp fiction.

Awed overstatement inadvertently poses not pristine beauty but obsessive-compulsive disorder: "She tended her body so carefully each night. Powder here. Perfume there. Sometimes she took as many as five baths in a day. She was lovely. 'Gemeni' could have been referred to as radiant."[25] The indiscretion puts cleanliness next to aesthetics with a rather mundane cause for all that luminosity, not the romanticism he had in mind. Coy contrivances like "could have been referred to as," like "as if it had been," enjoy the precious distance from effect that we find in camp, but so awkwardly that camp would have to distance itself from this writing too.

Yet we find kinship even between Wood's hit-and-run writing and flouting of the literary highway code and the pedestrian and precious but irregular English of Ronald Firbank. Brophy[26] finds, "Firbank was indeed grossly and gloriously ignorant not just of the forms of grammar but of its very terminology," which is merely "disdainful carelessness." Firbank's graphic inspiration from musical notation passed Wood by. Wood seems oblivious to the *look* of style on the page, and his prolific exclamation marks are driven by unconditional enthusiasm: what makes them reflective to the reader is their sheer excess, so incredible that they cannot be scanned without a double-take.

Firbank's mannered ellipses strike a contrast to Wood, who favors ellipses to signal an oncoming extravagance and simulate some ponderous conversational patterns. Firbank stops time and plot in its narrative tracks with his unique punctuation, and elliptical dialogue eavesdrops on impressionistic conversations. Like his use of questions, Ed Wood interjects ellipses to tighten suspense and promote plot but succeeds rather in highlighting the artless artifice — beautifully — augmenting unlikely figures of speech: "Besides the guy was paying her seventy-five bucks ... for ... a trip around the world ... a trip along the delights of the female frame."[27] Ellipses seep into the text, even creeping into a title, *Watt's ... After,* and dissipate the tension they aspire to generate. Like a smoke machine on a film set they give an occult air of mystery — as to what the author is intending to say — disorienting the sentence like the clauses of Kant or Hegel.

Camp and kitsch deal in excess and imitation (or quotation), but kitsch is garish with bad taste, void of the ironic inflections that dissociate from ego. It's the difference between theater and carnival, and Wood preferred carnival enough to set many stories there and draw characters from the playbill. And camp, kitsch and carnival share a characteristic identified by Sontag, "The whole point of camp is to dethrone the serious."[28] Mikhail Bakhtin's observations, too, raise the subversive and aesthetic and philosophic profile of the carnivalesque, and recommend a second look at the pages of Ed Wood, and not just a double-take. Kitsch is carnivalesque beyond camp but their close relation is demonstrated by Linda Mizejewski, who associates camp with "Bakhtin's theories of comedy and parody, particularly with regard to his well-known discussions of the carnivalesque as subversive body of discourse." Mizejewski notes how "Bakhtin sees every word enclosed in intonational quotation marks,"[29] another echo of Sontag's assertion, "Camp sees everything in quotation marks." Sontag declares finally, "The ultimate Camp statement: it's good *because* it's awful," and although I don't altogether hold with that, it promotes Ed Wood. I pose camp and kitsch along a continuum, not exclusively oppositional, but when Sontag contraposes kitsch as soulless against the camp *love* of its subjects, in this sense, in his love of the genres he exposes so haplessly and in his wondrous infatuation with the vision and the process, even in some of his pornographic exploitation, Ed Wood is camp.[30]

Jack Babuscio[31] sees the vulgarity of kitsch as "sensationalism, sentiment and slickness" — qualities that Ed Wood made paradoxically triumphant. Ross associates the camp revival of the 1960s with "the throwaway Pop aesthetic," like the aloof detachment of the throwaway line. Like the plastic construct of a cliché, kitsch is literally and materially a product of disposable culture, and so is Ed Wood, yet the value of his books escalates over time with ironic hindsight. Wood wrote books for the transient consumer at railway stations and newsstands; he specialized in the throwaway novel in throwaway genres of pulp fiction and sensational exploitation, and if you didn't catch his latest book, there will be another one along in a minute. The opening paragraph of short story "It Takes Two for Terror" in 1971 (take a moment to admire his titles) takes a disposable cliché and runs it off the thermometer, unforgettably. He literalizes the observation that camp sees everything in quotation marks—

> It was hot, the most humid day of the year. Beth got off the subway and walked slowly down the street to work. "Fry an egg on the sidewalk?" she said to herself, "heck, you could roast a whole ox and have plenty of heat to spare."[32]

That's *kitsch* heat.

If 50 percent of creativity is accident, in one draft Wood racks up that percentage with the breezy recklessness of a man who has nothing to lose, and in the process, finds his voice. Hunter S. Thompson himself would be hard pressed to let go with Ed Wood's fearlessness. He didn't rewrite, he didn't proof-read — how invigorating now that our cosmetic culture prefers image over substance. Like his film-making, his writing is a masterclass in simple pragmatism; sentences lead where they will with stark honesty that academic writers cannot imagine, so honest that his lack of control is exhilarating. His imperative pep talk to budding actors favors the Stanislavski method, and though lured further down the road of his rhetoric than he planned before leaving the house, Ed Wood was never one to turn back....

> You're a typist — learn to type! You're a laundress— do the laundry. You're a housewife — be one! You're a nurse or a doctor — don't become a nurse or a doctor, necessarily, but at least study their work.[33]

Compare his spontaneous associations to the discursive digressions of Goytisolo: we can be confident that Goytisolo will bring a clause to a coherent conclusion effortlessly. Wood achieves an impromptu conversational edge in sentences that rush headlong into the unknown, unplanned, and the incoherent meandering happens *between* sentences, without Goytisolo's fluency. It is as if Wood is victim to an inattentive, cursory translation, which is, in fact, his own treatment without as much as a conscientious editor to stand in the way of his mad dash to realize his hallucinations. Only a manic style too busy to think and too crazed with its own vision could rattle off passages like this, on Hollywood's decline and restoration:

> Recently an organization planted a few trees along Hollywood Boulevard, but it will take many years before any one of those trees gives shade to the midget who touts the Hollywood Wax Museum, which by the way is a very fine show.[34]

His rhetoric dramatizes extreme contrasts to make a point indelible; in this case, that Hollywood is so far gone it will take an age to recover. Local misfit detail juxtaposes a growing tree with a touting midget, which highlights his taste for the carnivalesque. The pace ambushes your critical faculty but an after-shock tells your nervous system that something is horribly wrong with that construction. But there isn't: it makes perfect sense, strange to say. The author recruits the most diminutive representative he can find to make the most extreme analogy. The pedestrian midget magnifies the contrast and distorts time and space along the way. A midget will be able to enjoy the shade of a sapling many years before taller homo sapiens can walk erect under the tree-lined boulevard, yet even he will have to wait many years, and so Hollywood's convalescence is more prolonged than we could have imagined. Only Ed Wood could have imagined it. He was writing high on his instinct for melodramatic relations and manic-depressive pacing that grabs the reader by the lapels before sobbing on your shoulder. The reader has *got* to keep turning those pages, the author's rent depends on it. His improbable strange-but-true rhetoric is emphatic with incontrovertible declamations. On the other hand, that midget was probably a close personal friend, and Wood, a noble and sensitive man, finds time to recommend his show at the Wax Museum — all in the same sentence: we skip over a comma from a fantastical metaphor to a breezy conversational aside. This is *weird camp.* When Wood portrays a prostitute in the throes of sexual and emotional abandon, "She clung to his neck as if it might fly away from his own shoulders."[35] In good faith, we ought to feel the desperation in this clutching embrace, but the abiding image is the zany suggestion, invoked by Wood's dramatic penchant for extremes and expressed with an uncouth and bizarre turn of phrase altogether congruent with the disfigured symbolism of his work, that the head of her lover might take off in decapitated flight. Yet this fantastic sentence is far more interesting and delightful than a conventional expression that allowed the reader to register the conventional image without batting an eyelid or bringing consciousness to bear on the wording. In consideration of plot and an inconspicuous aesthetic, we should move on to the next paragraph with subliminal facility — but camp, we know, is an exhibitionist aesthetic.

Another one-draft writer, Chloe Poems comes close to such carnivalesque imagery. The poet free associates with disconcerting incoherence and amphetamine verve in "Faith":

> Madness is the moment
> Friends become Stepford Wives,
> Hurricane building a house of cards
> Whilst tight roping on two left-footed roller skates

A razor-sharp stainless steel
Stepford knife edge of life.[36]

Inconsistent, outlandish imagery whimsically undermines the harrowing edge that these lines want to impress, kitsch enough to parade on Hollywood Boulevard, methinks. There is, though, a contextual congruence and tongue in cheek rambling design in Poems' case. Reading these authors is a dyslexic experience, as the disorienting associations displace a linear engagement with the text. I believe that Wood had no awareness of the hilarity he provoked with his disfigured expressions and earnest tone. His naiveté was as neat as his martini. You can hear the process of the author crafting his fiction, a camp and Brechtian exposure of his medium: hear the clatter in the manic depression of typewriter keys in every line. Friend and actor Paul Marco conjures the vision of the maestro at work: "He was always like a Liberace, banging away, bouncing up and down on the sofa, banging on the typewriter. I can just visualize, closing my eyes, his butt going up and down while he's banging on the damn typewriter. Just like Liberace did when he played the piano."[37]

Devil Girls rolled out of the typewriter in 1967: tough-talking pulp fiction with gender-bending girl gang machismo steeped in sex, drugs and crime. *Devil Girls* and *Hell Chicks* the following year pushed the boundaries of his screenplay for *The Violent Years* (1956) for the permissive society of the 1960s: violent females with aggressive sexuality. It's a curious counterpoint in the mainstream genre narrative that also features a masculine hero:

> Ruggedly handsome Sheriff Buck Rhodes raced his police car toward the well-lighted two-storey school building. He screeched his brakes on the gravel in front of the main entrance and behind one of his deputy's cars and a black sedan he knew belonged to school principal, Hal Carter.[38]

Typical of his forthright style, swift and thrifty punctuation doesn't inhibit the author from loading his sentences with freight: adjectives attend to a noun's every whim, pedantic, functional or sensational but never pretentious, from the full name and title of the hero and his stock pulp description to the color and make of car that he parks behind and the full name and title of its owner. A basic rule of point of view identifies closely with a character and the narrative shows only what he knows and experiences. Ed Wood makes sure by spelling out that (ruggedly handsome) Sheriff Buck Rhodes *knew* that sedan belonged to school principal Hal Carter in *Devil Girls,* which gives undue dramatic emphasis on an incidental fact and exposes the conscientious narrative that observes the rule so transparently. A scene earlier, spelling out a ship's propulsion, "He knew somewhere out

there a ship was carefully propelling its way toward the Texas coastline" ...
before pitching a hook that is not only anachronistic but belongs to another
genre altogether: "A ship which should have been flying the deaths head
and crossbones of the pirate from its mast head."[39]

Incidental description is smuggled in as naturalistic detail with naiveté
that inadvertently makes waves at the reader, a tad more gregarious than
on a need-to-know basis:

> The schoolroom they had entered was much the same as any schoolroom the
> country over, with the exception that since it was a small town school, the
> desks were a bit more crowded together.[40]

Amateur writing often crams adjectives and smuggles detail incidentally into the prose via lack of punctuation, which it is hoped will pass for
fluency. Ed Wood was a professional writer, but he never forgot his roots.
From *Side-Show Siren*, "She composed a meaningful smile on her twenty-
one year old features then smoothed the lines of the white angora sweater
down over the fire-engine red skirt."[41]

We are a long way from Oscar Wilde's aristocratic repartee, deft irony
and camp expositions on aesthetics — but not so far from the lush and gratuitous digressions of camp and Decadence. Look at Lord Berners' library,
recalled in memoir, "its elaborate gas chandeliers with their luminous globes
like gigantic incandescent fruit on Gothic branches...."[42] Camp or kitsch?
baroque or rococo? The overwhelming "gigantic" scale and "luminous"
lighting are garish, and the image of incandescent fruit is as kitsch as Liberace's candelabra — or Wood's Liberace bottom bouncing to the tune of his
typewriter. In the context of Berners' paragraph, classical references qualify the bad taste — details that Wood's schooling could not provide. Decadence and kitsch would be neighbors if kitsch could afford it, but instead
Wood types on the other side of town, where the vocabulary can't afford to
get precious. Yet there is camp here too. In *Watt's — the Difference* in 1966,
Wood assumes Oscar Wilde's effete position on a divan and indulges the
decadence of fetishism.

> He sighed, then, as he got up from the arm of Angie's chair, "Ahh, girls have
> so much more going for them — so much more fun than boys," he expounded
> while he lazily stretched out in his studio couch. "They're pretty to look at —
> Oh, so soft bodies.... The clothes...." he whispered and Angie thought he had
> climaxed just thinking about them.[43]

Sighing "Ahh" and "Oh" and "so's"and dashes and ellipses augment
the effeminate and aristocratic ennui pose, and "he expounded" is, for
Wood, a grandiose touch. But he takes the camp pose by the akimbo elbow
and lurches it into kitsch: there is no distance from the headlong drive of

desire. Wilde would never be so explicit: his society forbad it and his aesthetics snubbed vulgarity.

As transparently as the shop window reflection of his traveling film crew in *Glen or Glenda* (1953), our author highlights the artifice of the pulp genre and and makes it comic. Pauses are heavily pregnant, stilted like an actor's delivery cued by the worst director of all time. "Buck let the information sink in a moment before he spoke again. 'Okay, Bob. I'll take over now.'" I'm not sure how Wood manages consummately to labor the moment with a pace so ahead of itself but, later, Buck smiled "for the first time in several minutes."[44] Even fictional characters balk at the dialogue: "'What's up, Buck? You look like a ghost, and I don't mean the Holy one!'"[45] Firbank used punctuation to pace the prose silently and fluently (and in dialogue sometimes without intervening words), but Wood spells out the pause — and the language, pointedly — like cued speech, in *Killer in Drag:*

> She paused, then, "I'm a good shot."
> The little man batted his eyes a couple of times. "Shoot — Shoot? What is this shoot business?"
> Glenda moved the .32 a bit closer to the man. He took another step backward. "This is the kind of shoot to which I refer," replied Glenda pointedly, still with that beautiful smile.[46]

The little man is foreign, but his pigeon English sounds like a fantastic contrivance of our American writer rather than a foreign construction — laboring over "shoot" and the incongruent phrasing of the question but taking the colloquial use of "business" in his stride. Our all-American hero/ine sounds just as contrived, and between the characters we never get past the writer. The transaction reads the cues like a script-in-hand performance, exposing pulp conventions as clearly as Eric Berne revealed the socially programmed scripts and roles of everyday small-talk in transactional analysis. Watching any Ed Wood film, you are continuously aware of the calls, "Action!" and "Cut!" the only narrative reality that holds water, that unintended camp effect of actors waiting to exchange their lines on cue in the studied, rehearsed moment. His novels accomplish the same effect, as characters wait to go on and scenes are dressed by the author's vivid cinematic imagination. Narrative is shown to be a myth, a construct, as it is in reality; there are only events which the mind synthesizes into causes and effects. There is only ever this moment, the moment of punching a typeface to pulp fiction. There is no convincing history to his scenes or characters before the snap of a clapperboard or the page in the roller. "Reaction shots" are overstated, "Both men snapped their heads toward the tent as Herlie's voice came from the midway beyond,"[47] with the impression of characters on their mark *waiting* to react, making that sound mountainous.

Our absorption in narrative time surfaces and the moment of artifice suffuses our awareness as surely as in Firbank's crafted, isolated images that drop the plot.

Wood is so conscientiously exacting about a jail-break in *Side-Show Siren* that he distracts us with the process of spelling out the narrative. "They crouched on their legs, but those legs carried them fast — but not so fast as to attract attention from the occupants of the guard tower high above and behind them."[48] Clumsy even in precision, he lurches one way, "fast," and then the other, "but not so fast." The howling redundancy of stating what they were crouching on is missed by our author even as his emphatic rhetoric pointedly draws attention to it, typical of Wood's earnest voice, "but those legs carried them fast." As the escapees "lay there panting for air — gasping for that precious commodity," we will never take oxygen for granted again, or writing, as we scan "each taking deep, life-giving breaths of the fresh air." He leaves his readership in no doubt about how vital air is to his characters while the dramatic struggle for freedom is usurped by something more fascinating, a clear reflection of the mind of Ed Wood honing his craft.

As he gropes toward the end of a sentence in *Killer in Drag,* we passengers are as conscious of his difficulty as of a man lurching his way down the aisle of a moving bus:

> Although she really did like the rain she didn't relish driving in it even with an experienced driver such as the bus driver she knew to be an expert.[9]

He puts the reader on the bus in that sentence, a literary achievement, but he gives the reader no time to find a seat before he crashes the gears and goes. His style reads like a pitch to a Hollywood studio executive who gives our man just three minutes to sell his yarn. It's an oral pitch and the executive is long gone: this is the narrative of a writer talking to himself — talking, not thinking — so hooked on what he's going to say next he can hardly wait. The hooks are not merely manipulative; they express the author's enchantment with his vision:

> There had been no reason for Buck to take that road past Harriett Long's former home. But there had been something he couldn't explain which drew him in that direction ... a something which was all powerful enough to control his mind.[50]

An omnipotent stroke of excess: if it's "all powerful," it should be "enough." The strangely exhilarating melodrama is camp extravagance, bigger than the genre of the book. Wood does for the horror genre what he does for crime fiction. In a story from *Orgy of the Dead,* the mummy captures the heroine and we enjoy the obligatory "mad scientist" justification,

robbed of rationality by hysteria and appalling phrasing — you don't hear
the characters speak but you do hear the typewriter keys:

"Fiend! You're mad!"

"Mad is it! Why is it that I am mad?" The black creature's words were dangerously calm. "One is always considered mad when one says or does something which others cannot comprehend." He laughed, and the sound was the rattling of skeletons and the thunder of the tomb.[51]

That refutation of madness, punctured by crazy laughter (and despite the black creature's incongruously precious use of the pronoun "one"), is a genre headline — see Wood's own film *Bride of the Monster* (1955) — as the passage summons the entire genre to fortify the scene. True to camp style the book is bigger than itself in portraying the medium.

He subverts by accident: Wood himself is sold on the genre. Inspired, but not clever, he unwittingly makes the novel more interesting and entertaining than the seamless pulp of Ross Macdonald and Mickey Spillane, who follow convention more skilfully to keep our focus on what happens next. Ed Wood achieves the modernist goal of shifting our focus from narrative to process without spending any time on the process. The style is emblematically his own, as uniquely identifiable as any accomplished artist. Wood plays the role of pulp novelist sensationally: the prose follows the author's inspired, crazed pacing, his bouncing up and down at the typewriter. Like Liberace, he deals in kitsch superlatives that have everything but gravitas.... "Hollywood Boulevard is SWISH. The Sunset Strip is SWISHIER. And there are other places which are the most." That example leaps off the page of another 1967 novel, *It Takes One to Know One*.[52]

The easy act of answering the telephone is made ponderous by a pedantic heavy hand in *Devil Girls:* "He picked it up and put it in the using position"[53] — even more pronounced on a pay phone in *Killer in Drag*, "and when he located the object he moved immediately to it, pulled the glass door shut behind him then after depositing a coin in the proper slot, dialed a number. He waited impatiently listening to spaced ringing at the other end. During its fourth ring the other end receiver was lifted."[54] More scrupulous than documentary detail, this qualifies as a manual for foreigners. The style makes kitsch objects of everyday utilities. How removed is this from the alienation effect idealized by Brechtian Epic Theater? Leaving nothing to assumption, Wood's undue emphasis makes us intensely aware of social and mechanical actions: the portrayal of a character using the telephone is positively Brechtian....

"The actor must not only sing but show a man singing. His aim is not so much to bring out the emotional content of his song ... but to show gestures that are so to speak the habits and usage of the body," Brecht said in

1931.[55] "What is acting?" Ed Wood asks in *Hollywood Rat Race*, and his answer holds true for his writing too: "It is to portray with all your ability and sincerity a character, a *person*, with all your heart and soul."[56] The difference is in the design or intention, but the result, and dare I say perhaps the aesthetic experience, is equivalent. "Acting is an act not easily practiced," Wood says—rather like writing, he demonstrates.[57] Wood's identification with his subject is immediate, sweeping the reader along: "The glamor, the lights, the great silver screen of Hollywood. You must act! You must! You must! You must! But how?" Critical distance, an aesthetic goal of Brecht, would qualify as failure to Ed Wood, but those headline exclamations and obsessive repetitions are halted by such a show-stopping ponderous afterthought that the contrast (rather androgynous between the forceful exclamations and the effete question), as well as the showbiz rhetoric of a Broadway musical number, puts the writing itself on the stage.

Chloe Poems stages similar histrionics to halt the racing meter in "Me." The well-trodden device of the shocked afterthought appeals to the stalls, the gallery, the gods. Lines teeter on the brink of a showstopping revelation on the other side of the ego, in that Samadhi void, with punchy exclamation, repetition, ellipsis, and interrogation—after a little alliteration, naturally.

> Shining medals of valor and velour
> To prove I've lived and survived
> Survived!
> Survived...
> Survived?
> Survived what?[58]

These are the authors "Who dared to explore venture /Into the terrifying world of sexploitation."[59] True, Wood does not share Poems' political consciousness. The single hapless revelation triggered by Ed Wood is the fantastic artifice of the miraculous moment when improbable sentences form and slapdash across the page. These masters of the double-take make us scan the line again to check that we haven't missed a sentence.

In *Killer in Drag*, the immediacy of the man on the phone ("when he located the object he moved immediately to it") is sabotaged by the detail that prolongs the moment and distances the reader from any urgency that the author had in mind. The pulp fiction of Harry Stephen Keeler, early in the 20th century, shows some of this literal and self-conscious language; Ed Wood salutes that American heritage and runs it up the flagpole gloriously. An incongruent male voice reveals another killer in drag in *Side-Show Siren*: "It was Clay Warner's voice that dominated the rouged lips, that spat the words at the startled group."[60] The stark pointing at the voice, the kinky phrasing of "dominated the rouged lips" to incriminate a masculine tone behind a female impersonation, the whole declamation is so stilted yet casual yet as melodramatic as rebuttal court testimony that the speech sounds overtly like studio dubbing. Our credulity remains aloof even though the author is fully committed. Our perspective is not a matter of superiority but a privileged view from the wings. Wood is our guide to areas of the mind that we would otherwise need exotic stimulants to access. Thanks to Ed Wood, over time the modern reader sees the artifice askance, which offers delightful compensation of laugh after laugh and the revelation of rhetorical structures that other writers get away with but Wood, thankfully, cannot.

The definite article, never more definite than when asserted by Ed Wood, is a zooming device that looks to create suspense with dramatic close-ups. Even the indefinite article is emphatically definitive in narrative hooks, each emotive term hooking into the next sentence. In a paragraph spaced apart from the rest of the text in *Side-Show Siren,* "Not far from Judge Henry and the others, a set of eyes peered through a peep-hole in the side of a tent. Hatred burned in those eyes. A hatred steeped in memories that only death could erase. Death in the violent overtones of murder."[61] The emphatic rhetoric accumulates its melodramatic portent by echoing an emotive word in each successive sentence, which in turn propagates another charged term, from "those eyes" to "hatred," and from "hatred" to "death," cliff-hanging terminally on "murder." This is the narrative of matinee serials, each sentence another thrilling instalment, and we see through the device to fully appreciate the artifice. You could frame those indefinite articles in captioned panels in a comic strip sequence....

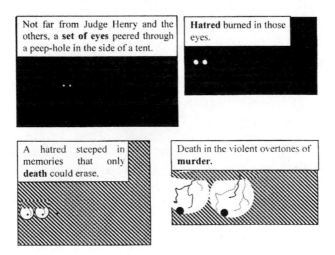

In today's market, Wood may have collaborated with an illustrator to specialize in the graphic novel — but Wood's amazing prose is already vividly visual.

Failing to achieve mediocrity, the innocuous benchmark of a "pass," he achieves by misadventure an extraordinary distinction that lives on like art. The modesty of a naturalistic or figurative aesthetic may not satisfy offbeat readers: for them Wood's appeal is his outlaw status. Even those furtive traits, slipped in as authentic detail, stand out as oddities: "Mr. Long began twitching slightly his left eyebrow — something one of the sub-curators warned her about. Whenever he did that, he was very annoyed."[62] It scans a tad too mannered, too pronounced for the reader to easily note and move on without arching a brow of his own — the arched brow, that camp signifier that sets itself aloof from identification. A kindred spirit, here is Sacher-Masoch in *Moonlight,* 1868: "And the proud woman, who rarely rewarded avowals of devotion with anything more than a contemptuous twitch of her eyebrow, walked up to him and spoke first."[63] Marie Corelli scales this peak of loftiness with her lips in 1896: "She smiled — a smile so slight and cold that it scarcely lifted the corners of her lovely lips."[64] Such graphic close-ups become another device that magnifies the pause — even when nothing is happening in *Side-Show Siren:* "It was several long minutes before either of them attempted to move as much as an eyebrow."[65] The character must not only raise an eyebrow, he must show a man raising an eyebrow, to paraphrase Brecht.

Yet seedy, frontline realism will occasionally convince the Ed Wood reader. *Devil Girls* investigates juvenile delinquency on the edge, wonders about social causes and worries about trends: its sensational account of the desperate influence of drugs no longer seems sensational. All the same, juxtaposed with the tough genre tone, a quaint gentleman's code is signaled by genteel compliments to a preening southern belle:

> "Miss O'Hara. You are a mighty lovely woman when you smile!"
> "Well, thank you Sheriff Rhodes."[66]

Occasionally the writing chokes on Lichtenstein tears, especially in denouements. Greeny lies dying after the shoot-out in *Side-Show Siren.* He was a greasy carnival underling in the plot, but he drenches the ending in kitsch sentiment. At the end of it all, "Pat was crying, and he didn't care who knew it." Sentiment was less conspicuous in Victorian romances, and so Marie Corelli gets away with Lionel's goodbye note in 1896 in *The Mighty Atom*—"I couldn't go on living — I was so very tired."[67]— but not in urbane retrospect, and not in 1966 when Wood wrote *Side-Show Siren.* This is a fey fragment of what Pat was crying about: "Greeny's eyes rolled — he looked out over the side area for a long time. 'I'm so very tired.'"[68]

But watch out in *Devil Girls,* a volatile masculine-feminine synergy, where Wood's taste for melodrama can swing hysterically away from sentiment:

> The sadness overwhelmed Mrs. Purdue's voice. She felt older than her years. Her entire life had collapsed before her eyes in a matter of moments. "Can't hurt me anymore." The tears twinkled in her tired old eyes. "Can't hurt me anymore.... " Then her voice rose to a screaming pitch. "How soon you have forgotten. LILA KILLED YOUR FATHER!" And with that outburst, Mrs. Purdue dived at the gun.[69]

Capital letters seem a kitsch way of raising the emotional tone, but then, screaming IS kitsch! The escalation is so schizoid—from maudlin pity to startling rage and the old woman's physical rise to heroic status—that it provokes incredulous detachment even from screaming capitals. Wood is adept at eliciting maximum hysteria from exclamations and italics in "Gore in the Alley":

> *She could be wrong!*
> *She had never been wrong before!*[70]

—a story whose opening sentence is marvelously crazed, juxtaposing a pedestrian act with a fantastic exclamation to headline the banality on a line of its own,

> She walked!

Even the conscientious reader must let go of any last trace of rational continuity, which induces the same effect as a punchline. The artless lurch from one extreme to the other is kitsch, but Wood gives a philosophical pay-off: ironic detachment from life's drama through performative overstatement and incongruous displacement. Elsewhere, hysteria provokes an eccentric phrase, "her voice was a high pitched entity of surprise,"[71] all the more original for provoking the reader's double-take. All writers struggle conscientiously with variations on the trite "she said," concealing the effort behind their naturalistic alternatives—but Wood does it all out loud in strained constructions like, "'You're in there,' she ventured through strained vocal cords."[72] The sleazy exploits and cynical dialogue of a tough girl biker gang in *Hell Chicks* do not restrain precious commentary like, "opined Flame," and, "'Where the hell do we go tomorrow, Flame?' expounded Cherry," where "expounded" is not only culturally incongruous but unrelated to the act of questioning. The author gets heavy-handed for a tougher tone, "Flame slammed her voice at the unseen adversaries."[73] No matter how sleazy the characters or thrusting the action, these aberrant elaborations continuously return us to the eccentric character of the writer at work.

Weird speech patterns that bedeviled his scriptwriting also distinguish his fiction:

> "Cops! Always cops! Why should I be so intimidated by such cops? How do I make money for the company when passes I gotta give because cops and big shots say I gotta?"[74]

Schizophrenic dialogue juxtaposes uncouth phrasing of the street in "gotta" and "big shots" (and, to nail it to the street, "gotta" again), with the unlikely choice of a rather objective "intimidated" and the "so" and "such" of a prim and very feminine English schoolteacher. Those insistent exclamations and interrogations "play it straight" despite the absurd, inverted contrivance, reaching the heights of deranged melodrama to model Wood's theatrical advice in *Hollywood Rat Race* to portray character "with all your heart and soul." The most wonderful incongruity is Wood's wholehearted investment and the reader's incredulous detachment from the narrative.

A driver speeds his passenger toward imminent collision in *Devil Girls*, toward her ever so eloquent and philosophical last words (she *is* a teacher):

> It was more than possible the last few seconds of her life were speeding toward her shaking body. Her stomach pumped violently up against her lower ribcage. Her breathing came in short gasps. She bit her trembling lower lip to keep from screaming. She had to speak and the words came out in a rush of air. "Don't you realize you're looking into eternity?"[75]

The phrasing thrusts *seconds* like projectiles in a bizarre but inventive construction. The teacher's learned last words undermine the simulation of adrenalin that Ed Wood is giving everything he's got to achieve. Once we disbelieve the credibility of the artifice, we are now watching the process of writing, not the narrative developments. We read the passage ironically, but this time the irony is the reader's, while the writer remains as fully committed to his vision as that speeding driver. The page-turning pulp fiction would have us ride the suspense and press on to the collision. Perhaps we *are* carried along in Wood's speedy slipstream, until that line releases a greater force of laughter than the narrative momentum: this moment climaxes the scene, regardless of what happens next.

Hell Chicks depicts hippy culture in a strange cultural exchange with biker girls, presenting dialogue like this:

> "Oh, now that ain't no way for anybody to talk to us, the 'Flower Children' of the world who look only for peaceful ways to live. We have come to the land of the open spaces to rid ourselves of the violent world beyond. But it is not beyond us to retaliate to some violence if it becomes necessary. Rather, however, girls of the leather fetish, we much prefer to toss flowers into your hair."[76]

Wood seems to borrow from North American Indian patois via Hollywood westerns, but the hippy talk feels so surrealistic in its stilted and totemic construction that not even LSD would account for it. It is not possible to suspend disbelief long enough to read this dialogue, as fiction readers dutifully try to do. These amazing contrivances project the author as he envisions the scene and then fashions what he imagines to be convincing dialogue: that is what we are reading here. Some wise words from the hippy leader:

> "Ah," grinned the bearded fat man. "The essence of true reality — it is what you desire. The weed — the pot — the grass — the heavy smoke with which one might visit the stars and the planets beyond and the finding of the center of the earth."

Massive cumulative synonyms on the potency of pot (which he goes on to dismiss in comparison to harder drugs), and the contrivances "with which one might" and "the finding of the center of the earth," fashion bizarre idioms that would seem out of place anywhere on earth. "— It is what you desire" is a favorite perverted Wood construction: its self-conscious pronoun seeks the spotlight in *Orgy of the Dead* ("'Mad is it! Why is it that I am mad?'"), where "it" inverts the subject in stilted disorientation.

Wood achieves the same incredulity with his similes, never subtle when contrasting extremes raise the stakes. "His words of attack had about as much effect on them as a fly's attack on an elephant," in *Devil Girls,* may recall the midget and the tree in *Hollywood Rat Race.* In a knife fight, the simile suddenly turns coy at a cliché, like feminine reserve at incongruous machismo: "Lila's entire movement was not unlike the rattlesnake." "Entire," like "complete," is a common all-or-nothing adjective in Wood's larger than life pitches. "The courage of a James Bond filled his entire frame," a boyish evocation of adventurous heroism that arm-links Ian Fleming's iconic secret agent into a cameo.[77]

Stake-outs and shoot-outs backfire beautifully in the pulp fiction of Ed Wood. After scenes of rape and murder, the biker girls in *Hell Chicks* are staked out: the sheriff's men make themselves heard through the dramatic darkness with some straight-talking to the renegades. "'We're tired of your nonsense! The likes of you have got to meet your fate.'"[78] The author's voice has the place surrounded. The finale of *Devil Girls,* a shoot-out and stand-off on a drug smuggler's boat, lines up the forces of good: Sheriff Buck Rhodes, the Reverend Steele, Jockey and a giant Indian chief. They have been waiting to act this moment for the whole novel. The crowning coup, shuffling out of the shadows, is Mrs. Purdue, the old mother of the delinquent girls. We are not prepared for this—"'Ma!' screamed Rhoda in utter disbelief," expressing the reader's gasp. The old woman is still carrying a bullet from an earlier mishap, but she bravely turns heroine and advances on her armed daughters....

> Mrs. Purdue grimaced suddenly in complete pain. She doubled over slightly.
> "You're hurt badly," shouted Buck. "Please come back here, Mrs. Purdue, or I'll have to come after you."
> She straightened again. "Don't do that Sheriff Rhodes. Don't risk your life. She will not shoot me."

Lurching from "complete pain" to the discrediting qualifier "slightly," not only can you see his vivid scenes, you see the mind's eye of the author visualizing them too. The accelerated pace amplifies the color and panel-busting action of a comic strip. Kitsch prose accelerates the narrative, sold on the same newsstands to a transient readership — yet over time these disposable paperbacks have become as collectable as comics. Comic strips are a spasmodic series of still life images. Wood replicates this abrupt action in prose. "Cherry reached her hand out with the swiftness of a striking snake and tore the boy's shirt from his body," in *Hell Chicks,* is fast narrative like the caption to an action comic panel.[79] He saturates still life scenes with simple, stark detail and ambience of the kind that comic strips encapsulate in a single panel. In a carnival tent in *Side-Show Siren,* at the peak of his literary powers in 1966, men are seated at an old table: "Jinx, Duke, Herlie and Pat viewed their cards by the dull illumination of a single yellowed bulb, stuck in a socket hanging on a cord from the tent ceiling," as simply vivid as a Hopper painting.[80] Like Hopper, he sets up a scene with figures that intimate a narrative, with simplistic detail and vivid, defining colors that exude atmosphere.

Roy Lichtenstein made the comic strip camp by isolating a panel in time and space, which stretched our distance from the narrative and made the kitsch impact of line and color and pixelated pulp seem mannered and iconic to the viewer in a gallery. Firbank isolated images to pause the plot and admire his painterly vignettes. In critically isolating passages of his novels, you might say we're doing the same for Ed Wood — and in making their construction so *conspicuous,* he is surely helping. In the finale of *Watts ... After* in 1967, after the hero's defense of democracy on live television, "Angie stood up and applauded. Sonny joined her, and as Rance let the tears flow freely, Rocky could read Angie's lips as they said, 'I'll marry you my darling....'"[81] You can picture the comic-strip panel encapsulating a genre, blown up to Lichtenstein proportions, the kitsch equivalent of Wilde's pithy epigrams.

Meanwhile, in *Devil Girls...*

Mrs. Purdue used every ounce of strength she had left as she pushed Lila's arm upward and the gun fired harmlessly into the air. She at the same time pushed her backward and both, losing their footing, went over the guard rail and into the speeding propeller at the fan tail.[82]

Foregrounding an old woman in a hard-boiled crime novel, like the little old lady who opens his wild-west story, "Pearl Hart and the Last Stage," signifies Wood's egalitarian world where the forgotten and the fugitive find a part to play. Sometimes it's a circus, but dwarves, giants, hermaphrodites, juvenile delinquents, prostitutes, junkies, and most of all transvestites are the author's beautiful people. His extraordinary repertory of film actors embraced heroin-addicted (and presumed dead) Bela Lugosi, camp goth Vampira, and the theatrical prophet with transsexual aspirations, Criswell ... all are welcome in his underworld of outcasts that rather recalls Quentin Crisp's wonderful misfit Soho social circle or Benson's familiar relations with *The Freaks of Mayfair*. And so "Gore in the Alley" raises the profile of the downbeat prostitute to the status of convincing protagonist and has no difficulty identifying intimately with her. Not the aristocratic lineage of camp but the everyman embracing the outcast, both down on their luck. Underworld realism and bizarre sensationalism is another diversion from the plot on the reader's eyeline. He secures pathos for the prostitute even on a razor blade killing spree. It even ends on a high, of a kind — that characteristically deranged, Ed Wood high, the freight train impetus of kitsch sensibility that only a train wreck can stop:

Perhaps there was another client lurking somewhere in those dark shadows. *Another client for her special brand of thrills!*[83]

Even the contrivance of a denouement (as life's real-time narrative unfolds without closure) is exposed as artifice.

Diary of a Transvestite Hooker fell somewhere between pornography and Walt Disney in 1974: "I can't wait to be had when I'm decked out like a cute little fuzzy bunny rabbit — remember the angora in my wardrobe?"[84] How could we forget? The Ed Wood reader must come to terms with his personal fetish sooner or later: like Alfred Hitchcock's walk-on appearances, angora is the exhibitionist cameo motif in all his work. He spells out his fetish with such pronunciation that the word itself becomes fetishistic, just as fetishism literalizes the symbol as the signified. "'Angora,' she said aloud. 'What a delightful sound. What a magnificent feeling.'"[85]

Even the sordid short story of a downbeat prostitute, nearly twenty years after *Glen or Glenda*, as she takes off her panties and stuffs them down her cleavage, the author smuggles in the detail with transparent legerdemain:

"They would remain there, held by the tight pink angora sweater she wore."[86] In Wood's work, angora becomes a symbol of redemption that bequeaths a state of grace on the wearer, a pagan holy icon, the chimera of indefatigable idealism for a better way of being. It is as conspicuous and elemental as furs in Sacher-Masoch. Such devoted fetishism is never a subliminal motif: it is noticed too frequently and reverently, despite an absurd pretense of incidental detail: their furs are stage props. Wanda in Sacher-Masoch's *Venus in Furs* is even seen exiting a furriers, as conspicuous a signifier as the shopfront. In that showcased signposting, behold camp. I don't know that Ed Wood read *Venus in Furs,* but I delight in the aesthetic similarities between texts over eighty years apart, one deemed classic, the other, trash. Ed Wood has Sacher-Masoch's venerating wonderment and idealistic rhetoric to boot, somewhere between eulogy and a confessional tone so open it borders on bombast. As Wood's close focus makes bizarre iconography of the raised eyebrow, Sacher-Masoch dedicates stop-motion saturation to the twitching, scornful lip of a Mistress.

Continuing a traditional association with camp, Wood's joyful obsession crosses gender codes in *Killer in Drag* and at least seven other books. Sometimes angora is smuggled into the prose as foxily as innuendo, only slightly odd here in *Side-Show Siren:* "'Mine too,' chimed in Shirley, pulling her angora cardigan tight around her, against a sudden, slight chill of the night." It gets more attentive twenty pages on, on the pretext of reassuring the woman, "Tom patted her angora sweater-covered arm attentively."[87] *Killer in Drag* saturates the indulgence. After a few clues—a protagonist called "Glen," as in *Glen or Glenda;* his "expensive, effeminately decorated apartment"; then, "'Yes?' The voice was almost too musical to be that of a man...." the transvestite revelation is dramatized with kitsch impact:

> He picked up the gun affectionately and slipped it smoothly into a pocket of the garment he was wearing. That garment was a fluffy, floor length, pink marabon negligee.[88]

Transvestism embellishes the pattern of incongruities as he evokes his clear vision of feminine finesse — without finesse. Tough-talking pulp fiction is bent to accommodate the trappings of effeminacy as the anti-hero turns *femme fatale.*

> Glenda's voice was low, but hard. A mixture of both hers and Glens. But there was no mistaking the expression on her face. Glenda was mad and could kill this Mousy creep with no more compunction than she would have stepping on a spider — perhaps less.[89]

His style can't resist the rhetorical afterthought — no matter how redundant. "Perhaps less" is even moreso in the simile: Ed Wood deals in excess. Naming the voice and an extra moment to first draw attention to a facial expression sets up the description emphatically, a technique of suspense that is endemic in the genre, made melodrama when the author oversteps the mark. He observes the masculine phrasing of the genre, direct and laconic, but there is always one laconic sentence too many, and often three laconic sentences in one, and emphasis falls on the incongruous. Action is never so important as what the protagonist is wearing, and when he prepares for masculine combat, the uniform is feminine. Dashiell Hammett in drag: "Glenda could really wear a sweater — and she usually did. Especially on jobs like this."[90]

His fixation diverts a sentence even in a shoot-out in *Side-Show Siren*, as a speeding car crashes into a Ferris Wheel: "Donna, still wearing the brown skirt and pink Mohair sweater, forced open the partly sprung door on the driver's side, and got out. She held a pistol in each hand."[91] There is a plotline expediency in identifying the female attire here, but it turns the prose into a fashion show at the most inopportune moments, like the "fur-trimmed sleeve" of Wanda's whip-hand, smuggling clauses that refuse to stay incidental, shifting the weighting and usurping the action of the sentence like scene-stealing stage asides. "The Negro, wearing a long flannel nightgown and robe, got to his feet and raced into the room."[92] Pausing on decorative detail contradicts the urgent action — Wood's illustration of how camp is more enamored of form than function.

Wood is infatuated with his transvestite vision, like Sacher-Masoch's lunar wonderment and epic Romanticism. Indeed, "[her] fur heaved and sank on her surging bosom like a moonlit wave" is Sacher-Masoch yet so consistent with Wood's sensibility. *Venus in Furs* sets up the subject: "Here she was— Venus. But without furs. No, this time it was the widow, and yet — Venus. Oh! What a woman!" before plunging into spellbound, moon-struck Romanticism, like Wagner in drag. "And now her eyes struck me like a bolt of green lightning. Yes, they were green, those eyes, with their indescribable gentle power; green, but green like precious stones, like deep, unfathomable mountain lakes."[93] He expresses the same enraptured exclamations, the melodramatic use of the dash, the epic, sky-high symbology. And here is Ed Wood: "To say that Glenda walked across the spacious lobby to an elevator is not enough." We know right there that an elaborate metaphor — or two or four — is on its way. Corelli signals her vision of femaleness in just this superlative way in 1892 in *The Soul of Lilith*: "To say merely that she was lovely would scarcely describe her —for the loveliness that is generally understood as such was here so entirely surpassed and intensified that it would be difficult, if not impossible to express its charm."[94] When we focus, we magnify; when we elaborate, we exaggerate: Ed Wood takes that principle on a world cruise:

Glenda didn't just walk. Watching her was to feel the pleasant roll of a luxury
liner; the smooth flow of an airplane high in the altitudes, entering silent
drifts of white cloud puffs over a clear day. She moved as though she were an
angel or a specter in a wonderful dream.[95]

The metaphor of a luxury ocean liner to trace her elegant wake is colossal, yet majestic, apropos of feminized masculinity, and succeeding
metaphors defy gravity and realism with simple naivete. The author may
have written that rapturous passage without once opening his eyes. Marie
Corelli exalts the peerless archetype with dreamy idealism again in 1889,
with an exotic nude dancer who is barely earthbound: "Then—like a
rainbow-garmented Peri floating easefully out of some far-off sphere of
sky-wonders—an aerial Maiden-Shape glided into the full luster of the
varying light...."[96] "Easefully" is the most lush adverb for effortlessness in
motion, and the wonderful fancy of "far-off sphere of sky-wonders" shows
how ethereal and elusive this enchanted vision of perfect femaleness must
be to preserve its phantom chastity. Rider Haggard's generation was
bewitched by romantic fantasy and the timeless archetype popularized as
Ayesha in *She,* and modern transvestism can see the attraction.

A transparent subtext in Wood's narrative speaks touchingly and honestly and comically of a deep need. For all his sensationalism, the author
broaches intimacy with his readers that is unprecedented in pulp crime
fiction and most other genres:

Rose hastened to add, "Please, Glenda. Take me with you. Oh not as a legal
wife, I know you don't want that sort of an arrangement. I would cook for
you. We could make your special kind of love."[97]

Her reaction to Glen's transformation is as uncritical as the author's
editorial capacity, emphatically indulging the transvestite fantasy of looking not only "convincing" but as irresistible as a Corelli heroine.

The aspiration to womanhood is reinforced by signifiers that spotlight
the effeminate manner as not-male and portray masculinity as uncouth as
a pig's trotter, according to camp's amenity to extreme contrasts and exhibitionist incongruities. The "man-womanly mind" of Virginia Woolf's ideal
never quite gets together for Wood, though all the constituents are there in
his books. The separatism is dramatized in Glen's psyche.

Glenda liked that. Glen never did. But Glenda appreciated the longer walk; she
enjoyed hearing those high heels click on hard cement. She could, and many
times did, walk for miles just listening to her spike heels as they clicked along
rhythmically.[98]

The high heels, clicking like his wishful typewriter, echo in *Death of
a Transvestite* and "Gore in the Alley," too: the call and response of a need

to be accepted as female. The author opens his heart and mind to bring his readership intimately close to the transvestite experience. The mirror image is never far away in *Killer in Drag,* but its affirmation is aloof from ego: the entranced identification with an archetype of the feminine ideal, and the focal length of the mirror, measures our distance from the identification — far enough for Brecht. Far enough, too, for transvestite pornographer Zack in *Hell Chicks,* who agrees with a girl who thinks he's cute, "'I always have. And only my mirror can tell for sure.'"[99]

Transvestism, the *staging* of femininity offset by masculine subtext (or vice versa), making masquerade of gender, is a typecast identifier of camp. This social incongruity is driven to extremes by stereotyped machismo and alluring femininity endemic in crime fiction. His transvestites do not deny their masculinity, an openness he shares with Chloe Poems. Wood's denouements are no less sensational for that. Masculine-feminine energies are always full-on and the tension between them sparks the dynamics and breaks the gender boundaries of the genre.

The murderer in *Side-Show Siren* is revealed as the carnival attraction Donna, half-man half-woman. His motivation for killing women is as unlikely as his dialogue in the final shoot-out and stand-off, but here goes: "'Not one that I put into the grave deserved the right to call themselves woman. My cousin, the real Donna and me — we are more woman than any I sent into oblivion!'" The murderer is wearing a woman's carnival costume but his wig is pulled off— a traditional exposing finale in camp transvestite performance. "'Donna was in himself a great person — but with little guts for ridding the world of creatures in the female form both of us should have possessed!'"

The unwitting genius of this denouement is the fantastic confluence of incoherence and incongruence in dialogue, motivation and situation. It climaxes earlier intimations of transvestism in *Side-Show Siren.* These are effeminate transformations of the most butch imagery, a monster and a brusque, patriarchal cop, whose extreme contrasts are a camp constituent: the Abominable Snowman, escaped, whose brute force stumbles into a women's clothes rack in a carnival tent and tries them on under the pretext of feeling the cold; and then, bashful Sheriff Myers prepares for an all-night vigil to protect the carnival and searches a woman's wardrobe for a cape (of black velvet): "He took it off the hanger and tossed it to Myers. 'The boys won't laugh at you wearin' Dolly's cape.'" Yes, and, "Gratefully, Myers draped the heavy garment over his shoulders."[100] Myers is a brave hero, nonetheless, just as Wood was a "decorated" war hero indeed who went into battle wearing women's underwear. These self-conscious flirtations with transvestism feel like innuendo, spotlit by our awareness of the

artless and educative subtext. Wood is incidentally showing his readers the
reality of transvestism through unrealistic contrivances in the novel.

The Glen/da dynamic is a schizoid dramatic contrast in *Killer in Drag,*
where, like Mister (or Sister) Hyde, "Glen was taking over more and more,"
and of course he pushes the dramatic tension too far and evokes that
deranged quality that is Ed Wood all over: "Glen laughed. Oh-oh — Too
musical."[101] One of Wood's inspired derangements is the borrowings of 19th
century Romanticism in his pulp fiction (culled from the romantic legacy
in culture rather than direct reading) because there is nothing in the genre
language of crime novels and horror tales to articulate the elevated femininity of transvestism. The most popular romantic fantasist of her time,
Marie Corelli fetishizes female couture in *Delicia* much as transvestism
would: "the care of this special gown was her delight; her mistress had only
worn it once, and then had looked such a picture of ethereal loveliness as
might have made 'Oberon, the fairy king,' pause in his flight over flowers
to wonder at her...."[102] Romantic idealism speaks the language of fairy tales,
and so Corelli's heroine in *Vendetta!* is "a veritable queen of the fairies...."[103]
And so, with some imagery from 19th century Romanticism, minus the
poetry, a transvestite in *Killer in Drag* "flounced around his apartment like
a fluttering old auntie, like a nymph in a flower bed; a fairy in the scented
woodlands."

Transvestites spend a quiet evening at home in *Killer in Drag* and glory
in camp: in their elevated femininity; innuendo couched in euphemism;
mirroring imagery and conversation; and gender incongruity that subverts
yet confirms a precious stereotype of womanliness— with heavier weighting than deft femininity and pauses more labored than subtle irony....

> "Are you comfortable?" Glenda asked diplomatically with a raised eyebrow.
> "Well — I should think so."
> "Good. So am I. We are dressed as we feel best for our own comfort."
> "You dear thing."[104]

Here in transvestite garb, in precious tones, is where we find the aristocratic lineage of camp. The raised brow arches the irony that is underscored "diplomatically"; the dash measures the poise before the response;
the theatrical garb of "attire" and the precious construction that puts the
consequence at arm's length from the conditional clause, "had I really fully
realized..." are all effeminate effects ... made a tad inane by that last remark
that is indeed an "old auntie" thing to say but doesn't quite follow from the
exchange. It's the characteristic moment of incoherence that transports us
to a phantom dimension uncharted by logic, literature or the laws of time
and space — the glorious pay-off for the modern Ed Wood reader. As much

as Brophy credits Firbank's isolated images, Wood succeeds in fashioning that ironic distance ... at least, in one out of three counts: "distancing of reader from book, of writer from book, and of reader from writer."[105] Incredulity, as much as hapless revelation of process and those incoherent juxtapositions, keeps our distance, yet this writer's oblivious commitment to his work is part of the charming irony. Lastly, the modern reader, like myself, is likely to feel not alienated but affectionately close to this wonderful writer. He is a cult figure now, and his books are cult artifacts.

> And what she didn't conjure up in her own mind was created by the newspaper accounts of her daring adventure into the badlands territory. Altogether, these made her break out into the cold sweats of fame.
>
> Time would be good in telling her just how famous she had become ["Pearl & the Last Stage"[106]].

Time, and the cold sweats of fame, came too late for Ed Wood. He declined into alcoholism and poverty, finally, as opportunities to finance his dreams deserted him. When he was evicted from his home in 1978, his last work in progress, a biography of his friend Bela Lugosi, with a publishing deal in place, was left behind and lost to history and literature. Lugosi's life is well documented now, but the facts are incidental to the irreplaceable style that was lost in that final document. We must take heart that the evicted master was working on his dreams to the end.

There was no obituary for Edward D. Wood, Jr. Inspired but unassuming, he was a noble eccentric and fearless dreamer with a gift for naiveté even in the face of his own sleaze. Ed Wood's fantastically preserved sense of wonder and his intoxicated enthusiasm bring the best out of life.

"Far fetched? Think about it!"[107]

Juan Goytisolo (1931–)

"What happened some hundred and forty-five years
later came out of the blue."
—*A Cock-Eyed Comedy,* 2000

Juan Goytisolo, camp?

Firbank and Saki and Berners and most of Wilde are camp. Most of Goytisolo's distinguished career takes no such interest. His prose is more muscular than the feminine styles of most camp writers— though he can be exquisitely lyrical. Goytisolo's stories seldom highlight female characters— though transvestite and transsexual characters, male-to-female, are prominent. All the same, Goytisolo is so prolific that his mature contribution to camp aesthetics enlightens the genre. He aspires to "a totalizing art" rather as Powell and Pressburger created "total cinema," and look how camp cinema became in *The Red Shoes* and *The Tales of Hoffmann* (1948, 1951). He intellectualizes camp in his Brechtian mission to reveal the manipulations of media —forging the novel with journalism, essay, memoir, drama. His craft is as studied as Ed Wood is naïve. There is a maturity about Goytisolo's prose beyond any other featured writer here, which makes his camp candidacy ingeniously problematic. Always edifying, with an educative remit where camp plays truant, he borders precipitously on being serious. For instance, camp fuses masculine-feminine energies and gender roles, androgynously, transsexually, effeminately, but it doesn't do it like this, by treatise, in *Quarantine:* "Who talks in the masculine and who in the feminine? Isn't the distinction between the sexes negated in the zone of subtlety? What can we do about the rules of grammar? Why do we refer to He and not She?"[1] Camp doesn't labor the question but lets style demonstrate. That's not to say that Goytisolo is never ironic or detached — only inconsistently so. His prose is often too dense to make space for the arched pause that signals irony. His long sentences maintain a conscientious grammatical cohesion, brilliantly, fluently, but cannot detach from their scrupulous concentration — just as the reader frowns to follow the subjects of sentences, sometimes through lists of intricate detail as dense as Naturalism.

Goytisolo's intellectual gravitas and political realism bravely confront stern, empirical home-truths beyond, say, Firbank's flights of fancy. Academic rigor shows in his multi-cultural diversity, in the erudite depth of research that authenticates his narratives, and in his incorporation of literary criticism of his own work. Ennui, a disinclination for the work ethic and a cavalier disregard for academia often deters such detailing in camp works. Firbank's travels barely inform the exotic cultures of his tales, and the only documentation that informed his novels was "the habit of writing down on long strips of paper any phrase that particularly struck him and hoarding these strips in his desk."[2]

Goytisolo frivolously rips up religious icons and juxtaposes genres and historic periods as if by cut-up method, a cavalier conjuring of anachronism and form. Goytisolo is an aesthetic anarchist, importing into his fiction any genre formula that suits his collage. His fantasy *The Marx Family Saga* integrates the essay form with more animation and ironic reflection than Kundera. "I must confess, I wanted to shut the book and declare it was one big leg-pull!"[3] expresses the critic's fear of being hoaxed that Arthur Waley identified in 1929. This chapter examines how Juan Goytisolo, in postmodern maturity, is occasionally miraculously camp.

Camp seems immature in its breezy frivolity and effeminate domesticity and attention to surface, preserving child-like distance from society: you can read the distance in Wood, Firbank, Poems, Berners, Saki ... even in Wilde's seasoned urbanity, paradoxically. Many constituents of camp aesthetics are variables. Goytisolo is camper than Ed Wood to this extent: artfully aware of the process, his narrative consciously discloses the writer writing: his books are a performance, a *tour de force*. Techniques such as multiple narratives in *The Garden of Secrets,* ostensibly written and read aloud by a writers' group, or the first-person character who passes on the M/S of *A Cock-Eyed Comedy* to the reader "just as it came" mailed to the character, or the conspicuous integration of historical authors into the fictional ensemble, all challenge the authority of the author and preserve skeptical distance from the medium.

Even Karl Marx may be someone else behind that beard. As the author interviews him in *The Marx Family Saga,* his character is under suspicion:

his professional actor style, of a man used to pacing the boards, to delivering the quick, precise retort, deepens your uncertainty, your unease
    is the man seated opposite the real Marx, the character in your novel, or

worse still the protagonist of the Euro-financed co-production soap written by two brilliant luminaries of the French intelligentsia?[4]

And that's aside from whether Marx stands up to examination in the light of contemporary history.

In 1997, *The Garden of Secrets* depicts the author himself as a work of fiction: after all, the author is defined by his books. This is the camp take on narcissism that preserves the focal length of the mirror image. Milan Kundera makes it palatable for serious critics: "All novels, of every age, are concerned with the enigma of the self. As soon as you create an imaginary being, a character, you are automatically confronted by the question: What is the self?"[5] The self is a fiction, and narcissism is a work of art. At the end of the collective narrative of *The Garden of Secrets,* the Reader's Circle invent an author for their collective tales, trying Goitisolo, Goitizolo, and arriving at Juan Goytisolo, with the author's actual biography and bibliography, whose very face on the dust jacket is "a clever montage."[6]

After establishing the authority of the author's voice, *Landscapes After the Battle* finally issues this disclaimer:

> Reader, beware: the narrator is not trustworthy. Beneath his shameless pose of frankness and forthrightness— as his multiple mea culpas and self accusations come pouring out — he does not scruple for a moment to dupe you.[7]

It is a disclaimer against all seeming authorial objectivity, a growing disillusion, I suspect, with the cult of seriousness and its social equation with truth that is so open to manipulation now by unscrupulous politicians and, in *The Marx Family Saga,* the make-believe of news media. The perspective is fantastic. Goytisolo's novels stage the overview, beyond the motivations that skew information, by disorienting the customs of genre and historic and grammatical context, making theater of media rhetoric and the processes of persuasion, be it fiction, journalism, politics, even history. "'What happened some hundred and forty-five years later came out of the blue.'"

In 1975, Goytisolo was talking about crafting a new literature. The last time he talked like that was 1956 when he moved to Paris, his formative period with Jean Genet and the Parisian literati. Back then, "developing a political conscience" in "a literary form which was suited to the didactic and revolutionary purpose which guided my pen," Goytisolo had heartfelt, intellectual and left wing things to say about Franco's Spain and the state of the world. He contends that society shapes the literature of its authors, specifically politicized in times of malcontent: *Nineteen Eighty-Four* in the wake of Nazi Germany and under threat of Russian totalitarianism. Otherwise, describing England in the 19th century, Goytisolo incidentally sets the balmy conditions for flourishing camp and Decadence (and for its demise through the Depression and World War II rationing): "She had obtained religious liberty, resolved religious conflict, begun the Industrial Revolution (full of injustices, of course, but necessary nonetheless), and the result was that its intellectuals began to draw away from the national problem." Likening the mood to 1970s Spain, in his forties in exile, Goytisolo began to think of more ornate aesthetics. In the camp British revival that began in the 1960s, most authors were showboating their craft as screenwriters in film and television, so Goytisolo translations were rare literary representatives. Now his extrovert and highbrow manipulations of genre and language put high camp on display.

Makbara flourishes a sunlit passage as flowerful as Firbank, layering camp accessories in delicate yet vivid visual prose,

> a symphony of colors in mauve, lilac, violet tones, coordinated bridesmaids' gowns in a delightfully old-fashioned, romantic silk-print: ostrich plumes tinted to match rose, fuchsia, daffodil dresses in mousseline de soire: Calais lace, embroidered tulle veils, flowered bridal wreathes, an exquisite parasol:

and so on, gloriously inconsequential. *Makbara* invites feminine identification with a character's theatrical entrance; an alternating narrative address flexes third and second person just as the author flexes gender variables. Already fashioned here in 1980, this is a solution to the gender case problem he would pose in *Quarantine* in 1991 (see [1]), yet hardly exploited in Goytisolo's busy itinerary of literary experiments. For male readers, at least, it is a rare transgender invitation, and the reader even gets to flutter a camp accessory: "she waited until the dark shadows gathered before making her appearance: as you descended the staircase you fluttered your fan before your face with a queen's genteel decorum and reserve...."[8]

Makbara is also fraught with anxiety and political conscience and distorted by grotesquerie that is more carnival than camp — more postmodern too. Camp and postmodernism have been seen taking tea together but they are not intimate, and Goytisolo is more postmodernist, which offers a serious intellectual subtext amenable to angst and destruction, a more reactive, dynamic aesthetic for his profound anarchy. Bradley Epps says of *Makbara*, "In tune with so many of the values of postmodernism, the Angel advocates the nomadic wandering of the Pariah ... 'walking on and on, losing oneself in the desert.'"[9] Camp finds itself on the divan — a victim of outrageous flirting from Goytisolo without any commitment.

Quarantine turns the text inside out to put language and genre up for proscenium inspection, setting the stage for his later camp career. The Preface to *The Picture of Dorian Gray* declared Wilde's aesthetic principles, but

Goytisolo's prose is a commentary on his actual technique. "That rash venture of assembling and ordering the elements of a text in a vague, imprecise zone, establishing a fine web of relationships, weaving a net of meanings beyond time and space, ignoring the laws of verisimilitude, rejecting worn-out notions of character and plot, abolishing the frontiers between reality and dream, destabilizing the reader by multiplying the levels of interpretation and registers of voice, appropriating historical events and using them to fuel his purpose...."[10] This passage plots the narrative structure of *A Cock-Eyed Comedy* ten years later, which demonstrates these disfigurements with style.

A lecturer on classic European literature preaches Spartan aesthetics with bombastic rhetoric in *A Cock-Eyed Comedy*, on the quest of minimalism and realism and values antithetical to camp ... at which point the lecturer's microphone is unplugged — transparently, by Goytisolo himself, who is rather fond of arabesque turns of phrase in long and winding sentences.[11]

A conspicuous aside in *The Marx Family Saga* challenges the author with a familiar criticism to Goytisolo, and particularly of the very novel where it appears: "Why all those long, unpunctuated paragraphs? didn't I tell you once and for all, it upsets the punters, puts them off reading your books?"[12]

Its inclusion in this prime culprit speaks of his confident and cavalier intent, with inverse narcissism, like Firbank's whimsical inclusion of *his* critics in *The Flower Beneath the Foot*. Mark Currie's revisionist, dialectic definition of metafiction, which invents a collaboration between novelist and critic, could cite this example as supporting evidence. I see it rather as an example of the author's multiple genre approach and a disdainful aside that notes the common criticism of his density and carries on nonetheless.

These stylistic contrivances do cultivate detachment from the story. A dissenting character criticizes Goytisolo's depiction of homosexuality in *A Cock-Eyed Comedy* and doesn't trust his "contradictions and ambivalence" or his lyrical depictions of the underworld.[13] In the composite narrative of *The Garden of Secrets*, the author (that is, the latest character to assume the role of narrator and write the next chapter), criticizes the hitherto loose style, sounding like a realist objection to camp and a parody of the diligent attention to function and politics to be found in Marxist literature:

> A story-line never on line or a leisurely way of beating about the bush: that's what I think of the tale told this night. A digression, with literary pretensions, diverting us from the search for Eusobio, the true aim of our Circle and its weekly meetings in this delightfully cultivated garden.[14]

The passage is preparing to resume the plot but can't resist admiring the garden even in making the point.

In 1975, Goytisolo told a reporter, "The only 'novelistic' works which I am interested in now are those which show a new and audacious elaboration; those in which the creative imagination of the writer manifests itself not through an outside referent in reality, but above all, through the use of language."[15] I recall the Symbolist movement that reformed Naturalism and refined Decadence, emphasizing imagination over realism. He wants syntax that is "Baroque, a language which uses discourse rather than referent and which centers its attention on the sign rather than on the thing designated."

Ronald Firbank was surely not the writer Goytisolo had in mind. Firbank, who resided in Paris for a spell, would surely have been ejected from the Parisian left-wing literary set had he lived and been audacious enough to flirt with them. Yet Firbank's flamboyant language and images suspended from narrative that Jones calls the "counterpoint to the Joycean *epiphany*,"[16] the flight from banality so characteristic of camp, certainly rejects an outside referent in everyday social reality. Kundera[17] credits James Joyce with analysing the elusive present, "Joyce's great microscope manages to stop, to seize, that fleeting instant and make us see it." Firbank (and camp) doesn't use a microscope, nothing so scientific; perhaps he uses a lorgnette, but the aesthetic saturation in the sign, the self and the moment is the same. Goytisolo elaborates on this picturesque penchant for crystallized images, layered in more detail with a wider vocabulary, and no room for ellipses, yet summary and equally detached from time and plot. Staged on a dais of eloquent prose, *Makbara* flourishes the signatures of showbusiness,

> an enigmatic, sybiline figure lurking backstage, waiting to make a sensational entrance: feathers, sequins, satin slippers, a sexiloquent dance: enthusiastic cheers from the audience, cries of encore, encore, waves of applause, flowers, a diva's deep curtsies: sinuous hands, promissory curves, suggestive writhings, slow pubic oscillation.[18]

His decadent listing is not the flat and exhaustive detailing of naturalism, but rather lush montages highlighted with esoteric and memorable phrases, the sexiloquent dance and promissory curves of prose that embroider the emblematic page. *Landscapes After the Battle* had pursued naturalism with endless listings of detail to wear out even his adoring critics. *Makbara* reflects on the aesthetic and finally gives up, "patiently setting down nouns, adjectives one after the other, parts of speech fighting a losing battle with the perfect simultaneity of the photograph," and seeks instead to emulate the creative potential within the space between events, the space between the narrative in "a precarious combination of signs whose message is uncertain: infinite possibilities of play opening up in the space that is now vacant: blackness, emptiness, the nocturnal silence of the page that is still blank."[19] And so Goytisolo finds the path that questions naturalism and traditional structure. Although he doesn't find the graphic patterning that Firbank creates with his aerated style in this space — a white space, never black, and a surface, not a void — Goytisolo too crystallizes the signature moment suspended from narrative time, larger than life.

At last a camp character makes an appearance in *The Marx Family Saga*, "as he smokes and lolls back in his chair," made more vivid by the dearth of camp characters in this novel, as we read the closing section. A photographic moment captured: "as in Serge Levitski's photo, dressed half-bohemian, half-romantic, full of lordly disdain, his voluminous yet feathery form now apparently swanning it among the ducks in Hispanic dishwater," and later, "preening like a swan in a lake of serenity."[20] (With some carnivalesque touches that became a specialty of later Goytisolo) his dégagé timing and flamboyance is welcome relief in this work. The prose often preens itself critically but never really fans its feathers. Here, though, the character's divorce from the pace and cares of the novel halts its progress, momentarily for all time.

Goytisolo's emblematic listings of sights and subjects show a camp eye for signature detail: characters who wear their cultural context like icons — *Landscapes After the Battle:*

> a somewhat older woman, wearing one of those berets tilted to one side so often seen in war films of the forties. When she rises from her seat to make certain that the projector is working properly, her silhouette suddenly calls to mind a cheap, romantic photo engraving: thin, narrow-hipped, bony, like an old ungainly gasoline pump.[21]

You can find this iconic type of woman in Crisp's *The Naked Civil Servant,* a cameo appearance as a Czech artist's model whose "black beret balanced at the ultimate degree of obliquity,"[22] which is also one of Glen/da's guises in *Death of a Transvestite* by Ed Wood. And don't forget Benson's Georgie in *Lucia's Progress:* "Georgie had on his fur-trimmed cape and a new bright blue beret which he wore a little sideways on his head."[23] The petrol pump in Goytisolo's piece is a kitsch association — perhaps a crude symbol of American imperialism over crude oil — which qualifies her European and rather Left Bank look, but the pump does suggest an arm akimbo, an iconic camp pose.

Masculinity is butch sculpture in Goytisolo's work, all overstated posturing and cloying loins, yes, all Leni Riefenstahl and Albert Speer (sans the gauche Nazism),

> the vision of dozens of fierce, brawny fellows, alone or grouped together, hands clasped as if sealing a peace treaty; weight-lifters with flexed, bulging

muscles; strapping, mustachiod lads, arms akimbo, lusty pectorals, radiating a glow from their leather breeches and foursquare physique.[24]

This lusty caricature from *Quarantine* is similarly mustachiod in *The Garden of Secrets* and *A Cock-Eyed Comedy,* as elegiac as Sunday morning worship. It is all tightly clichéd with a fetishized gloss from those leather breeches, with an admiring feminine touch that complements and distances the machismo, where the genteel noun "fellows" underplays the brawny force. Intellectual sophistication notwithstanding, many Goytisolo scenes are simple signal emblems writ as large and visual as Firbank's isolated images. The vision is captured like an art pose by literary portrayal, like this narcissistic voice that prefigures a show of masculinity in *The Garden of Secrets:* "'You'll learn the virtues of manliness, the longing after perfection of Greek philosophers and German artists.'"[25]

Academic critics like Bradley Epps[26] worry that "his stereotypical figures can continue to signify simply as stereotypes." This is a "problem," speaking from an aesthetic and moral obligation to social realism and political revisionism. To camp, social realism is material for theatrical drama, gay identity is a performance like any other, and stereotypes are a reality (at least insofar as reality is fiction). The brush-strokes of real people are really rather broad. When we discuss the work of Chloe Poems, it's easy to forget that this archetypal fictional character was penned by Gerry Potter, but Goytisolo too offers his author's persona as a fiction.

Even the peacock strutting of masculinity before the wry, admiring writer, as theatrical a presentation of gender as transvestite femininity, is predated by Saki early in the 20th century. On a trip to Russia Saki encounters "hundreds of well-built, healthy-looking men, ranging from eighteen years upwards, but mostly in the prime of early manhood," whose domestic chores include door-keeping and sweeping and errand-running, yet, "In their peaked caps, gay shirts, and high Blucher boots, they convey the impression of a sort of Praetorian Guard in undress...."[27] It's a domestic-fantastic vision of homoeroticism, understated and symbolized by cultural necessity in Saki's time. Goytisolo can be explicit about masculinity in uniform even as he parades the posturing of it all that keeps the vision camp. The homosexuality of the writing transfixes the detail, and may be tongue in cheek about making an artistic homage of the author's admiration, but what conjures camp is how men sport their masculinity like an iconic fashion accessory.

Chloe Poems takes this tongue in cheek depiction to extremes in "Some of My Best Friends Are Straight."

> We're a real hardhitting, ball kicking, beer swilling
> Sunday League team
> But some of those boys really are cads
> Because they're straight acting, non scene
> Sunday League queens.

"Some of My Best Friends Are Straight" puns on the showboating physicality of disco clubbing — "I love to shake my bootie" — and the sporty bravura of football with rather ambiguous manly lads, "displaying our masculine powers" and scoring innuendos in cheeky jinky parley:

> but believe me
> there's a lot more dribbling
> going on in the showers.[28]

This is what happens when masculinity is represented theatrically.

Masculinity turns transvestite in Goytisolo's *The Virtues of the Solitary Bird*, exchanging one gay stereotype gaily for another, like a change of costume. Prisoners in a labor camp achieve high camp in a production of *Swan Lake:* "Preening like a swan in a lake of serenity" once more, the men attain that divan disposition in suspension of ego, desire and narrative, in another photographic glimpse of eternity:

> the death throes of the swan exalted us and we acted without ulterior motives, we aspired only to attain the concise lightness of her fluttering wings, the ethereal equilibrium of steps en pointe, that ineffable expression of languor at the cruel instant of her decline, the boots and uniform had been transmuted into the tutis and gauze skirts of ballerinas.[29]

"Languor" is the expression that suspends time in the ether, and equilibrium is the camp ideal in posture and attitude. As soon as the narrative resumes, the spell is broken and *The Virtues of the Solitary Bird* drops the camp aesthetic.

Out of the ballet and into the Church, in the new century Juan Goytisolo may be taking the miter from Firbank as patron saint of ecclesiastical camp. The permissive passage of time since Firbank overwhelms the adroit understatement of innuendo in Goytisolo's carnival of perversity. Expiation conjoins with exploitation in orgiastic religious ritual — I feel I should prepare you for the Catholic culture shock. *A Cock-Eyed Comedy* perverts the language of the Church into lewd innuendo: "proselytising a parishioner of mine," a gay encounter becomes an act of communion, "whilst Abdekadir fanned the flames of his own and our pleasure with ejaculatories and quotations from my breviary." His fusion of carnality and religion is generously subversive in its embrace of the flesh as well as mind and spirit. Goytisolo implicates grammar in fluent sexual innuendo — and of course it *is* incriminated by the nature of innuendo, a play on words: "We conjugated the verb *sikis* and all its modes and tenses and I didn't stumble over difficult gerunds and participles." Ironic highlighting of form distances the passion.

Firbank "dealt in porcelain hints" (Harold Nicolson),[30] while modern innuendo is more rascallion than risqué, a tad kitsch. Blasphemy embarrasses the altered state of religious ecstasy, teasing the ideal of "ascension" as both holy elevation and a phallic erection, "mortification" as self-effacing penitence and self-indulgent masochism; flirting with figures of speech like "ace of spades" which, stripped now of their disguising function in the repressive society of Firbank's day, sound even more ironic against the flagrant debauchery of the text ("ace of spades and balls" seems to discard discrete innuendo half-way through the phrase). The camp tradition of French phrasing lends an exotic expression of the pleasures of the flesh.

Firbank kept his flagellation scenes light, but they come out in welts with Goytisolo, given the Church's penchant for penitence. Nuns manufacture whips "to mortify the flesh in pursuit of a healthy soul." He loves to list excesses, "belts, studded leather straps and bracelets, collars, gauntlets, lashes and flails."[31] This exhibitionism streaked through *Count Julian* in 1970:

> self-flagellation will now be performed, with ritual exactitude: at each blow, her pious gasps grew louder, accompanied by the musical erection of an explosive, paroxysmal Negro rhythm, the repeated muscular contractions apparently bringing on orgasm: progressing from the vulgar and common periphery toward the epicenter of dogma: slow, persistent, dialectical rotary motions: a corkscrew or a propeller: pleading for masculine help with parched lips, provoking a sudden flux of blood with her frenzied eyes: a sweet love wound, a cruel dart transfixing the soul![32]:

This is the Catholic camp that Ken Russell put controversially on film a year later in *The Devils*. Pious gasps, the paroxysmal Negro rhythm, motions delectably described to transmute a "dialectical" philosophical term into physical gyrations, fuse the purging ritual with overt sexual pleasure ironically. Goytisolo embraces another wonderful perversity in the diversity of sexuality, another theatrical performance of passion masquerading as piety yet achieving a state of bliss in orgasm. Sadomasochism, with extremes of dominance and submission, its exhibitionistic fetishism, its performance of roles, is potentially camp; especially ironic when juxtaposed against the punitive restraints of holy repression (and inquisition) made kinky bondage and torture. The fusing of compassion-cruelty and masculine-feminine socialized polarities is as keen in sadomasochism as in camp, and just as tongue in cheek in *A Cock-Eyed Comedy*. Feminine hands made larger than life by close focus and the extreme contrast of "making cakes, buns, marzipan whirls and other delicious tidbits" and also exquisite instruments of divine torture to "stiffen weak, wavering souls."[33] The delicacy of a devout woman's domestic touch that yet can tame animal passions in deviant holy men. What a spectacular domestic-fantastic conceit, where sadomasochism provides the fantasy. I do hear an embellishment of Sade in Goytisolo's academic dialectic between flamboyant indulgence and intellectual discourse: I hear it in Goytisolo's discursive sentences, in his heavenly relish in atonement through punishment, and the decadent hypocrisy of sadomasochism at the heart of Puritanism: I hear Sade's sharp tongue in cheek casuistry, with which Sade's libertines rationalize their motives in audacious parody of theology. Yes, but Goytisolo's ironic narrative transcends Sade's fixated, centrifugal force that repeats exhaustively until the reader is desensitized: Sade's prose is a succubus to suffering and death that cannot find relief from its lusty Decadence. Goytisolo finds distance in asides, domestic-fantastic conceits, and flamboyant language beyond the reach of Sade.

There follows a rapturous passage in *A Cock-Eyed Comedy* whose rhythm swells in orgiastic climax like a rising hosanna, with wry right wing jingoism:

> The confessor to one of the convent Mother Superiors, informed by a common friend won over by my silent preaching by example in North American territories— where I studied for a Masters in Business Sciences and Soul Merchandising — exhorted me to encourage adepts of extreme ardours to persevere in their fine work and not yield in their efforts till Communism fell and Russia was converted according to the prophecies of Our Lady of Fatima.[34]

In Goytisolo's book tour of England in 2002, this passage was performed by Chloe Poems, whose ebullient yet tongue in cheek delivery steered an artful course, charted by the author, between theater and pantomime, camp and kitsch. The cheerleading sadomasochism is as zealous as McCarthyism, but a frivolous digression about a Masters degree distances the reader from the rapture. Extravagant sentences swell the rapturous enthusiasm even as clauses displace our alignment with carnal nature, a signal of Goytisolo's showboating penmanship that draws attention to itself. The opening sentence in *The Garden of Secrets,* like the opening sentence of *Landscapes After the Battle,* is a curtain-raiser fourteen lines long, occupying a paragraph with much incidental detail in attendant chattering clauses that would be separated into sentences or struck out altogether under more stringent aesthetics.

The Marx Family Saga begins each sentence with a new paragraph, in lieu of capital letters. Each collage of detail, a paragraph long, is an overt challenge to the writer's powers of grammatical coherence, which Goytisolo articulates like a maestro before his audience, aided only by commas and brackets:

> a bejeweled finger pointed to the misty horizon and the vaporous silhouette of a boat, its luxury cabins, funnels, radar, aerials, bridge looming into view opposite the select beach, as if by some trick or special effect.[35]

The special effect glosses realism to blend genres and styles, however unlikely bedfellows. This novel flirts promiscuously with exclamation marks, which defuses its content — as camp is wont to do — but raises the profile of the stylistic mark itself. I find this agreeable and interesting, though others may object from the tradition of artistic guile when style so conspicuously relegates content. Goytisolo's bejeweled finger directs our attention to the sign and not the referent, another still-life of the moment. Quentin Crisp describes his own extended hand "weighed down with coral and turquoise,"[36] his writing hand, I deduce, dripping with provocative irony and colorful and frivolous exhibitionism. Goytisolo's bejeweled indexing of decadent detail is more concentrated camp, more descriptive, and penetrative even unto innuendo.

More than Genet, more than Joyce, Aubrey Beardsley set the camp precedent for Goytisolo's pornographic tradition a century past in his elaborate prose in *Under the Hill,* made obscure and bowdlerized by obscenity laws. Now *Landscapes After the Battle* pictures a man in a trenchcoat in a pornographic cinema, camply offset by "his eternal felt hat." Goytisolo demonstrates that any encounter with social realism may yet be made camp — the style, not the content, determines the aesthetic. Stark naming of the unceremonious sex act on screen is not camp but our ironic removal from the immediacy makes it so. Through the character's detachment, the absurd choice of a Strauss waltz to juxtapose grace with animal exertions, and the contrast of precious allusions to masturbation in the audience ("a not at all mysterious maneuver with their flies") with kitsch close-ups of the stark screen image, are all carried off with Goytisolo's vulgar gusto in prose that begins to parody itself as his work finally embraces camp. As if on a divan in the pornographic cinema, "he is sprawled out comfortably in his seat and is contemplating with detachment and apparent anaphrodisia the laborious, interminable fucking of an individual...."[37]

"Dignity" often depends on disowning animal instinct, and carnival upstages civic dignity by exposing what has been repressed and crowning it king, at least for a day. Like camp, carnival is theatrical. Juan Goytisolo, like Firbank, is carnivalesque in dethroning religious figures and putting vestments to flamboyant and frivolous use. Father Trennes, protagonist of

A Cock-Eyed Comedy, is a modern Cardinal Pirelli. Goytisolo indulges desire and mocks decorum in passages as riotous as Rabelais and as sensual and fantastic as Beardsley. In this scene, another passage ear-marked for recital by Chloe Poems, Father Trennes plays an unlikely bull-man — a traditional feature of carnival — in another "performance" of carnal nature:

> Pigtail brandished with brio the foulard of Cuckoo who'd purloined a pair of fans from the glass-cabinet, and was whirling them like *banderillas.* Then, Father Trennes turned Miura bull. A red quilt! I fetched a faded pink specimen which I handed to Pigtail. The good priest pawed the parquet with his elegant hoofs before making for the cloth. Cuckoo goaded him roaring like a lioness on heat. Our pedigree youngster wasn't afraid of ridicule. Flustered and rather unbuttoned, he performed to script with the fury of the possessed. The *paso doble* turned us on: its crescendo *bien arrosé* with gin was a perfect arouser.[38]

Strutting masculinity in bullfighting is the camp metaphor that animates the passion under the cassock, in eccentric contrast with a *paso doble* dance. The camp accessory of fans in a simile of *banderillas* reminds me of Firbank's substitution of a fan for a riding crop in *The Princess Zoubaroff.* Figures of speech like "Pigtail brandished with brio the foulard of Cuckoo" take on a totemic, iconic, mnemonic posturing that owes acknowledgement to English translator Peter Bush, whose words pose like figures in the narrative. Tongue in cheek phrasing in translation matches Goytisolo's intent and scores images like an arranger who complements a composer, with the sensual sonorance that we find in the English tradition of Polari, that burlesque code of gay linguistics that smuggles the subculture into the mainstream by innuendo and contrived euphemism.

Goytisolo takes the oral tradition of gossip and fashions a hubbub of prose poetry in later monologue narratives with sinuous clauses and chattering digressions, not the dialogue of Firbank but a pointedly spoken address to the reader that Goytisolo encourages you to read aloud. His eloquent consciousness meanders between Joyce's ponderous, introspective murmurings and Firbank's externalized and pastoral-pretty prose: intellectual and lascivious, metaphysical and sensual, decadent yet naturalistic in cumulative lists of detail that spill over into street scenes or political rhetoric or orgy. When Noël Coward remarks of a camp character in *Quadrille,* "Whenever you embark on a sentence I feel as though you were off on a long journey and that I must wave you goodbye,"[39] he could be speaking for Goytisolo's readership. The kind of reader drawn to camp may be happy to depart from the predestination of plot-driven narrative. With Goytisolo, though, we may find ourselves railroaded by another momentum, driven by argument. After all, the singular focus of plot or argument tightens and trims narrative, for better or worse. For all his bluffing diversions, Goytisolo always has a thesis up his sleeve that recovers the meaning of his meanderings. Confident in his artistry now, he lets sentences course where they will in no more of a rush to find the terminus than Firbank, though more definite in the precision of his detail and the assertion of his intent. Experimental punctuation in pieces like *Count Julian* and *Makbara* substitutes colons for full stops to fuse associations of sentences in the seamless way that ideas blend in the moment. Susurrant sentences in *Count Julian* sublimate dialogue into patterns of prose by omitting quotation marks—a fashion he still wears—so that individual speakers contribute to a choral narrative in a collective consciousness. This oral variation makes harmonious chorus out of gossip, another refraction of the unitary consciousness of the author—like the polyphonic narrative of *The Garden of Secrets.* (Anything monolithic may be upstaged by camp or upended by carnival.) Sometimes the immediacy of dialogue without framing quotation marks closes the camp distance on his subject—camp puts everything in quotation marks—but Goytisolo is not bound by the rules of any particular aesthetic any more than he remains bound by genre. The narrative choral voice becomes a *tour de force* that develops a consciousness of its own music, even the reader's voice, in a narcissistic and cumulative posturing of excess.

> her lips murmur prayerful ejaculation, orisons rich in privileges and blessings, especially if recited for an entire month and accompanied by the sacrament of confession, a visit to a church, and prayers for the Pope:

Sacrilegious double entendres like "ejaculation" and the lush excess of "orisons rich in privileges and blessings" strut before ascetic values of nunnery and monastery. The passage leads directly to the self-flagellation scene that we read—and enjoyed, I can only hope—in *Count Julian*.[40]

"As I was translating *A Cock-Eyed Comedy,* I was very conscious of the musicality of the language, its orality," Peter Bush remarks. "The themes live through a language buzzing with resonance and cadence, a hallucinatory, burlesque fusion that demands to be read aloud."[41] *The Independent* (12 October 2002) reviewed *A Cock-Eyed Comedy* and judged, "there's no better match than that between the translation and the original."

Succeeding Helen Lane, Peter Bush translated Goytisolo's later, camper work. Bush shows a fine ear for camp aesthetics and a Rabelaisian gusto that Goytisolo enjoys. Political and historic sensitivity to the author's word and scholastic attention to detail are tenets of his translation, but Bush also emphasizes "Music not meaning!" along with "ambiguities, images, wordplay," crucial to camp. He notes the tradition of archaic English in British comedy (citing Frankie Howerd, Cyril Fletcher, the Goons, *Black Adder*), as well as innuendo popularized by Benny Hill, and so Bush researched Shakespeare before translating *A Cock-Eyed Comedy*. "The writing itself depended on a drafting procedure where the playful enjoyment had to prevail."[42]

His treatise on "The Translator as Writer"[43] samples early draft translations of *A Cock-Eyed Comedy,* including the *paso doble* passage where Father Trennes turns Miura bull. "Colita brandished with brio Cacu's cravate" became the signal and stylized "Pigtail brandished with brio the foulard of Cuckoo." "Pawed the carpet" developed into the more alliterative "pawed the parquet," whose plosives tread the page and act out the priest's behavior. The translator, in camp aesthetics, is also a performer. Regarding the paso doble, "nothing was more arousing than its crescendo well-watered with gin" in the first draft translation. Developed, "its crescendo *bien arrosé* with gin was a perfect arouser," whose ironic, blasé rephrasing has a stylish, lighter touch, where "perfect" is a more contented superlative than the emphatic negative "nothing was more" ... altogether more camp between first and sixth draft.

In another passage, "Exiled three times from the Court by those who feared his biting wit, he had returned with all attributes of his spirited stock: riding a fine roan, wearing a hat adorned with a flameanto diablo...." became, by draft three, "Thrice exiled from Court by those who feared his biting satire and burned with envy before him, he had returned with all the fire of his spirited stock: astride a fine roan, wearing a hat adorned with a fluttering pennant...." Remember that camp is not the only sensibility at play here in the translator's work, and indeed in Goytisolo—but the changes highlight some features of camp. Peter Bush raises the exhibitionist self-consciousness of the writing. "Thrice" is trimmer than the first draft but it has a theatrical flourish. "Fire" sets "attributes" alight dramatically and the imagery is developed overtly by the addition of "burned with envy." "Riding" yields to the explicit posture "astride." Less camp, I feel, the change of phrasing from "a flameanto diablo" to "a fluttering pennant" is less visible, less flamboyant.

A first draft tells of a character who, attending a bullfight, "to offend the monarch and scandalize the tittle-tattlers he hoisted the legend My Loves are right royal, boldly playing with ambiguity...." In draft two, "to insult the monarch and scandalize idle hangers-on he hoisted the legend I love right royally, in a bold play of ambiguity...." reads less camply, loaded with the judgemental term "idle hangers-on" in place of the frivolous "tittle-tattlers"; also, "insult" feels more biting and less effete than "offend." But then, "in a bold play of ambiguity" parades ambiguous camp, not hurried as in draft one: taking the adverb away from "bold" slows the text and gives

the play of ambiguity time to register. These changes, in translation or edit-
ing, are the equivalent of stage lighting or stage direction where subjects
and performances are foregrounded, played up. We'll find the burlesque
contrivance "right royally" echoed in Chloe Poems' verse. However, by the
third draft it is trimmed to "I love royally, in a bold play of double entendre," where "royally" sounds banal standing alone, although double entendre spells out the ambiguous play even more. These draft translations show
the artful exaggeration of artifice, such as alliteration and word-play, which
conventional literary aesthetics would artfully conspire to disguise. Such
emphasis of surface and symbol makes a translator's role more crucial than
in plot-driven narrative or minimalist prose. A translator with Spartan or
realist aesthetics would be a misalliance with a camp text that calls for theatrical excess and style over content. And so very vice versa: Milan Kundera, who frowns like Goytisolo but with a furrowed not arching brow, tells
us, "*The Joke* was translated into all the Western languages. But what sur-
prises! In France, the translator rewrote the novel by ornamenting my
style."[44] Ornamentation is an acquired taste, all surface and not at all pedantic.

   Here is an extract from *Landscapes After the Battle*, translated by Helen
Lane: "When his turn comes, our man — I use yet again, as always, the plural possessive so as to avoid being the butt of vulgar jokes on the part of
malicious and spiteful readers that the use of the adjective in the first person singular might give rise to...."[45] whose conscientious disclosure feels
heavier than camp. A camp treatment may be phrased less emphatically, "I
shall use once again" ... and a tardy pause or two would defuse the frown-
ing concern over misinterpretation that strains the narrative to pose a more
aloof tone ... but is this tone Goytisolo's? The text would further highlight
the self-conscious persona of the designer (and therefore the artifice) by,
say, "I should like to avoid...." After another nonchalant stop, "After all,
unhelpful readers might...." could take out the uncouth bitterness of "malicious and spiteful" to maintain a distant poise from the text that is somewhat set up by the voice. However, we are bordering on rewriting and
reinterpreting the author's voice, a particular pitfall with this writer of multiple voices in multiple genres with complex aesthetics.

   We have browsed the camp and decadent libraries of Lord Berners and
Wilde's Lord Henry. *Count Julian*'s library shows no such attention to ornate
décor, or to the book covers that we find in Firbank: Goytisolo is ornate
instead in his eulogy of the history and potential of literature, "in a per-
petual state of rapture: capital carefully preserved here behind glass cases:
catalogued, arranged in the proper order, lined up in neat rows: on shelves
within reach of your hand or accessible with the aid of a library ladder."

Goytisolo's decadent catalogue of lush and loving phrases is as intimate and intellectual as his stream of consciousness, and somewhat narcissistic given his own meandering style...

> a river constantly seeking, and finding, the course that best suits it: the robust octosyllable, the perfect hedecasayllable, the immortal sonnet; a powerful abundant stream: narrowing at times and occasionally descending underground for a certain distance, bending back upon itself and meandering, but never ceasing to flow.[46]

Bradley Epps[47] browses the library in *The Virtues of the Solitary Bird.* In this repressive, censorious environment, he cites "the 'ghostly décor of the library, an immense necropolis of books doomed to annihilation and oblivion, reading rooms plunged into darkness.'" Addressing the "significant violence" of Goytisolo's mature writing, Epps describes his "stylistic experimentation that does violence to the word itself." It's a weighty consideration that applies equally to Poems' language in our next chapter. Goytisolo's carnival grotesquery would support that view, and he does wear a hard hat for deconstruction, but Epps doesn't give any weight to superficiality. Epps' busy erudition is not detained by shallowness, and so overlooks the camp aesthetic. On the surface, it is apparent that Goytisolo *loves* words and adores literature. His dense prose is more masculine than effeminate, "the robust octosyllable" indeed, penetrating the aerated spaces of Firbank's effeminate text, yet his poeticism caresses the ear. Grammatical constraints and genre convention provoke his masculine force to rip into the page — in order to get closer to the word and more intimate with the truth in all its forms. He makes love to language, romancing sentences in stylistic foreplay and fucking words in every conjugation. Such lavish attention to surface makes it possible to enjoy later novels by Goytisolo without always knowing what he is talking about, I know, if you drop the educated hang-up over a laborious "struggle for meaning [that] implicates author, reader, and text," which Epps pursues impressively and Sisyphus admires. Goytisolo's poetic prose, in his relish of *Count Julian*'s library and throughout the author's oeuvre, in long, shapely sentences and those continual colons that link associations in this stream of consciousness, showboats his penmanship and mirrors the library's literature so that the style *is* the content, and to this extent Goytisolo hints at camp potential in 1970. The carnival came later.

Professor Epps did go on to invite Chloe Poems to address Harvard, streets ahead of academia. Poems, Wood and Goytisolo, like Beardsley before them, are carnivalesque in their cheering procession of misfit sexuality and the warm welcome that their prose and poetry extends to those driven underground by society. In its exuberance, carnival is not always aloof enough for camp, and camp is more eloquent than the mime and slapstick of carnival: Goytisolo is too articulate, too erudite, too fond of poetic excess, to be carnivalesque only, but has a natural bent for camp.

Only irony restrains the cavalier narrative from getting carried away with ecstasy. A characteristic address to the reader catalyses reflection on the process of reading as well as writing,

> Those penetrating pages, those personal experiences of harsh, acerbic devotions are meant for you, discreet reader. Meditate on the lives of those saints and on the multiple access routes to the inner dwelling till their juicy marrow impregnates you.[48]

Goytisolo's exhortations, somewhat detached by narrative voice, urge a rather tantric translation of "all roads lead to Rome," where "the inner dwelling" may be soul or anus, an egalitarian acceptance of the body and all its functions rarely found in the Church but often sanctioned in a temple of convenience. Public toilets are something we all have in common; we visited them in Part One. Makeshift dressing-room for Quentin Crisp's flamboyant alter-ego, the public toilet is, in gay culture at least, a rejuvenating place of transformation, satirized by Goytisolo in *The Marx Family Saga*, camp and kinky:

> he went into the lavatories and after a while emerged transformed, as if an accomplice looking after his wardrobe in there had got him a new outfit, a clown disguised as an operatic divo, in plumed hat, doublet, sable-fur cape and calf-length boots.[49]

These unceremonious haunts of lusty and illicit encounters, stripped of innuendo, are venerated as havens of underground truth and honest desire by Goytisolo as they are in Poems: kitsch bad taste made lyrical with exquisitely stylized literary excellence. Goytisolo glories in decadence, juxtaposed incongruously up tight against religious orthodoxy — Catholic ritual in *A Cock-Eyed Comedy* in 2000, Moslem ritual in *Makbara* in 1980. He continues, too, the camp depiction of religion as theater that Firbank excelled in to excelsior, and makes it multi-cultural in *Makbara*, "a theatrical spectacle: the calls of muezzino in the minarets of the mosques as an accompaniment in the background: shoddy footlights, stage sets, backdrop: joining in the rejoicing of the chorus bidding farewell to the fast of Ramadan."[50]

I am persuaded that Salmon Rushdie could have avoided a fatwah if only his prose was more frivolous and his scenes too theatrical for orthodoxy to attack with any credibility. Camp can be disarming even in subversion.

Alliteration, from murmurings of muezzino to the farewell fast, facil-
itates the fluency and lavishes further excess on Goytisolo's exotic and decadent detail. By the time we get to *A Cock-Eyed Comedy*, the flair of *Makbara*
seems restrained. *A Cock-Eyed Comedy* flirts with anachronism to satirize
the modern cult of celebrity. Will Self did it in *Dorian*, but Goytisolo likens
the act of worship in religion to the magazine adulation of fame. Narcissism, anointed tongue in cheek: "Though it was not my good fortune to be
born in a media century, I performed like a professional artiste in the spotlight, confronted the quizzical eyes of press and cameras."[51]

Grim political and social realism dogs *Dorian* and preoccupies Goytisolo. AIDs, literally and as a metaphor for social decay, darkens *Dorian* and
A Cock-Eyed Comedy. *Landscapes After the Battle* in 1982, only infrequently
camp, compares with *Dorian* in politicizing the camp motif of smoking,
heavy handedly: "the woman takes several deep drags on a cigarette which,
unlike the sort manufactured by cancer-spreading Yankee multinationals,
has been produced by a healthy and simple people knowing nothing of the
ravages of sickness."[52] Goytisolo is often so committed to his subject that
an aloof stance is not accessible; like Chloe Poems, on the harrowing edge
of uncouth political home-truths that transgress drawing-room decorum,
he doesn't always allow himself the aesthetic luxury of a lighter touch when
his perception of injustice is so acute. The oppressive reality of political
internment in *The Garden of Secrets* prefers tragedy to camp and prevents
the reader's escape through detachment or stylistic distraction; only as multiple narrative develops does he allow stylistic distance. This is an age where
frivolity has lost its innocence. The world's media brings politics and the
plight of the disenfranchised into our homes, and Goytisolo considers it a
literary obligation too. In *Landscapes After the Battle*, "As the proclamation
of martial law in Warsaw brutally sweeps away, with one stroke of the pen,
the noble aspirations of people to a just and humane socialism, our hero
indifferently files his fingernails." He could be a Firbank hero, but Goytisolo makes an indictment out of the observation that is not allowed to
remain camp. "The Vietnamese people have victoriously assumed their destiny, and you, what the fuck have you done?"[53]

After foregrounding his political conscience for decades, with the lifting of a publication ban in his home country post–Franco Spain, his later
period is more attentive to surface aesthetics. *A Cock-Eyed Comedy* delights
more than ever in camping it up in language, holiness and sexuality. The
"Dramatis Personae" of the novel continues his mature penchant for casting historical figures, flouting historical context with frivolous anachronisms perverted timelines, transplanting period literary characters and authors
themselves in his carnivalesque procession of humanity and creativity. *A*

Cock-Eyed Comedy is subtitled like a theater bill, "Starring Friar Bugeo Montesino and other faeries of motley feather and fortune," stretching the skeptical distance between performance and existence, closing the conceptual difference between altar and stage. Critics— and the author —find philosophical and political subtexts in all this, naturally, but let's not forget that it is, above all, a lark. This acclaimed intellectual savant, weighty with kudos and learning, is skylarking in his senior years.

The "Dramatis Personae" of *The Marx Family Saga* includes the birth and death of each Marx family member, promenading the anachronism of the premise. Karl Marx watches television play out history, the collapse of the Soviet Union and associated communism all around the Eastern Bloc, "the dismantling of the systems supposedly based on his thought, the collapse of walls and watchtowers." Historic determinism has become an anachronism. This is intellectual camp. Full of political enquiry, demanding of Marx what the hell went wrong, the dramatic layering of questions— "a pathetic exile on Dean Street, what could he do against the engines of omnipotent authoritarianism and the propaganda machine of a superpower?"— recalls cliff-hangers in a soap opera: *The Marx Family Saga*. Marx's plight, as his daughters channel-hop with the remote control, is all part of the teleplay. Karl Marx arrives home like a sitcom protagonist, dumps his learned books and slumps in his armchair with supper on his intellectual mind—

> a good day's work? (Jenny)
> the usual.[54]

What a spoofing confluence of domestic-fantastic detail, as history plays out its drama for television viewers. All it lacks is a kitsch presenter. In this postmodern revision of history, Marx must be wondering, what is the point, really, in a plot?

A Cock-Eyed Comedy cocks a snoop at content: "Plot is the least of his worries," Father Trennes discusses the writer. Goytisolo is happy to expose his aesthetic mission and reflect on his technique in the best tradition of camp. "He wanted to transcribe his cruising experiences in church language, including that of the author of the contemporary Kempis, in order to parody it from within and strip bare its hypocrisy...."[55] Not an interview extract after publication but a narrative declaration in, an instant photograph of method and process captured in prose, fulfilling the portent declared ten years before in *Quarantine* by demonstrating the aesthetic manifesto.

Take the author's disquisition on gender dogma in *Quarantine* that we cited earlier, an un-camp laboring of the question of masculine-feminine variables. Compare it with *A Cock-Eyed Comedy:* here the author develops the metaphysics of the transmigration of souls to animate transgender consciousness, distinguished from identity. The protagonist has a variable identity, living several lives over generations. The novel features a portrait of narcissism as admiration of the female form, before a full-length mirror, by a consciousness aroused to masturbation yet estranged from the self-image of this latest transsexual incarnation — while devotees genuflect outside.[56]

Like Ed Wood's transgender narcissism, transposed to his protagonists, ego has little to do with this worship and ownership of the female form and psyche by a formerly male consciousness (in terms of both the transmigrant biography of the character and the shadow of the author himself). The exhibitionist discrepancy between holy veneration of this saintly character by the adoring crowd outside and her masturbatory narcissism behind closed doors exposes the underside of human nature that so many religions deny with dogma sustained by hypocrisy. Ironic contrast, the mirror image and metaphysical transcendentalism are all counterpoints to her new female narcissism, projecting camp distance.

Speaking of another incarnation, the actual story is disregarded altogether, the narrative never enters linear time: "I wasn't fired straight from the gun-carriage into the uterus but created with a flourish of the pen within the pages of a manuscript which threaded me seamlessly from cradle to grave," drawing attention to the textual simulation of the world. The character in this existence is "pure entelechy" without narrative events or motivation or any relationship beyond his readership and his connection to his creator, which is narcissism when we realize that the protagonist is, like all characters, the author's projection, holding court until the story's end. Suspended from further drafts, he is spared "my sentence to the galleys...."[57] Camp loves a pun, and Peter Bush makes sure that the translation of characters as galley slaves sentenced to serve sentences alludes to galley proof pages of a manuscript. *A Cock-Eyed Comedy* is as postmodern as it is camp. Even as entelechy, a rather feminine accessory to identity asserts itself in the protagonist's consciousness: "I wandered the skies lost in the immense void populated by stars and meteorites, trying to divine the signs of the Zodiac and which was mine." It's a frivolous reduction of our metaphysical quest for primal origins and portents in the universe to astrology.

Goytisolo's metaphysical socialism morphs the identities of his characters and narrative point of view, blending disparate historical contexts and changing gender, until even "you," the reader, becomes the writer himself, pseudonymously. Camp isn't particularly socialist, but it does love playing in wardrobes.

Goytisolo's long, distinguished career shows a graduation — or relapse, depending on your aesthetics—from academic and political gravitas to the whimsy and wonder of (second) childhood. It massages his muscular prose and assuages his political indignation with a delightfully feminine and ironic light touch. His critical acclaim is internationally high. He got away with his camp proclivities by borrowing on his literary kudos, and critics have yet to recognize the camp aesthetics in his mature work, preferring to call it "postmodern."

The Garden of Secrets dethrones the cult of the hero with an investigative and anecdotal narrative that traces the identity of Eusabio, an enigmatic, schizoid and ultimately somewhat camp protagonist: "His ostentatious extravagances won over the European fauna flourishing at the time"—fauna being a flamboyant metaphor for fashionable society. His biography is a masquerade: "He posed as a prince, poet, artist, as a spy in the pay of the Intelligence Service, and a few other roles besides. Daily he constructed himself a character and lived it with the conviction of an actor on stage," rather like Crisp. In the presence of the protagonist, at least, the pages are dripping with baroque and rococo, camp and kitsch: "His rococo salon suffocated newcomers with a profusion of furniture, carpets, vases, all manner of refined or kitsch bric-a-brac."[58] His "on-the-sleeve sincerity" is a kitsch attribute. Camp would refrain from such unseemly exertions for the sake of sincerity or sentiment. His home "looked like a diva's luxurious dressing-room packed with faded glories and distant memories," projecting favorite films, as camp and kitsch as *Sunset Boulevard.* In the book's final analysis, like Will Self in *Dorian,* Goytisolo asserts such camp accessories as pathological lies, camp readers may be disturbed to find.

I find this tension pulling between his erudite pedigree and his anarchic artistic experiments— though it is open to question whether the tension is in the art or the critic. I read it as ambivalence that sacrifices aesthetic coherence when different aesthetics clash on the page unresolved. Coherence in this sense means not narrative resolution but consistent aesthetic principles. I'm embarrassed to own this conservative expectation, which may be too restricting for Goytisolo; his exciting strides in narrative invention may be worth the sacrifice of coherence. I may change my mind. Another critic will see a complementary layering of aesthetics and genres, or see irresolution as a satisfying coda: the value of discord that Schoenberg sounded. And perhaps irresolution finds coherence in 21st century camp. For thirty years, Goytisolo has been moving toward that distorted hybrid aesthetic that is *weird camp.* Bradley Epps[59] applauds subversion of "dominant discourse, with its emphasis on linearity, logic, stability, clarity, order [that] rejects ambivalence and ambiguity...." And it's true, works of complex inconsistency require great concentration and invention. Goytisolo's later pages begin to tear up the contractual obligations of all aesthetic schools ingeniously. All the same, consistency and simplicity have aesthetic appeal. The close focus of complexity can block the gloriously supercilious overview, the proscenium vision.

The notion of resolution may be an expendable artifice, but artifice, in camp, is what art is all about. *The Blind Rider* closes the chapter on this illustrious novelist, his latest and his last, he says. It's beautifully harrowing. *The Garden of Secrets* conspired to name "Goytisolo" as the phantom unitary pseudonym of a writer's group; now *The Blind Rider* exposes the Deity as a contrivance, a false god by its own cynical testimony, voiced by Goytisolo. The godforsaken protagonist awaits death in the final theatrical sentences of Juan Goytisolo's historic career. "The appointment would be for another day: when the safety curtain was raised and he confronted the vertiginous void. He was, was still among the spectators in the stalls." The writing glitters—but it isn't camp, too embittered by the demise of idealism, ominous with awesome nihilism and tormented by ageing. "The magic tracery of constellations gave way to a savage universe of sound and fury...."[60] And so *A Cock-Eyed Comedy* is his last luscious fling with camp. If camp is to reflect the bountiful horrors of the 21st century, a new aesthete generation must fulfil its literary potential. How timely, then, when Goytisolo took his crowning camp achievement to Britain and shared a stage with Chloe Poems, the latest libertarian torch-bearer of this fickle flame...

Chloe Poems (1962–)

"Time for more than just window dressing."
"Ooh Matron,"
—*How to Be a Better Gay*, 2006

As Juan Goytisolo was redesigning his writing in mid-life exile, in the 1970s, an effeminate boy in exile from patriarchy was playing truant to find an education in youth theater in Liverpool. This rogue schooling taught him the trappings of camp, the witnessing audience, the stage, curtains, spotlight and wardrobe of the glorious masquerade. Writing from an oral tradition older than calligraphy, Gerry Potter fashioned a poetic style for the creation of his avenging character, Chloe Poems, the woman behind the man, a subpersonality and something of a Muse. This agent of transformation would so transform camp that camp becomes startled by its own reflection in this 21st century chapter.

Goytisolo arrived in England in 2002 with Parisian literary pedigree and international academic kudos—and the most camp book of his life tucked under his arm — to meet Chloe Poems and launch his book. Poems was making the uncertain transition from camp performance poetry in theaters and clubs to promoting publications like *Adult Entertainment* in their own right. Of course, most authors don't pose naked in bob wig and makeup on their book covers, astride a chair a la Christine Keeler, but this author was bringing to literature a theatrical tradition older than literature itself.

The pseudonym is sonorous with oral tradition and the tongue in cheek embouchure of camp: "Chloe Poems" sounds an onomatopoeic lipstick pout with a powder-puff plosive, mirrored promiscuously in assonance like a kiss blown to one's reflection, or at least, to the author's alter ego. Poems will demonstrate, through the cosmetics of ego and in grandstanding, iconic style, that narcissism and masquerade are on intimate terms.

239

Like Goytisolo, Poems negotiates a dilemma between aloof style over content so essential to camp and radical political commitment that aesthetes like Wilde and Firbank and Crisp would never entertain. The feminized, aspirate protagonist of "The Effeminate" with the divan demeanor is not ineffectual, and the subtext warns that camp will not always defer to its effete stereotype but may be contentiously political ... even with one eye on style. As Goytisolo exposes genre convention by juxtaposing the novel with the essay or letter or play or even the interview, so *How to Be a Better Gay* masquerades in multiple genres in 2006. It relates to Alan Bennett's Christmas inspiration for his latest heartwarming anthology of memoirs, diaries, lectures and the odd play and monologue: "those long-forgotten annuals which lured you on from story to story through pictures and puzzles, a real box of delights."[1] Poems frames a collage of interpersonal narratives discreetly, each piece suspended in its own time and space, like Acts in a theatrical revue. Not the interwoven intellectual text of Goytisolo, but *How to Be a Better Gay* has elements of the soap opera format that is satirized in *The Marx Family Saga*. Characters like the N.H.S. Matron and Old Willow Pantomime morph in and out of short stories, poetry, monologue, song, interview; conceptual instructions cross Yoko Ono's *Grapefruit* with a self-help manual. The very title is conscious of the satirical take on self-help that Quentin Crisp flags in *How to Become a Virgin; How to Have a Lifestyle; How to Go to the Movies;* and his one-man show *How to Make It in the Big Time.*

Chloe Poems affirms and decries the legacy of this Edwardian effeminate ambiguously. "Good manners would demand that on no account, even by implication, should I bring to light a subject offensive to other people," Quentin Crisp believes.[2] Poems seems to believe those are the only subjects worth writing about, flouting discretion to provoke political and aesthetic conservatism, sensationally. Our Introduction to Part One watched society overtake camp generation after generation, as critics and fashion set aside the anachronisms of Saki and Lord Berners and Firbank and Beerbohm and Coward. Now, camp has an author who outstrips fashion and sets aside conservatism to steal a lead on the status quo.

"Time for more than just window dressing," Poems asserts against the culture of spin, beyond Crisp's early book on that very subject and beyond his book on its literary equivalent, calligraphy, and perhaps beyond Wilde's attention to surface and symbol? It's a pun with a point: the dressing required is tended by a nurse to a wounded society. *How to Be a Better Gay* features a matron's monologue in the beleaguered National Health Service in a society busy "Shutting down buildings of hope and healing." Conspicuous language catalyses consciousness behind the noun, beyond desensitizing assumptions: "Hospitals" would not give us pause to consider the significance of those buildings to the social psyche; "Buildings of hope and healing" makes their closure more telling. The matron is sister to the nurse in Alan Bennett's *Untold Stories* who knows she's in a "Carry On" film — but Poems delivers the outraged tantrum that is beyond the remit of Bennett's decorum. Is it camp? The title suggests, yes, it is: "Ooh, Matron." It begins with a pastiche of Gilbert and Sullivan that plays on excessive alliteration, puns on "general," and courts a theatrical analogy both whimsical and profound:

> I am a modern major matron in a modern major general
> Twenty years in the theater
> Of life and death.[3]

Three puns, a popular operatic echo, and the humming momentum of melodic alliteration lead us to expect chattering flippancy in the camp tradition — but we take a terminal turn instead. The workmanlike writings of George Orwell, even an article on how to make a perfect cup of tea, show no such inclination or aptitude for camp, but he does champion the subtext of socialism in literature. For Orwell, the promise of socialism was the spoils of war: if men were yet again called upon by governments to wage world war in the name of civilization and justice, then those men who made it back wanted to bloody well see social justice in their own land. And so Churchill was ousted and, for a while, the British Welfare State became a paragon of the civilized world. *How to Be a Better Gay* and Poems' preceding books look to bring Orwell's pamphleteering idealism back into fashion with a style that would have bemused Orwell himself. I'm as surprised as Orwell: socialism seems an unlikely affiliation to an aesthetic whose aloof disposition rises above the lowest common denominator. Two World Wars had devastated the aesthetic and rendered it redundant — but Orwell would be more bemused that socialism itself has been ruthlessly expelled. A paradox of Poems' work is the incongruous integration of two anachronisms in a driving modern form: camp socialism. Many of the poems in this chapter are chronicles of our time that press camp into public service: topical verses pronounce an editorial position, tabloid titles proclaim sensational headlines, lines are as throwaway as the dailies— and yet they transcend the transience of current affairs in their camp iconography, as "Crash! Bang! Wallop! What a Picture!" survives 1997 and the demise of its royal subject.

"True camp is always connected, not divorced," Poems insists in the Introduction to *I'm Kamp* in 2003, stressing a connection to humanity in a book that is skeptically detached from society. Poems' engagement is possible in modern gay culture that is "coming out." Forty years after the Berlin novels, Christopher Isherwood indicts his own self-effacing narrative as a device to cloak his homosexuality. His passive voyeurism is "wistful impotence," though many a camp author stands further aloof from his prose, even in a "coming-out" culture, as a matter of style. In fact, an aloof tone requires presence: Isherwood's character in the Berlin novels is transparent, not aloof. Citing his famous metaphor, "I am a camera," when his disguised sexuality forestalled engagement with his characters, and referring to himself in third person now, Isherwood laments, "From that moment on, whenever he published a book, there would always be some critic who would quote it, praising Mr. Isherwood for his sharp camera-eye but blaming him for not daring to get out of his focal depth and become humanly involved with his sitters."[4] Yet Susan Sontag[5] rather romanticizes camp when she asserts, "Camp taste is a kind of love, love for human nature," and Poems politicizes the connection with socialist verse that engages popular culture. Mindful of the camp dynamic of distance (of relativist distance from judgement, too) and the barbed wit that Kenneth Williams called the *acid drop*, I'd say that Sontag's assertion is variably somewhat so. It does find confirmation with Ed Wood, who engages wholeheartedly in process, and Chloe Poems, who engages wholeheartedly with humanity. But popular culture in the Poems oeuvre is, *au contraire, counter*culture, and it questions my own assertion in Part One that camp, so aloof and dégagé, seldom *opposes* anything. The Poems reader is addressed by appealing and confrontational second person pronouns more personally than with any other camp writer excepting Goytisolo. Can we reconcile this intimate immediacy with Quentin Crisp's advocacy (in Part One), "A true humorist is so totally disengaged that he can relax in any situation and evaluate every crisis— even those that are brought about by his own folly —from at least two (possibly opposed) points of view"?

Let's start at the very beginning, with beautiful transparency. "I was in such a befuddle about what to write for an introduction," Poems introduces *Adult Entertainment*, reflecting the process and then echoing the reflection, "and so turned to Betty, my trusted colleague and equal, and said 'Betty, my trusted colleague and equal, I'm in such a befuddle about what to write for this introduction, what do I do?' Betty quickly, succinctly, without even opening her mouth, said 'Just write what you believe in.'"[6] The perplexity is genuine — the author takes the address as seriously as some take the opening of Parliament or the State of the Union speech — but the term "befuddle" is pantomime confusion, and its repetition in quotation dramatizes the dilemma fit to tread the boards and wring Cinderella hands before the reader. Ironic echo distances every sentence. Betty's reply is related tongue in cheek: a miraculous innuendo makes telepathy sound like sphincter ventriloquism, "without even opening her mouth"; even "succinctly" is incriminated by lewd onomatopoeia. Betty's advice, clear and simple, sets the stage for a manifesto: personal, political and paradoxical beliefs given equal coverage, as genuine and simply whimsical as a child's heart. "I believe in my family. I believe there is still a working class. I believe in Easter Egg chocolate."

Belief in the working class is a socialist sentiment, but socialism might be expected to relegate the family in favor of the state. The affirmation of Easter Egg chocolate symbolizes a childlike openness to delight, wonderment, and perhaps the potential of a new beginning — and Easter Egg chocolate. Incongruities are posed with barely a comma or a conjunction, with never a "However" and barely a "because." Iconic incongruities such as family and socialism and Easter Eggs align with equivalent weighting in separate sentences within the same paragraph. Made random by design, the manifesto achieves the philosophy of equivalence that Quentin Crisp conveyed in deadpan irony and fatalism. The politicized difference is that Poems applies the equivalence to socialism. This is the essence of aloof disposition, not indifference to events exactly, but aspiring to be as indifferent to their priority as socialism is supposed to be to hierarchy. It's a world: things happen. Framing each sentiment in its own space — as equilateral as a gingham design, which is the author's iconic motif in performance — the Introduction sustains equilibrium from polarities and hierarchies even in a highly political posing of heroes and villains. This list of iconicized, fetishized favorite things is spiked with antipathy. A demonizing disavowal of the American presidency contrasts with a belief in Doctor Who. Doctor Who, reputed to be nine hundred years old, is a cult science fiction wizard with two hearts and a penchant for regeneration who occasionally materializes in the poems with shamanic significance. These icons of beliefs are amulets against the closed and clinical realism of the unacceptable status quo. The open naivete of language and symbolism may be dismissed as puerile by some academicians, but these elements are too elemental for the author to intellectualize the aesthetic. "The Effeminate" defines the art,

> out of his silliest dillies and dallyings
>   A marrying of wit and movement,[7]

where the silliest dillies and dallyings are the very aesthetic. My own analysis in this chapter is, even if valid, quite beside the point.

The litany of idealism that introduces Poems' thoroughly modern camp in *Adult Entertainment* sounds like lyrics for Julie Andrews, to help the revolution go down. It soars above the status quo and banishes banality with visions both domestic and fantastic, simplistic and radical: Mary Poppins on poppers. It has the transparency of truth yet reads like a Jackanory rendition of a fairy tale, with all the wonder and drama and morality and simplicity that charms fairy tales, that favorite camp genre. It even has a Wicked Witch: "I believe Margaret Thatcher to be the ultimate personification of evil." The political antagonism is so melodramatic — Thatcher's own extremism was dogmatically unqualified by doubt, compromise or mercy — that it recalls pantomime performance, especially when we read, "I believe if she was a drag king she would dress as Tony Blair. I believe Tony Blair would see this as a compliment." The poise between political indictment and whimsical nonchalance is perfectly equidistant. The masculine-feminine confluence, the air of aloof irony and foxy paradox that sees beyond each declaration, the dramatic excess ... this is the surest indication so far that thoroughly modern camp aesthetics may even in detachment declare political assertions — not nearly as somber as Brecht but every bit as alienated and left wing. The political indictments in Chloe Poems' work suggest that perhaps society is not synonymous with civilization as we had assumed, that society may be closer to barbarism than we care to concede. Only Poems and Goytisolo among camp practitioners address the barbarism of humanity. If modern camp can express this damning radicalism, it suggests a wider political remit than in Firbank's daydreams — or in the disdainful appraisals of critics who have yet to get with it (what they're forgetting is, this isn't 1922).

There is one sweet, horticultural sentiment that Firbank could endorse in his flowerful fancy; its cunning innocence looks so aesthetically agreeable, poised beautifully on a line of its own, that Firbank would be taken quite by surprise when it blooms in socialist colors: "I believe everyone should have a garden."

Heavens, who could argue with that?

The writing achieves a fairy tale wedding of camp and ethics that was divorced in Oscar Wilde's camp plays and moralistic fairy tales. Though both authors might agree in principle on amorality in art, Poems does contravene Wilde's view that we reviewed in Part One, "To art's subject matter we should be more or less indifferent," with "no preferences, no prejudices, no partisan feeling of any kind." Yet the matter of fact simplicity of the Introduction to *Adult Entertainment* breezes through Crisperanto, too. "As a well-mannered listener to your dogmas and catastrophes, I bring an engagement and a detachment at the same time," Crisp proposes in his book on good manners.[8] Paradoxical notions like detached engagement work on the insight that every truth incubates its inverse mirror image. Hence, "I believe showbusiness is a cancer and riddled with disease. I believe in entertainment." Crisp too flirts capriciously with paradox and confesses, tongue in cheek, that, before he has finished writing a book, "I am over-taken by the fear that I have begun to state the opposite of what I said at the outset."[9] *Adult Entertainment* pre-empts all that by contradicting every-thing before the book proper begins.

The contrast between political cynicism and child-like wonderment is a most intriguing thematic paradox. Aesthetically, detached engagement works by declaring a judgement or a concern and then putting ironic dis-tance between the expression and consciousness ... by whimsical aside, extreme contrasts, conscious contradiction, irreverent innuendo, allusions beyond the present consideration (generally or historically or even cosmi-cally), not to disown the assertion but to set it in context — and the con-text is paradox. "His position is crystal unclear" describes "The Effeminate," a landmark poem that signaled an explosion of new *fin de siècle* creativity. "It's what gives him his unerring vision /And makes his inaccuracies hit bull's-eye."[10]

Camp aloof disposition expresses itself preciously, a feminine touch to arch the irony and lighten the proclivity and suggest that distinctive superior tone in rising above partisanship. We found it expressed through ironic qualifiers in Part One — "quite [extreme]" or "somewhat [extreme]" — achieved through unequivocal simplicity in Poems' Introduction, unquali-fied by the dissembling clauses and sophistry that often passes for reasoned judgement in politics. The author indicts western culture and Very Impor-tant politicians with fantastic and sensational imagery — George Bush is six of the Seven Horses of the Apocalypse and Tony Blair makes up the num-bers — yet all in simple sentences free of interim punctuation and patterned on serial repetition that prefaces each belief with "I believe." After this sub-jective refrain, each declaration is entirely free from persuasive argument, presented with simple clarity normally reserved for factual statements and so ironically appearing aloof from personal prejudice! Of course, we are continually reminded by the mantra "I believe," a canny incongruence between subjectivity and impervious impartiality, posed by an innocent bystander to any unpalatable indecorum caused by reality; it is, after all, truth as the author sees it, decorated and dramatized with poetic symbol-ism, just like the Bible, where the Horsemen of the Apocalypse also gave us a bumpy ride. There were only four of them in the Bible but a magnificent seven in the analogous Introduction. Camp flashes its rhetorical license for galloping excess and style over content. Seven riders look so much more impressive, and the numeral itself seems aesthetically complete. Only eccle-siastical camp would have the nerve to revise the Bible and flaunt the car-dinal sin.

In Part One ecclesiastical camp attended The Temple of Convenience in the graffiti verse of "Faith Is A Toilet" and the revelation of "No Stranger to Sequins." Public toilets are "Piss smelly cathedrals" in "The Effeminate," "where real men kneel /And find the answers /To their wet knee'd, piss-smelly prayers." Seedy religiosity strikes an ironic genuflection and dwells in decadent deliberation just enough to be too much. Poems' holiness opens all orifices, embracing bodily functions that Christian civilization suppresses, that even Crisp judged ill-mannered and uncouth to speak of. Another sermon that revises Christendom, "Faith," echoes a modulated line break on "But beyond that, faith is

> Beyond that faith is
> Beyond that
> Faith is beyond that
> Faith is beyond that
> Faith is.[11]

Excess in "Faith" is beyond even repetition, faith is beyond even that. There it ends, in a child-like idiom that restates the subject at the end of a sentence (like "That's mine, that is"), even adapting Beerbohm's penchant for swaggering music-hall refrain (in the cockney formula of "'Enery the Eighth I am, I am!") to a church-hall context. (*I'm Kamp* warns, "Don't Put Your Laurels on the Page, Mr. Birmingham." "Crash! Bang! Wallop! What a Picture!" echoes a rousing cockney musical number. You can find a seaside shanty in "The Silk Weaver" and another music-hall number nested like a pun in "No Stranger to Sequins'" when the author discloses his past: "My old man disappeared / Followed the van and cleared off with my mother's money," a bonny working class nod to "My Old Man Said Follow the Van," and so, gratuitously, for a line or two, "He dillied, he dallied." This lyric is parodied again by Rosie Lugosi in "My Friend Gwen.")

"Faith" testifies to the herenow presence of the author's faith, and, too, the pagan affirmation of excess, "beyond that," beyond conceptualizing. Letting the mind tick over the irregular repetition, the trippy ditty leaps into the void without a circumscribing adjective or noun to limit the statement, epistemologically or morally. It's a *Doctor Who* thing to do.

"In Celebration of Poo" canonizes toilet humor. It affirms and "outs" shit, as "Some of My Best Friends are Straight" affirms and "outs" gay fellatio (whose "Omni, Omni, Omni" onomatopoeic masticating mantra relishes the act and the outrage) and "Kinky Boy" affirms and "outs" prostituted polymorphous perversion and "My Effeminate Bottom" speaks for itself ("it whistles a better Pink Panther than Henry Mancini") — all collected in *Universal Rentboy.* With Carry On camp "In Celebration of Poo"[12] preaches scatological evangelism. Evangelism is so exhibitionist in its proscenium pulpit, it converts naturally to camp. This devout sermon on shit takes camp beyond innuendo to come to terms with its inevitable waste subject matter for all men engaging in anal penetration. Likening repression to constipation, it challenges the anal-retentive denial of at least two thousand years of culture, in fluent verse. It's true:

> It's no mystery
> we've poo'd through history,

and history itself is human waste. Wordsworth is celebrated for his paeans to nature, but he never came near to acknowledging our basic natural function that binds our bowels to the earth. Poems discloses the secret yet everyday pleasure in the life of mankind deemed unfit for literature. It's true: "It's so fulfilling squeezing it out." "Poo" is preferred over "shit" because the childish term is not spattered by stigmatic use as a curse, and its simplicity ridicules our intense and (to Freud anyway) complex antipathy to it. By the end of the poem it will become as personable as Pooh Bear. The characteristic tone of naivete is genuine and tongue in cheek: outside the centrifugal social force of fundamental assumptions and cyclic thinking. Naiveté gives the author's voice license to speak the unspeakable and question the integrity of convention, not unaware of the moral and philosophical turbulence in its wake ... in fact, rather delighted with it. The audacious thrust of camp excess escapes the peer pressure of collusion and assumption.

Quentin Crisp, another nonconformist, declines the invitation to celebrate. "All bodily functions are unpleasant," he wrote in 1984, approving of closeted privacy and disdaining the modern trend toward "tasteless behavior that aspires to being Rabelaisian but which, in fact, is merely revolting."[13] It is hard to see how Crisperanto decorum could approve Rabelais himself. "In Celebration of Poo" subverts the heavenly supremacy of the incorporeal world and the puritan separation of body and spirit, as Poems embraces the physicality of being gay that Crisp pathologized despite himself. "It's time our poo was elevated /to its highest state," flouting decorum to envision the profound poos of the Virgin Mary and baby Jesus, reclaims the purity of our desanctified bodily functions. It is a plea to humanity for acceptance of its own nature, a Rabelaisian cry against the last refuge of snobbery, "don't turn your nose up," as the out-house comes in from the cold. It heals a schizoid dichotomy in modern man of feminine mother nature disowned by masculine intellect, restoring the primacy of regenerative energy. The author reaffirms this in "Autumn" (a reconciliation with ageing), "I Wanna Be Fucked By Jesus" (a gay supplication in search of an immaculate conception), and "All God's Children" (a decadent embrace of deviant varieties of pornography).

Degrading, or just biodegradable? The subject matter of waste matter appears vulgar, and vulgarity in excess is kitsch. Milan Kundera thinks not. Au contraire, Kundera defines the "original and metaphysical meaning" of "kitsch" in 19th century Germany as "the absolute denial of shit, in both the literal and the figurative senses of the word." The obfuscation of honest and earthy humanity is replaced with plasticity. Kundera paraphrases the kitsch rejection of nature, including human nature, "The daily defecation session is daily proof of the unacceptability of Creation."[14] He rejects the kitsch equation with vulgarity.

"In Celebration of Poo" suddenly sounds celestial. The whimsical yet earnest conclusion, "What a wise thing poo is," gives our poo a Tibetan air of mystery. Rabelais spread the word long ago. In Harvard Professor Epps analyzes "waste" matter in Juan Goytisolo's *Juan the Landless:* "It celebrates a more socially determined inversion of values in which the base elements of the body — everything considered unproductive and improper — are vindicated."[15] Ditching analysis itself as anal retentive, Poems puts it simply, "so open your arse /let your bowels be free." Spreading "its dusky allure /and provocative perfume," sensual onomatopoeic alliteration recommends "the soft moist joys /of your fascinating sphincter." Finally, the poem sends up its message, "as the old saying goes /Poo does, as Poo knows /what a profound thing Poo is!" capitalizing the Subject that has by now attained archetypal resonance and spiritual divinity. The theatrical scale of the flagrant faux pas redresses the imbalance of repression, after the unorthodox evangelism of Lenny Bruce. A great leveler in its everyday pertinence to us all yet the euphoric elevation of its subject transcends banality. Girly and flippant in its airey rhyming and toilet posing,

> flicking through your Vanity Fair
>   smiling contently
>   not giving a care

not even to correct the adverb (style over content, rhythm over grammar), yet "In Celebration of Poo" pinches a crack in civilized man's self-acceptance. Ethereal spirituality must be grounded in earthy nature, our roots.

> "If we deny our natural bodily endeavor
>   then naturally
>   we'll be crippled for ever and ever,"

a whimsical echo of "natural" with a line break as fatalistic as a Gallic shrug at the crippling consequences. Contrived bravery in the phrase "bodily endeavor" mocks our penchant for fancy euphemisms for the crudely unspeakable and makes trench warfare of toilet-training. Sensational impact, set up by delayed timing after an unassuming conditional proposition, is a signature trait of this provocative poet, who sticks his bottom over the parapet time and again: showstopping rhetoric shocks our conditioning.

The Introduction to *Adult Entertainment* too grounds wisdom in the earth and takes exception to the clinical intellect to be found trowelled under mortar boards. Despite a Harvard rendezvous in 2004, "Also I believe intellect without instinct is akin to having the finest pedigree dog without a sense of smell," the precious diction, domestic, bourgeois analogy and a measured accumulation of clauses charge the impact of the final taboo (yet simple) word: "for no matter how well turned out it is, or how may tricks it's been taught, it's only half a dog if it can't sniff out, and therefore understand, the very many different types of shit." Howard Gardner's research into the very many different types of creative intelligence would support the point; *Frames of Mind* (1983) prizes kinaesthetic intelligence, say, as highly as the analytic kind that holds court in Oxbridge. Poems distrusts a scheme of understanding the world that denies our organic nature as easily as suppressing the first person pronoun, and that seeks a divorce from the grounding earthiness of our origins, our feelings and our shit. Such divorce proceedings facilitate man's inhumanity to man as well as bad dress sense.

When Kundera suggests, "The true opponent of totalitarian kitsch is the person who asks questions," kitsch is the "spin" culture of marketing bylines and tabloid headlines, propaganda for the masses. Camp asserts the distinction of exposing artifice, not covering it up, but kitsch, as *objective* camp not conscious of process, exposes artifice too, unwittingly. In order to concur with Kundera, which has its uses, we would have to separate kitsch and camp altogether and deny the observable relation between them. Poems observes camp and kitsch as neighbors—"They don't share a house, but they borrow the odd cup of sugar from each other"*—and leans over the fence to jangle with kitsch. Incongruous working class noises of family life, "the moaning and groaning /Of a tone-deaf orchestra /Warming up to performance," commandeer camp from its aristocratic lineage. Kitsch may even be essential for the rare camp writer who documents urban underclass culture that can ill-afford finery and must make do with cheap imitation, where "Beauty was knee-capped before it could walk /Was second-hand before it was worn," in "No Stranger to Sequins."[16] "Those bloody French windows" are not on the set and Poems doesn't care to take tea with Saki in china cups and crested saucers. "Underlit by multi-colored

*Conversations with Chloe Poems and the author during 2004.

neon," "Bingo Jesus"[17] is a tramp who specializes in "the street theater of polystyrene tea and sympathy." The poem becomes a kitsch artifact by association when it notices kitsch objects like a polystyrene cup. Breaking with elite camp tradition, the style becomes "common," as Bennett's generation puts it. The very title is a real juxtaposition of two signs on a desperate building in a street in godforsaken Manchester: "Bingo" in bric-a-brac lettering besides a solemn "Jesus."

Yet Poems is the antithesis to Kundera's kitsch, questioning culture more than any other camp writer. "No Stranger to Sequins" poses a conundrum on behalf of every child taken into care and every psychiatric patient and any "client" of any "chartered" social service: "But how can you trust people who are paid to care." Something more fundamental is at work here, personal and political, than interrogating the establishment only. Kundera's take on kitsch "describes the attitude of those who want to please the greatest number, at any cost," while Poems' work upsets as many people as it delights.[18] "Liverpool City of '?'" questions the European City of Culture award amid all the congratulations. The very title "Are We Myra Hindley?" refuses to set the community righteously apart from the demons of tabloid headlines: they are magnifying mirrors of our own psyches that call our collective responsibility to account. A whimsical conundrum is just as insistent: "Oh why do roughs have such tight buns? /Why do dominatrixes dress as nuns?"[19] In the philosophy of equivalence, gravity and frivolity skip hand in hand and one question is as good as another: natural selection is a construct that fabricates a linear genealogy from undifferentiated events. Poems, like Crisp, perceives that God, or his impersonator, reclines on a divine divan, aloof. Interconnectedness of all matter and energy sweeps aside any distinguishing footprint in the sand, like the beach in "No Stranger to Sequins," "As much a part of everything as anything was."

Many a provocative question challenges the Chloe Poems reader and baits controversy with accustomed exhibitionism. The question in celebration of poo is rhetorical: "how can we love ourselves /if we can't love our shit!" I'm bound to say, it's a tall order.

So is growing older. "Autumn" reflects on the mirror image of aging as we may expect of an aesthetic that exposes process by detachment and exhibitionism. Like Coward and Crisp, Poems disputes the legacy of Wilde, unimpressed by the cult of *The Picture of Dorian Gray* and the seeming obsession with youth and its equation with beauty and associations of aging lines and hollows with damning ugliness. (The rhetorical question here was asked by Rasputin, too: "What's a wrong for /If it can't be forgiven." It smoothes away the furrows of guilt, taking exception to Wilde's moral allegory, those stigmatic lines of decadent experience that mar Dorian Gray's portrait.) Youth is an enduring subject in the surface aesthetic. Saki's serial protagonist makes the point: "Reginald in his wildest lapses into veracity never admits to being more than twenty-two."[20] In *The Watched Pot,* René bemoans that his mother didn't delay his birth by four years, whereupon, "I should be nineteen now, which is the only age worth being."[21] "Autumn" petitions the camp cult of youth. "A Pop psychologist with allusions to Wilde" might agree that youth was wasted on the young, "But surely Oscar's greatest delusion /Was to continually give so much kudos /To nothing more than the aging child."[22] With camp diction, the pouting, parodying verse rolls those mulled "u's"and "l's"around the palette like a fruity wine, "allusions ... surely ... continually ... delusion ... kudos...." One feels Oscar Wilde couldn't have disagreed with himself better.

"Autumn" makes melodrama of the phobia of growing old in our youth culture, punning on vanity's crisis. Time passes "With the ferocity of a hungry housewife /With the wind taken out of her January sales." The desperate aspirate analogy domesticates shipping and sailing with sales shopping. "It can be all consuming" inflates the metaphor of consumerism where the appearance of youth is a lucrative commodity in fashion and cosmetics and celebrity, and fear of aging is a driving consumer motivator. These are the ravages not of time but capitalist exploitation.

We saw Will Self blunt the camp aesthetic of *The Picture of Dorian Gray* to address harrowing political realities. Poems, and this poem in particular, exposes realities behind the new culture of "spin" with camp social commentary. The poem has implications for Ronald Firbank, who, like Dorian Gray, presents a vain sensibility that can't bear another line of aging. He "had a horror of growing old," perhaps inevitable in surface aesthetics. Ifan Kyrle Fletcher[23] suspects that Firbank's "fear of age may account for the narcissistic habit of having his portrait painted.... The swift passage of the years made personal his theory that only art was enduring." "The Effeminate" attributes the trait generically to effeminacy, "On what he hopes is his ever youthful face," just as "Autumn" satirizes effeminate hysteria, "You're getting older /Something's got to give /Head's pounding a beat /You're in trouble." Hear an echo of *The Naked Civil Servant:* there is nobility in a receding hairline, "but when you are noble all the way to the crown of your head, you're in trouble." At the time, Crisp was in his "Havisham twilight" (unaware of another thirty years of experience ahead), writing with humorous hindsight at the Canute posturing of ego against a rising tide, with a refrain as inevitable as high tide, "I was growing old." Crisp stylized personhood cosmetically but, unlike modern youth culture, did not airbrush away the years. In his "blue period," an overtly artificial tint does not hide his grey hair.[24] His stylized fatalism demands that he accept aging without protest or denial. "Autumn" goes further than fatalism to *embrace* this stage of life — by romanticizing it, with the equivalent of blue dye. Yet Poems and Crisp look at the world and the mirror without flinching. A bitchy scratch on another day is, in "The Effeminate," simply and poignantly the unflinching truth: "Years are reaching stretching /Like Virginia Creepers /Trailing around your once bonny baby blue peepers." Virginia Creepers turn to gold in autumn. Art nouveau embroiders the traits of aging in the poem and makes them pretty with a superabundant aesthetic.

> A leafing legacy of vines
> You're now more inclined to call laughter lines.

Camp's two-hundred year love-affair with Romanticism will always prefer autumn colors to bleak winter. Kitsch is the delinquent influence on the stately, senior aesthetic: an uncouth analogy jumps ship from the maritime imagery to take up the beat, "As a thousand thought policemen's feet /Trample down the wisdom you wore so well /For so few decades." Those clod-hopping agents of ageism are flagrantly inconsistent with the image system ... but this author poses a dilemma in seeming kitsch by design. If we imagine gradients of excess and (un)awareness, these poems traverse the continuum from camp to kitsch: the author as camp subject fashions a showboating artifact that reflects itself, then loses itself in kitsch excess, a camp object. "Half-mast, yardarms creaking," with a pun on "fleeting reminder," waves of seafaring imagery swell our apprehension. A pick-yourself-up admonition is no less maternal for being assertive: "So you're floundering /In a shallow bay /Be a castaway grounded /On some certain unsure." The certain unsure is a punning paradox of the surety of age that yet leads to the undiscovered country of the next moment and beyond — and more seafaring.

Whole stanzas of this poetry would be under threat from many a parsimonious editor, but, in the last rays of sunset or an autumn leaf, "Autumn" finds coherence in gilding advancing age gold, a prized commodity in the same consumer culture that devalues old age. (Gold is glamor in camp aesthetics, too.) Deriding nostalgia and even repentance that avoid the herenow of any given moment, "Autumn" has a metaphorical reach. It challenges the remit of literary criticism and the editorial process that would revise spontaneity, stem the tide of life and spurn the abundant offering of energy and diversity that life represents to the end; it validates the spirit of Ed Wood. Quentin Crisp endeavored to live in the continuous present, an admirable lifestyle,[25] though his most iconic works are retrospective memoirs. Poems achieves present focus *in the text,* an adroit balance of immediacy and distance in one draft. Like "Faith," where "madness is a moment ... ego is a moment ... truth is a moment," so "Autumn" resolves time into "golden moments ... a growing old moment...." and the silence of a line break when "Life itself has stopped," like "The tock between the tick of time" in "Volcano II,"[26] like eternal moments in "The Insomnia Suite," "An Eternity of...." in "Volcano IV,"[27] like Wilde's lament in "De Profundis," "Suffering is one very long moment"[28] ... so camp aesthetics undresses narrative down to flimsy instants that take the spotlight and dilate when we stop the plot.

Kundera's analysis of the moment "still more ungraspable than Proust's 'lost time': the present moment," he says, "eludes us completely. All the sadness of life lies in that fact."[29] Kundera congratulated Joyce on managing "to stop, to seize, that fleeting instant and make us see it." We have seen camp aesthetics perform this magic show all the time by dropping the plot, cause and effect and all ... in the smoky slow motion arising from Wilde's divan ... Firbank's picturesque saturation in the Bigger Picture ... Goytisolo montages of signature detail suspended in decadence ... and the classic Ed Wood moment of unwitting revelation that exposes itself, caught in the act: "Three minutes and ten seconds can seem a very long time when one knows exactly how long three minutes and ten seconds are...."[30]

"It can't be less than now" is the line in "Autumn" that enlightens this moment, at whatever time of life it is experienced, as not only measurably equal to any other, it is also all there is: all these years come down to this. Biographical narrative (which underpins the ego) is a myth, and the comparative evaluation of this moment with other moments that do not exist, in nostalgia, regret, ambition and apprehension, is delusory. Poems' argument stays true to surface aesthetics, ironically, digging no deeper than the present and the first draft.

"Crash! Bang! Wallop! What a Picture!" snaps the most photographic moment of the 1990s, and the most photographed celebrity since Jaqueline Kennedy Onassis, the spectacular death of Princess Diana. This was a moment when Britain wailed a wall of grief, so the riotous title (from a rousing cockney musical) and the tone of this camp provocateur may seem unseemly. Chirpy Tommy Steele in *Half a Sixpence* (1968) sang the original chorus, "Stick it in your family album!" which, through no fault of chirpy Tommy's, suddenly sounds outrageous.

Souvenir broken bone china and porcelain fragments of Diana's royal crest and visage merge "into the twisted metal /that contorted the fairytale lovely /until she was splattered on more than /just our front pages."[31] Acerbic and plosive and welding words together in clashing assonance, buggering the vowels with consonants, Poems approaches what Bradley Epps observed in Goytisolo, the "significant violence" of his "stylistic experimentation that does violence to the word itself." A natural disciple of decadence driven into labor by his art, this performer writes his own lines from expediency, so perhaps this "significant violence" reflects the author's antagonism to the writing process. Words are spat, bludgeoned, distorted, and yet, stylized even in excess, the poetry is never consumed by aggression, for dramatic irony gives us distance. "Crash! Bang! Wallop! What a picture!" is the sensational headline, and the first stanza is the leader that captures the lurid public imagination, smash and grab, "embittered ... shattered ... battered ... splattered" in a fraught and winding narrative, speed unchecked by punctuation, wrought like the twisted royal wreckage of the high speed collision. The kitsch pun splattered on the front page is no more horrific than the frenzied paparazzi reality of the pursuit of a great story all the way to the grave. In this instance, in reality, larger than life is just about the size of it.

The poem strips the seemly hypocrisy of the moment to relieve us of all that maudlin sentiment that mourned a tragedy while indulging the saturated publicity and celebrity culture that manufactured it. Outrageous impropriety bucks social collusion to free us from the tyrannous obligations of a tragedy. The second stanza takes a distanced perspective on the historical significance of the event but shows no faith in history to get it right. Instead, like Ed Wood, Poems summons the horror genre to suggest the grotesque disfigurement of the royal figurehead as a pathetic object of the public imagination, outfitted for martyrdom, in that lurid moment when the tabloid "love affair" with the princess became a shade necrophiliac.

Rhetorical questions are the customary vehicle for leading his readers to radical realizations. "Crash! Bang! Wallop! What a Picture!" touts the ghoulish hypocrisy beyond the grief:

> Is this Saint Frankenstein
> an unfortunate creature of our own making
> lumbering clumsily through a soft-focused
> rose-tinted insistence of England
> so green and pleasant
> or a graveyard where they still shoot pheasants.

The syntax of that stanza, the gross extremes of comparative images, and the whimsical timing of the final line break that presents itself as a pointed afterthought, feels like another Ed Wood moment, where the subject of the question switches distractedly from Princess to country — until you step back and see the alternatives are posed in the two images of England, rose-tinted or brutish, not in the terms of the rhetorical question of whether the Princess is a grotesque artifice of our own making. Coherence is stretched to include a disorienting objection to blood sports (which does belie the image of a decorous and precious royal sensibility) in the same sentence that questions the Frankenstein construct of royalty and gives pathos to society's celebrity martyr, all in the context of the most famous car crash in history. The runaway style is exhilarated with more than the sensational subject matter: the spontaneity of a free hand flies with the Muse on a single draft. All the reflection happens in gestation, rehearsed in life, in observation and conversation, before putting pen to paper.

"Crash! Bang! Wallop! What a Picture!" indulges fairy tale princesses and pageantry that Firbank and Wilde and Beardsley and Berners indulged, but takes a right royal detour. The "porcelain hints" that Harold Nicolson found in Firbank's precious innuendo are shattered by this "porcelain precise" portrayal of a Princess. Disinterring the gruesome details of August 31, 1997, it strips bare the cosmetics of celebrity and parodies the press coverage in an exposé of the insidious impropriety of royalty. What an analogy, "Princess Pretty" glossing shameless exploitation, equated with the gothic skeletal structure that underpins the romantic face of royalty ripped off by the crash. "Oh, such macabre poetry," indeed, reflecting on itself, driving underground poetry to a Parisian underpass and henceforth, graveside. All very kitsch, all very vulgar, but then, monarchy is kitsch: it has the audacious bad taste to flaunt its plundered riches before the dispossessed.

In reality, before tax deductions, our day-to-day lives have nothing to do with royalty, a world apart. That's the real distance that the poem observes, decorum to the wall. The great delusion of bereavement that Britain bought into, courtesy of the media, calls on the master of eulogies:

> How can we struggle on
> now that our hope has gone?
> Thank God we've still got Elton John.

It stages a funereal masquerade, "Crash! Bang! Wallop! What a Picture!

> Saint Frankenstein you floored a nation
> with your oh so dramatic exit.

The mirror held up to society does not flatter or collude; first person plural sends us all up, "We're fighting back the crocodile tears /because we mustn't miss the souvenirs," a fair summary of kitsch culture. Time for one more dramatic pause and an irresistible tasteless pun on "Lady Di /Lady dead," before a forlorn epitaph gives society the benefit of the doubt despite the poet's better judgement: "I hope we were mourning a woman of compassion /and not Princess Pretty and the death of fashion."

This is one of many fixated poems that indicts royalty. The poet rather relishes "this no-good monarchy business,"[32] but in no way that Noël Coward could recognize. Coward epitomizes the genuflecting generations that have, until late, defined British patriotism with compelling peer pressure. *Pomp and Circumstance,* although set in an idyllic pagan island community liberated from hang-ups over sex and poo, prepares for a British royal visit with bourgeois fussiness. The narrator opines for Coward, "Royal snobbery, in moderation, is rather a good thing and I am all in favor of it. The crown is a symbol and as such is, or should be, of tremendous importance." You begin to appreciate the combustible culture clash between British monarchism and Poems' damning of the royal family that may be indicted as treason in Coward's United Kingdom. Coward: "I, being thoroughly British and sentimental to the core, would hate to live in a country in which there was no regal pageantry and no chance of suddenly seeing the Queen drive by."[33]

Actually, Poems celebrates pageantry as an opulent subject for flamboyant writing, "Limousine wealthy /Parisian couture," courting the tantrums and lush detail and flagrant controversy of camp temperament. Camp has an aesthetic affinity with the ostentatious decadence of royalty. The royal series, "Harry, King of Smack," "Margaret — A Royal Love Gory," "The Queen Sucks Nazi Cock," "Whore," and "Crash! Bang! Wallop! What a Picture!" condemns the iniquity from a socialist perspective but pauses to relish the decadence, squaring the difference in "Whore" by equating royalty with whoredom,

> Streetwalking threadbare
> The bejeweled corridors
> Of her own red carpet district.[34]

It interrogates the coherence of "good taste" that applauds the exhibitionism of the monarchy yet stigmatizes honest exhibitionism on other red light streets—and turns it on its crown. A bitter pun on acid reign poses the monarchy "Shining down brassily /Shirley Bassily." (Shirley Bassey is a camp and kitsch facsimile of royalty, celebrated and imitated in gay queen culture.) "Whore" admires "the baroque Edwardian splendor" while regretting that the Queen Mother is, "Sadly not the last of the great big spenders," tarnishing the royal gilt with ironic echoes of that seedy, brassy Bassey song. Camp is iconic but Poems is also iconoclastic. Camp just loves a tiara, and Poems indulges the bejeweled enchantment of a thousand and one fairy stories, refracted by black magic into the imagery of classic gothic myth,

> Diamonds mined by slaves
> The blood of colonized culture
> Soaked in every ruby
> The bold souls of workers
> Trapped within the amber of her jewelery.

"Volcano I," from a forthcoming collection (as I write),[35] reflects the contradiction, "Dreaming of being working class English /Day Dreaming of being royalty," with no urgency to resolve it. Royal, decadent and socialist, all are fictional in the masquerade of being.

The most notorious, and popular, piece of lese majesté is "The Queen Sucks Nazi Cock." The title is emblematic of the author's disorienting associations that thrust us into a strange world where poet laureates dare not stray. Prince Phillip's right-wing racist faux pas are more notorious than the poem; this right royal gaff is juxtaposed against a second premise that the Queen and her husband engage in sex, which sounds so radical in itself that one wonders why. The notion of a sexual Queen transgresses the propriety that raises the royals above the world of the flesh — and we now know how the author feels about denial of our physical functions. This poem aims to bring the throne down to earth, demythologizing its divinity. With poetic license, the last premise of "The Queen Sucks Nazi Cock" also assumes royal foreplay.

And so, envisioning the royal figurehead giving head to her stately husband, and equating him to a Nazi, we begin the strange journey of the poem's protagonist, a royalist rudely disillusioned of patriotic values. From this character's point of view, with the author's seething anti-royalism primed to explode, the poem lurches schizophrenically from idyllic naivete to treasonable outrage. The emotional range is operatic.

> How I adore
> the lush green amour
> of my England[36]

The poem satirizes the privileged delusion of an idyllic England nestled in pastoral Wordsworth. Ornate use of "amour" flouts semantics to rhapsodize in a rhythmic rhyming of "adore," with camp's penchant for French and for style over content or impression over meaning. Lush and genteel language basks, tongue in cheek — a dissonant reference to foxgloves is more hand over fist than hand in hand with nature — in a rapturous eulogy to country and, reflexively, to the poem's own poetry:

> where whispering breezes
> go hand in hand
> with foxgloves
> and the gentle down of
> dandelion feather
> the heather
> pinks and purples...

with a lullaby sense of security,

> streams rhyme and gurgle
> hares chase and hurdle
> across her morning moist dewy fields...

The gay tone plays up the author's effeminacy, preciously satirizing the genre but audibly loving the language. The stanza imitates the England of the pastoral poets who omitted only one detail — society. Patriotism is a public performance: being seen to be dutiful before the readership, "I salute my England," the speaker pantomimes nationalism. The first stanza sets up the devastating impact of a political storm on the horizon with pastoral escapism in an unsustainable ideal of nation, "floating o'er moor and lake /impervious to trouble." Little could Wordsworth have suspected that the picturesque stream that gurgles musically through stanza one is about to burble obscenely into the onomatopoeia of fellatio on the page.

Melodrama is a dynamic of extremes. Poems attenuates this volatility to perform moods larger than life and catalyse reflective awareness of the action and the medium. It's a tad Zen in the tradition of shocking the unenlightened into awareness. Real anger is made theater, performed to excess and crafted ironically: pink punk. Before riding the amazing ejaculation of energy in the rest of the poem, let's contemplate how this author's characteristic dynamism squares deftly with camp.

There is a festive generosity in Poems' work that replenishes the cornucopia of poetry with a decadent overspill of similes and syllables, "Dodecahedron in currency,"[37] like "the robust octosyllables" in Goytisolo's *Count Julian.* It testifies to a schooling in theater: the stage, altar of a dramatic catharsis of man's lifetime of suppressed energy. The momentum of "Crash! Bang! Wallop! What a Picture!" is urgent like a car chase or a sensational news deadline; "The Queen Sucks Nazi Cock" and "Celebrities Are Shits" are infused with anger; "Kinky Boy" is driven by exhibitionist polymorphous sexuality; "London Is Paranoid" pulses with seething fear and contempt for all things London; merrymaking "Mirrorballin" and "Manchester Queen, Glittery Top" swing with good-time girly pop poppers and groove; "I Wish You Life" and "What Is This Thing Called Gay?" launch waves of allegiance and affirmation and toss bouquets from the heart to the needy and meritorious.... The languid language of Wilde and Beardsley and Saki and Firbank and Berners and Coward and Crisp is scarce here. There is, though, showmanship; even angry, the uncontainable momentum is as generous as theater, martialing the indignation of oppressed minorities that, put together, represents a faction greater than the whole. Euphoric, with a dash of whimsy, his Byronic verve revels in wordplay, joie de vivre and outrage, conscious of style even on the brink of insurrection. The immediacy is stylized in improvization, as live as an ad lib and as reckless as nothing-to-lose, unrevised, off the lace cuff, as it were. Tumultuous vitality, with judo turns of phrase and its demands on epic and incongruous imagery, contrasts dramatically with reflections on style with ironic élan, to fashion camp-going-on-kitsch.

At the kitsch end of the spectrum, "I needed help /Like a bomb needs a target" in "No Stranger to Sequins" brandishes Ed Wood's precious heavy-handedness like an effeminate Thor, like a cartoon *Blam!* Sounding like a trip down Tin Pan Alley, "Faith" proclaims an invocation to sing your promises as openly as "A lung-busting trash can opera /A pitched perfect indecipherable Italian aria /Performed for the thousandth time /But always heartfelt, always meant /By gutter-hearted divas," kitsch by Andrew Ross's definition (see Edward D. Wood chapter).

"I Wish You Life" wishes you, the reader, joy,

> The electrified high flying bewildering wonderment of
> Its spine tingling ecstatic pomposity
> The blinding cor blimey flash of its bombastic optimistic slapstick
>   Generosity....[38]

As bombastic as its word, like Goytisolo's curtain-raisers, the fluent lack of conjunctions and articles between bric-a-brac detail compounds the decadent saturation. Unlike Goytisolo, liberated clichés like "high flying" and "spine tingling" and folksy "cor blimey" lubricate the lush deluge unto "The firework display of its floristry." Poetic resonance gives proscenium elevation to every enunciation. Cascading syllables recall the oratorical caprioles of Leonard Sachs, host of B.B.C. music hall program *The Good Old Days,* whose renowned bombastic badinage brought "ooohs" and "aaahs" from the audience: showmanship.

Fireworks is Poems' favored symbolism to spark this combustible high energy. It may even cite Guy Fawkes as a revolutionary anti-hero. Yes, this skylarking firebrand *wants* to get caught in the Act and be celebrated for such cavalier penmanship and radicalism.

> I light the blue touchpaper
> And reluctantly
> Stand well back,[39]

describes the poet's ambivalence in "Volcano III," engaged yet detached. Fireworks catalyse a crystallized moment of enlightenment and chaos, ephemeral and timeless, saturated in color and sound. The starburst leads to the line, "I start to understand fantasy." Fireworks convey the wonderment that transports banality skywards. Many an inflammable poem by our gingham Guy Fawkes lights the fuse in stanza one and explodes, colorfully, across the rest of the page.

On rude awakening, the second stanza of "The Queen Sucks Nazi Cock" swings from idyllic peace to riotous indignation, from conservatism to anarchy, with a diva's temperament. Archaic rhetoric steps up the reaction to royal treachery with Frankie Howerd-style escalation:

> So you must understand my surprise,
> nay, my horror, my shock
> when I found out that
> the Queen sucks Nazi cock.

Pastoral poetry has been well and truly left behind, inadequate to articulate the modern urban and political experience. Only vulgarity, that is to say, kitsch language, can convey, and parody, the author's outrage — the explicit vision of fascist fellatio in excessive alliteration and pun:

> Your Royal Heinous, Elizabeth
> the bastion of majesty
> orally caressing her husband's erectile racist penis
> a right royal travesty
> an unequivocal tragedy
> of unimaginable proportions.

This is fantastic manipulation of language and rhetoric, though not the Pomp and Circumstance that Coward could parade. The poet's oral heritage spits like a curse the emphatic assonance and plosive impact of "bastion of majesty." "R's" roll around the tongue and tonguing sibilants relish the fellatio on the palette; the lines even dribble, I fancy. "Right royal" is camp rhetoric, and the echo of "bastion of majesty" in "travesty" amplifies the outrage at a bastardized country betrayed by its monarchy. "Gorging on national identity," decadent innuendo stretches the culpable erection with gobbling syllables, gullible no more. The poem opens its mouth Jagger-wide on "Gorging" and gnashes its teeth on "National," explicitly dental and palatine on "identity," as the words pose for a lipstick close-up. Extending from "unequivocal" to "unimaginable proportions," the overblown scale and provocative vulgarity may disguise the brilliance of this poem from conservative sensibility — it was, after all, released as a kitsch artifact, a single vinyl record — but really, what a magnificent exploitation of the polemic potential of camp.

It's a matter of mime, implicit on the page of this poet — melodramatic mime, that is, pantomime, where actions speak louder than words, so, on the camp page, orotund "O's" and somersaulting "R's" act out the process to access the overview. This mime of letters has a Pierrot presence as prevalent as in the art of Aubrey Beardsley, cipher to sadness and gaiety and rage but above all to reflection. Poems' latest creation is the archetypal idiot savant Old Willow Pantomime, where this oldest of English theatrical traditions, and perhaps the earliest camp form, is personalized as protagonist in *How to Be a Better Gay*. On the page, mime can be read into high-wire line breaks or finely poised ambiguity; in the toppling stanza spacing that may displace one state (a false sense of security, say) with its opposite (a false sense of anxiety); in repetition and overstated synonyms that impersonate incredulous realization; in the showboating simile that mirrors the artist as well as itself; in the rhetorical question that embodies its own call and response between the raised brow and open mouth, assuming assent to a dissenting voice from the silent majority. Assonance, alliteration and rhyme reflect the exhibitionist narcissism of the wordsmith and even moreso the poetic medium, preening itself. And so Echo and Narcissus get together after all.

In the aftermath of ideological havoc, in "The Queen Sucks Nazi Cock," a fey theatrical sentiment stages the protagonist bravely facing the truth, isolated and alienated, martialing his powers of survival: a narcissistic self bereft but still standing, girly and mannish, surveying the ruins of false consciousness, pausing only to pun on this sceptic isle,

> I stand
> stranded a million miles away
> observing this septic isle
> saddened lonely

...and open now to a deluge of damning home truths about his homeland, "where an Englishman's castle /is the crumbling housing /on a drug-run council estate." The moment of aftermath stops biographical narrative and opens up to revelation, just as Firbank stops the plot to saturate his prose and consciousness in eternity within the crystallized moment.

Poems stands like the dramatic personification of camp itself when the aesthetic was devastated by two World Wars. You can find the same epic and outcast narcissism, fey with world-weariness yet still showboating defiance, posed on a pedestal in "Love, Sex, Drugs, Rock 'n' Roll and Honesty," "I'm somehow still standing though the rug's pulled from under me"[40]— and in "Spud-u-Like in Monochrome," "I stand proud /resplendent in my gingham gown"[41]— and again by the opening lines in "Me": "I stand sometimes noble /As I survey with dignified relish /The battlefield of my life."[42] Suffering is so uncouth, but camp adores martyrdom because it stages suffering in the spotlight: metaphoric martyrdom not only gets religious billing but is made iconic by art too: it makes the subject aloof from suffering. Elevated as it is, the pose carries the kitsch public masochism of the Crucifixion, like the coda to Poems' play *Miracle* (unpublished, pre-miered at the Green Room Theater in godforsaken Manchester, England, 2000), with the crucified choreography of three figures and the effeminate turn of their heads; like Saint Sebastian pierced exquisitely to the core as in "No Stranger to Sequins" when "Heart stops as if punctured by an arrow"; like Corelli's Christ; like Oscar Wilde in "De Profundis"; like dead Lady Di; like the transvestite's implacable poise on the way to public execution in Wood's *Death of a Transvestite.* Quentin Crisp too posed this theatrical public masochism, turning his persecution in an ugly society into glorious passive resistance; transforming stigma into heavenly stigmata, suffering for his effeminate art — on the streets taking the blows of a vicious mob, in a shoe shop trying on dainty shoes two sizes too small, or triumphing over oppression with a magnificent performance of a homosexual in court, mod-eled after Imogen in *Cymbeline.* In a lecture and again in an essay, Alan Bennett sends up the penchant with Anglican camp when he notices that paintings of Christ seldom depict hair anywhere but on his head, not even armpit hair. He likens the paintings to his own late development with a transsexual metaphor about "this protracted pregnancy of puberty" and a depiction of our effeminate martyr in physical exercise, "crucified twice-weekly on the wall bars."[43] "Twice-weekly" domesticates the crucifixion. Poems is reluctant to relinquish the epic scale of martyrdom in so cavalier a fashion.

"Me," poised between survival and vulnerability and looking quite magnificently devastated and altogether star-struck in the spotlight, reflects (to me) the grandstanding ego of Shirley Bassey, parading her sequins and legend ("I Who Have Nothing")—or Sinatra on the farewell/come-back trail with a valedictory "My Way" or a valiant Judy Garland holding a note while fending off a nervous breakdown or Elton John Still Standing. A flamboyant effeminate fantasy sweeps by majestically,

> A most Florid Florence Nightingale
> Flagrantly singing a lament
> To the brave dying boys of the massacre
> I'm the last face many of them will see,

minted in memory like a sovereign. A martyr's exhibitionism, sacrificed on the altar of theater, yields his privacy to express and accept his psyche's secrets and, by association, what we impersonally call the human condi-tion, that is, yours and mine.

When *Crisp* goes public with an autobiography, it sets him apart: as society closes ranks on the outcast, he stands aloof in exiled eccentricity. Au contraire, "Me," beyond its flagrant egotism, through its very narcissism, offers the self as mirror to the reader. It is epic. In a dramatic development, "Me" strips the trappings and defenses of the privatized ego. "I'm reminded by my eyes /Just how many times I have failed love." Narcissism seems incomplete if it is exclusive: "I can't give wholly of myself /Even to myself." As far as Crisp can see, "When Miss Barbra Streisand says that people who need people are the luckiest people in the world, she is being a very funny girl,"[44] and Chloe Poems is just such a funny girl. "Me" blows a kiss to Sontag's romantic ideal of camp as a kind of love of human nature and its subjects, repairing the "significant violence" to the word itself, as "robust octosyllables" subside and silence speaks up. Mirror-gazing into one's original face, Poems discovers that narcissism is only self-contained if it is transcendental, that is, only if narcissism leads to universal identification, only if there is such thing as society. By going epic, larger than life à la camp, the personal becomes political. In a rendezvous (on public transport: the last bus) with what might be left standing behind the masquerade, "Has the last bus taken me to us

> And does that mean
> It's not just me
> That perhaps
> Perhaps
> It may be
> We.

The masquerading notion of a unitary ego ghost-dances before the unassuming yet o so awesome backdrop, the horizon of oneness between I and thou. "Perhaps" tentatively ventures a self-conscious presumption: precipitous graphics edge one step forward, two steps back on the page, courting the reader's consent to universalize the author's personal vulnerabilities in the public arena. This is a rare offering in camp, closing the distance between author and reader as the poem strips the words line by line and performs the hesitancy like an Ed Wood cliff-hanger, until ten stanzas of epic melodrama and wordy syllables close on a speculative "We." The poet comes out in search of acceptance with disarming honesty, initiating the risk of intimacy. Ego is an expression and an offering of self to others. Narcissism has never looked so vulnerable.

"Me" holds a musical note while fending off a nervous breakdown, a note given meaning in relation to other notes and to silence. Being camp, the note is operatic in scale:

> ME
> Me Me Me Me Me Me Me Meeeee....

In "Me," the dawning revelation is intimately personal, even with consciousness finally nationalized; in "The Queen Sucks Nazi Cock," it is political. The tide turns and sovereign cynicism swells in sweeping statements with lines that break like breakers on the page, reinforced by more damning revelations. "The Queen Sucks Nazi Cock" ends on the emphatic refrain, pacing the rhetoric dramatically toward the inevitable disillusionment made iconic by the title,

> When the head of the highest
> Family in all the land
> Our Mother Protector
> Her Royal Heinous the Queen
> Sucks Nazi cock.

"The Queen Sucks Nazi Cock," "London Is Paranoid," "Me," "Drag Is Dead," "Faith," "The Effeminate," "Are We Myra Hindley?" and "No Stranger to Sequins," speak from an alienated perspective that lives with paradox, "As alien as it." This state of mind destabilizes moral, political, philosophical and aesthetic assumptions, and unseats the ego. It strikes an ambivalent relationship with every subject from royalty to homosexuality, from Christianity to camp, from society and country to the self.

"London Is Paranoid," another landmark title, revels like an anarchist in London's typographic collapse on the page. Verses look chiseled like epitaphs in desiccated stone, "hanging on a precipice

> of insufficient power
> an imposing edifice
> rocking, rotting
> second by minute
> minute by hour[45]

in irregular lines that landslide down the page. In Poems, line breaks can signify a sigh of ennui or a heart-stopping moment of melodrama, the fey posturing of despair or the stage silence of a suspenseful pause; line breaks can signpost the rhetorical dialectic of call-and-response or paradox, the flip side of an incongruous juxtaposition, the tease before a punning punchline or saucy innuendo; line breaks arch the barbed wit of a quip taking aim and linebreaks stand aloof from the context of a sentiment and gather the second wind for another layer of excess. In "London Is Paranoid," lines break under the cumulative weight of a capital landfill site for the chic waste of consumerism. Terrorism has nothing to do with it. This graphic metaphor mirrors the moral and cultural downfall of the capitalist capital, a systemic nervous breakdown recalling the decline of the Roman and British Empires and anticipating the corrupted decay in *A Cock-Eyed Comedy* and *Dorian.* Counting the hours second by minute augurs a warning to the nation with no time to lose. The pace and doom is precipitated by terse, unalterable (and unrevised) lines. For a new slant on style over content, turn the text sideways and see London's crumbling skyline, the anarchy of free verse made graphic in agitated lines, looking like telemetry that measures the capital erosion or exposes the quaking lie of the body politic.

The key hanging image foreshadows the national presentiment, paranoid or prophetic, as stanzas fall under seismic scansion:

> but give a city enough rope
> and it will hang a nation
> starved of emotional nourishment.
> Now that's what I call
> Capital Punishment.

The timing of each acidic indictment is devastating, like bitching at its Bette Davis best, but this is a political blitzkrieg. Bette Davis took on Warner Brothers; Chloe Poems takes on London. Urbane, effeminate rap compresses its lips in a lipstick pun, sending chic packing,

> So magazine
> So limousine
> Has Been
> And Maybeline.

Our foundation is quaking, "for London is the epicenter /of Cruel Brittania." Decay dissolves into liquefaction as the warning leaks out of London; paranoia spreads paranormally, its corrosive influence as insidiously pervasive as some radioactive sci-fi substance from the '50s culture of paranoia:

> London is creeping
> dripping, seeping
> into the consciousness
> of us all.

London is the amorphous symbol of what Brecht called false consciousness, and it's headed our way. Yet the final injunction, that would have us rise above consumerism, is positive, valuing the reader more highly than material calculation, and urging you, personally, to remember, always,

> you're much more important
> than the last thing you bought.

The paranoid tone pervades the graphic decay — yet of all the political symptoms of corruption and dissolution in the poem, is it ever demonstrated that London *is* particularly paranoid? Celebrities, another caste of royalty prone to queeny tantrums in "Celebrities Are Shits," are *seen* imprisoned by their own egos in that poem, "Marooned on Paranoid Island."[46] "*London Is Paranoid*" is only asserted emphatically: even when London "looks over its own cold shoulder ... /it just wants to check out /what you're wearing." Is "London Is Paranoid" prophetic? Seven years later, defense of democracy requires the restriction of civil liberty. How can we refuse? A shoot-to-kill policy at point-blank range now protects commerce in the capital. Evacuations, dawn raids, internments—London *is* paranoid. The speaker too inhabits paranoia, by my reading: not a clinical diagnosis but a theatrical response. The tone makes receptive readers paranoid too, on the look-out for the plague of mercenary commercialism in our own towns. We are made conspicuous by our awareness. If we do not subscribe to the culture of false consciousness, we are *other:* we stand out: in the milieu of *Invasion of the Body Snatchers,* people will stare.

There's a lot of it about. The democratic odds are stacked against the individual by the colluding appearance of a mandate. Even the author's socialism is too spiritual for socialists and too individualist for communists. Naturally, in "No Stranger to Sequins," from the domestic disillusion of ruptured family life to the corrupted life of the nation on to the infinite freefalling of paradox and religious uncertainty ("What if he's not there?"), "Doubt is inseparable from paranoia." Performing "London Is Paranoid" on stage, warning a nation caught up in capital values, Poems names the godforsaken variable noun of the last stanza as the home town of the audience — Manchester, Leeds, Liverpool.... In 2005, "Liverpool City of '?'" questions whether the European City of Culture award is beneficial to Liverpool. This time, property developers and big business swoop on the poet's home town, leaving the Liverpudlian alienated as another city is displaced by capital culture. What looks like paranoia is the conspicuous awareness of the cultural take-over of an entire city under the auspices of an award, amid the kickbacks and backslaps of Liverpool City Council.

"Faith" observes the projecting pathology of madness as disownership that leaves society looking kitsch like plastic. Warily we scan the lines left and right (for hidden meaning) as "Friends become Stepford Wives." The poem declares allegiance to the integrity of madness,

> Surely they know madness is a moment
> We all share
> I know they've been there.

I'm using "paranoia," like "schizophrenia," as emblematic of every diagnostic term that sets the misfit apart from society, that is, from normality. "Florid," which describes the generous prose and flowery poesy of camp, has become an unlikely psychiatric term for a full-blown exhibition of blooming psychosis. And what are the well-adjusted conforming to? The question posed in the rhetorical structures of these poems is just this, How does one become well-adjusted to injustice, plasticity, denial? Paranoia is the only rational response of a seditionist, a citizen made outcast by visions and values unrepresented by Parliament, the media or mainstream culture. Camp's penchant for incongruous juxtaposition lends its aesthetic to such a voice, but it was never stretched so far. Camp masquerade acts out those terms to reflect the projecting culture, giving as good as it gets.

While Firbank strolled on the sunny side of life under pink skies, Poems demonstrates transcendental insomnia — "Forever started too short a time ago" in "The Insomnia Suite 3"[47]— "Often awake /I'll dream for dreaming's sake" in "Volcano II"[48]— and in the short story "The Matron's Revolution," the Matron and keeper of the conscience of society "shot bolt upright at the nightmare visions of dim and not too distant pasts."[49] "The Cocktail Hour" and "Something Red in a Tart's Glass" street-walk underworld haunts and recurring themes where lines solicit an outrage or a promiscuous paradox or a provocative question. Even pastoral passages prickle in Poems and seascapes espy fantastic constructs ahoy. In Part One, Ronald Firbank peered over the garden wall of a fairy tale princess to notice the hardship of the people in 1905. Firbank puts (mis)fortune down to the cruel laws of life, nothing to do with politics. Poems works on the other side of that wall, where political prospects are dark and only the realm of gothic myth will do for a metaphor, as horrific as the tales of Hoffmann: with wicked queens and ugly royal sisters ("Because towards the end she looked a lot like Tobermory," "Margaret — A Royal Love Gory"),[50] with Orwellian anthropomorphic capitalist pigs and a bogey-man Prime Minister ... a nightmare envisioned by an insomniac while society shuts its eyes to the forces of darkness.

When melodrama heightens this mindset, it plays with pathology and questions normality as another masquerade, rather as seriousness masquerades as truth.

> Hilarious
> While at the same time tiptoeing precarious
> Through the fragmented, crystalline world of the introspective.
> He is detective" ("The Effeminate"),

sleuthing the psyche like a master of disguise, but brittle like Usher. Quentin Crisp equalized his author's voice with an acutely rational and staid perspective. Chloe Poems throws the reader off balance with paradox and hystrionics. Nursery rhymes cradle conspiracy theories in "Mirrorballin": "poor old Humpty Dumpty /did he fall or was he pushed?" Bent juxtapositions and outcast observations are dramatized by the Muse of hallucinogenics: "I choose an image then I grab it /and there's Richard Gere as Alice /being fist-fucked by a white rabbit."[51]

In our Introduction, Susan Sontag classified camp as the most frivolous of three distinct aesthetics. Poems is trespassing on this demarcation to make melodrama of the aesthetic of distorted seriousness. Deranged, yet prescient: "The Effeminate" "knows his crazy business /His odd agenda." Sontag describes it as Kafkaesque, not camp, contorted by asymmetrical angst, but this irregular poet is accustomed to transgression from an exiled yet activist perspective. Juxtaposing two anachronisms in aesthetics and politics, camp and socialism, sets the radical tone. A strange and florid metamorphosis: ironic detachment, whimsical exaggerations and domestic-fantastic scansions promenade the bizarre disharmony of Sontag's second aesthetic beautifully, like grotesque pantomime, enacting trauma as melodrama, frought with political indignation, iconic and iconoclastic. In Part One, in defense of the frivolous and my skepticism of seriousness-equated–with-truth, I described the angst of meaning-lessness not as lack of meaning but the telling deceit of unsustainable false meaning that leaves us displaced, in a state of ideological yearning. Agitating the text, Poems voices this misfit, asymmetrical angst that is alienated by the well-adjusted media structures of prefabricated meaning. Poems opens a fissure in the surface aesthetic. It was there all along. Those memorable authors who were camp by misadventure — Sacher-Masoch, Corelli, Ros, Wood — happened on the possibilities in their deranged seriousness but didn't recognize the potential, since they didn't recognize camp. Only now does this fanciful fusion express the political, spiritual and psychological displacement of a camp idealist. A hundred years ago, in Beardsley's *Under the Hill,* we find bizarre portents of camp's potential as a deviant (not merely decadent) aesthetic. Beardsley's fantastic world of picturesque grotesquerie layers the text exquisitely with terms like "the extravagant monstrous poetry, the heated melodrama, and splendid agitation of it all!... a world of strange preciousness ... unearthly fops ... troubled with an exquisite fear...."[52]

Poems finds fantastic visions in the realms of radical politics and the unconscious unearthed, charting the underground that Beardsley envisioned, "a passport, as it were, from the upper to the lower world."[53] In "Volcano I," Poems validates the daydream that Firbank found so vital to camp, and befriends alienation. This is the dream state that knows it is dreaming:

> A most important dream.
> It allows me to surf
> A plane of hypocrisy
> And journey flights of infantasy,

which is why, in "No Stranger to Sequins," flagging the necessary naivete of this vision, "A single stride takes me from the beach /Into fairyland," which is why the mantra "I believe," in the Introduction to *Adult Entertainment,* is as fanciful as it is skeptical.

> There's a full moon somewhere with my name on it.

The first line of "Drunks and the Ghosts" makes this enchanting declaration of idealism, narcissistic and naïve, stargazing like Judy Garland on the brink of a song. "Somewhere" is just aimless enough to stay open to the planetary wiles of fate, like a first draft that somehow finds its way home to an unedited resolution. Ambiguity makes the uncertain space where transformation takes place. Like innuendo, ambiguity courts being coy, a camp and fey way of making eye-contact with truth, of winking at signifiers, like a geisha behind her fluttering fan. Ambiguity, the nebulous derangement of approximation that navigates a paradigm by the stars, beguiles the establishment patterns of thinking to generate androgyny, paradox, potential, and moonlight.... "Silver-white glamor of the moon," Marie Corelli called it in one of her idealized moonstruck moments.[54] "Drunks and the Ghosts" carouses in the ether and claims the moon for the dispossessed. The author shows the full moon reflected in a puddle like "a scene from *Hobson's Choice,*" bringing idealism street-level by cobbling a localized reference to this northern, working-class play and film. Yet by the same light, the moon alludes to spellbound hallucinations too, the lunar wonderment that shines on Sacher-Masoch, an emblem of madness. It is the glowing catalyst to fantasy and sexual transgression and gender-role reversal in *Venus in Furs.* Poems venerates the full moon as an agent of transformation — as madness is catalyst to change, as alcohol liberates inhibition. Banality, in these terms, is a constipated lack of transforming potential, the sobriety of seriousness, conformism and industrial regularity. "Drunks and the Ghosts" is a pedestrian meditation on the spiritual camaraderie of drunkenness. Drunks are as socially untouchable as ghosts and socialists, but the poem approximates that intoxication and raises it to a state of grace, a rite of passage to eternity. We accompany the poet on a merry dance, Sufi style, "Twisting with a thousand imponderables /And an almost infinite capacity to rejoice." "Almost infinite" is reaching for the stars like Emerson's ambition or Melies' rocket, just out of reach but within the poet's vision, intangible but not impossible, not unthinkable. "Almost always ... almost infinite" is tempted by camp's cavalier inclination to generalize outrageously, yet the refrain qualifies "always" and sounds paradoxically more emphatic!

"And I almost always find it here /Among the neon and the cobbles," open-mouthed and wide-eyed vowels in "Almost always" are awed by the proximity of the infinite — the greatest exaggeration — and, after several sauntering stanzas, the magnetic compass of lunar mysticism points homeward ... home to one's fate, home to one's original, starbound state of existence:

> And I almost always find my way
> Using these almost seen signposts
> And they almost always seem to point
> To the drunks and the ghosts.[55]

Fantastical irregularities counter the oppressive propaganda and banality of corporate society, including the notion of single, corporate identity. Undermining the ego and the exclusive laws of logic leaves many a Chloe Poems stanza and its reader in metaphysical freefall. This effeminate in a man's-man's world challenges the delusion of singular and separate identity that camp loves to denude through masquerade. In Coward's *Relative Values,* a mother is asked her opinion on her prospective daughter-in-law, an actress: "I've only seen her as a hospital nurse, a gangster's moll, a nun, and Catherine the Great, so it's a little difficult to form any definite opinion."[56] Poems pairs the masquerade down to the doppelganger to explore multiple personality in monologue, a motif that shadows many a fantasy from Hoffmann to Dostoevsky.

"Me" stages a nervous blind date with one's self. It was written in three hours on speed, unrevised in the best traditions of Ed Wood. "Me" exploits the imagery of two World Wars with trench warfare and tunneling escapees and Florence Nightingale — analogous of the poet's lifetime of struggle and close encounters with the Bigger Picture. During my research, in conversation, the author reflected whimsically on the artillery of imagery, crafting an Ed Wood moment, "But then it stops being about a war and starts being about a bus." Like the switch in tone between stanzas in "The Queen Sucks Nazi Cock," the disorienting change of mood and imagery lurches like a bus as one stanza grinds to a halt....

> I am moribund.
> I am catalepsy.
> I am coma.

...and begins again,

> I am waiting for the last bus
> And the last bus is me.
> Ding ding!
> I've got a ticket to ride.

The domestic-fantastic juxtaposition is a local bus ride to rendezvous with the self. In schizoid scansion, from one mask to its opposite in theater's symbology of sorrow and joy, Poems goes beyond the Brechtian "A" Effect and the "Ahh" Effect of the divan perspective to realize the "*Aarrghh*" Effect that distorts perception and assumption even in the mirror image. Deconstruction is destructive, and in Poems' work this is a personal and political aesthetic, even in whimsy. In "Stupid Intellectual," a literary critic imputes the author's transvestite persona as a prop to prop up limp poetry, else why go drag? The poet disagrees, for if modern poetry is the deconstruction and reconstruction of language, "Then surely he must understand you can do the same with the poet."[57] Like a fist on a limp wrist, the author identifies his transvestite effeminate persona, though not shy of asserting his manhood as a matter of sexuality and gender. Vitriolic verse in "Drag Is Dead," performed in drag by the author, condemns drag as frequently misogynistic and altogether unaesthetic. While critics and authors cite the trendy concept of deconstruction, Poems' naïve world view leaves no assumption left standing.

This seeming paranoid schizophrenia knows itself well enough to *play* itself on the page, refracting its own image — as "Mirrorballin" smashes "a million shards and more /each reflecting a piece of me," offering infinite possibilities to narcissism. (Camp excess ensures that the estimate ends, "and more.") In "Me" the mirror image is the transcendental portal to universal consciousness. Going within is going beyond. "The Effeminate" as self-portrait is absorbed by the generic, iconic portrayal of universal effeminacy. When Poems in excess goes beyond, larger than life, he manifests the marginalized processes of psyche and society, bringing subpersonalities and outcasts out of the shadows into the footlights. Our final mirror image in camp literature is a two-way mirror, and it matters not which side we stand on, for looking within is looking beyond. The artist's reflection and performance of the self also enacts the self of those onlookers, the readers, the audience. The two-way mirror takes us into the world of weird camp. The unerring distortions of a fairground mirror reflect on one side while the other side sees through it. Is the universal scale of the reflection a megalomaniacal distortion, or is the real megalomania the notion of singular and separate identity? Whose image is reflected in the paranoid projection? the outsider or society? London or the speaker? Is the traumatized speaker in "The Queen Sucks Nazi Cock" saner in pretty, pastoral stanza one or when rudely disillusioned in the rest of the poem? In "Liverpool City of '?'" the question mark displaces the lucrative award that disenfranchises traditional Liverpool culture — or are these the alarmist and outlandish suspicions of a befuddled Liverpudlian? This question exists in the social aftermath of

1980s' Britain and the media stigmatizing of "the loony left" in the onslaught on socialism. Poems observes the symptoms of obsessive-compulsive disorder in the capitalist system, in the cult of acquisitions, where buying and selling and selling more and buying more is the normal state of mind for more than half the world: Poems is contending that capitalism must germinate obsessive-compulsive consumers to survive.

Insanity itself may be the only rational response to society. "With a broken pencil I draw me," "Volcano II"[58] dramatizes the formative fashioning of the author's ego against the cultural battering of banality, lies and oppression. The tyranny of banality is a matter of uniformity, an imposed mean average leveled by herding, unenlightened assumptions and suppressed creativity. Insanity is the ultimate antidote to banality, yet not escapist in camp, where even madness is grounded in domesticity: "Tidy up /Find space amongst my emotional debris /Mind was overcrowded /With people who couldn't think," even with such distracted syntax and images as here in "No Stranger to Sequins," "Cars without wheels /Dishes corrupted every kitchen sink /And broken crockery industry touched the sky." Domestic, yet quite fantastic.

Ed Wood pioneered psycho-melodrama in camp — incidentally. The political paranoia of the 1960s, on the verge of Nixon, in the middle of the Watts riots and civil rights demonstrations and political assassinations that brought the sci-fi invasions of the '50s down to earth, charges and distorts the narratives of *Death of a Transvestite, Watts ... the Difference* and *Watts ... After.* The radical social milieu conspires with Ed Wood's overactive penmanship and disfigures his expressions. Even Wood's treasured transvestism is incriminated in criminology and pathologized in *Death of a Transvestite* and *Side-Show Siren.* Glen and Paul, protagonist and antagonist of *Death of a Transvestite,* enjoy alter egos as Glenda and Pauline — with an angora fetish — and both are contract killers. Wood's unstable passages of focalization suddenly surge into vilification or paranoia and throw the reader off balance. In casual conversation, Glenda reflects on her respect for the police but raises her contempt for corruption. "Let them rot in hell. The world was better off without them ... the bastards! Let them rot in HELL!" Repetition and capitalized exclamation escalates the crazed tirade that seems to worry the author until, "Glenda vowed to herself that she would write a letter, anonymous of course, divulging their true characters."[59] The letter feminizes those masculine exclamations instantly, lurching from the codes of one gender to the other melodramatically. The passage sounds off-key, like the atonal shift between stanzas of "The Queen Sucks Nazi Cock," though not at all tongue in cheek: Wood is pitching dramatic characterization, not irony. Yet both Poems and Wood demand such mercurial attitudinal shifts that we dissociate from the focalized mindset of the character and focus on author, medium and process.

In "Faith," madness is the conscientious objection to collusion; madness is the truth of intransience and the integrity of transformation; the nervous breakdown that demolishes the lie like the distracted lines and disorienting irony, like the deconstruction and reconstruction of the poet. The text is displaced by the reader's double-take. The sense of displacement, depending on reflective distance and on black and white exclusive possibilities refracted into colorful paradoxes, is a key experience in the Chloe Poems canon. It poses as weird, then justifies itself with domestic and disarming simplicity, like the Introduction to *Adult Entertainment,* before counterposing everyday, accepted phenomena such as war, rabid avarice or schizoid denial, to suggest ironically, in effect, "now how weird is that?" Poems outpaces the rhetoric of Quentin Crisp, yet both artists demonstrate the insights of alienation, free from the gravitational pull of society but still in eavesdropping orbit, engaged yet detached.

The zen and zany energy of Poems, mescalin and feminine, conjures a baroque headspace in camp literature, beyond Wilde yet heir to camp heraldry. Here is Chloe Poems in 2002 in "Are We Myra Hindley?" surveying the corporate assault on truth and compassion even in sponsoring charity, where the author's violence on the word simulates the cultural bludgeoning of the senses:

> Bastardized, advertized, homogenized, dramatized, brutalized, traumatized
> Lies, lies, lies, lies, lies, lies, lies.[60]

And this is Max Beerbohm in 1935 in "London Revisited,"

> London has been cosmopolitanized, democratized, commercialized, mechanized, standardized, vulgarized, so extensively that one's pride in showing it to a foreigner is changed to a wholesome humility. One feels rather as Virgil may have felt in showing Hell to Dante.[61]

"London Is Paranoid" drops the classical niceties and simply descends into hell to report the conditions. The escalating language, evident in Beerbohm's dramatic, polysyllabic listing before irony removes itself, is made yet more extreme as thoroughly modern camp speaks to a society desensitized, desensitized, desensitized. It's time for more than just window dressing.

We have traced camp's catwalking prose across the pages, or at least the margins, of modern literature. Now, if only modern writers can find the superficial talent, this rare art beckons in new directions, the most dynamic development since the aesthete generation of Wilde and Beardsley, I fancy. The melodramatic camp temperament is now reacting to the artifice and reality of society-as-grotesque-theater. Poems' headline conclusion, "Society Is Evil," demands it. Susan Sontag's lucid delineation of the three aesthetics—the classical ideal; disharmony; and frivolous artifice—has been breached. *Weird camp* responds to mainstream extremism in modern society, that is, the mandatory vulgarity of the citizenry of a grotesque system. The miraculous paradox, to me, is that camp remains engaged with the theater of life and death from its folly-tower over the 21st century, and remains, distinctly, Camp.

> I treated art as the supreme reality and life as a mere mode of fiction.
> —Oscar Wilde, "De Profundis." 1896

> All, was it vanity; these pointing stars and spectral leaning towers, this miter, this jeweled ring, these trembling hands, these sweet reflected colors, white of daffodil and golden rose. All, was it vanity?
> —Ronald Firbank, *Concerning the Eccentricities of Cardinal Pirelli.* 1926

> Of course the most obvious explanation for my total lack of success was that I was a bad writer. This idea I did not entertain for a moment.
> —Quentin Crisp, *The Naked Civil Servant.* 1968

> Aim for the stars and if, at the end of your life, you've only reached Mars, remember one thing. Stars flicker in and flash out. Mars is a planet. A constant light. A stable entry that will be here as long as life itself.
> A character even in our own solar system!
> —Edward D. Wood, *Hollywood Rat Race.* Posthumous, circa 1960s

> an enigmatic, sybiline figure lurking backstage, waiting to make a sensational entrance: feathers, sequins, satin slippers, a sexiloquent dance: enthusiastic cheers from the audience, cries of encore, encore, waves of applause, flowers, a diva's deep curtsies:
> —Juan Goytisolo, *Makbara.* 1980

> He knows his crazy business
> His odd agenda
> It's almost a sacred knowledge
> It allows the true effeminate
> To transcend gender.
> —Chloe Poems, "The Effeminate." 2002
> Curtain

Notes

Preface

1. Nicholls, M. *The Importance of Being Oscar.* 1981, London: Robson. p39

2. Brophy, B. *Prancing Novelist: A Defense of Fiction in the Form of a Critical Biography in Praise of Ronald Firbank.* 1973, London: Macmillan. pp12, 73, 104

An Introduction to Camp

1. Meyer, M. Introduction in Meyer, M. (ed.) *The Politics & Poetics of Camp.* 1994, London: Routledge. pp11, 1, 5

2. Booth, M. *Camp.* 1982, London: Quartet. pp18–19

3. Meyer, M. "Under the Sign of Wilde: An Archaeology of Posing," in Meyer M. (ed.) *The Politics & Poetics of Camp* (London: Routledge, 1994), pp80, 78

4. Booth, M. *Camp* (London: Quartet, 1982), p33

5. Lord Berners, G. *First Childhood* (1934) in *First Childhood & Far from the Madding War.* 1983, Oxford University Press. pp54–5

6. Beerbohm, M. "Comedy in French & English" (1902) in *Around Theaters* (1924) 1953, London: Rupert Hart-Davis. p218

7. Benson, E.F. *Lucia's Progress.* (1935) 1967, London: Hodder & Stoughton. p145

8. Benson, E.F. *The Oakleyites.* 1915, London: Hodder & Stoughton. p55

9. King, T.A. "Performing Akimbo: Queer Pride & Epistomological Prejudice," in Meyer M. (ed.) *The Politics & Poetics of Camp* (London: Routledge, 1994), p27

10. Crisp, Q. *Manners from Heaven.* 1984, New York: Harper & Row. p44

11. Le Gallienne, R. *Retrospective Reviews Vol.1 1891–93.* 1896, London: The Bodley Head. pxvii

12. Crisp, Q. *The Naked Civil Servant.* (1968) 1985, London: Flamingo. p49

13. Woolf, V. *A Room of One's Own* in *A Room of One's Own & Three Guineas.* (1929, 1938) 1993, London: Penguin. p93

14. Watson, J.R. *English Poetry of the Romantic Period 1789–1830.* 1985, Essex: Longman. pp268, 270

15. Wilde, O. *The Picture of Dorian Gray* (1890) in *The Works of Oscar Wilde.* 1987, Leicester: Galley Press. p32

16. Praz, M. *The Romantic Agony.* [Trans. Angus Davidson] (1933) 1985, Oxford University Press. pp356, 357

17. Huysmans, J.K. *Against Nature.* (1884) 1971, Harmondsworth: Penguin [1959 Trans. Robert Baldick] p36

18. Barthes, R. *Sade, Fourier, Loyola.* (1971) 1997, London: Johns Hopkins University Press. p162

19. Benson, E.F. *As We Were.* (1930) 1932, London: Longmans. p317

20. Masters, B. *The Life of E.F. Benson.* 1991, London: Chatto & Windus. p99

21. Fletcher, I.K. (from *Ronald Firbank: A Memoir*, 1930) in Horder, M. (ed.) *Ronald Firbank: Memoirs & Critiques.* 1977, London: Duckworth. p26

22. Amory, M. *Lord Berners: The Last Eccentric.* 1998, London: Chatto & Windus. p178

23. Benson, E.F. *Queen Lucia* (1920) in *Lucia Rising* (London: Penguin, 1991), p6

24. Coward, N. Introduction in Munro, H.H. (Saki), *The Complete Works of Saki.* (1976) 1986, Harmondsworth: Penguin. pxiv

25. Coward, N. *Future Indefinite* (written 1947–53) in *Autobiography.* 1986, London: Methuen. p397

26. Huxley, A. "Euphues Revisited" in *On the Margin.* 1923, London: Chatto & Windus. pp136–7

27. Wilde, O. "The Decay of Lying" (1889) in *The Works of Oscar Wilde* (Leicester: Galley Press, 1987), p917

28. Sontag, S. "Notes on Camp" (1964) in *Against Interpretation.* (1967) 1994, London: Vintage. pp286–7

29. Watson, J.R. *English Poetry of the Romantic Period 1789–1830* (Essex: Longman, 1985), p261

30. Grushow, I. *The Imaginary Reminiscences of Sir Max Beerbohm.* 1984, Ohio University Press. p111

31. Crisp, Q. *Manners from Heaven* (New York: Harper & Row, 1984), p50

32. Wilde, O. "The Decay of Lying," in *The Works of Oscar Wilde* (Leicester: Galley Press, 1987), p911

33. Morrill, C. "Revamping the Gay Sensibility: Queer Camp & dyke noir," in Meyer, M. (ed.) *The Politics & Poetics of Camp* (London: Routledge, 1994), p114

34. Maude, C. Preface to *The Watched Pot* (1914) in Munro, H.H. *The Complete Works of Saki* (Harmondsworth: Penguin, 1986), p865

35. Crisp, Q. *How to Go to the Movies.* (1989) 1990, London: Hamish Hamilton. pp201, 146

36. Huysmans, J.K. *Against the Grain.* 1969, New York: Dover [Trans. John Howard] Introduction, Havelock Ellis, pxxxviii

37. Brophy, B. *Prancing Novelist: A Defense of Fiction in the Form of a Critical Biography in Praise of Ronald Firbank.* 1973, London: Macmillan. pp10, 8

38. Wilde, O. "The Decay of Lying," in *Works of Oscar Wilde* (Leicester: Galley Press, 1987), p911

39. "An Interview with Juan Goytisolo by Julia Ortega" (trans. Joseph Schraibam), *Texas Quarterly* Spring 1975: University of Texas Press. pp56–77

40. Goytisolo, J. *The Marx Family Saga.* (1993) 1999, San Francisco: City Lights. [Trans. Peter Bush] p109

41. Kundera, M. "The Depreciated Legacy of Cervantes" (1984) in *The Art of the Novel.* (1986) 1990. London: Faber & Faber p6

42. Wilde, O. *An Ideal Husband* (1895) in *Works of Oscar Wilde* (Leicester: Galley Press, 1987) p509

43. Benson, E.F. *The Babe.* (1893) 1984, London: Garland. p38

44. Coward, N. "Rules of Three" (1928) in *Collected Sketches & Lyrics.* 1931, London: Hutchinson. p182

45. Coward, N. *We Were Dancing* (from *Tonight at 8.30*) (1935) in *Collected Plays: Seven: Quadrille; "Peace in Our Time"; Tonight at 8.30 (III).* 1999, London: Methuen. p281

46. Crisp, Q. *Manners from Heaven* (New York: Harper & Row, 1984), p87

47. Lord Berners, G. *First Childhood* in *First Childhood & Far from the Madding War* (Oxford University Press, 1983), p28

48. Lord Berners, G. *Far from the Madding War* (1941) in *First Childhood & Far from the Madding War* (Oxford University Press, 1983), pp54–5

49. Amory, M. *Lord Berners: The Last Eccentric* (London: Chatto & Windus, 1998), p36

50. Benson, E.F. *Trouble for Lucia.* (1939) 1968, London: Hodder & Stoughton. p13

51. Beerbohm, M. *Zuleika Dobson.* (1911) 1964, London: Heinemann. pp108, 1, 23, 175, 208, 212, 214

52. Babuscio, J. "Camp & the Gay Sensibility" in Dyer, R. (ed.) *Gays & Film.* 1977, London: British Film Institute. pp43, 44

Critics and Clerics

1. Crisp, Q. *How to Become a Virgin.* 1981, London: Duckworth. p26

2. Beerbohm, M. *Observations.* (1925) 1971, New York: Haskell House. p9

3. Beerbohm, M. "Music Halls of My Youth" (1942) in *Mainly on the Air* (1946) 1957, London: Heinemann. p42

4. Beerbohm, M. "Why I Ought Not to Have Become a Dramatic Critic" (1898) & "Comparisons" (1899) in *Around Theaters* (London: Rupert Hart-Davis, 1953), pp1, 2–3, 27

5. Coward, N. *Conversation Piece* (1933) in *Collected Plays: Three: Design for Living; Cavalcade; Conversation Piece; Tonight at 8.30 (I).* 1979, London: Methuen p215

6. Coward, N. *Relative Values* (1949) in *Collected Plays: Five: Relative Values; Look After Lulu!; Waiting in the Wings; Suite in Three Keys.* 1983, London: Methuen. p16

7. Coward, N. *Design for Living* (1932) in *Collected Plays: Three: Design for Living; Cavalcade; Conversation Piece; Tonight at 8.30 (I)* (London: Methuen, 1979), p123

8. Siegfried Sassoon (from *Siegfried's Journey 1916–1920,* 1945) in Horder, M. (ed.) *Ronald Firbank: Memoirs & Critiques.* 1977, London: Duckworth. p151

9. Amory, M. *Lord Berners: The Last Eccentric* (London: Chatto & Windus, 1998), p94

10. Lord Berners, G. *Far from the Madding War* in *First Childhood & Far from the Madding War* (Oxford University Press, 1983), p188

11. Amory, M. *Lord Berners: The Last Eccentric* (London: Chatto & Windus, 1998), p182

12. Masters, B. *The Life of E.F. Benson* (London: Chatto & Windus, 1991) pp189, 190, 276

13. Benson, E.F. *The Babe* (London: Garland, 1984), pp67, 75, 108, 109

14. Benson, E.F. *The Inheritor.* (1930) 1992, Brighton: Millivres Books. p140

15. Praz, M. *The Romantic Agony.* [Trans. Angus Davidson] (1933) 1985, Oxford University Press. pp359, 358

16. Wilde, O. *The Picture of Dorian Gray* in *The Works of Oscar Wilde* (Leicester: Galley Press, 1987), p110

17. Saki, "Reginald at the Theater" in *The Bodley Head Saki.* (1963) 1973, London: The Bodley Head. p65

18. Lord Berners, G. *First Childhood* in *First Childhood & Far from the Madding War* (Oxford University Press, 1983), p110

19. Lambert, J.W., Introduction in *The Bodley Head Saki* (London: The Bodley Head, 1973), pp39

20. Saki, *The Unbearable Bassington* (1912) in *The Bodley Head Saki* (London: The Bodley Head, 1973), p366

21. Crisp, Q. *The Naked Civil Servant* (London: Flamingo, 1985), p119

22. Coward, N. *Present Indicative* (1937) in *Autobiography.* 1986, London: Methuen. p11

23. Isherwood, C. *Goodbye to Berlin* (1935) in *The Berlin of Sally Bowles.* (1975) 1978, London: Hogarth Press. pp290, 354

24. Beerbohm, M. *Zuleika Dobson* (London: Heinemann, 1964), p23

25. Bennett, A. *The Laying On of Hands.* 2001, London: Profile Books. pp19, 18, 20

26. Benson, E.F. *Mapp & Lucia.* (1931) 2004, London: Penguin. p154

27. Bennett, A. *The Laying On of Hands* (London: Profile Books, 2001), p47

28. Bennett, A. *A Question of Attribution* (1988) in *Plays 2: Kafka's Dick; The Insurance Man; The Old Country; An Englishman Abroad; A Question of Attribution.* 1998, London: Faber. p311

29. "Going to the Pictures" (1993) in Bennett, A. *Untold Stories.* 2005, London: Faber/Profile. pp458, 461, 470

30. Benson, E.F. *The Babe.* (London: Garland, 1984) p177

31. Firbank, R. *The Artificial Princess* (1934) in *Five Novels: Valmouth; The Flower Beneath the Foot; Prancing Nigger; Concerning the Eccentricities of Cardinal Pirelli; The Artificial Princess.* 1951, London: Duckworth. p417

32. Poems, C. "Faith Is a Toilet" in *Universal Rentboy.* 2000, Manchester: Bad Press. p70

33. Poems, C. "No Stranger to Sequins" in *How to Be a Better Gay.* 2005, Author's draft copy.

34. Bennett, A. *Forty Years On.* 1969, London: Faber. p63

35. Brophy, B. *In Transit.* (1969) 1989, London: GMP Publishers. p116, 117

36. Poems, C. Introduction in *Adult Entertainment* (Glasshoughton: Route, 2002), pp13, 14

37. Firbank, R. *Concerning the Eccentricities of Cardinal Pirelli* (1926) in *Three Novels: The Flower Beneath the Foot; Sorrow in Sunlight; Concerning the Eccentricities of Cardinal Pirelli.* 2000, London: Penguin. p216

38. Carter, A. "A Self-Made Man" (1984) in *The Curious Room.* 1996, London: Chatto & Windus. p147

39. Wilde, O. "The Remarkable Rocket" (1888) in *The Works of Oscar Wilde* (Leicester: Galley Press, 1987), p317

40. Munro, H.H. (Saki), "Reginald's Choir Treat" in *The Complete Works of Saki* (Harmondsworth: Penguin, 1986), p17

41. Munro, H.H. (Saki), "Clovis on the Alleged Romance of Business" in *The Complete Works of Saki* (Harmondsworth: Penguin, 1986), pp559, 560

42. Munro, H.H. (Saki), *When William Came* (1913) in *The Complete Works of Saki* (Harmondsworth: Penguin, 1986), p692

43. Munro, H.H. (Saki), *The Watched Pot* in *The Complete Works of Saki* (Harmondsworth: Penguin, 1986), pp906, 884

44. Munro, H.H. (Saki), "The Infernal Parliament" in *The Complete Works of Saki* (Harmondsworth: Penguin, 1986), p551

45. Beardsley, A. *Under the Hill* (posthumous, 1904) in *In Black & White: The Literary Remains of Aubrey Beardsley* (Stephen Calloway & David Colvin, eds.) 1998, London: Cypher Press. pp27, 19

46. Brophy, B. *Beardsley & His World.* 1976, London: Thames & Hudson. p6

47. Glassco, J. Introduction in Beardsley, A. *Under the Hill.* (1959) 1966, London: New English Library/Olympia. p11

48. Beardsley, A. *Under the Hill* in *Black & White: The Literary Remains of Aubrey Beardsley* (London: Cypher Press, 1998), pp27, 39, 38

49. Beardsley, A. "The Three Musicians" (1896) in *In Black & White: The Literary Remains of Aubrey Beardsley* (London: Cypher Press, 1998), p144

50. Saki, "Gabriel-Ernst" in *Tobermory & Other Stories.* 1998, London: Phoenix. p13

51. Saki, "The Philanthropist and the Happy Cat" in *Tobermory & Other Stories* (London: Phoenix, 1998), p308

52. Coward, N. *Point Valaine* (1944) in *Collected Plays Volume Six: Point Valaine; South Sea Bubble; Ace of Clubs; Nude with Violin; Waiting in the Wings.* 1962, London: Heinemann. p17

53. Beerbohm, M. *Zuleika Dobson* (London: Heinemann, 1964), p6

54. Isherwood, C. *Goodbye to Berlin* in *The*

Berlin of Sally Bowles (London: Hogarth Press, 1978), pp364, 324

55. Corelli, M. *Ziska.* 1897, Bristol: Arrowsmith. p294

56. Corelli, M. *Ardath.* 1889, London: Richard Bentley. p204

57. Corelli, M. *Barabbas* (London: Methuen, 1912), p131

58. Corelli, M. *The Secret Power.* 1921, Toronto: Ryserson Press. p1

59. Crisp, Q. *The Naked Civil Servant* (London: Flamingo, 1985), p134

60. Coward, N. *Bitter Sweet* (1929) in *Collected Plays Volume One: Cavalcade; Bitter Sweet; The Vortex; Hay Fever; Private Lives; Post-Mortem; Design for Living.* (1934) 1952, London: Heinemann. pp156–7

61. Coward, N. *Blithe Spirit* (1941) in *Collected Plays Volume Five: Pacific 1860; "Peace in Our Time"; Relative Values; Quadrille; Blithe Spirit.* 1958, London: Heinemann. p591

62. Munro, H.H. (Saki), *The Watched Pot* in *The Complete Works of Saki* (Harmondsworth: Penguin, 1986), pp883, 886

63. Munro, H.H. (Saki), "The Bull" in *The Complete Works of Saki* (Harmondsworth: Penguin, 1986), p487

64. Lord Berners (*Ronald Firbank: A Memoir*) in Horder, M. (ed.) *Ronald Firbank: Memoirs & Critiques* (London: Duckworth, 1977), p81

65. Firbank, R. *The Flower Beneath the Foot* (1923) in *Three Novels: The Flower Beneath the Foot; Sorrow in Sunlight; Concerning the Eccentricities of Cardinal Pirelli* (London: Penguin, 2000), p8

66. Amory, M. *Lord Berners: The Last Eccentric* (London: Chatto & Windus, 1998), p181

67. Crisp, Q. *Love Made Easy* (1952) 1977, London: Duckworth. p59

68. Waley, A. "Introduction to Limited Edition of *Collected Works of Ronald Firbank*" (1929) in Horder, M. (ed.) *Ronald Firbank: Memoirs & Critiques* (London: Duckworth, 1977), p166

69. Masters, B. *The Life of E.F. Benson* (London: Chatto & Windus, 1991) p279

70. Richards, G. "Ronald Firbank" (from Richards' book, *Author Hunting,* 1934) in Horder, M. (ed.) *Ronald Firbank: Memoirs & Critiques* (London: Duckworth, 1977), p120

71. Crisp, Q. *How to Become a Virgin* (London: Duckworth, 1981), pp20, 18

72. Coward, N. *The Noël Coward Diaries.* (Graham Payn & Sheridan Morley, Eds.) 1982, London: George Weidenfeld & Nicolson. (17 February 1957) p350 (20 November 1955) p293, (7 January 1961) p462, (28 February 1960) p430

73. Coward, N. Introduction in *Collected Plays Volume One: Cavalcade; Bitter Sweet; The Vortex; Hay Fever; Private Lives; Post-Mortem; Design for Living.* (London: Heinemann, 1952), pvii

74. Vonnegut, K. *Palm Sunday.* 1981, London: Jonathan Cape.p320

75. Munro, H.H. (Saki), "Reginald's First Drama" in *The Complete Works of Saki* (Harmondsworth: Penguin, 1986), p28

76. Coward, N. *Pomp & Circumstance.* 1960, London: Heinemann. p99

77. Currie, M. Introduction in Currie, M. (ed.) *Metafiction.* 1995, London: Longman. p2

78. Lodge, D. "The Novel Now" (1990) in Currie, M. (ed.) *Metafiction* (London: Longman, 1995) p146

79. Waugh, P. "What Is Metafiction & Why Are They Saying Such Awful Things About It?" (1984) in Currie, M. (ed.) *Metafiction* (London: Longman, 1995), pp40, 41

80. Le Gallienne, R. "Some First & Second Principles of Criticism" in *Retrospective Reviews Vol.1 1891–93* (London: The Bodley Head, 1896), pxv

81. Vechten, C. van "Ronald Firbank" (from van Vechten's book, *Excavations,* 1924) in Horder, M. (ed.) *Ronald Firbank: Memoirs & Critiques* (London: Duckworth, 1977), pp162, 163

82. Le Gallienne, R. "Some First & Second Principles of Criticism" in *Retrospective Reviews Vol.1 1891–93* (London: The Bodley Head, 1896), pxvii

83. Corelli, M. *The Life Everlasting.* 1911, London: Methuen. p35

84. Masters, B. *Now Barabbas Was a Rotter: The Extraordinary Life of Marie Corelli.* 1978, London: Hamish Hamilton. p115

85. Ros, Amanda McKittrick, *St. Scandalbags.* 1954, Surrey: The Merle Press. p26

86. Louden, J. *O Rare Amanda!* 1954, London: Chatto & Windus. p61

Shakespeare's Sister

1. Benson, E.F. *Lucia in London.* (1927) 1968, London: Heinemann. p108

2. Firbank, R. *Concerning the Eccentricities of Cardinal Pirelli* in *Three Novels: The Flower Beneath the Foot; Sorrow in Sunlight; Concerning the Eccentricities of Cardinal Pirelli* (London: Penguin, 2000), p227

3. Munro, H.H. (Saki), *The Watched Pot* in *The Complete Works of Saki* (Harmondsworth: Penguin, 1986), p870

4. Lakoff, R. "Extract from *Language & a Woman's Place,*" in Cameron, D. (ed.) *The Feminist Critique of Language.* 1990, London: Routledge. p223

5. Moore, S. *Ronald Firbank: An Annotated Bibliography of Secondary Materials, 1905–1995.* 1996, Illinois: Dalkey Archive Press. *Glasgow Herald* 1916 review of *Odette: A Fairy Tale for Weary People,* p4

6. Huysmans, J.K. *Against Nature* (Harmondsworth: Penguin, 1971), pp96, 31

7. Beardsley, A. *Under the Hill* in *In Black & White: The Literary Remains of Aubrey Beardsley.* (Stephen Calloway & David Colvin, eds.) (London: Cypher Press, 1998), p29

8. Wood, E.D. "It Takes One to Know One" (1967) in Grey, R. *Nightmare of Ecstasy: The Life & Times of Edward D. Wood, Jr.* (1994) 1995, London: Faber & Faber p183

9. Poems, C. "No Stranger to Sequins" in *How to Be a Better Gay.* 2005, Author's draft copy.

10. Poems, C. "London Is Paranoid," in *Universal Rentboy* (Manchester: Bad Press, 2000), p21

11. Beerbohm, M. "London Revisited" (1935) in *Mainly on the Air* (London: Heinemann, 1957), pp4, 5, 6

12. Beerbohm, M. "The Pervasion of Rouge" (1894) in *The Works of Max Beerbohm.* 1922, London: Heinemann. p105

13. Crisp, Q. *Manners from Heaven* (New York: Harper & Row, 1984), pp92, 44, 54

14. Huysmans, J.K. *Against Nature* (Harmondsworth: Penguin, 1971), p125

15. Brophy, B. *Prancing Novelist: A Defense of Fiction in the Form of a Critical Biography in Praise of Ronald Firbank.* (London: Macmillan, 1973), p133

16. Beardsley, A. *Under the Hill* in *In Black & White: The Literary Remains of Aubrey Beardsley* (London: Cypher Press, 1998), pp66, 109, 45, 27, 20, 98

17. Saki, "Excepting Mrs. Pentherby" in *Tobermory & Other Stories* (London: Phoenix, 1998), p174

18. Jones, D. "*Gossip:* Notes on Women's Oral Culture," in Cameron, D. (ed.) *The Feminist Critique of Language* (London: Routledge, 1990), pp246–7

19. Benson, E.F. *Mapp & Lucia* (London: Penguin, 2004), p48

20. Benson, E.F. *Lucia's Progress* (London: Hodder & Stoughton, 1967), p71

21. Benson, E.F. *Trouble for Lucia.* (London: Hodder & Stoughton, 1968), p232

22. Benson, E.F. *Trouble for Lucia* (London: Hodder & Stoughton, 1968), p21

23. Benson, E.F. "The Jamboree" (1924) in *Fine Feathers & Other Stories* (1994) 1995, Oxford University Press. p144

24. Munro, H.H. (Saki), *The Watched Pot* in *The Complete Works of Saki* (Harmondsworth: Penguin, 1986), p876, 907

25. Coward, N. *Blithe Spirit* in *Collected Plays Volume Five: Pacific 1860; "Peace in Our Time"; Relative Values; Quadrille; Blithe Spirit* (London: Heinemann, 1958), p503

26. Coward, N. *Bitter Sweet* in *Collected Plays Volume One: Cavalcade; Bitter Sweet; The Vortex; Hay Fever; Private Lives; Post-Mortem; Design for Living.* (London: Heinemann, 1952), p140

27. Crisp, Q. *The Naked Civil Servant* (London: Flamingo, 1985), p29

28. Crisp, Q. *Resident Alien.* (1996) 1997, London: Flamingo. p141

29. Corelli, M. *Jane.* (1900) 1911, London: Methuen. p84

30. Corelli, M. *Delicia* (1896) in *Delicia & Other Stories.* London: Constable, 1907. pp8–9

31. Corelli, M. *Delicia* in *Delicia & Other Stories* (London: Constable, 1907), pp195–5

32. Corelli, M. *Delicia* in *Delicia & Other Stories* (London: Constable, 1907), p59

33. Corelli, M. *Delicia* in *Delicia & Other Stories* (London: Constable, 1907), pp29, vii

34. Crisp, Q. *The Naked Civil Servant* (London: Flamingo, 1985), p218

35. Poems, C. "The Effeminate" in *Adult Entertainment* (Glasshoughton: Route, 2002), pp20, 17, 19

36. Brophy, B. *The Finishing Touch.* 1963, London: Secker & Warburg. pp11,45,8,7,13–14

37. Brophy, B. *In Transit* (London: GMP Publishers, 1989), pp86, 67

38. Lugosi, R. "there's a plaice for us" in *Coming Out at Night.* 2000, Manchester: purpleprosepress, p28

39. Garland, R. "Coming Out at Night — Performing as Lesbian Vampire Rosie Lugosi" in: *Journal of Lesbian Studies* 1998, Vol. 2, 2/3: The Haworth Press. p205

40. Lakoff, R. "Extract from *Language & a Woman's Place,*" in Cameron, D. (ed.) *The Feminist Critique of Language* (London: Routledge, 1990), p232

41. Lugosi, R. "favorite things" in *Coming Out at Night* (Manchester: purpleprosepress, 2000), p23

42. Beerbohm, M. "Poor Romeo" (1896) in *The Works of Max Beerbohm* (London: Heinemann, 1922), p119

43. Louden, J. *O Rare Amanda!* (London: Chatto & Windus, 1954) p61

44. Masters, B. *Now Barabbas Was a Rotter: The Extraordinary Life of Marie Corelli* (London: Hamish Hamilton, 1978), p101

45. Woolf, V. *A Room of One's Own* in *A Room of One's Own & Three Guineas.* (London: Penguin, 1993), p61

46. Wilde, O. "The Decay of Lying" in *The Works of Oscar Wilde.* 1987, Leicester: Galley Press. p909

47. Saki, *The Unbearable Bassington* in *The Bodley Head Saki* (London: The Bodley Head, 1973), p349

48. Munro, H.H. (Saki), "Louise" in *The Complete Works of Saki* (Harmondsworth: Penguin, 1986), p398

49. Munro, H.H. (Saki), "The Elk" in *The Complete Works of Saki* (Harmondsworth: Penguin, 1986), p360

50. Saki, "Tea" in *Tobermory & Other Stories* (London: Phoenix, 1998), p226

51. Hadlow, G.C. (University of Toronto Quarterly January 1955) in Moore, *S. Ronald Firbank: An Annotated Bibliography of Secondary Materials, 1905–1995* (Illinois: Dalkey Archive Press, 1996), p69

52. Crisp, Q. *Chog.* 1979, London: Duckworth. pp110, 67

53. Poems, C. "Something Red in a Tarts Glass" in *How to Be a Better Gay.* 2005, Author's draft copy.

54. Crisp, Q. *How to Have a Lifestyle.* (1975) 1998, Los Angeles: Alyson Books. pp123, 167

55. Coward, N. *Blithe Spirit* in *Collected Plays Volume Five: Pacific 1860; "Peace in Our Time"; Relative Values; Quadrille; Blithe Spirit* (London: Heinemann, 1958) p549

56. Coward, N. "The English Lido" (1928) in *Collected Sketches & Lyrics* (London: Hutchinson, 1931), pp211, 212

57. Isherwood, C. *Goodbye to Berlin* in *The Berlin of Sally Bowles* (London: Hogarth Press, 1978), pp326, 2, 348

58. Benson, E.F. "Bootles" (1904) in *Fine Feathers & Other Stories* (Oxford University Press, 1995), pp102, 105

59. Benson, E.F. *Mapp & Lucia* (London: Penguin, 2004), pp102, 45

60. Benson, E.F. *Lucia's Progress* (London: Hodder & Stoughton, 1967), pp9–10

61. Ros, Amanda McKittrick, *Helen Huddleston* in Louden, J. *O Rare Amanda!* (London: Chatto & Windus, 1954), p137

62. Benson, E.F. "Mr. Carew's Game of Croquet" in *Fine Feathers & Other Stories* (Oxford University Press, 1995), p193

63. Benson, E.F. *Queen Lucia* (1920) in *Lucia Rising.* 1991, London: Penguin. p25

64. Benson, E.F. *Mapp & Lucia* (London: Penguin, 2004), pp23, 172, 238

65. Benson, E.F. *The Babe.* (London: Garland, 1984) pp208–9

66. Benson, E.F. *Mapp & Lucia* (London: Penguin, 2004), pp180, 145, 105, 249

67. Benson, E.F. *Trouble for Lucia* (London: Hodder & Stoughton, 1968), p180

68. Benson, E.F. *Lucia's Progress* (London: Hodder & Stoughton, 1967), pp287, 291

69. Benson, E.F. *Lucia's Progress* (London: Hodder & Stoughton, 1967), pp284, 220, 308

70. Benson, E.F. *Mapp & Lucia* (London: Penguin, 2004), p72

71. Benson, E.F. "The Exposure of Pamela" (1924) in *Fine Feathers & Other Stories* (Oxford University Press, 1995), p58

72. Benson, E.F. "The Male Impersonator" (1929) in *Fine Feathers & Other Stories* (Oxford University Press, 1995), pp205, 217

73. Benson, E.F. "The Male Impersonator" in *Fine Feathers & Other Stories* (Oxford University Press, 1995), p217

74. Benson, E.F. *Final Edition.* 1941, London: Longmans. p162

75. Benson, E.F. *As We Were* (London: Longmans, 1932), pp170, 177, 178, 180

76. Firbank, R. *Caprice* (1917) in *The Complete Firbank.* (1961) 1973, London: Duckworth. p328

77. Praz, M. *The Romantic Agony.* (Oxford University Press, 1985), p312

78. Munro, H.H. (Saki), "The Elk" in *The Complete Works of Saki* (Harmondsworth: Penguin, 1986), p358

79. Munro, H.H. (Saki), "The Easter Egg" in *The Complete Works of Saki* (Harmondsworth: Penguin, 1986), p154

80. Munro, H.H. (Saki), *The Watched Pot* in *The Complete Works of Saki* (Harmondsworth: Penguin, 1986), pp921, 868–9, 865, 919

81. Beerbohm, M. "Kipling's Entire" (1903) in *Around Theaters* (London: Rupert Hart-Davis, 1953), p246

82. Coward, N. *Hay Fever* (1925) in *Collected Plays Volume One: Cavalcade; Bitter Sweet; The Vortex; Hay Fever; Private Lives; Post-Mortem; Design for Living* (London: Heinemann, 1952), p250

83. Crisp, Q. *How to Become a Virgin.* 1981, London: Duckworth. p19

84. Ross, A.M. *Irene Iddesleigh* in: Ormsby, F. (ed.) *Thine in Storm & Calm* (Belfast: Blackstaff, 1988), p42

85. Benson, E.F. *Trouble for Lucia* (London: Hodder & Stoughton, 1968), p224

86. Corelli, M. *Jane* (London: Methuen, 1911), p119

87. Corelli, M. *Ziska* (Bristol: Arrowsmith, 1897), p231

88. Corelli, M. "Mademoiselle Zephyr" in *Cameos.* (1896) 1919, London: Methuen

89. Corelli, M. *Vendetta!* (London: Methuen, 1919), p288

90. Corelli, M. *God's Good Man.* 1904, London: Methuen. p201

91. Corelli, M. *A Romance of Two Worlds.* (1886) 1976, London: Garland. p162

92. Firbank, R. *The Flower Beneath the Foot* (1923) in *Three Novels: The Flower Beneath the Foot; Sorrow in Sunlight; Concerning the Eccentricities of Cardinal Pirelli* (London: Penguin, 2000), pp8, 52

93. Firbank, R. *The New Rythum* (posthumous) in *The New Rythum.* 1962, London: Duckworth. p79

Saki's Cat

1. Gide, A. "In Memoriam" (1949) in Ellmann, R. (ed.) *20th Century Views: Oscar Wilde, A Collection of Critical Essays.* 1969, New Jersey: Prentice-Hall. p34
2. Wilde, O. "De Profundis" (1896) in *The Works of Oscar Wilde* (Leicester: Galley Press, 1987), p867
3. Benson, E.F. *The Freaks of Mayfair.* 1916, London: T.N. Foulis. pp33, 35, 38, 42, 46, 47
4. Grushow, I. *The Imaginary Reminiscences of Sir Max Beerbohm* (Ohio University Press, 1984), pp13, 18
5. Benson, E.F. *The Oakleyites* (London: Hodder & Stoughton, 1915), pp75, 80
6. Benson, E.F. *Lucia in London* (London: Heinemann, 1969), p162
7. Corelli, M. *Delicia* in *Delicia & Other Stories* (London: Constable, 1907), p4
8. Corelli, M. *Delicia* in *Delicia & Other Stories* (London: Constable, 1907), pp2, 221
9. Corelli, M. *The Sorrows of Satan.* (1895) 1918, London: Methuen. p173
10. Corelli, M. *The Soul of Lilith* (1892) 1958, London: Methuen. pp193, 194
11. Acton, R. Preface in Lord Berners, G. *First Childhood & Far from the Madding War* (Oxford University Press, 1983), pvi
12. Cunard, N. "Thoughts About Ronald Firbank" (1954) Horder, M. (ed.) *Ronald Firbank: Memoirs & Critiques.* 1977, London: Duckworth.
13. Crisp, Q. *The Naked Civil Servant* (London: Flamingo, 1985), p14
14. Lord Berners, G. *First Childhood* in *First Childhood & Far from the Madding War* (Oxford University Press, 1983), pp13, 4
15. Wolff, L. Introduction in Sacher-Masoch, L.von, *Venus in Furs.* (1870) 2000, London: Penguin [Trans. Joachim Neugroschel] pxiv
16. Firbank, R. *Odette: A Fairy Tale for Weary People* (1905) in *The Complete Firbank* (London: Duckworth, 1973), p17
17. Firbank, R. *Odette: A Fairy Tale for Weary People* in *The Complete Firbank* (London: Duckworth, 1973), pp22, 25
18. Wilde, O. "The Fisherman & His Soul" (1891) in *The Works of Oscar Wilde* (Leicester: Galley Press, 1987), p254
19. Huysmans, J.K. *Against Nature* (Harmondsworth: Penguin, 1971), p33
20. Munro, H.H. (Saki), *The Watched Pot* in *The Complete Works of Saki* (Harmondsworth: Penguin, 1986), p670
21. Munro, H.H. (Saki), "For the Duration

of the War" in *The Complete Works of Saki* (Harmondsworth: Penguin, 1986), pp532, 533
22. Wilde, O. *The Importance of Being Earnest* (1895) in *The Works of Oscar Wilde* (Leicester: Galley Press, 1987), p330
23. Crisp, Q. *The Naked Civil Servant.* (London: Flamingo, 1985), p15
24. Crisp, Q. *How to Become a Virgin* (London: Duckworth, 1981), pp58, 154
25. Crisp, Q. *How to Go to the Movies* (London: Hamish Hamilton, 1990), p18
26. Beerbohm, M. *Zuleika Dobson* (London: Heinemann, 1964), p61
27. Benson, E.F. *Dodo Wonders.* 1921, London: Hutchinson. pp88, 90, 99
28. Fletcher, I.K. in Horder, M. (ed.) *Ronald Firbank: Memoirs & Critiques* (London: Duckworth, 1977), pp11, 13
29. Brophy, B. *Prancing Novelist: A Defense of Fiction in the Form of a Critical Biography in Praise of Ronald Firbank* (London: Macmillan, 1973), p307
30. Bennett, A. *The Laying On of Hands* (London: Profile Books, 2001), p43
31. Brophy, B. "Baroque-'n'-Roll" in *Baroque-'n'-Roll & Other Essays.* 1987, London: Hamish Hamilton. pp149, 147, 156
32. Benson, E.F. *Dodo Wonders* (London: Hutchinson, 1921), p117
33. Crisp, Q. *Manners from Heaven* (New York: Harper & Row, 1984), p44
34. Crisp, Q. *Resident Alien* (London: Flamingo, 1997), pp224, 140
35. Coward, N. *Blithe Spirit* in *Collected Plays Volume Five: Pacific 1860*; "Peace in Our Time"; *Relative Values; Quadrille; Blithe Spirit* (London: Heinemann, 1958), pp511, 512, 507, 571, 568, 616, 565
36. Coward, N. "The Tube" (1928) in *Collected Sketches & Lyrics* (London: Hutchinson, 1931), pp251–2, 253
37. Saki, "Tobermory" in *Tobermory & Other Stories* (London: Phoenix, 1998), pp83, 84
38. Munro, H.H. (Saki), "The Reticence of Lady Anne" in *The Complete Works of Saki* (Harmondsworth: Penguin, 1986), pp46, 47
39. Saki. "Reginald on Worries" in *The Bodley Head Saki* (London: The Bodley Head, 1973), p69
40. Saki, "Tobermory" in *Tobermory & Other Stories* (London: Phoenix, 1998), pp83, 84
41. Williams, K. Preface in *The Complete Acid Drops.* (1999) 2000, London: Orion. pxv
42. Isherwood, C. *Goodbye to Berlin* in *The Berlin of Sally Bowles* (London: Hogarth Press, 1978), pp319–20
43. Saki, "Tobermory" in *Tobermory & Other Stories* (London: Phoenix, 1998), p87
44. Crisp, Q. *The Naked Civil Servant* (London: Flamingo, 1985), pp26, 189

45. Huysmans, J.K. *Against Nature* (Harmondsworth: Penguin, 1971), p25

46. Beardsley, A. *Under the Hill* in *In Black & White: The Literary Remains of Aubrey Beardsley*. (Stephen Calloway & David Colvin, eds.) (London: Cypher Press, 1998), pp22, 82

47. Beerbohm, M. *Zuleika Dobson* (London: Heinemann, 1964), pp11, 20

48. Saki, "The Byzantine Omelette" in *The Bodley Head Saki* (London: The Bodley Head, 1973), p269

49. Corelli, M. *Ziska* (Bristol: Arrowsmith, 1897), pp148–9

50. Amory, M. *Lord Berners: The Last Eccentric* (London: Chatto & Windus, 1998), p121

51. Lord Berners, G. *First Childhood* in *First Childhood & Far from the Madding War* (Oxford University Press, 1983), p1

52. Coward, N. *Present Indicative* (1937) in *Autobiography* (London: Methuen, 1986), p74

53. Crisp, Q. *Manners from Heaven* (Harper & Row, 1984), p61

54. Coward, N. Introduction in *Collected Plays Volume One: Cavalcade; Bitter Sweet; The Vortex; Hay Fever; Private Lives; Post-Mortem; Design for Living* (1952, London: Heinemann, 1952), px

55. Coward, N. *Present Indicative* in *Autobiography* (London: Methuen, 1986), p136

56. Firbank, R. *A Study in Temperament* (1905) in *The New Rythum* (London: Duckworth, 1962), p21

57. Wilde, O. *Salomé* (1893) [Trans. Lord Alfred Douglas] in *The Works of Oscar Wilde* (Leicester: Galley Press, 1987), pp545, 556

58. Goytisolo, J. *The Garden of Secrets*. (1997) 2002, London: Serpent's Tail.p135

59. Wood, E.D. *Killer in Drag* (1963, A.K.A. *Black Lace Drag*). 1999, London: Four Walls Eight Windows.p27

60. Corelli, M. *The Young Diana* (London: Hutchinson, 1953), p228

61. Corelli, M. *Delicia* (A.K.A. *The Murder of Delicia*) (1896) in *Delicia & Other Stories* (London: Constable, 1907), p132

62. Poems, C. "Me," in *Adult Entertainment* (Glasshoughton: Route, 2002), p72

63. *Diaries 1997* in Bennett, A. *Untold Stories* (London: Faber/Profile, 2005) p199

64. Willett, J. (ed.) *Brecht on Theater: The Development of an Aesthetic*. (1964)1987, London: Methuen. p139

The "Ahh" Effect

1. Willett, J. (ed.) *Brecht on Theater: The Development of an Aesthetic* (London: Methuen, 1987), p139

2. Saki. "Reginald's Christmas Drama" in *Saki: The Unrest, The Cure, & Other Beastly Tales*. 2000, London: Prion. p9

3. Willett, J. (ed.) *Brecht on Theater: The Development of an Aesthetic* (London: Methuen, 1987), pp70, 34, 44

4. Saki, *The Watched Pot* in *The Complete Works of Saki* (Harmondsworth: Penguin, 1986), pp917, 902, 922–3

5. Saki, "The Unrest Cure," in *The Complete Works of Saki* (Harmondsworth: Penguin, 1986), pp128, 131

6. Corelli, M. *The Mighty Atom*. 1896, London: Hutchinson. p177

7. Coward, N. *Conversation Piece* (1933) in *Collected Plays: Three: Design for Living; Cavalcade; Conversation Piece; Tonight at 8.30 (I)* (London: Methuen, 1979), p271

8. Druten, J.van *I Am a Camera*. 1955, New York: Dramatist's Play Service. p20

9. Beardsley, A. *Under the Hill* in *In Black & White: The Literary Remains of Aubrey Beardsley*. (Stephen Calloway & David Colvin, eds.) (London: Cypher Press, 1998), p100

10. Crisp, Q. *Manners from Heaven* (New York: Harper & Row, 1984), p23

11. Poems, C. "Why Do Roughs Have Such Tight Buns?" in *I'm Kamp*. 2003, Manchester: Bad Press

12. Coward. N *Waiting in the Wings*. 1960, London: Heinemann. pp31, 72

13. Lord Berners, G. *First Childhood* in *First Childhood & Far from the Madding War* (Oxford University Press, 1983), p118

14. Bennett, A. *An Englishman Abroad* (1988) in *Plays 2: Kafka's Dick; The Insurance Man; The Old Country; An Englishman Abroad; A Question of Attribution* (London: Faber, 1998), p277

15. Bennett, A. "Unsaid Prayers" & "No Mean City" in *Telling Tales*. (2000) 2001, London: B.B.C. Worldwide. p87; p94

16. "An Average Rock Bun" in Bennett, A. *Untold Stories* (London: Faber/Profile, 2005), p605

17. "Untold Stories" in Bennett, A. *Untold Stories* (London: Faber/Profile, 2005), p44

18. Bennett, A. *Forty Years On*. 1969, London: Faber. p24

19. "Seeing Stars" in Bennett, A. *Untold Stories* (London: Faber/Profile, 2005) p166

20. "Seeing Stars" in Bennett, A. *Untold Stories* (London: Faber/Profile, 2005) pp169–70

21. Sitwell, O. Introduction in Firbank, R. *Five Novels: Valmouth; The Flower Beneath the Foot; Prancing Nigger; Concerning the Eccentricities of Cardinal Pirelli; The Artificial Princess* (London: Duckworth, 1951), pxviii

22. Firbank, R. *The Artificial Princess* in *Five Novels: Valmouth; The Flower Beneath the Foot; Prancing Nigger; Concerning the Eccentricities*

of Cardinal Pirelli; The Artificial Princess (London: Duckworth, 1951), p437

23. Wilde, O. *The Picture of Dorian Gray* in *The Works of Oscar Wilde* (Leicester: Galley Press, 1987), p58

24. Wilde, O. *An Ideal Husband* in *The Works of Oscar Wilde* (Leicester: Galley Press, 1987), pp473, 480

25. Saki, "The Occasional Garden" in *Tobermory & Other Stories*. 1998, London: Phoenix p194

26. Sontag, S. "Notes on Camp" in *Against Interpretation* (London: Vintage, 1994), p280

27. Goytisolo, J. *Quarantine.* (1991) 1994, London: Quartet. [Trans. Peter Bush] p93

28. "Peter Bush Interviews Juan Goytisolo." *Book Forum* Winter 2002. New York: Art Forum Publishing.

29. Poems, C. "Whore" in *Adult Entertainment* (Glasshoughton: Route, 2002), p51

30. Fletcher, I.K. in Horder, M. (ed.) *Ronald Firbank: Memoirs & Critiques* (London: Duckworth, 1977), p55

31. Lambert, J.W. Introduction in Saki, *The Bodley Head Saki* (London: The Bodley Head, 1973), p40

32. Coward, N. *The Vortex* (1923) in *Collected Plays Volume One: Cavalcade; Bitter Sweet; The Vortex; Hay Fever; Private Lives; Post-Mortem; Design for Living* (London: Heinemann, 1952), pp192, 188

33. Coward, N. *Quadrille* (1952) in *Collected Plays: Seven: Quadrille; "Peace in Our Time"; Tonight at 8.30 (III)* (London: Methuen, 1999), p73

34. Firbank, R. *Caprice* in *The Complete Firbank* (London: Duckworth, 1973), p369

35. Firbank, R. *Inclinations* (1916) in *The Complete Firbank* (London: Duckworth, 1973), p230

36. Isherwood, C. *Goodbye to Berlin* in *The Berlin of Sally Bowles* (London: Hogarth Press, 1978), pp306–7

37. Robertson, P. *Guilty Pleasures: Feminist Camp from Mae West to Madonna.* 1996, Durham: Duke University Press. pp12, 12

38. Laughlin, K. "Brechtian Theory & American Feminist Theater" in Kleber, P. & Visser, C. (eds.) *Re-Interpreting Brecht: His Influence on Contemporary Drama & Film.* (1990) 1992, Cambridge University Press. p150

39. Kaplan, K. "Language & Gender" in Cameron, D. (ed.) *The Feminist Critique of Language.* 1990, London: Routledge p60

40. Coward, N. *Point Valaine* in *Collected Plays Volume Six: Point Valaine; South Sea Bubble; Ace of Clubs; Nude with Violin; Waiting in the Wings* (London: Heinemann, 1962), p10

41. Losey, J. "The Individual Eye," March 1961 in Harowitz, C., Mile, T. & Hale, O. (eds.) *New Theater Voices of the Fifties and Sixties: Selections from Encore Magazine 1956–63.* (1965) 1981, London: Methuen. p204

42. Willett, J. (ed.) *Brecht on Theater: The Development of an Aesthetic* (London: Methuen, 1987), p14

43. Brophy, B. *In Transit* (London: GMP Publishers, 1989), p66

44. Crisp, Q. *Manners from Heaven* (New York: Harper & Row, 1984), p119

45. Benson, E.F. *The Babe.* (London: Garland, 1984) p306

46. Saki, "The Byzantine Omelette" in *The Bodley Head Saki* (London: The Bodley Head, 1973), p265

47. Lord Berners, G. *Percy Wallingford* in *Collected Tales & Fantasies.* 1999, New York: Turtle Point Press/Helen Marx Books. p22

48. Crisp, Q. *How to Have a Lifestyle* (Los Angeles: Alyson Books., 1998), p73

49. Crisp, Q. *The Naked Civil Servant* (London: Flamingo, 1985), p122

50. Wilde, O. "The Decay of Lying" in *The Works of Oscar Wilde* (Leicester: Galley Press, 1987), pp915–16

51. Benson, E.F. *The Babe* (London: Garland, 1984), p93

52. Saki, *The Unbearable Bassington* in *The Bodley Head Saki* (London: The Bodley Head, 1973), p367

53. Saki, *The Watched Pot* in The Complete Works of Saki (Harmondsworth: Penguin, 1986), p928

54. Epps, B. S. *Significant Violence: Oppression & Resistance in the Narratives of Juan Goytisolo 1970–1990.* 1996, Oxford: Clarendon Press. p349

55. Coward, N. "The English Lido," in *Collected Sketches & Lyrics* (London: Hutchinson, 1931), p202

56. Amory, M. *Lord Berners: The Last Eccentric* (London: Chatto & Windus, 1998), p149

57. Crisp, Q. *The Naked Civil Servant* (London: Flamingo, 1985), p186

58. Crisp, Q. *Resident Alien* (London: Flamingo, 1997), pp41

59. Epps, B. S. *Significant Violence: Oppression & Resistance in the Narratives of Juan Goytisolo 1970–1990* (Oxford: Clarendon Press, 1996), p428

60. Crisp, Q. *The Naked Civil Servant* (London: Flamingo, 1985), p206

61. Bennett, A. *Getting On* (London: Faber, 1972), p24

62. *Diaries 2003* in Bennett, A. *Untold Stories* (London: Faber/Profile, 2005) p325

63. Isherwood, C. *Mr. Norris Changes Trains* (1935) in *The Berlin of Sally Bowles* (London: Hogarth Press, 1978), pp83, 91, 94

64. Amory, M. *Lord Berners: The Last Eccentric* (London: Chatto & Windus, 1998), pp27, 94
65. Crisp, Q. *The Naked Civil Servant* (London: Flamingo, 1985), pp107, 118
66. Wood, E.D. "The Sexecutives" (1968) in Hayes, D.C. & Davis, H. *Muddled Mind: The Complete Works of Edward D. Wood, Jr.* (Shreveport: Ramble House, 2001), p76
67. Poems, C. "Whore" in *Adult Entertainment* (Glasshoughton: Route, 2002), p51
68. Coward, N. *Relative Values* in *Collected Plays: Five: Relative Values; Look After Lulu!; Waiting in the Wings; Suite in Three Keys* (London: Methuen, 1983), p113
69. Poems, C. "What Is This Thing Called Gay?" in *How to Be a Better Gay*. 2005, Author's draft copy
70. Ros, Amanda McKittrick, *Irene Iddesleigh* in Louden, J. *O Rare Amanda!* (London: Chatto & Windus, 1954) p48

Camp by Misadventure

1. Sacher-Masoch, L.von, *Venus in Furs* (London: Penguin, 2000) p3
2. Sacher-Masoch, L.von, *Don Juan of Kolomea* (1864) in *Love: The Legacy of Cain.* (1878) 2003, Riverside: Ariadne. [Trans. Michael T. O'Pecko] p42
3. Sacher-Masoch, L.von, *Venus in Furs* (London: Penguin, 2000) p12
4. Sacher-Masoch, L.von, *Venus in Furs* (London: Penguin, 2000), pp, 109, 41
5. Wood, E.D. *Purple Thighs* (1968) in Hayes, D.C. & Davis, H. *Muddled Mind: The Complete Works of Edward D. Wood, Jr.* 2001, Shreveport: Ramble House. p65
6. Sacher-Masoch, L.von, *Venus in Furs* (London: Penguin, 2000), pp6, 66
7. Sacher-Masoch, L.von, *The Man Who Re-Enlisted* (1868) in *Love: The Legacy of Cain* (Riverside: Ariadne, 2003), p70
8. Sacher-Masoch, L.von, *Venus in Furs* (London: Penguin, 2000), p15
9. Sacher-Masoch, L.von, *Moonlight* in *Love: The Legacy of Cain* (Riverside: Ariadne, 2003), pp144, 167, 148
10. Sacher-Masoch, L.von, *Venus in Furs.* (London: Penguin, 2000), pp75, 76
11. Wolff, L. Introduction in Sacher-Masoch, L.von, *Venus in Furs* (London: Penguin, 2000), ppxiv, xiii
12. Corelli, M. *The Sorrows of Satan.* (1895) 1918, London: Methuen. p227
13. Corelli, M. *Ardath* (London: Richard Bentley, 1889) p163
14. Corelli, M. *Temporal Power* (London: Methuen, 1902), p175
15. Corelli, M. *Delicia* in *Delicia & Other Stories* (London: Constable, 1907), p1
16. Corelli, M. *Delicia* in *Delicia & Other Stories* (London: Constable, 1907), p211
17. Corelli, M. *Delicia* in *Delicia & Other Stories* (London: Constable, 1907), pp99–100
18. Corelli, M. *The Young Diana* (1918) 1953, London: Hutchinson. p5
19. Corelli, M. *Ziska* (Bristol: Arrowsmith, 1897), pp256, 13
20. Corelli, M. *Barabbas* (London: Methuen, 1912), pp218, 120
21. Corelli, M. *Barabbas.* (1893) 1912, London: Methuen. pp132
22. Masters, B. *Now Barabbas Was a Rotter: The Extraordinary Life of Marie Corelli* (London: Hamish Hamilton, 1978), p15
23. Corelli, M. *Vendetta!* (1886) 1919, London: Methuen. p362
24. Corelli, M. *Ziska* (Bristol: Arrowsmith, 1897), p358
25. Benson, E.F. *Queen Lucia* in *Lucia Rising* (London: Penguin, 1991), p7
26. Corelli, M. *Temporal Power.* 1902, London: Methuen. p177
27. Benson, E.F. *Mapp & Lucia* (London: Penguin, 2004), p178
28. Benson, E.F. *Queen Lucia* in *Lucia Rising* (London: Penguin, 1991), p6
29. Corelli, M. *The Sorrows of Satan* (London: Methuen, 1918), p484
30. Corelli, M. *Temporal Power* (London: Methuen, 1902), pp98, 135
31. Corelli, M. *Delicia* in *Delicia & Other Stories* (London: Constable, 1907), p6
32. Corelli, M. *Delicia* in *Delicia & Other Stories* (London: Constable, 1907), p224
33. Corelli, M. *Barabbas* (London: Methuen, 1912), p131
34. Corelli, M. *Delicia* in *Delicia & Other Stories* (London: Constable, 1907), pp92, 40
35. Corelli, M. *Ziska* (Bristol: Arrowsmith, 1897), pp236, 239
36. Corelli, M. "The Song of Miriam" in *Cameos* (London, 1919), p222, 224
37. Corelli, M. *The Sorrows of Satan* (London: Methuen, 1918), p173
38. Corelli, M. *Delicia* in *Delicia & Other Stories* (London: Constable, 1907), pix
39. Corelli, M. *Delicia* in *Delicia & Other Stories* (London: Constable, 1907), p188
40. Corelli, M. (ed.) *The Avon Star: A Literary Manual for the Stratford-on-Avon Season of 1903.* 1903, Stratford: J. Stanley. pp1, 4
41. Corelli, M. *Temporal Power* (London: Methuen, 1902), pp172, 370
42. Corelli, M. (ed.) *The Avon Star: A Literary Manual for the Stratford-on-Avon Season of 1903.* 1903, Stratford: J. Stanley. pp126, 124, 125
43. Masters, B. *Now Barabbas Was a Rotter: The Extraordinary Life of Marie Corelli* (London: Hamish Hamilton, 1978), p216

44. Ros, A.M. *Helen Huddleston* in Ormsby, F. (ed.) *Thine in Storm & Calm*. 1988, Belfast: Blackstaff. p98

45. Huxley, A. "Euphues Revisited" in *On the Margin* (London: Chatto & Windus, 1923), p137

46. Ros, A.M. *Helen Huddleston* in Ormsby, F. (ed.) *Thine in Storm & Calm* (Belfast: Blackstaff, 1988), pp98–9

47. Ros, A.M. *Delina Delaney* (1898) 1935, London: Chatto & Windus. pp8, 13

48. Ros, A.M. *Irene Iddesleigh* in Ormsby, F. (ed.) *Thine in Storm & Calm* (Belfast Blackstaff, 1988), p48

49. Ros, A.M. *Helen Huddleston* in Louden, J. *O Rare Amanda!* (London: Chatto & Windus, 1954), p47

50. Louden, J. *O Rare Amanda!* (London: Chatto & Windus, 1954), p3

51. Louden, J. *O Rare Amanda!* (London: Chatto & Windus, 1954) p14

52. Ros, A.M. *Delina Delaney* (London: Chatto & Windus, 1935), p263

53. Ros, A.M. *Helen Huddleston* in Ormsby, F. (ed.) *Thine in Storm & Calm* (Belfast: Blackstaff, 1988), pp101–2

54. Ros, A.M. *Irene Iddesleigh* in Ormsby, F. (ed.) *Thine in Storm & Calm* (Belfast Blackstaff, 1988), p48

55. Louden, J. *O Rare Amanda!* (London: Chatto & Windus, 1954), p49

56. Ros, A.M. "On Visiting Westminster Abbey" (1933) in Ormsby, F. (ed.) *Thine in Storm & Calm* (Belfast: Blackstaff, 1988), p28

57. Louden, J. *O Rare Amanda!* (London: Chatto & Windus, 1954), p94

58. Ros, A.M. *Irene Iddesleigh* in Ormsby, F. (ed.) *Thine in Storm & Calm* (Belfast: Blackstaff, 1988), pp42–3

59. Ros, A.M. *Irene Iddesleigh* in Ormsby, F. (ed.) *Thine in Storm & Calm* (Belfast: Blackstaff, 1988), p44, 45

60. Ros, A.M. *Delina Delaney* (London: Chatto & Windus, 1935), ppxviii, xiv-xv

61. Ros, A.M. *Delina Delaney* (London: Chatto & Windus, 1935), ppxviii, xvii

62. Ros, A.M. *Delina Delaney* (London: Chatto & Windus, 1935), ppxii, v

63. Ros, A.M. *Delina Delaney* (London: Chatto & Windus, 1935), ppix, x

64. Ros, A.M. *Saint Scandalbags*. (1927) 1954, Surrey: The Merle Press. pp7–8

65. Ros, A.M. *Saint Scandalbags* (Surrey: The Merle Press, 1954), pp28, 34, 31

66. Ros, A.M. *Saint Scandalbags* (Surrey: The Merle Press, 1954), p20

67. Ros, A.M. *Delina Delaney* (London: Chatto & Windus, 1935), p1

68. Ros, A.M. *Delina Delaney* (London: Chatto & Windus, 1935), pp40, 42

69. Ros, A.M. *Helen Huddleston* in Ormsby, F. (ed.) *Thine in Storm & Calm* (Belfast: Blackstaff, 1988), p55

70. Ros, A.M. *Donald Dudley*. 1954, Surrey: The Merle Press. p61

71. Ros, A.M. *Donald Dudley* (Surrey: The Merle Press, 1954), p32

72. Ros, A.M. *Donald Dudley* (Surrey: The Merle Press, 1954), pp29–30

73. Ros, A.M. *Donald Dudley*. 1954, Surrey: The Merle Press. p54

Oscar Wilde

1. Beerbohm, M. "The Pervasion of Rouge" in *The Works of Max Beerbohm* (London: Heinemann, 1922), p88

2. Ellmann, R. *Oscar Wilde*. (1987) 1988, London: Penguin. p347

3. Woodcock, G. "The Social Rebel" (1950) pp155,159 in Ellmann, R. (ed.) *20th Century Views: Oscar Wilde, a Collection of Critical Essays*. 1969, New Jersey: Prentice-Hall.

4. Beerbohm, M. *1880* (1894) in *The Works of Max Beerbohm* (London: Heinemann, 1922), pp39–40

5. Coward, N. *The Noël Coward Diaries* (London: George Weidenfeld & Nicolson, 1982), (11 November 1949) p135

6. Coward, N. *Bitter Sweet* in *Collected Plays Volume One: Cavalcade; Bitter Sweet; The Vortex; Hay Fever; Private Lives; Post-Mortem; Design for Living* (London: Heinemann, 1952), p149

7. Benson, E.F. *As We Were* (London: Longmans, 1932) p234

8. Wilde, O. "De Profundis" in *The Works of Oscar Wilde*. 1987, Leicester: Galley Press. pp858, 853, 881

9. Williams, K. *The Complete Acid Drops* (London: Orion, 2000), p101

10. Wilde, O. *The Picture of Dorian Gray* in *The Works of Oscar Wilde* (Leicester: Galley Press, 1987), p41

11. Wilde, O. "The Decay of Lying" in *The Works of Oscar Wilde* (Leicester: Galley Press, 1987), p914

12. Hart-Davis, R. *The Letters of Oscar Wilde*. 1962, New York: Harcourt, Brace & World. Letter to Ralph Payne, p352

13. Crisp, Q. *How to Have a Lifestyle* (Los Angeles: Alyson Books, 1998), pp91, 74

14. Wilde, O. *The Picture of Dorian Gray* in *The Works of Oscar Wilde* (Leicester: Galley Press, 1987), p36

15. Wilde, O. *An Ideal Husband* (1895) in *The Works of Oscar Wilde* (Leicester: Galley Press, 1987), p510

16. Crisp, Q. *The Naked Civil Servant* (London: Flamingo, 1985), p90

17. Ellmann, R. *Oscar Wilde.* (London: Penguin, 1988), p296
18. Crisp, Q. *How to Have a Lifestyle* (Los Angeles: Alyson Books, 1998), p90
19. Wilde, O. *Lady Windermere's Fan* (1892) in *The Works of Oscar Wilde* (Leicester: Galley Press, 1987), p410
20. Wilde, O. "De Profundis" in *The Works of Oscar Wilde* (Leicester: Galley Press, 1987), p887
21. Bentley, E. *"The Importance of Being Earnest"* (from *The Playwright as Thinker,* 1946) in Ellmann, R. (ed.) *20th Century Views: Oscar Wilde, a Collection of Critical Essays* (New Jersey: Prentice-Hall, 1969), p115
22. Amory, M. *Lord Berners: The Last Eccentric* (London: Chatto & Windus, 1998), p95
23. Wilde, O. *The Picture of Dorian Gray* in *The Works of Oscar Wilde* (Leicester: Galley Press, 1987), p112
24. Bennett, A. *An Englishman Abroad* in *Plays 2: Kafka's Dick; The Insurance Man; The Old Country; An Englishman Abroad; A Question of Attribution* (London: Faber, 1998), p291
25. St John Hankin, "Wilde as a Dramatist" (from *The Dramatic Works of St John Hankin, vol III,* 1912) in Ellmann, R. (ed.) *20th Century Views: Oscar Wilde, A Collection of Critical Essays* (New Jersey: Prentice-Hall., 1969), p69
26. Hollinghurst, A. Introduction in Firbank, R. *Three Novels* (London: Penguin, 2000), pxi
27. Coward, N. *Quadrille* in *Collected Plays: Seven: Quadrille; "Peace in Our Time"; Tonight at 8.30 (III).* p73
28. Wilde, O. *An Ideal Husband* in *The Works of Oscar Wilde* (Leicester: Galley Press, 1987), p472
29. Wilde, O. *An Ideal Husband* in *The Works of Oscar Wilde* (Leicester: Galley Press, 1987), pp469, 470, 468
30. Wilde, O. *The Picture of Dorian Gray* in *The Works of Oscar Wilde* (Leicester: Galley Press, 1987), p20
31. Wilde, O. "The Fisherman & His Soul" in *The Works of Oscar Wilde* (Leicester: Galley Press, 1987), p260
32. Wilde, O. *The Picture of Dorian Gray* in *The Works of Oscar Wilde* (Leicester: Galley Press, 1987), p44
33. Wilde, O. *The Picture of Dorian Gray* in *The Works of Oscar Wilde* (Leicester: Galley Press, 1987), p19
34. Firbank, R. *Concerning the Eccentricities of Cardinal Pirellii* in *Three Novels.* (London: Penguin, 2000), p202
35. Munro, H.H. (Saki) "Reginald" in *The Complete Works of Saki* (Harmondsworth: Penguin, 1986), p8
36. Crisp, Q. *Love Made Easy* (1952) 1977, London: Duckworth. p46

37. Crisp, Q. *Manners from Heaven* (New York: Harper & Row, 1984), p62
38. Corelli, M. *Delicia* (A.K.A. *The Murder of Delicia*) (1896) in *Delicia & Other Stories* (London: Constable, 1907), p100
39. Apter, E. "Sexological Decadence: The Gynophobic Visions of Octave Mirbeau," in Hustvedt, A. (ed.) *The Decadent Reader: Fiction, Fantasy, & Perversion from Fin-de-Siecle France.* 1998, New York: Zone. p964
40. Bentley, E. *"The Importance of Being Earnest"* (from *The Playwright as Thinker,* 1946) in Ellmann, R. (ed.) *20th Century Views: Oscar Wilde, a Collection of Critical Essays* (New Jersey: Prentice-Hall, 1969), p115
41. Wilde, O. "The Decay of Lying" in *The Works of Oscar Wilde* (Leicester: Galley Press, 1987), p911
42. Crisp, Q. *How to Go to the Movies* (London: Hamish Hamilton, 1990), p117
43. Crisp, Q. *Love Made Easy* (London: Duckworth, 1977), p57
44. Huysmans, J.K. *Against Nature* (Harmondsworth: Penguin, 1971), pp78, 79
45. Corelli, M. *Ziska* (Bristol: Arrowsmith, 1897), p306
46. Wilde, O. *The Picture of Dorian Gray* in *The Works of Oscar Wilde* (Leicester: Galley Press, 1987), pp21, 116
47. Wilde, O. *An Ideal Husband* in *The Works of Oscar Wilde* (Leicester: Galley Press, 1987), p502
48. Firbank, R. *The New Rythum* in *The New Rythum* (London: Duckworth, 1962), p78
49. Munro, H.H. (Saki) "Reginald's First Drama" in *The Complete Works of Saki* (Harmondsworth: Penguin, 1986), p28
50. Munro, H.H. (Saki) *The Westminster Alice* in *The Complete Works of Saki* (Harmondsworth: Penguin, 1986), p819
51. Corelli, M. *Ziska* (Bristol: Arrowsmith, 1897), pp299–300
52. Corelli, M. *The Sorrows of Satan* (London: Methuen, 1918), pp88, 132
53. Munro, H.H. (Saki) *The Watched Pot* in *The Complete Works of Saki* (Harmondsworth: Penguin, 1986), p887
54. Munro, H.H. (Saki) *The Watched Pot* in *The Complete Works of Saki* (Harmondsworth: Penguin, 1986), p935
55. Wilde, O. *The Picture of Dorian Gray* in *The Works of Oscar Wilde* (Leicester: Galley Press, 1987), p114
56. Brophy, B. *Baroque-'n'-Roll & Other Essays* (London: Hamish Hamilton, 1987), "Baroque-'n'-Roll," p161
57. Firbank, R. *Santal* in *The Complete Firbank* (London: Duckworth, 1973), p498
58. *Diaries 1996* in Bennett, A. *Untold Stories* (London: Faber/Profile, 2005), p180

59. Wilde, O. "Lord Arthur Savile's Crime" (1887) in *The Works of Oscar Wilde* (Leicester: Galley Press, 1987), p176

60. Wilde, O. *The Picture of Dorian Gray* in *The Works of Oscar Wilde* (Leicester: Galley Press, 1987), p85

61. Wilde, O. *The Picture of Dorian Gray* in *The Works of Oscar Wilde* (Leicester: Galley Press, 1987), p103

62. Wilde, O. *The Picture of Dorian Gray* in *The Works of Oscar Wilde* (Leicester: Galley Press, 1987), p79

63. Wilde, O. *The Picture of Dorian Gray* in *The Works of Oscar Wilde* (Leicester: Galley Press, 1987), p46

64. Huysmans, J.K. *Against Nature* (Harmondsworth: Penguin, 1971), p30

65. Roditi, E. "Fiction as Allegory: *The Picture of Dorian Gray*" (from *Oscar Wilde*, 1947) in Ellmann, R. (ed.) *20th Century Views: Oscar Wilde, A Collection of Critical Essays* (New Jersey: Prentice-Hall, 1969), p50

66. Wilde, O. *The Picture of Dorian Gray* in *The Works of Oscar Wilde* (Leicester: Galley Press, 1987), p48

67. Wilde, O. *The Picture of Dorian Gray* in *The Works of Oscar Wilde* (Leicester: Galley Press, 1987), pp63, 65

68. Wilde, O. *An Ideal Husband* in *The Works of Oscar Wilde* (Leicester: Galley Press, 1987), pp479, 522

69. St John Hankin, "Wilde as a Dramatist" in Ellmann, R. (ed.) *20th Century Views: Oscar Wilde, A Collection of Critical Essays* (New Jersey: Prentice-Hall, 1969), pp62, 66

70. Wilde, O. *Salome* in *The Works of Oscar Wilde* (Leicester: Galley Press, 1987), p539

71. Corelli, M. *Ziska* (Bristol: Arrowsmith, 1897), p134

72. Wilde, O. *An Ideal Husband* in *The Works of Oscar Wilde* (Leicester: Galley Press, 1987), pp481, 480

73. Wilde, O. *An Ideal Husband* in *The Works of Oscar Wilde* (Leicester: Galley Press, 1987), pp505–6

74. Wilde, O. *The Picture of Dorian Gray* in *The Works of Oscar Wilde* (Leicester: Galley Press, 1987), p21

75. Wilde, O. *The Picture of Dorian Gray* in *The Works of Oscar Wilde* (Leicester: Galley Press, 1987), p121

76. Wilde, O. *The Picture of Dorian Gray* in *The Works of Oscar Wilde* (Leicester: Galley Press, 1987), pp141, 144, 91

77. Wilde, O. *The Picture of Dorian Gray* in *The Works of Oscar Wilde* (Leicester: Galley Press, 1987), p84

78. Sontag, S. "Notes on Camp" in *Against Interpretation* (London: Vintage, 1994), p287

79. Wilde, O. *The Picture of Dorian Gray* in *The Works of Oscar Wilde* (Leicester: Galley Press, 1987), p81

80. Wilde, O. "The Decay of Lying" in *The Works of Oscar Wilde* (Leicester: Galley Press, 1987), p917

81. Coward, N. *Quadrille* in *Collected Plays: Seven: Quadrille; "Peace in Our Time"; Tonight at 8.30 (III)*. p9

82. Coward, N. *Point Valaine* in *Collected Plays Volume Six: Point Valaine; South Sea Bubble; Ace of Clubs; Nude with Violin; Waiting in the Wings* (London: Heinemann, 1962), p101

83. Brophy, B. *Prancing Novelist: A Defense of Fiction in the Form of a Critical Biography in Praise of Ronald Firbank* (London: Macmillan, 1973), p120

84. Fletcher, I.K. (from *Ronald Firbank: A Memoir*) in Horder, M. (ed.) *Ronald Firbank: Memoirs & Critiques* (London: Duckworth, 1977), p12

85. Amory, M. *Lord Berners: The Last Eccentric* (London: Chatto & Windus, 1998), p75

86. Lambert, J.W. Introduction in Saki, *The Bodley Head Saki* (London: The Bodley Head, 1973), p37

87. Crisp, Q. *The Naked Civil Servant* (London: Flamingo, 1985), pp35, 51

88. Beerbohm, M. *Zuleika Dobson* (London: Heinemann, 1964), p137, 20

89. Roditi, E. "Fiction as Allegory: *The Picture of Dorian Gray*" in Ellmann, R. (ed.) *20th Century Views: Oscar Wilde, A Collection of Critical Essays* (New Jersey: Prentice-Hall, 1969), p55

90. Wilde, O. *The Picture of Dorian Gray* in *The Works of Oscar Wilde* (Leicester: Galley Press, 1987), p43

91. Wilde, O. "Lord Arthur Savile's Crime" in *The Works of Oscar Wilde* (Leicester: Galley Press, 1987), p177

92. Wilde, O. "The Model Millionaire: A Note of Admiration" (1891) in *The Works of Oscar Wilde* (Leicester: Galley Press, 1987), pp220, 219

93. Wilde, O. "Lord Arthur Savile's Crime" in *The Works of Oscar Wilde* (Leicester: Galley Press, 1987), p168

94. Wilde, O. *The Picture of Dorian Gray* in *The Works of Oscar Wilde* (Leicester: Galley Press, 1987), p45

95. Self, W. *Dorian*. 2002, London: Penguin. p228

96. Self, W. *Dorian*. (London: Penguin, 2002), p7

97. Self, W. *Dorian*. (London: Penguin, 2002), p20

98. Firbank, R. *The Flower Beneath the Foot* in *Three Novels* (London: Penguin, 2000), p50

99. Nicholson, H. "Lambert Orme" (from *Some People*, 1930) in Horder, M. (ed.) *Ronald*

Firbank: Memoirs & Critiques (London: Duckworth, 1977), p94

100. Beerbohm, M. *Zuleika Dobson* (London: Heinemann, 1964), p157

101. Munro, H.H. (Saki) *When William Came* in *The Complete Works of Saki* (Harmondsworth: Penguin, 1986), pp806–7

102. Munro, H.H. (Saki) *The Watched Pot* in *The Complete Works of Saki* (Harmondsworth: Penguin, 1986), p879

103. Isherwood, C. *Mr. Norris Changes Trains* in *The Berlin of Sally Bowles* (London: Hogarth Press, 1978), p85

104. Druten, J. van. *I Am a Camera* (New York: Dramatist's Play Service, 1955), p16

105. Egerton, G. "A Cross Line" (1893) in Showalter, E. (ed.) *Daughters of Decadence.* 1993, London: Virago. p54

106. Wood, E.D. *Death of a Transvestite* (New York: Four Walls Eight Windows, 1999), pp8, 167

107. Wood, E.D. *Hell Chicks* (Shreveport: Woodpile, 2001), p64

108. Wilde, O. *The Picture of Dorian Gray* in *The Works of Oscar Wilde* (Leicester: Galley Press, 1987), pp18, 70, 139

109. Wilde, O. *The Importance of Being Earnesti* (1895) in *The Works of Oscar Wilde* (Leicester: Galley Press, 1987), p325

110. Self, W. *Dorian* (London: Penguin, 2002), pp7, 128, 179, 40

Ronald Firbank

1. Fletcher, I.K. (from *Ronald Firbank: A Memoir*) in Horder, M. (ed.) *Ronald Firbank: Memoirs & Critiques* (London: Duckworth, 1977), pp24, 32

2. Firbank, R. "A Study In Temperament" in *The New Rythum* (London: Duckworth, 1962), p22

3. Firbank, R. *The Flower Beneath the Foot* in *Three Novels* (London: Penguin, 2000), p45

4. Beerbohm, M. *Zuleika Dobson* (London: Heinemann, 1964), p72

5. Firbank, R. *The Flower Beneath the Foot* in *Three Novels* (London: Penguin, 2000), pp7, 9, 11, 14, 92, 59

6. Brophy, B. *Prancing Novelist: A Defense of Fiction in the Form of a Critical Biography in Praise of Ronald Firbank* (London: Macmillan, 1973), pp80, 82

7. Firbank, R. "Lady Appledore's Mésalliance" (juvenilia) in *The New Rythum* (London: Duckworth, 1962), pp50, 64

8. Firbank, R. *Caprice* in *The Complete Firbank* (London: Duckworth, 1973), pp346, 347

9. Fletcher, I.K. (from *Ronald Firbank: A Memoir*) in Horder, M. (ed.) *Ronald Firbank:*

Memoirs & Critiques (London: Duckworth, 1977), pp14, 25

10. Crisp, Q. *How to Have a Lifestyle* (Los Angeles: Alyson Books, 1998), p46

11. Gross, J. (1969) in Moore, S. (ed.) *Ronald Firbank: An Annotated Bibliography of Secondary Materials, 1905–1995* (Illinois: Dalkey Archive Press, 1996), p69

12. Hollinghurst, A. Introduction in Firbank, R. *Three Novels.* (London: Penguin, 2000), p.ix

13. Powell, A. Introduction in Firbank, R. *The Complete Firbank* (London: Duckworth, 1973), p10

14. Firbank, R. *The Mauve Tower: A Dream Play in VII Scenes* (1904) in *Complete Plays.* 1994, Illinois: Dalkey Archive Press. p8

15. Holland, V. (from *Ronald Firbank: A Memoir*) in Horder, M. (ed.) *Ronald Firbank: Memoirs & Critiques* (London: Duckworth, 1977), p56

16. Brophy, B. *Prancing Novelist: A Defense of Fiction in the Form of a Critical Biography in Praise of Ronald Firbank* (London: Macmillan, 1973), pp13, 28, 68, 69

17. Firbank, R. *The Flower Beneath the Foot* in *Three Novels* (London: Penguin, 2000), pp61, 116

18. Firbank, R. *The Artificial Princess* (1934) in *Five Novels: Valmouth; The Flower Beneath the Foot; Prancing Nigger; Concerning the Eccentricities of Cardinal Pirelli; The Artificial Princess* (London: Duckworth, 1951), p416

19. Firbank, R. *The New Rythum* in *The New Rythum* (London: Duckworth, 1962), p82

20. Firbank, R. *The Mauve Tower: A Dream Play in VII Scenes* in *Complete Plays* (Illinois: Dalkey Archive Press, 1994), pp13, 14

21. Coward, N. *Pomp & Circumstance* (London: Heinemann, 1960), p78

22. Powell, A. Introduction in *The Complete Firbank* (London: Duckworth, 1973), p15

23. Lord Berners (*Ronald Firbank: A Memoir*) in Horder, M. (ed.) *Ronald Firbank: Memoirs & Critiques* (London: Duckworth, 1977), p83

24. Wilde, O. *The Picture of Dorian Gray* in *The Works of Oscar Wilde* (Leicester: Galley Press, 1987), p33

25. Firbank, R. *The Flower Beneath the Foot* in *Three Novels* (London: Penguin, 2000), p48

26. Firbank, R. *Odette: A Fairy Tale for Weary People* in *The Complete Firbank* (London: Duckworth, 1973), p20

27. Firbank, R. *Inclinations* in *The Complete Firbank* (London: Duckworth, 1973), p311

28. Hollinghurst, A. Introduction in Firbank, R. *The Flower Beneath the Foot* in *Three Novels* (London: Penguin, 2000), pxviii

29. Firbank, R. *Santal* (1921) in *The Complete Firbank* (London: Duckworth, 1973), p483

30. Firbank, R. 1924 Preface to 1st American Edition in *The New Rythum* (London: Duckworth, 1962), p4

31. Firbank, R. *The New Rythum* in *The New Rythum* (London: Duckworth, 1962), p71

32. Firbank, R. *The Mauve Tower: A Dream Play in VII Scenes* (1904) in *Complete Plays* (Illinois: Dalkey Archive Press, 1994), p9

33. Sitwell, O. (from *Ronald Firbank: A Memoir*) in Horder, M. (ed.) *Ronald Firbank: Memoirs & Critiques* (London: Duckworth, 1977), p68

34. Firbank, R. "Lady Appledore's Mésalliance" in *The New Rythum* (London: Duckworth, 1962), p49

35. Firbank, R. *Odette: A Fairy Tale for Weary People* in *The Complete Firbank* (London: Duckworth, 1973), p20

36. Benson, E.F. *Lucia in London* (London: Heinemann, 1969), p225

37. Firbank, R. *Santal* in *The Complete Firbank* (London: Duckworth, 1973), p497

38. Firbank, R. *The Flower Beneath the Foot* in *Three Novels* (London: Penguin, 2000), p9

39. Firbank, R. *Concerning the Eccentricities of Cardinal Pirelli* in *Three Novels* (London: Penguin, 2000), p192

40. Brophy, B. *Prancing Novelist: A Defense of Fiction in the Form of a Critical Biography in Praise of Ronald Firbank* (London: Macmillan, 1973), pp396, 397, 232

41. Firbank, R. *The Flower Beneath the Foot* in *Three Novels* (London: Penguin, 2000), p39

42. Crisp, Q. *How to Become a Virgin* (London: Duckworth, 1981), p180

43. Hollinghurst, A. Introduction in Firbank, R. *Three Novels* (London: Penguin, 2000), pxxiii

44. Freud, S. *The Complete Introductory Lectures on Psychoanalysis.* (1921) 1971, London: George Allen & Unwin. p541

45. Jung, C.G. *Symbols of Transformation: The Collected Works of C.G. Jung Vol 5.* 1995, London: Routledge. p437

46. Firbank, R. *The Flower Beneath the Foot* in *Three Novels* (London: Penguin, 2000), p37

47. Brophy, B. *Prancing Novelist: A Defense of Fiction in the Form of a Critical Biography in Praise of Ronald Firbank* (London: Macmillan, 1973), p378

48. Ros, Amanda McKittrick, *Helen Huddleston* in Louden, J. *O Rare Amanda!* (London: Chatto & Windus, 1954) p131

49. Firbank, R. *The Flower Beneath the Foot* in *Three Novels* (London: Penguin, 2000), p12

50. Firbank, R. *Santal* in *The Complete Firbank* (London: Duckworth, 1973), p497

51. Firbank, R. *The Flower Beneath the Foot* in *Three Novels* (London: Penguin, 2000), pp103, 63

52. Firbank, R. *The Princess Zoubaroff* (1920) in *The Mauve Tower: A Dream Play in VII Scenes* (1904) in *Complete Plays* (Illinois: Dalkey Archive Press, 1994), p54

53. Firbank, R. *The Flower Beneath the Foot* in *Three Novels* (London: Penguin, 2000), p15

54. Firbank, R. "Lady Appledore's Mésalliance" in *The New Rythum* (London: Duckworth, 1962), p65

55. Brophy, B. *Prancing Novelist: A Defense of Fiction in the Form of a Critical Biography in Praise of Ronald Firbank* (London: Macmillan, 1973), p79

56. Firbank, R. *The Flower Beneath the Foot* in *Three Novels* (London: Penguin, 2000), p48

57. Firbank, R. *Concerning the Eccentricities of Cardinal Pirelli* in *Three Novels* (London: Penguin, 2000), p203

58. Firbank, R. *Caprice* in *The Complete Firbank* (1973, London: Duckworth, 1973), p330

59. Firbank, R. *The Flower Beneath the Foot* in *Three Novels* (London: Penguin, 2000), p81

60. Firbank, R. *The New Rythum* in *The New Rythum* (London: Duckworth, 1962), p77

61. Firbank, R. "Mister White-Morgan the Diamond King" (age approx. 14) in *The New Rythum* (London: Duckworth, 1962), p116

62. Firbank, R. *The New Rythum* in *The New Rythum* (London: Duckworth, 1962), p101

63. Firbank, R. *Caprice* in *The Complete Firbank* (1973, London: Duckworth, 1973), p330

64. Firbank, R. *Concerning the Eccentricities of Cardinal Pirelli* in *The Flower Beneath the Foot* in *Three Novels* (London: Penguin, 2000), p211

65. Firbank, R. "A Discipline from the Country" in *The New Rythum* (London: Duckworth, 1962), p120

66. Firbank, R. *Caprice* in *The Complete Firbank* (London: Duckworth, 1973), pp374, 345, 367

67. Firbank, R. *The New Rythum* in *The New Rythum* (London: Duckworth, 1962), pp97, 99

68. Firbank, R. *The Flower Beneath the Foot* in *Three Novels* (London: Penguin, 2000), p69

69. Firbank, R. *The Flower Beneath the Foot* in *Three Novels* (London: Penguin, 2000), p18

70. Firbank, R. *Concerning the Eccentricities of Cardinal Pirelli* in *Three Novels* (London: Penguin, 2000), pp223, 227

71. Firbank, R. "A Discipline from the Country" in *The New Rythum* (London: Duckworth, 1962), p121

72. Firbank, R. *Concerning the Eccentricities of Cardinal Pirelli* in *Three Novels* (London: Penguin, 2000), p202

73. Firbank, R. *The Flower Beneath the Foot* in *Three Novels* (London: Penguin, 2000), p70

74. Firbank, R. *Inclinations* in *The Complete Firbank* (London: Duckworth, 1973), p261

75. Firbank, R. *The Artificial Princess* in *Five Novels: Valmouth; The Flower Beneath the Foot; Prancing Nigger; Concerning the Eccentricities of Cardinal Pirelli; The Artificial Princess* (London: Duckworth, 1951), pp453, 452

76. Firbank, R. *Caprice* in *The Complete Firbank* (London: Duckworth, 1973), p328

77. Firbank, R. *Santal* in *The Complete Firbank* (London: Duckworth, 1973), p487

78. Firbank, R. *Five Novels: Valmouth; The Flower Beneath the Foot; Prancing Nigger; Concerning the Eccentricities of Cardinal Pirelli; The Artificial Princess. Valmouth*, p23

79. Firbank, R. *Concerning the Eccentricities of Cardinal Pirelli* in *Three Novels* (London: Penguin, 2000), pp85, 71

80. Firbank, R. *The Flower Beneath the Foot* in *Three Novels* (London: Penguin, 2000), p11

81. Firbank, R. *The Flower Beneath the Foot* in *Three Novels* (London: Penguin, 2000), p16

82. Firbank, R. *The New Rythum* in *The New Rythum* (London: Duckworth, 1962), p73

83. Firbank, R. *The Princess Zoubaroff* in *Complete Plays* (Illinois: Dalkey Archive Press, 1994), p70

84. Carter, A. "A Self-Made Man" in *The Curious Room* (London: Chatto & Windus, 1996) p123

85. Firbank, R. *The Flower Beneath the Foot* in *Three Novels* (London: Penguin, 2000), p49

86. Beardsley, A. *In Black & White: The Literary Remains of Aubrey Beardsley. Under the Hill*, pp84–5

Quentin Crisp

1. Crisp, Q. *How to Become a Virgin* (London: Duckworth, 1981), p16

2. Crisp, Q. *The Naked Civil Servant* (London: Flamingo, 1985), pp215, 114, 160, 216

3. Crisp, Q. *The Naked Civil Servant* (London: Flamingo, 1985), p129

4. Crisp, Q. *How to Become a Virgin* (London: Duckworth, 1981), p132

5. Crisp, Q. *Love Made Easy* (London: Duckworth, 1977), pp10, 6

6. Crisp, Q. *Love Made Easy* (London: Duckworth, 1977), pp57, 66, 41, 80

7. Crisp, Q. *The Naked Civil Servant* (London: Flamingo, 1985), p106

8. Crisp, Q. *Resident Alien* (London: Flamingo, 1997), p6

9. Crisp, Q. *The Naked Civil Servant* (London: Flamingo, 1985), p16

10. Crisp, Q. *Manners from Heaven* (New York: Harper & Row, 1984), p36

11. Crisp, Q. *How to Become a Virgin* (London: Duckworth, 1981), p5

12. Crisp, Q. *The Naked Civil Servant* (London: Flamingo, 1985), p194

13. Crisp, Q. *How to Become a Virgin* (London: Duckworth, 1981), p141

14. Crisp, Q. *How to Go to the Movies* (London: Hamish Hamilton, 1990), p129

15. Crisp, Q. *Resident Alien* (London: Flamingo, 1997), p72

16. Crisp, Q. *The Naked Civil Servant* (London: Flamingo, 1985), p133, 222

17. Crisp, Q. *How to Become a Virgin* (London: Duckworth, 1981), p189

18. Crisp, Q. *The Naked Civil Servant* (London: Flamingo, 1985), pp129, 222, 128

19. Crisp, Q. *The Wit & Wisdom of Quentin Crisp.* (Ed. Guy Kettelhack) (1984) 1985, London: Century. p131

20. Crisp, Q. *The Wit & Wisdom of Quentin Crisp* (London: Century, 1985), pp99–100

21. Crisp, Q. *Love Made Easy* (London: Duckworth, 1977), p121

22. Coward, N. *Blithe Spirit* in *Collected Plays Volume Five: Pacific 1860; "Peace in Our Time"; Relative Values; Quadrille; Blithe Spirit* (London: Heinemann, 1958), p502

23. Crisp, Q. *Manners from Heaven* (New York: Harper & Row, 1984), pp119, 12

24. Crisp, Q. *Love Made Easy* (London: Duckworth, 1977), p152

25. Crisp, Q. *Resident Alien* (London: Flamingo, 1997), p124

26. Crisp, Q. *The Naked Civil Servant* (London: Flamingo, 1985), p122

27. Crisp, Q. *Resident Alien* (London: Flamingo, 1997), p94

28. Beardsley, A. *Under the Hill* in *In Black & White: The Literary Remains of Aubrey Beardsley* (London: Cypher, 1998), pp32, 19

29. Crisp, Q. *Chog* (London: Duckworth, 1979), p18

30. Crisp, Q. *Chog* (London: Duckworth, 1979), p76

31. Carroll, D. Introduction in Crisp, Q. *Resident Alien* (London: Flamingo, 1997), p2

32. Crisp, Q. *Resident Alien* (London: Flamingo, 1997), p7

33. Crisp, Q. *The Wit & Wisdom of Quentin Crisp* (London: Century, 1985), p42

34. Crisp, Q. *Manners from Heaven* (New York: Harper & Row, 1984), p73

35. Crisp, Q. *Manners from Heaven* (New York: Harper & Row, 1984), p62

36. Crisp, Q. *Chog* (London: Duckworth, 1979), p150

37. Crisp, Q. *The Wit & Wisdom of Quentin Crisp* (London: Century, 1985), p42

38. Crisp, Q. *How to Become a Virgin* (London: Duckworth, 1981), pp190, 7, 29

39. Crisp, Q. *How to Become a Virgin* (London: Duckworth, 1981), p13

40. Crisp, Q. *How to Become a Virgin* (London: Duckworth, 1981), p90
41. Crisp, Q. *The Naked Civil Servant* (London: Flamingo, 1985), pp46, 16–17
42. Crisp, Q. *Chog* (London: Duckworth, 1979), p153
43. Crisp, Q. *Resident Alien* (London: Flamingo, 1997), p41
44. Crisp, Q. *Resident Alien* (London: Flamingo, 1997), p151
45. Crisp, Q. *The Naked Civil Servant* (London: Flamingo, 1985), p197
46. Crisp, Q. *How to Become a Virgin* (London: Duckworth, 1981), pp179, 26
47. Crisp, Q. *Manners from Heaven* (New York: Harper & Row, 1984), pp131–2
48. Coward, N. *Relative Values* in *Collected Plays: Five: Relative Values; Look After Lulu! Waiting in the Wings; Suite in Three Keys* (London: Methuen, 1983), pp16, 19, 38
49. Crisp, Q. *The Naked Civil Servant* (London: Flamingo, 1985), p176
50. Crisp, Q. *How to Become a Virgin* (London: Duckworth, 1981), pp179, 26
51. Crisp, Q. *The Naked Civil Servant* (London: Flamingo, 1985), p119
52. Crisp, Q. *Resident Alien* (London: Flamingo, 1997), p89
53. Crisp, Q. *How to Go to the Movies* (London: Hamish Hamilton, 1990), p128
54. Crisp, Q. *Manners from Heaven* (New York: Harper & Row, 1984), p24
55. Crisp, Q. introduction in *Resident Alien* (London: Flamingo, 1997), p3
56. Crisp, Q. *Chog* (London: Duckworth, 1979), p98
57. Crisp, Q. *How to Have a Lifestyle* (Los Angeles: Alyson Books, 1998), pp12, 25
58. Crisp, Q. *How to Become a Virgin* (London: Duckworth, 1981), p158
59. Crisp, Q. *The Naked Civil Servant* (London: Flamingo, 1985), p199
60. Crisp, Q. *How to Become a Virgin* (London: Duckworth, 1981), p186
61. Crisp, Q. *How to Become a Virgin* (London: Duckworth, 1981), p14
62. Crisp, Q. *The Wit & Wisdom of Quentin Crisp* (London: Century, 1985), p127
63. Crisp, Q. *Chog* (London: Duckworth, 1979), p145
64. Crisp, Q. *Chog* (London: Duckworth, 1979), pp120, 103, 112
65. Crisp, Q. *The Wit & Wisdom of Quentin Crisp* (London: Century, 1985), p120
66. Crisp, Q. *All This and Bevin Too.* (1943) 1978, London: The Mervyn Peake Society. p8
67. Crisp, Q. *Resident Alien* (London: Flamingo, 1997), p7
68. Crisp, Q. *How to Have a Lifestyle* (Los Angeles: Alyson Books, 1998), pp49, 90

69. Crisp, Q. *The Naked Civil Servant* (London: Flamingo, 1985), pp114, 123
70. Crisp, Q. *The Naked Civil Servant* (London: Flamingo, 1985), p92
71. Crisp, Q. *The Naked Civil Servant* (London: Flamingo, 1985), p34
72. Crisp, Q. *How to Become a Virgin* (London: Duckworth, 1981), pp152, 154
73. Crisp, Q. *Resident Alien* (London: Flamingo, 1997), p86
74. Crisp, Q. *How to Become a Virgin* (London: Duckworth, 1981), p182
75. Crisp, Q. *Resident Alien* (London: Flamingo, 1997), p51
76. Crisp, Q. *Love Made Easy* (London: Duckworth, 1977), p5
77. Crisp, Q. *How to Become a Virgin* (London: Duckworth, 1981), p186
78. Crisp, Q. *Manners from Heaven* (New York: Harper & Row, 1984), p19
79. Crisp, Q. *How to Go to the Movies* (London: Hamish Hamilton, 1990), p78
80. Crisp, Q. *Love Made Easy* (London: Duckworth, 1977), pp71, 55, 107, 102
81. Crisp, Q. *Resident Alien* (London: Flamingo, 1997), p128
82. Crisp, Q. *How to Have a Lifestyle* (Los Angeles: Alyson Books, 1998), p122
83. *Diaries 1999* in Bennett, A. *Untold Stories* (London: Faber/Profile, 2005), p251
84. "Untold Stories" in Bennett, A. *Untold Stories* (London: Faber/Profile, 2005), pp12, 118
85. Crisp, Q. *How to Go to the Movies* (London: Hamish Hamilton, 1990), pp10, 13
86. Crisp, Q. *The Naked Civil Servant* (London: Flamingo, 1985), p65
87. Crisp, Q. *The Naked Civil Servant* (London: Flamingo, 1985), p154
88. Poems, C. "Whore" in *Adult Entertainment* (Glasshoughton: Route, 2002), p52
89. Crisp, Q. *Chog* (London: Duckworth, 1979), p97
90. Crisp, Q. *The Naked Civil Servant* (London: Flamingo, 1985), p53
91. Crisp, Q. *Resident Alien* (London: Flamingo, 1997), p218
92. Crisp, Q. *The Naked Civil Servant* (London: Flamingo, 1985), p30
93. Crisp, Q. *Chog* (London: Duckworth, 1979), p126
94. Crisp, Q. *How to Have a Lifestyle* (Los Angeles: Alyson Books, 1998), pp47–8, 166
95. Crisp, Q. *How to Have a Lifestyle* (Los Angeles: Alyson Books, 1998), pp122, 149, 23
96. Crisp, Q. *Resident Alien* (London: Flamingo, 1997), p77
97. Crisp, Q. *How to Have a Lifestyle* (Los Angeles: Alyson Books, 1998), p47
98. Crisp, Q. *The Naked Civil Servant* (London: Flamingo, 1985), pp170–5

99. Crisp, Q. *The Naked Civil Servant* (London: Flamingo, 1985), p69
100. Crisp, Q. *Manners from Heaven* (New York: Harper & Row, 1984), p42

Edward D. Wood, Jr.

1. Goytisolo, J. *The Marx Family Saga* (San Francisco: City Lights, 1999), p77
2. Grey, R. *Nightmare of Ecstasy: The Life & Times of Edward D. Wood, Jr.* (1994) 1995, London: Faber & Faber. pp175,139
3. Wood, E. *Watts ... After* (1967) in Hayes, D.C. & Davis, H. *Muddled Mind: The Complete Works of Edward D. Wood, Jr.* (Shreveport: Ramble House, 2001), p46
4. Grey, R. *Nightmare of Ecstasy: The Life & Times of Edward D. Wood, Jr.* (London: Faber & Faber, 1995), pp18,139
5. Wood, E.D. *Hollywood Rat Race.* 1998, London: Four Walls Eight Windows/Turnaround. p124
6. Wood, E.D. *Hollywood Rat Race* (London: Four Walls Eight Windows/Turnaround, 1998), pp5, 46, 112
7. Wood, E.D. *Death of a Transvestite* (A.K.A. *Let Me Die in Drag*). (1967) 1999, New York: Four Walls Eight Windows. pp146, 7, 13
8. Wood, E.D. *Hollywood Rat Race* (London: Four Walls Eight Windows/Turnaround, 1998), p37
9. Sontag, S. "Notes on Camp" in *Against Interpretation* (London: Vintage, 1994), p283
10. Kundera, M. *The Art of the Novel* (London: Faber & Faber, 1990), pp163, 135
11. Kundera, M. ("Jerusalem Address: The Novel & Europe," 1986, & "Sixty Three Words," 1986) in *The Unbearable Lightness of Being.* (1984) 1985, London: Faber & Faber. p254
12. Wood, E.D. "Bum's Rush Terror" (1971) in *The Horrors of Sex* (Shreveport: Woodpile, 2000), p65
13. Poems, C. "Are We Myra Hindley?" in *Adult Entertainment* (Glasshoughton: Route, 2002), p99
14. Wood, E.D. "The Night the Banshee Cried" (1966) in *The Horrors of Sex* (Shreveport: Woodpile, 2000), p81
15. Wood, E.D. [as N.V. Jason] *Hell Chicks* (Shreveport: Woodpile, 2001), p29
16. Beerbohm, M. "Relic" (1918) in *And Even Now.* (1920) 1950, London: Heinemann. p6
17. Wood, E.D. "To Kill a Saturday Night" (1966) in *The Horrors of Sex* (Shreveport: Woodpile, 2000), p111
18. Crisp, Q. *Love Made Easy* (London: Duckworth, 1977), pp8, 34
19. Wood, E.D. "Domain of the Undead" (1971) in *The Horrors of Sex.* 2000, Shreveport: Woodpile. p99
20. Wood, E.D. "Final Curtain" (1966) in *The Horrors of Sex* (Shreveport: Woodpile, 2000), pp3, 5
21. Booth, M. *Camp* (London: Quartet, 1983), p20
22. Ross, A. *No Respect: Intellectuals & Popular Culture.* 1989, London: Routledge. pp140,136
23. Wood, E.D. "Gemeni" in *The Horrors of Sex* (Shreveport: Woodpile, 2000), p22
24. Wood, E.D. *Killer in Drag* (1963, A.K.A. "Black Lace Drag.") 1999, London: Four Walls Eight Windows. p51
25. Wood, E.D. "Gemeni" in *The Horrors of Sex* (Shreveport: Woodpile, 2000), pp20, 22
26. Brophy, B. "Baroque-'n'-Roll" in *Baroque-'n'-Roll & Other Essays* (London: Hamish Hamilton, 1987), pp231–2
27. Wood, E.D. "Gore in the Alley" (1977) in *The Horrors of Sex* (Shreveport: Woodpile, 2000), p33
28. Sontag, S. "Notes on Camp" in *Against Interpretation* (London: Vintage, 1994), p288
29. Mizejewski, L. *Divine Decadence: Fascism, Female Spectacle & the Makings of Sally Bowles.* 1992, Princeton University Press. pp63, 70
30. Sontag, S. "Notes on Camp" in *Against Interpretation* (London: Vintage, 1994), pp291, 292
31. Babuscio, J. "Camp & the Gay Sensibility" in Dyer, R. (ed.) *Gays & Film* (London: British Film Institute, 1977), p44
32. Wood, E.D. "It Takes Two for Terror" (1971) in *The Horrors of Sex* (Shreveport: Woodpile, 2000), p45
33. Wood, E.D. *Hollywood Rat Race* (London: Four Walls Eight Windows/Turnaround., 1998), p10
34. Wood, E.D. *Hollywood Rat Race* (London: Four Walls Eight Windows/Turnaround, 1998), p138
35. Wood, E.D. "Gore in the Alley" in *The Horrors of Sex* (Shreveport: Woodpile, 2000), p34
36. Poems, C. "Faith" in "Are We Myra Hindley?" in *Adult Entertainment* (Glasshoughton: Route, 2002), p95
37. Grey, R. *Nightmare of Ecstasy: The Life & Times of Edward D. Wood, Jr.* (London: Faber & Faber, 1995), p139
38. Wood, E.D. *Devil Girls* (London: Gorse, 1995), p30
39. Wood, E.D. *Side-Show Siren* (Shreveport: Woodpile, 2000), p182
40. Wood, E.D. *Devil Girls* (London: Gorse, 1995), p14
41. Wood, E.D. *Side-Show Siren* (Shreveport: Woodpile, 2000), p46

42. Lord Berners, G. *First Childhood* in *First Childhood & Far from the Madding War* (Oxford University Press, 1983), p4
43. Wood, E.D. *Watts ... the Difference* (1966) in Grey, R. *Nightmare of Ecstasy: The Life & Times of Edward D. Wood, Jr.* (London: Faber & Faber, 1995), pp177–78
44. Wood, E.D. *Devil Girls* (London: Gorse, 1995), pp30, 34
45. Wood, E.D. *Devil Girls* (London: Gorse, 1995), p75
46. Wood, E.D. *Killer in Drag* (London: Four Walls Eight Windows, 1999), p20
47. Wood, E.D. *Devil Girls* (London: Gorse, 1995), p7
48. Wood, E.D. *Side-Show Siren.* (1966) 2000, Shreveport: Woodpile. pp13, 14
49. Wood, E.D. *Killer in Drag* (London: Four Walls Eight Windows, 1999), pp160–1
50. Wood, E.D. *Devil Girls* (London: Gorse, 1995), p11
51. Wood, E.D. *Orgy of the Dead* (1966) in Grey, R. *Nightmare of Ecstasy: The Life & Times of Edward D. Wood, Jr.* (London: Faber & Faber, 1995), p177
52. Wood, E.D. *It Takes One to Know One* (1967) in Grey, R. *Nightmare of Ecstasy: The Life & Times of Edward D. Wood, Jr.* (London: Faber & Faber, 1995), p181
53. Wood, E.D. *Devil Girls* (London: Gorse, 1995), pp30, 34
54. Wood, E.D. *Killer in Drag* (London: Four Walls Eight Windows, 1999), p7
55. Willett, J. (ed.) "Conversations with Bert Brecht" in *Brecht on Theater: The Development of an Aesthetic* (London: Methuen, 1987), p44
56. Wood, E.D. "It Takes Two for Terror" (1971) in *The Horrors of Sex* (Shreveport: Woodpile, 2000), p45
57. Wood, E.D. *Hollywood Rat Race* (London: Four Walls Eight Windows/Turnaround, 1998), p3
58. Poems, C. "Me" in *Adult Entertainment* (Glasshoughton: Route, 2002), p69
59. Poems, C. "The Cocktail Hour" in *Adult Entertainment* (Glasshoughton: Route, 2002), p82
60. Wood, E.D. *Side-Show Siren* (Shreveport: Woodpile, 2000), p200
61. Wood, E.D. *Side-Show Siren* (Shreveport: Woodpile, 2000), p53
62. Wood, E.D. "It Takes Two for Terror" in *The Horrors of Sex* (Shreveport: Woodpile, 2000), p55
63. Sacher-Masoch, L.von, *Moonlight* (1868) in *Love: The Legacy of Cain* (Riverside: Ariadne, 2003) [Trans.Michael T. O'Pecko] p148
64. Corelli, M. *The Sorrows of Satan* (London: Methuen, 1918), p86
65. Wood, E.D. *Side-Show Siren* (Shreveport: Woodpile, 2000), p14
66. Wood, E.D. *Devil Girls* (London: Gorse, 1995), p32
67. Corelli, M. *The Mighty Atom* (London: Hutchinson, 1896). p319
68. Wood, E.D. *Side-Show Siren* (Shreveport: Woodpile, 2000), pp206, 205
69. Wood, E.D. *Devil Girls* (London: Gorse, 1995), pp151–2
70. Wood, E.D. "Gore in the Alley" in *The Horrors of Sex* (Shreveport: Woodpile, 2000), p37
71. Wood, E.D. *Devil Girls* (London: Gorse, 1995), p179
72. Wood, E.D. "Gore in the Alley" in *The Horrors of Sex* (Shreveport: Woodpile, 2000), p37
73. Wood, E.D. *Hell Chicks* (Shreveport: Woodpile, 2001), pp11, 93, 126
74. Wood, E.D. *Side-Show Siren* (Shreveport: Woodpile, 2000), pp49–50
75. Wood, E.D. *Devil Girls.* (1967) 1995, London: Gorse. pp132–3
76. Wood, E.D. *Hell Chicks* (Shreveport: Woodpile, 2001), pp136, 138–9
77. Wood, E.D. *Devil Girls* (London: Gorse, 1995), pp70,119,174
78. Wood, E.D. *Hell Chicks* (Shreveport: Woodpile, 2001), p185
79. Wood, E.D. *Hell Chicks* (Shreveport: Woodpile, 2001), p115
80. Wood, E.D. *Side-Show Siren* (Shreveport: Woodpile, 2000), pp173–4
81. Wood, E. *Watts ... After* in Hayes, D.C. & Davis, H. *Muddled Mind: The Complete Works of Edward D. Wood, Jr.* (Shreveport: Ramble House, 2001), p47
82. Wood, E.D. *Devil Girls* (London: Gorse, 1995), pp186,188,189
83. Wood, E.D. "Gore in the Alley" in *The Horrors of Sex* (Shreveport: Woodpile, 2000), p44
84. Wood, E.D. *Diary of a Transvestite Hooker* (1974) in Grey, R. *Nightmare of Ecstasy: The Life & Times of Edward D. Wood, Jr.* (London: Faber & Faber, 1995), p35
85. Wood, E.D. *Killer in Drag* (London: Four Walls Eight Windows, 1999), p30
86. Wood, E.D. "Gore in the Alley" in *The Horrors of Sex* (Shreveport: Woodpile, 2000), p38
87. Wood, E.D. *Side-Show Siren* (Shreveport: Woodpile, 2000), pp48, 67
88. Wood, E.D. *Killer in Drag* (London: Four Walls Eight Windows, 1999), pp7,8
89. Wood, E.D. *Killer in Drag* (London: Four Walls Eight Windows, 1999), pp15–16
90. Wood, E.D. *Killer in Drag* (London: Four Walls Eight Windows, 1999), p12

91. Wood, E.D. *Side-Show Siren* (Shreveport: Woodpile, 2000), p53

92. Wood, E.D. *Killer in Drag* (London: Four Walls Eight Windows, 1999), p37

93. Sacher-Masoch, L.von, *Venus in Furs.* (London: Penguin, 2000), pp16, 17, 44

94. Corelli, M. *The Soul of Lilith* (London: Methuen, 1958), p28

95. Wood, E.D. *Killer in Drag* (London: Four Walls Eight Windows, 1999), p31

96. Corelli, M. *Ardath* (London: Richard Bentley, 1889) p195

97. Wood, E.D. *Killer in Drag* (London: Four Walls Eight Windows, 1999), pp131

98. Wood, E.D. *Killer in Drag* (London: Four Walls Eight Windows, 1999), pp28–9

99. Wood, E.D. [as N.V. Jason] *Hell Chicks* (Shreveport: Woodpile, 2001), p60

100. Wood, E.D. *Side-Show Siren* (Shreveport: Woodpile, 2000), pp202, 180, 183

101. Wood, E.D. *Killer in Drag* (London: Four Walls Eight Windows, 1999), pp82,73

102. Corelli, M. *Delicia* (A.K.A. *The Murder of Delicia*) (1896) in *Delicia & Other Stories* (London: Constable, 1907), p172

103. Corelli, M. *Vendetta!* (London: Methuen, 1919), p362

104. Wood, E.D. *Killer in Drag* (London: Four Walls Eight Windows, 1999), pp33,34

105. Brophy, B. *Prancing Novelist: A Defense of Fiction in the Form of a Critical Biography in Praise of Ronald Firbank* (London: Macmillan, 1973), p398

106. Wood, E. "Pearl & the Last Stage" in Hayes, D.C. & Davis, H. *Muddled Mind: The Complete Works of Edward D. Wood, Jr.* (Shreveport: Ramble House, 2001), p96

107. Wood, E.D. *Hollywood Rat Race* (London: Four Walls Eight Windows/Turnaround, 1998), p76

Juan Goytisolo

1. Goytisolo, J. *Quarantine* (London: Quartet, 1994), p30

2. Kennard, C. "Introduction to *The Artificial Princess* (1934)" in Horder, M. (ed.) *Ronald Firbank: Memoirs & Critiques* (London: Duckworth, 1977), p108

3. Goytisolo, J. *The Marx Family Saga* (San Francisco: City Lights, 1999), p64

4. Goytisolo, J. *The Marx Family Saga* (San Francisco: City Lights, 1999), p126

5. Kundera, M. "Dialogue on the Art of the Novel," (1983) in *The Art of the Novel* (London: Faber & Faber, 1990), p23

6. Goytisolo, J. *The Garden of Secrets* (London: Serpent's Tail, 2002), p147

7. Goytisolo, J. *Landscapes After the Battle.* (1982) 1987, London: Serpent's Tail. [Trans. Helen Lane] p144

8. Goytisolo, J. *Makbara.* (1980) 1991, London: Serpent's Tail [Trans. Helen Lane] pp85–5, 62

9. Epps, B. S. *Significant Violence: Oppression & Resistance in the Narratives of Juan Goytisolo 1970–1990* (Oxford: Clarendon Press, 1996), p236

10. Goytisolo, J. *Quarantine* (London: Quartet, 1994), p92

11. Goytisolo, J. *A Cock-Eyed Comedy.* (2000) 2002, London: Serpent's Tail. [Trans. Peter Bush] p71

12. Goytisolo, J. *The Marx Family Saga* (San Francisco: City Lights, 1999), p61

13. Goytisolo, J. *A Cock-Eyed Comedy* (London: Serpent's Tail, 2002), pp134–5

14. Goytisolo, J. *The Garden of Secrets* (London: Serpent's Tail, 2002), p59

15. "An Interview with Juan Goytisolo by Julia Ortega" (trans. Joseph Schraibam), *Texas Quarterly* Spring 1975 (University of Texas Press), pp56–77

16. Jones, E. "Introduction to *Three Novels*" (1950) in Horder, M. (ed.) *Ronald Firbank: Memoirs & Critiques* (London: Duckworth, 1977), p193

17. Kundera, M. "Dialogue on the Art of the Novel" in *The Art of the Novel* (London: Faber & Faber, 1990), p25

18. Goytisolo, J. *Makbara* (London: Serpent's Tail, 1991), pp216–17

19. Goytisolo, J. *Makbara* (London: Serpent's Tail, 1991), p270

20. Goytisolo, J. *The Marx Family Saga* (San Francisco: City Lights, 1999), pp145, 147

21. Goytisolo, J. *Landscapes After the Battle* (London: Serpent's Tail, 1987), p31

22. Crisp, Q. *The Naked Civil Servant* (London: Flamingo, 1985), p88

23. Benson, E.F. *Lucia's Progress* (London: Hodder & Stoughton, 1967), p125

24. Goytisolo, J. *Quarantine* (London: Quartet, 1994), p59

25. Goytisolo, J. *The Garden of Secrets* (London: Serpent's Tail, 2002), p29

26. Epps, B. S. *Significant Violence: Oppression & Resistance in the Narratives of Juan Goytisolo 1970–1990* (Oxford: Clarendon Press, 1996), p15

27. J.W. Lambert, Introduction in Saki, *The Bodley Head Saki* (London: The Bodley Head, 1973), pp32–3

28. Poems, C. "Some of My Best Friends Are Straight" in *Universal Rentboy* (Manchester: Bad Press, 2000). pp25–6

29. Goytisolo, J. *The Virtues of the Solitary Bird.* (1988) 1991, London: Serpent's Tail [Trans. Helen Lane] p30

30. Richards, G. *Ronald Firbank* in Horder,

M. (ed.) *Ronald Firbank: Memoirs & Critiques* (London: Duckworth, 1977), p120

31. Goytisolo, J. *A Cock-Eyed Comedy* (London: Serpent's Tail, 2002), p60

32. Goytisolo, J. *Count Julian.* (1970) 1989, London: Serpent's Tail [Trans. Helen Lane] p139

33. Goytisolo, J. *A Cock-Eyed Comedy* (London: Serpent's Tail, 2002), p60

34. Goytisolo, J. *A Cock-Eyed Comedy* (London: Serpent's Tail, 2002), pp60–1

35. Goytisolo, J. *The Marx Family Saga* (San Francisco: City Lights, 1999), p3

36. Crisp, Q. *The Naked Civil Servant* (London: Flamingo, 1985), p106

37. Goytisolo, J. *Landscapes After the Battle* (London: Serpent's Tail, 1987), p78

38. Goytisolo, J. *A Cock-Eyed Comedy* (London: Serpent's Tail, 2002), p5

39. Coward, N. *Quadrille* in *Collected Plays: Seven: Quadrille; "Peace in Our Time"; Tonight at 8.30 (III)* (London: Methuen, 1999), p15

40. Goytisolo, J. *Count Julian.* (1970) 1989, London: Serpent's Tail [Trans. Helen Lane] p139

41. "Peter Bush Interviews Juan Goytisolo." *Book Forum.* Winter 2002. New York: Art Forum Publishing

42. Bush, P. "The Act of Translation: The Case of Juan Goytisolo's *A Cock-Eyed Comedy*" in: *Quaderns,* No. 10, 2003: Universitat Autònoma de Barcelona. pp132–3

43. Bush, P. *The Translator as Writer: The Case of Juan Goytisolo's* A Cock-Eyed Comedy. Online. 2002, British Council Literature Department/ British Center for Literary Translation: *http://www.literarytranslation.com/index2.html* (accessed: 1 March 2004)

44. Kundera, M. "Sixty Three Words" in *The Art of the Novel* (London: Faber & Faber, 1990), p121

45. Goytisolo, J. *Landscapes After the Battle* (London: Serpent's Tail, 1987), p40

46. Goytisolo, J. *Count Julian* (London: Serpent's Tail, 1989), pp22–3

47. Epps, B. S. *Significant Violence: Oppression & Resistance in the Narratives of Juan Goytisolo 1970–1990* (Oxford: Clarendon Press, 1996), pp433, 2, 26

48. Goytisolo, J. *A Cock-Eyed Comedy* (London: Serpent's Tail, 2002), p47

49. Goytisolo, J. *The Marx Family Saga* (San Francisco: City Lights, 1999), p20

50. Goytisolo, J. *Makbara* (London: Serpent's Tail, 1991), p250

51. Goytisolo, J. *A Cock-Eyed Comedy* (London: Serpent's Tail, 2002), p104

52. Goytisolo, J. *Landscapes After the Battle* (London: Serpent's Tail, 1987), p31

53. Goytisolo, J. *Landscapes After the Battle* (London: Serpent's Tail, 1987), p115

54. Goytisolo, J. *The Marx Family Saga* (San Francisco: City Lights, 1999), pp14, 10–11

55. Goytisolo, J. *A Cock-Eyed Comedy* (London: Serpent's Tail, 2002), p8

56. Goytisolo, J. *A Cock-Eyed Comedy* (London: Serpent's Tail, 2002), p105

57. Goytisolo, J. *A Cock-Eyed Comedy* (London: Serpent's Tail, 2002), pp98, 112

58. Goytisolo, J. *The Garden of Secrets* (London: Serpent's Tail, 2002), pp135, 136, 138

59. Kennard, C. "Introduction to *The Artificial Princess* (1934)" in Horder, M. (ed.) *Ronald Firbank: Memoirs & Critiques* (London: Duckworth, 1977), p108

60. Goytisolo, J. *The Blind Rider.* (2003) 2005, London: Serpent's Tail. [Trans. Peter Bush] pp118, 36

Chloe Poems

1. Bennett, A. *Untold Stories* (London: Faber/Profile, 2005), pix

2. Crisp, Q. *Manners from Heaven* (New York: Harper & Row, 1984), p13

3. Poems, C. "Ooh, Matron" in *How to Be a Better Gay.* Author's Draft Copy, 2005

4. Isherwood, C. *Christopher & His Kind.* (1977) 1993, London: Minerva. p57

5. Sontag, S. *Notes on Camp* in *Against Interpretation* (London: Vintage, 1994), pp291–2

6. Poems, C. Introduction in *Adult Entertainment* (Glasshoughton: Route, 2002), pp13–15

7. Poems, C. "The Effeminate," in *Adult Entertainment* (Glasshoughton: Route, 2002), p17–21

8. Crisp, Q. *Manners from Heaven* (New York: Harper & Row, 1984), p27

9. Crisp, Q. *How to Become a Virgin* (London: Duckworth, 1981), p179

10. Poems, C. "The Effeminate," in *Adult Entertainment* (Glasshoughton: Route, 2002), p17–21

11. Poems, C. "Faith" in *Adult Entertainment* (Glasshoughton: Route, 2002), pp92–8

12. Poems, C. "In Celebration of Poo" in *Universal Rentboy* (Manchester: Bad Press, 2000), pp27–9

13. Crisp, Q. *Manners from Heaven* (New York: Harper & Row, 1984), pp59–60

14. Kundera, M. *The Unbearable Lightness of Being* (London: Faber & Faber, 1985), pp248, 254

15. Epps, B. S. *Significant Violence: Oppression & Resistance in the Narratives of Juan Goytisolo 1970–1990* (Oxford: Clarendon Press, 1996), p14

16. Poems, C. "No Stranger to Sequins" in *How to Be a Better Gay.* Author's Draft Copy, 2005

17. Poems, C. "Bingo Jesus" in *How to Be a Better Gay*. Author's Draft Copy, 2005

18. Kundera, M. "Jerusalem Address: The Novel & Europe" (1986) in *The Art of the Novel* (London: Faber & Faber, 1990), p163

19. Poems, C. "Why Do Roughs Have Such Tight Buns?" in *I'm Kamp* (Manchester: Bad Press, 2003)

20. Munro, H.H. (Saki) "Reginald" in *The Complete Works of Saki* (Harmondsworth: Penguin, 1986), p7

21. Munro, H.H. (Saki) *The Watched Pot* in *The Complete Works of Saki* (Harmondsworth: Penguin, 1986), p884

22. Poems, C. "Autumn" in *Adult Entertainment* (Glasshoughton: Route, 2002), pp22–5

23. Fletcher, I.K. "Ronald Firbank: A Memoir" in Horder, M. (ed.) *Ronald Firbank: Memoirs & Critiques* (London: Duckworth, 1977), p17

24. Crisp, Q. *The Naked Civil Servant* (London: Flamingo, 1985), pp416, 219, 178

25. Crisp, Q. *The Naked Civil Servant* (London: Flamingo, 1985), p133

26. Poems, C. "Volcano II" in *How to Be a Better Gay*. Author's Draft Copy, 2005

27. Poems, C. "Volcano IV" in *How to Be a Better Gay*. Author's Draft Copy, 2005

28. Wilde, O. "De Profundis" in *The Works of Oscar Wilde* (Leicester: Galley Press, 1987), p853

29. Kundera, M. "Dialogue on the Art of the Novel" (1983) in *The Art of the Novel* (London: Faber & Faber, 1990), pp24, 25

30. Wood, E.D. *The Casual Company: The Laugh of the Marines* (1948) in Hayes, D.C. & Davis, H. *Muddled Mind: The Complete Works of Edward D. Wood, Jr.* (Shreveport: Ramble House, 2001), p25

31. Poems, C. "Crash! Bang! Wallop! What a Picture!" in *Universal Rentboy* (Manchester: Bad Press, 2000), pp36–8

32. Poems, C. "Harry, King of Smack" in *Adult Entertainment* (Glasshoughton: Route, 2002), p56

33. Coward, N. *Pomp & Circumstance* (London: Heinemann, 1960), p85

34. Poems, C. "Whore" in *Adult Entertainment* (Glasshoughton: Route, 2002), p51

35. Poems, C. "Volcano I" in *How to Be a Better Gay*. Author's Draft Copy, 2005

36. Poems, C. "The Queen Sucks Nazi Cock" in *Universal Rentboy* (Manchester: Bad Press, 2000), pp30–2

37. Poems, C. Introduction in *Adult Entertainment* (Glasshoughton: Route, 2002), pp13–15

38. Poems, C. "I Wish You Life" in *Adult Entertainment* (Glasshoughton: Route, 2002), p104

39. Poems, C. "Volcano III" in *How to Be a Better Gay*. Author's Draft Copy, 2005

40. Poems, C. "Love, Sex, Drugs, Rock 'n' Roll & Honesty" in *Adult Entertainment* (Glasshoughton: Route, 2002), p67

41. Poems, C. "Spud-u-Like in Monochrome" in *Universal Rentboy* (Manchester: Bad Press, 2000), p85

42. Poems, C. "Me" in *Adult Entertainment* (Glasshoughton: Route, 2002), pp69–74

43. "Wriiten on the Body" & "Portrait or Bust" in Bennett, A, *Untold Stories* (London: Faber/Profile, 2005) pp133, 130, 500

44. Crisp, Q. *How to Have a Lifestyle* (Los Angeles: Alyson Books, 1998), p50

45. Poems, C. "London Is Paranoid" in *Universal Rentboy* (Manchester: Bad Press, 2000), pp21–4

46. Poems, C. "Celebrities Are Shits" in *Adult Entertainment* (Glasshoughton: Route, 2002), p32

47. Poems, C. "The Insomnia Suite 3" in *I'm Kamp* (Manchester: Bad Press, 2003), p16

48. Poems, C. "Volcano II" in *How to Be a Better Gay*. Author's Draft Copy, 2005

49. Poems, C. "The Matron's Revolution" in *How to Be a Better Gay*. Author's Draft Copy, 2005

50. Poems, C. "Margaret — A Royal Love Gory" in *Adult Entertainment* (Glasshoughton: Route, 2002), p48

51. Poems, C. "Mirrorballin" in *Universal Rentboy* (Manchester: Bad Press, 2000), p13

52. Beardsley, A. *Under the Hill* in *In Black & White: The Literary Remains of Aubrey Beardsley* (London: Cypher, 1998), pp82, 66, 77, 19, 81, 102, 32, 105

53. Beardsley, A. *Under the Hill* in *In Black & White: The Literary Remains of Aubrey Beardsley* (London: Cypher, 1998), p23

54. Corelli, M. *Temporal Power* (London: Methuen, 1902), p256

55. Poems, C. "Drunks & the Ghosts" in *How to Be a Better Gay*. Author's Draft Copy, 2005

56. Coward, N. *Relative Values* in *Collected Plays: Five: Relative Values; Look After Lulu! Waiting in the Wings; Suite in Three Keys* (London: Methuen, 1983), p53

57. Poems, C. "Stupid Intellectual" in *Adult Entertainment* (Glasshoughton: Route, 2002), p31

58. Poems, C. "Volcano II" in *How to Be a Better Gay*. Author's Draft Copy, 2005

59. Wood, E.D. *Death of a Transvestite* (New York: Four Walls Eight Windows, 1999), p26

60. Poems, C. "Are We Myra Hindley?" in *Adult Entertainment* (Glasshoughton: Route, 2002), p99

61. Beerbohm, M. "London Revisited" in *Mainly on the Air* (London: Heinemann, 1957), p7

Bibliography

Amory, M. *Lord Berners: The Last Eccentric*. 1998, London: Chatto & Windus

Armstrong, A. http://www.oddbooks.co.uk/amanda/

Barthes, R. *Sade, Fourier, Loyola* (1971) 1997, London: Johns Hopkins University Press

Beardsley, A. *Under the Hill*. (1959) 1966, London: New English Library

_____. *Under the Hill & Other Essays*. 1977, London: Paddington Press

_____. *In Black & White: The Literary Remains of Aubrey Beardsley*. (Ed. S. Calloway and D. Colvin) 1998, London: Cypher

Beerbohm, M. *The Happy Hypocrite*. 1897, London: The Bodley Head

_____. *Zuleika Dobson*. (1911) 1964, London: Heinemann

_____. *And Even Now*. (1920) 1950, London: Heinemann

_____. *The Works of Max Beerbohm*. 1922, London: Heinemann

_____. *Around Theaters* (1924) 1953, London: Rupert Hart-Davis

_____. *Observations*. (1925) 1971, New York: Haskell House

_____. *Mainly on the Air* (1946) 1957, London: Heinemann

Bennett, A. *Forty Years On*. 1969, London: Faber

_____. *Getting On*. 1972, London: Samuel French

_____. *Plays 2: Kafka's Dick; The Insurance Man; The Old Country; An Englishman Abroad; A Question of Attribution*. 1998, London: Faber

_____. *Telling Tales*. (2000) 2001, London: B.B.C. Worldwide

_____. *The Laying On of Hands*. 2001, London: Profile Books

_____. *Untold Stories*. 2005, London: Faber/Profile

Benson, E.F. *The Babe* (1897) 1984, London: Garland

_____. *The Oakleyites*. 1915, London: Hodder & Stoughton

_____. *The Freaks of Mayfair*. 1916, London: T.N. Foulis

_____. *Dodo Wonders*. 1921, London: Hutchinson

_____. *Lucia in London*. (1927) 1968, London: Heinemann

_____. *As We Were*. (1930) 1932, London: Longmans

_____. *The Inheritor*. (1930) 1992, Brighton: Millivres Books

_____. *Mapp & Lucia*. (1931) 2004, London: Penguin

_____. *Lucia's Progress*. (1935) 1967, London: Hodder & Stoughton

_____. *Trouble for Lucia*. (1939) 1968, London: Hodder & Stoughton

_____. *Final Edition*. 1940, London: Longmans

_____. *Lucia Rising*. 1991, London: Penguin

_____. *Fine Feathers & Other Stories*. (1994) 1995, Oxford University Press

Lord Berners, G. *First Childhood & Far from the Madding War*. 1983, Oxford University Press

_____. *Collected Tales & Fantasies*. 1999, New York: Turtle Point Press/Helen Marx Books

Booth, M. *Camp*. 1983, London: Quartet

Brophy, B. *The Finishing Touch*. 1963, London: Secker & Warburg

_____. *In Transit*. (1969) 1989, London: GMP Publishers

_____. *Prancing Novelist: A Defense of Fiction in the Form of a Critical Biography in Praise of Ronald Firbank*. 1973, London: Macmillan

_____. *Beardsley & His World*. 1976, London: Thames & Hudson

_____. *Baroque-'n'-Roll & Other Essays*. 1987, London: Hamish Hamilton

Bush, P. *The Translator as Writer: The Case of Juan Goytisolo's* A Cock-Eyed Comedy. Online. 2002, British Council Literature Department/ British Center for Literary Translation: http://www.literarytranslation.com/index2.html. (Accessed 1 March 2004)

_____. 'The Act of Translation: The Case of Juan Goytisolo's *A Cock-Eyed Comedy*' in: *Quaderns,* No.10, 2003: Universitat Autònoma de Barcelona

Cameron, D. (ed.) *The Feminist Critique of Language*. 1990, London: Routledge

Carter, A. *The Curious Room*. 1996, London: Chatto & Windus

Corelli, M. *A Romance of Two Worlds*. (1886) 1976, London: Garland

_____. *Vendetta!* (1886) 1919, London: Methuen

_____. *Wormwood* (1890) 1891, London: Richard Bentley

_____. *The Soul of Lilith* (1892) 1958, London: Methuen

_____. *Barabbas*. (1893) 1912, London: Methuen

_____. *The Sorrows of Satan*. (1895) 1918, London: Methuen

_____. *Cameos*. (1896) 1919, London: Methuen

_____. *The Mighty Atom*. 1896, London: Hutchinson

_____. *Delicia & Other Stories*. (1896) 1907, London: Constable

_____. *Ziska*. 1897, Bristol: Arrowsmith

_____. *Ardath*. 1889, London: Richard Bentley

_____. *Jane*. (1900) 1911, London: Methuen

_____. *Temporal Power: A Study in Supremacy*. 1902, London: Methuen

_____. *The Avon Star: A Literary Manual for the Stratford-on-Avon Season of 1903*. 1903, Stratford-on-Avon: J. Stanley

_____. *God's Good Man*. 1904, London: Methuen

_____. *The Life Everlasting*. 1911, London: Methuen

_____. *The Young Diana* (1918) 1953, London: Hutchinson

_____. *The Secret Power*. 1921, Toronto: Ryserson Press

Coward, N. *Collected Sketches & Lyrics*. 1931, London: Hutchinson

_____. *Collected Plays Volume One: Cavalcade; Bitter Sweet; The Vortex; Hay Fever; Private Lives; Post-Mortem; Design for Living*. (1934) 1952, London: Heinemann

_____. *Star Quality*. 1951, London: Heinemann

_____. *Collected Plays Volume Five: Pacific 1860; 'Peace in Our Time'; Relative Values; Quadrille; Blithe Spirit*. 1958, London: Heinemann

_____. *Waiting in the Wings*. 1960, London: Heinemann

_____. *Pomp & Circumstance*. 1960, London: Heinemann

_____. *Collected Plays Volume Six: Point Valaine; South Sea Bubble; Ace of Clubs; Nude with Violin; Waiting in the Wings*. 1962, London: Heinemann

_____. *Collected Plays: Three: Design for Living; Cavalcade; Conversation Piece; Tonight at 8.30 (I)*. 1979, London: Methuen

_____. *The Noël Coward Diaries*. (Eds. Graham Payn and Sheridan Morley) 1982, London: George Weidenfeld & Nicolson

_____. *Collected Plays: Five: Relative Values; Look After Lulu!; Waiting in the Wings; Suite in Three Keys*. 1983, London: Methuen

_____. *Autobiography*. 1986, London: Methuen

_____. *Collected Plays: Seven: Quadrille; 'Peace in Our Time'; Tonight at 8.30 (III)*. 1999, London: Methuen

Crisp, Q. *All This & Bevin Too.* (1943) 1978, London: The Mervyn Peak Society

_____. *Love Made Easy* (1952) 1977, London: Duckworth

_____. *The Naked Civil Servant.* (1968) 1985, London: Flamingo

_____. *How to Have a Lifestyle.* (1975) 1998, Los Angeles: Alyson Books

_____. *Chog.* 1979, London: Duckworth

_____. *How to Become a Virgin.* 1981, London: Duckworth

_____. *Manners from Heaven.* 1984, New York: Harper & Row

_____. *The Wit & Wisdom of Quentin Crisp.* (Ed. Guy Kettelhack) (1984) 1985, London: Century

_____. *How to Go to the Movies.* (1989) 1990, London: Hamish Hamilton

_____. *Resident Alien.* (1996) 1997, London: Flamingo

_____. Currie, M. (ed.) *Metafiction.* 1995, London: Longman

Doyle, A. C. *The Sign of Four.* (1890)1982, Harmondsworth: Penguin

Druten, J. van *I Am a Camera.* 1955, New York: Dramatist's Play Service

Dyer, R. (ed.) *Gays & Film.* 1977, London: British Film Institute

Ellmann, R. (ed.) *Twentieth Century Views: Oscar Wilde, A Collection of Critical Essays.* 1969, New Jersey: Prentice-Hall

_____. *Oscar Wilde.* (1987) 1988, London: Penguin

Epps, B. S. *Significant Violence: Oppression & Resistance in the Narratives of Juan Goytisolo 1970–1990.* 1996, Oxford: Clarendon Press

Firbank, R. *Five Novels: Valmouth; The Flower Beneath the Foot; Prancing Nigger; Concerning the Eccentricities of Cardinal Pirelli; The Artificial Princess.* 1951, London: Duckworth

_____. *The Complete Firbank.* (1961) 1973, London: Duckworth

_____. *The New Rythum.* 1962, London: Duckworth

_____. *Complete Plays.* 1994, Illinois: Dalkey Archive Press

_____. *Three Novels: The Flower Beneath the Foot; Sorrow in Sunlight; Concern-ing the Eccentricities of Cardinal Pirelli.* 2000, London: Penguin

Freud, S. *The Complete Introductory Lectures on Psychoanalysis.* (1921) 1971, London: George Allen & Unwin

Goytisolo, J. *Count Julian.* (1970) 1989, London: Serpent's Tail [Trans. Helen Lane]

_____. *Makbara.* (1980) 1991, London: Serpent's Tail [Trans. Helen Lane]

_____. *Landscapes After the Battle.* (1982) 1987, London: Serpent's Tail. [Trans. Helen Lane]

_____. *Quarantine.* (1991) 1994, London: Quartet. [Trans. Peter Bush]

_____. *The Marx Family Saga.* (1993) 1999, San Francisco: City Lights. [Trans. Peter Bush]

_____. *The Garden of Secrets.* (1997)2002, London: Serpent's Tail. [Trans.Peter Bush]

_____. *The Virtues of the Solitary Bird.* (1988) 1991, London: Serpent's Tail [Trans. Helen Lane]

_____. *A Cock-Eyed Comedy.* (2000) 2002, London: Serpent's Tail. [Trans. Peter Bush]

_____. 'Peter Bush Interviews Juan Goytisolo.' *Book Forum* Winter 2002. New York: Art Forum Publishing

_____. *The Blind Rider.* (2003) 2005, London: Serpent's Tail. [Trans. Peter Bush]

Grey, R. *Nightmare of Ecstasy: The Life & Times of Edward D. Wood Jr* 1995, London: Faber & Faber

Grushow, I. *The Imaginary Reminiscences of Sir Max Beerbohm.* 1984, Ohio University Press

Harowitz, C., Mile, T., and Hale, O. (eds.) *New Theater Voices of the Fifties and Sixties: Selections from Encore Magazine 1956–63.* (1965) 1981, London: Methuen

Hart-Davis, R. *The Letters of Oscar Wilde.* 1962, New York: Harcourt, Brace & World

Hayes, D.C., and Davis, H. *Muddled Mind: The Complete Works of Edward D. Wood Jr.* 2001, Shreveport: Ramble House

Hopkinson, A. 'Amanda Hopkinson hails the satirical subversive Spain' in: *The Independent* 12 October 2002

Horder, M. (ed.) *Ronald Firbank: Memoirs & Critiques.* 1977, London: Duckworth

Hustvedt, A. (ed.) *The Decadent Reader: Fiction, Fantasy, & Perversion from Fin-de-Siecle France.* 1998, New York: Zone

Huysmans, J.K. *Against Nature.* (1884) 1971, Harmondsworth: Penguin [1959 Trans. Robert Baldick]

_____. *Against the Grain.* (1884) 1969, New York: Dover [Trans. John Howard]

_____. *Becalmed.* (1887) 1992, London: BCM Atlas Press [Trans. Terry Hale]

_____. *Down There.* (1891) 1972, London: Dover [Trans. Keene Wallace]

_____. *Downstream & Other Works.* (1927) 1975, New York: Howard Fertig [Trans. Samuel Putnam]

_____. *The Road from Decadence: from Brothel to Cloister. Selected Letters of J.K. Huysmans* (Ed. and trans. Barbara Beaumont). 1989, London: The Athlone Press

Huxley, A. *On the Margin.* 1923, London: Chatto & Windus

Isherwood, C. *The Berlin of Sally Bowles.* (1975) 1978, London: Hogarth Press

_____. *Christopher & His Kind.* (1977) 1993, London: Minerva

Jung, C.G. *Symbols of Transformation: The Collected Works of C.G. Jung Vol 5.* 1995, London: Routledge

Kleber, P., and Visser, C. (eds.) *Re-Interpreting Brecht: His Influence on Contemporary Drama & Film.* (1990) 1992, Cambridge University Press

Kundera, M. *The Unbearable Lightness of Being.* (1984) 1985, London: Faber & Faber [Trans. Michael Henry Heim]

_____. *The Art of the Novel.* (1986) 1990. London: Faber & Faber [Trans. Linda Asher]

Le Gallienne, R. *Retrospective Reviews Vol.1 1891–93.* 1896, London: The Bodley Head

_____. *Attitudes & Avowals.* 1910, London: The Bodley Head

_____. *The Romantic '90s.* 1926, London: G.P. Putnam's

Lloyd, C. *J.K. Huysmans & the Fin-De-Siecle Novel.* 1990, Edinburgh University Press

Louden, J. *O Rare Amanda!* 1954, London: Chatto & Windus

Lugosi, R. *Coming Out at Night.* 2000, Manchester: purpleprosepress

_____. As Rosie Garland: 'Coming Out at Night — Performing as Lesbian Vampire Rosie Lugosi' in: *Journal of Lesbian Studies* 1998, Vol 2, 2/3: The Haworth Press.

Masters, B. *Now Barabbas Was a Rotter: The Extraordinary Life of Marie Corelli.* 1978, London: Hamish Hamilton

_____. *The Life of E.F. Benson.* 1991, London: Chatto & Windus

Meyer, M. (ed.) *The Politics & Poetics of Camp.* 1994, London: Routledge

Mirbeau, O. *Torture Garden.* (1899) 2000, New York: Re/Search

Mizejewski, L. *Divine Decadence: fascism, female spectacle & the makings of Sally Bowles.* 1992, Princeton University Press

Moore, S. *Ronald Firbank: An Annotated Bibliography of Secondary Materials, 1905–1995.* 1996, Illinois: Dalkey Archive Press

Nicholls, M. *The Importance of Being Oscar.* 1981, London: Robson

Ormsby, F.ed. *Thine in Storm & Calm.* 1988, Belfast: Blackstaff

Ortega, J. 'An Interview with Juan Goytisolo by Julia Ortega.' *Texas Quarterly* Spring 1975: University of Texas Press (Trans.Joseph Schraibman)

Poems, C. *Universal Rentboy.* 2000, Manchester: Bad Press

_____. *Adult Entertainment.* 2002, Glasshoughton: Route

_____. *I'm Kamp.* 2003, Manchester: Bad Press

_____. *How to Be a Better Gay.* 2005, Author's draft copy

Praz, M. *The Romantic Agony.* [Trans. Angus Davidson] (1933) 1985, Oxford University Press

Robertson, P. *Guilty Pleasures: Feminist Camp from Mae West to Madonna.* 1996, Durham: Duke University Press

Ros, A.M. *Delina Delaney.* (1898) 1935, London: Chatto & Windus

_____. *Saint Scandalbags.* 1954, Surrey: The Merle Press

_____. *Donald Dudley.* 1954, Surrey: The Merle Press

Sacher-Masoch, L. von, *Love: the Legacy of Cain.* (1878) 2003, Riverside: Ariadne [Trans.Michael T. O'Pecko]
_____. *Venus in Furs.* (1870) 2000, London: Penguin [Trans. Joachim Neugroschel]
Sade, Marquis de, *The Mystified Magistrate: Four Stories.* (1963) 1992, London: Peter Owen. [Trans. Margaret Crosland]
Saki. *The Bodley Head Saki.* (1963) 1973, London: The Bodley Head
_____. *Tobermory & Other Stories.* 1998, London: Phoenix
_____. *Saki: The Unrest, the Cure, & Other Beastly Tales.* 2000, London: Prion as Munro, H.H. *The Complete Works of Saki.* (1976) 1986, Harmondsworth: Penguin
Self, W. *Dorian.* 2002, London: Penguin
Shakespeare, W. *The Complete Works of William Shakespeare.* (1951) 1973, London: Collins
Showalter, E. (ed.) *Daughters of Decadence.* 1993, London: Virago
Smith, D. *The One Hundred and One Dalmatians.* (1956) 2000, London: Egmont
Sontag, S. *Against Interpretation.* (1967) 1994, London: Vintage
Vonnegut, K. *Palm Sunday.* 1981, London: Jonathan Cape

Watson, J.R. *English Poetry of the Romantic Period 1789–1830.* 1985, Essex: Longman
Wilde, O. *The Works of Oscar Wilde.* 1987, Leicester: Galley Press
Willett, J. (ed.) *Brecht on Theater: The Development of an Aesthetic.* (1964) 1987, London: Methuen.
Wood, E.D. *Killer in Drag.* (1963, A.K.A. 'Black Lace Drag.') 1999, London: Four Walls Eight Windows
_____. *Side-Show Siren.* (1966) 2000, Shreveport: Woodpile
_____. *Death of a Transvestite* (A.K.A. *Let Me Die In Drag*). (1967) 1999, New York: Four Walls Eight Windows
_____. *Devil Girls.* (1967) 1995, London: Gorse
_____. *Hell Chicks.* [as N.V. Jason] (1968) 2001, Shreveport: Woodpile
_____. *Hollywood Rat Race.* (Posthumous) 1998, London: Four Walls Eight Windows/Turnaround
_____. *The Horrors of Sex.* 2000, Shreveport: Woodpile
Woolf, V. *A Room of One's Own & Three Guineas.* (1929, 1938) 1993, London: Penguin
Williams, K. *The Complete Acid Drops.* (1999) 2000, London: Orion

Index